"What a wonderful story concerning your D-Day experiences! I'll never forget you standing in the door of your C-47 on June 6, 1944 over Normandy. Keep writing – you are good at it. And keep the copies of what you write on the war coming down to me. I can't get enough of them."
   - *Stephen E. Ambrose, historian and author*

"*The Cow Spoke French* provides some tantalizing insights into the wartime experiences of one American paratrooper and in so doing, provides the reader with a greater understanding of the men who belonged to one of the most successful combat units of World War II. I highly recommend this book."
   - *Chris Anderson, Editor*
   World War II Magazine

"Whether you're a combat veteran yourself, as I am, or just someone who'd like to know more about genuine wartime experiences, *The Cow Spoke French* is for you. Veterans will recognize its truth, and rare taste of reality. You may not smell the cordite of an exploding 88mm shell from a German tank, or feel the hot air from machine gun tracers brushing your hair, but you'll have a real sense of it. Bill True's experiences in Fox Company, closest unit in the regiment to our Easy Company, were of course similar to many of mine. Close cousins to our Band of Brothers, this story of the Fox men had to be told. As a guy who was there, I can tell you this is the real thing. Man, I loved this book!"
   - *Sgt. William ""Wild Bill" Guarnere, Co. E.*
   506th PIR, 101st Airborne

"After interviewing over 930 WWII survivors of the 101st Airborne, I can attest that there is no more personable storyteller than Bill True. His easygoing and humorous approach to viewing even the most terrifying events is reflected in the title of the book itself. It also runs throughout his narrative and helps explain how he was able to mentally cope with his WWII experiences. His detailed account of the training at Camp Toccoa is the best I've seen, and there are other surprises in the battle-related stories. In all, a fascinating reading experience."
- *Mark Bando, historian and author*

"*The Cow Spoke French* is a joint endeavor between a father and son. Bill True, the father, served as a paratrooper in Fox Company of the 2nd Battalion of the famous 506th Parachute Regiment of the 101st Airborne Division. True relates his wartime experiences as a member of the First Platoon fitting them in with the experiences of close members of his squad. The son, Deryck True, provides an overview in third-person and fits the actions of his father and buddies into the big picture."
- *George E. Koskimaki, veteran of and widely regarded as the "first historian" of the 101st Airborne Division.*

"Bill True's book, *The Cow Spoke French*, is a vivid, personal account of colorful and sometimes humorous experiences as a 506th paratrooper of World War II. It includes training in Toccoa, the night before the D-Day jump into Normandy, Bastogne, the end of the war. A longtime buddy of Easy Company's David Kenyon Webster, author of *Parachute Infantry* and Band of Brothers fame, Bill True tells it like it was."
- *Barbara Webster Embree, widow of David Kenyon Webster and world renowned artist.*

THE COW SPOKE FRENCH

A Paratrooper's Story of World War II

Bill True

William True
and
Deryck Tufts True

Deryck Tufts True

THE COW SPOKE FRENCH
A Paratrooper's Story of World War II

FIRST TRADE PAPER EDITION

ISBN 0-9773606-0-1

Cover designed by Teresa A. Shuff
Printed in the United States of America by
Mighty Designs, Fullerton, CA

Inquiries may be directed by email to:
info@thecowspokefrench.com

Web site: http://thecowspokefrench.com/
(secure online ordering)

Contents

Dedication

We wish to dedicate this work to our family. It was for them that these stories were recorded, and their enjoyment and approval of this book are more important to us than any commercial success we may or may not achieve. They are:

Bill's wife, Clarissa Jane (Janey) Tufts True.

His daughter, Dedra Lynn True-Scheib, along with her husband, Gerald Paul Scheib, and their son, Adam True Scheib.

Bill's second son, Devin Paul True, his wife Catherine Louise Dobry True, and son Devin Paul True Jr.

Bill's youngest child, Dean Leslie True, his wife Kimberly Carol Ann Garay True and their offspring Keenan William True, and Cadence Aleece True.

Deryck's wife, Anna Margaret (Peggy) Burnette True.

Deryck and Peggy's son, Colin Burnette True, and his wife Jelizabeth Guinto True.

Deryck and Peggy's daughter, Kelly Jane True.

It's obvious that many of these people would not be here at all if it weren't for the good fortune that young Sergeant William True miraculously enjoyed during many long months of combat in Europe. But miracles sometimes do abound, and the loving, supportive family members named here count chief among them in the hearts of the authors. It is they that make the going to war and the writing of books worthwhile.

Foreword to the Narrative

These are true stories. By that I mean that beyond the play on our family name, they are truthful depictions of real events, lived by real people. And truth is, in many ways, more important than fact.

This book is about my father and his generation. It is based almost exclusively on first-person accounts by the people who lived these events. I was, and am, extremely fortunate that my parents are both alive and in full possession of their faculties. While writing this I was able at a moment's notice to clarify a point, or fill in a narrative, with a simple phone call. But they were not the only sources for story material. Over the years my Dad has collected a very large body of personal correspondence from the men he fought beside during World War II. The 101st Airborne Association played a major role in this regard, keeping the men connected to each other and their own histories. Much of that personal correspondence has found its way into this book. I have also been fortunate to meet and interview many of the veterans who were my father's comrades-in-arms. Consequently, this is the story of numerous people, whose lives intertwined during a time of great and desperate world events.

Now that I've told you what this book is, I will tell you what it is not: facts. That's not to say there are no facts in it. Quite to the contrary, it's full of them. But they can be slippery things when gleaned from memories often removed from the occurrence by many years. Some recollections remain clear and sharp, yielding a nice, fleshy narrative. Others are fuzzy and less distinct, yet useful nonetheless. They often have enough meat clinging to their bones to be added to the stew pot for flavor. I have used them all, and tried my best honestly to portray events in the way they were experienced and afterward remembered.

The purpose of assigning the "third person" narrative to me in this project was deliberate. Individual soldiers are, to a degree, always isolated on the battlefield. It's common for them to beg news from the home front to discover the big picture of which they are playing a vital part. My task was to weave the soldier's story into context within the broader military events and movements surrounding it. This in no way relieved me of the obligation to tell the story in accordance with my father's personal recollections. As each chapter was completed, my Dad reviewed it carefully to answer my questions: "Did I get this right? Is that how it felt?" A negative answer invariably resulted in rewriting and renders that aspect of the work a genuine collaboration.

But we wanted to have our cake and eat it, too. The immediacy and poignant truth of a first-person "diary" carries drama that cannot be matched. Accordingly, my father wrote more than 20 short stories which are interspersed within the narrative as they fall chronologically. The "Prologue" is among them. These writings are his alone, and the reader will no doubt appreciate their value as records of these historic events from the perspective of one who lived them.

I remain, as should we all, in awe of the men and women who faced the challenge of fascism and unblinkingly withstood and overcame it—often sacrificing everything in the effort. It must never become cliché to say that my father's generation literally saved the world. I am deeply honored to be trusted with my Dad's stories, and hope with all my heart that I have rendered them faithfully here.

Deryck Tufts True

Foreword to the Personal Accounts

My interest in recording wartime experiences was not awakened until a couple of decades after those transforming events. About the same time in life—my early forties—I became interested in both family genealogy and the idea of making some written record of my days as a paratrooper.

My initial writings about life in the Army were simple notes of specific happenings, or recollections of feelings and reactions that were particularly momentous or memorable. This gradually expanded into making chronological notes of my experiences ranging from entry into the service to my discharge.

Correspondence with wartime buddies and the exchange of stories at 101st Airborne Association reunions further whetted my interest in recreating those exciting thirty-seven months of my life. After retirement in 1988 from my profession as a hospital executive, I took some writing classes at our local community college.

In those classes we practiced writing about actual experiences using some of the techniques of fiction. I found that approach to be very satisfying. It allowed me to convey both the true facts as well as the real tenor and flavor of the emotions connected with them.

My personal accounts herein follow that mode.

Decades afterward it's impossible to recall the exact language of specific conversations. Details of actions are sometimes not totally clear either, but the basic stories are factual and true. By using probable dialogue, and likely details of connected actions, I believe I am able to give the listener a truer experience of happenings and the associated feelings than would otherwise be conveyed by mere recitation of clearly remembered facts.

The misery and terrors of war aren't always in battles. Sometimes it is the things that never happen. My story "Outpost" in Chapter VI is a clear example of this. The conversations between Joe, George, Linus and me are obviously reconstructed, but the dialogue is true to the event and the emotions. As with my other writings, I have tried to bring the reader into the event with me. I hope I have, at least to some extent, succeeded.

Bill True

Authors' Note

The stories depicted here are accurate accounts of real deeds by real men and women in a time of tremendous global, as well as personal, stress. There is no softening or covering up behavior which, in the calm security of hindsight, might be construed by the self-righteous as "bad" or "immoral." In order to protect individuals and their descendants from anguish or criticism, we have chosen to use pseudonyms for some of the characters portrayed in this book. When used, the first occurrence of a name will be identified by this symbol: †. All other names are genuine.

Prologue

By Bill True

Uppottery Airfield, Southwest England
June 5, 1944, approximately 10:00 p.m.
Beside an Army Air Corps C-47, serial #849

"Dammit, Johnny, I don't know whether I can get up."

I'm on my back like an upended turtle. My ponderously heavy equipment is a giant magnet welding me to the ground. The sky is still light because of the double daylight saving time instituted with the war. Hundreds of our two-engine C-47s stretch out on the tarmac as far as you can see.

We're strapping and rigging our equipment and gear in final preparation before boarding planes for the flight to Normandy. Our first combat action.

"Roll over on your knees, TyTy, and I'll give you a hand," Johnny says. Johnny Jackson is second mortarman in the squad, and has managed to get his paraphernalia secured without the ludicrous expedient of lying flat on his back as I've done.

We've been in the marshalling area at this airfield for a week. Days spent poring over sand table mock-ups of our precise objectives in the D-Day invasion, cleaning and polishing and oiling our weapons, and especially sharpening our knives. I don't know why the knives became such an obsession, but everyone has spent hour upon hour whetting a razor edge that will slice a hair. "I hope to hell I never get close enough to use this on a German," I've thought to myself several times.

"Where'd you put your detonator, TyTy?" It's Joe Flick, buck sergeant and our squad leader. He's asking about the detonator for the Hawkins Land Mine each of us will carry. Our training has not included experience with mines, and we've never jumped with one. We're all pretty leery about it and concerned with strapping the detonator far from the mine itself and in a spot where it's least likely to go off. "Dude put his above his boot on the outside of his leg, but I've got mine out of the way and taped here inside my thigh," Joe says.

"If the damn thing goes off you're gonna lose a lot more than I will, Joe," Dude says. Dude Stone is the squad's first mortarman, and always handy with the quip. The kidding remark draws our smiles, but no laughter.

Come to think of it, I haven't heard anybody laugh all day long. The term "hushed atmosphere" crosses my mind. Clowning and banter has always preceded our many practice jumps. Not tonight.

Minimal talk has been almost eerily subdued as each of us secured M-1 rifle, bayonet, bandoleers of rifle clips, hand grenades, phosphorus grenade, disassembled sections of the mortar itself, mortar rounds, gas mask, entrenching tool, canteen and numerous other combat items onto and into our webbing and uniform. By the time my main parachute and a reserve are buckled into my chute harness I figure my 155 pounds has hit a cumbersome 300. Thank God we'll drop about 50 pounds of that when we land and get out of our chutes, I'm thinking.

"We just got the signal to start boarding, so let's move over to the plane," Joe announces. Light is lowering in the cloudless sky as we help each other to our feet and shuffle clumsily toward our C-47. The co-pilot and another crewman are pushing troopers up the steps which we cannot mount without help.

Lights are on in the plane as we slump in the bucket seats in accordance with the numbered order of our jump. Our pilot, Wayne King, is passing out a paper to each of us. "A message from the big boss," he says. SUPREME HEADQUARTERS ALLIED EXPEDITIONARY FORCE is the letterhead, and glancing at the bottom I see it is signed, Dwight D. Eisenhower.

My stomach butterflies have become flapping condors, accompanied perhaps not incongruously by a star spangled spine chill, as I read.

"Soldiers, Sailors, and Airmen of the Allied Expeditionary Force!

"You are about to embark on the Great Crusade...The eyes of the world are upon you. The hopes and prayers of liberty-loving people everywhere march with you..."

One of the plane's crewmen is passing out pills which he says are for air-sickness. Seems odd since we've never had those before. Wonder if they're really tranquilizers to help calm a few jagged nerves? He's also providing empty round cardboard ice-cream containers "in case the pills don't work," he says. I pass on the containers since I've never had even a touch of air-sickness, but several of the guys seem to welcome having them. Might as well take the pill though, I'm thinking, as I swallow it and light up a cigarette. The crewman now has a camera with flash attachment in hand and walks to the rear of the plane and says "Look back here and say cheese." I lean forward around Joe Flick as the flash goes off, and notice Rusty Houck making the Churchill "V for Victory" sign. The flash caught me taking a drag on my Lucky Strike and I'm wishing I could get a commercial endorsement fee for the advertisement.

The engines are whining as we taxi to our departure

position on the runway. The metal bucket seats vibrate under our butts as the pilot stops and revs for takeoff. We're moving. Nearly two years of rugged and intensive paratroop training culminate in tonight's purpose. "This is it! This is it!" The cliché ricochets 'round my skull.

Fear clutches my chest and flies with me as our grossly loaded C-47 lifts slowly from the tarmac. The darkening English countryside that has been our home for nine months flashes past the plane's open door as we bank into formation. The beaches and hedgerows of Normandy lie in wait.

Precisely three years prior, life had been very different for Bill "TyTy" True.

SUPREME HEADQUARTERS
ALLIED EXPEDITIONARY FORCE

Soldiers, Sailors and Airmen of the Allied Expeditionary Force!

You are about to embark upon the Great Crusade, toward which we have striven these many months. The eyes of the world are upon you. The hopes and prayers of liberty-loving people everywhere march with you. In company with our brave Allies and brothers-in-arms on other Fronts, you will bring about the destruction of the German war machine, the elimination of Nazi tyranny over the oppressed peoples of Europe, and security for ourselves in a free world.

Your task will not be an easy one. Your enemy is well trained, well equipped and battle-hardened. He will fight savagely.

But this is the year 1944! Much has happened since the Nazi triumphs of 1940-41. The United Nations have inflicted upon the Germans great defeats, in open battle, man-to-man. Our air offensive has seriously reduced their strength in the air and their capacity to wage war on the ground. Our Home Fronts have given us an overwhelming superiority in weapons and munitions of war, and placed at our disposal great reserves of trained fighting men. The tide has turned! The free men of the world are marching together to Victory!

I have full confidence in your courage, devotion to duty and skill in battle. We will accept nothing less than full Victory!

Good Luck! And let us all beseech the blessing of Almighty God upon this great and noble undertaking.

Dwight D Eisenhower

CHAPTER I

The Wild Blue Yonder
Transition to Army Life

"Time is the longest distance between two places."
Tennessee Williams, *The Glass Menagerie*, 1945

———————————

William Richard True graduated from Omaha Central High School on June 6, 1941. It was a seminal time indeed, with the Japanese attack on Pearl Harbor just months away, and the largest military invasion in history—one in which he would participate—exactly three years to the day in the future.

He and his father, Leslie Arthur True, were planning to move to California as soon as his dad completed a sheet metal course he was taking at night. That skill would make him eligible to work in one of the numerous aircraft plants that were constantly looking for workers. But classes would not be completed for at least another month.

The two of them had been "batching it" through Bill's high school years. There had been some very rough times; even beyond the endemic stress of living in the Great Depression. In 1934 Les had been diagnosed with tuberculosis. This news was not altogether a shock, as his sister had died of the disease a few years before, and several aunts and uncles were also infected. For the next two years the elder True was confined to the county hospital, while his wife Ruth, son Billy, and daughter Betty Jean survived mainly on public assistance. Then in '36 he was sent west to Arizona

7

for a year, on the chance that a change in climate might improve his condition. It was there that he discovered Christian Science and received an apparent miraculous "healing" of his ailment. This was the defining moment of his life and made him a permanent believer in the power of mind over matter.

Les returned home in 1937, healthy but with a whole new set of troubles. During the recuperation his wife had taken up with another man. She and Max Hoopes soon left Omaha, themselves bound for the promise of work in California. Leslie filed for divorce and tried his best to make a normal home for his son and daughter.

The two guys found they could get along pretty well by themselves, but it was different when it came to Bill's younger sister, Betty Jean. She was only 9 years old and the "bachelor" lifestyle seemed unlikely to meet the needs of a growing young woman. As a result, she was placed in a county-assisted home for girls—Minerva Cottage—that was recommended by church friends. This arrangement was never entirely satisfactory. Betty Jean eventually became quite unhappy, and finally went to live with her mother and Max in California.

The men became proficient in handling most of their domestic chores, but cooking was never a strong point. This was evidenced by a notable lack of variation in menus. Frequently, dinner consisted simply of a home-made combination of cranberries and apple sauce, with chipped-beef gravy on toast.

Bill intended to work full time in Omaha right after graduation, and save as much money as possible during the month before the trip to California. He had carried two Omaha World Herald paper routes all through high school, but the earnings were only about five dollars a week at best. He hoped he could do a bit better than that with a full time, regular job.

Outside of his night school sheet metal course, Leslie worked part-time for the WPA and also in a barber shop cutting hair. A customer at the shop managed a big laundry in town. One day it was made known that there was an opening in their tumbler section. Bill applied for the job and immediately went to work at 20 cents an hour. With a nine-hour work day five days a week, and five hours on Saturday, his earnings came to an even ten dollars: Not exactly heady wealth, but it was double what the paper routes paid.

Operating the big tumbler dryers was hard, hot work, but fairly simple. Bill became proficient in short order. He found the work not only physically demanding, but abysmally boring as well. Knowing that it was to be only a short-time employment made the slow passage of work hours endurable. At least he was saving some money.

At the end of his first month at the laundry, the manager called Bill into his office and complimented him on his work. In recognition of the progress he was making the manager granted him a 2-cent per hour raise. Bill thanked him and as he walked back to his tedious work he calculated his new weekly pay at eleven dollars. "Oh well, Dad is about to complete his sheet metal class," he thought, "and then I'll be out of here and heading for California."

Leslie purchased a 1933 Plymouth sedan shortly before Bill's graduation. The family had been without an auto for several years and this one looked great for an eight-year-old car. The salesman had emphasized that it was a "late" '33, in tip-top shape, and more than adequate for a trip to California.

Les was somewhat short on patience in teaching his son to drive. As Bill confused the coordination of clutch, gear shift, and accelerator, the car would lurch heavily. Then the instructions would come to an early halt. Nevertheless, they both persisted, and eventually Bill managed to pass his driver's test and become licensed shortly before the California journey was scheduled.

The plan was to drive from Omaha down through Nebraska and Kansas and visit several Oklahoma relatives before catching Route 66 and heading west. Thus on a bright, early morning in July, 1941, the "late" '33 Plymouth was finally loaded. Goodbyes were said to friends and neighbors, and the two Trues headed for sunny California.

↾   ↾   ↾

The first day's trip was long but uneventful. Just before sunset they pulled into the Oklahoma farm yard of Mabel and Herman Walbaum, sister and brother-in-law of Leslie. Their homestead sat right on Route 66 about 40 miles west of Oklahoma City. Bill had spent several summers there as he was growing up. In 1933 he had watched with fascination as construction of the famous highway came right through the middle of the Walbaum's 160 acres.

Leslie and Bill were welcomed warmly by the Walbaums. Soon the farm's home-grown meal of fried chicken, sweet corn, boiled potatoes, sliced tomatoes, and thick slabs of sour dough bread was hot on the table. Bill and his first cousin Ray were almost exactly the same age. They had lots to reminisce about from their summers of riding bare-backed mules, building tree houses, and helping out on the many farm chores. Even the routine tasks of milking cows, slopping hogs, and hoeing corn seemed fun to Bill in retrospect.

After supper Leslie and Herman played checkers, as they had many times in the past. The two had always been a pretty close match. But after three games, Les suggested a change.

"Let's play chess. I'll show you how," he said.

Leslie had learned the game during his stay at the county hospital, and came to love its intellectual challenge. He showed Herman all the moves of each piece and talked a little about strategy. Then they began. It soon became clear that Herman did not share his enthusiasm for such a "brainy" contest. Finally he had had enough. "This here's way more involved than any game for fun ought to be," he said. And that was that.

They spent the next couple of days driving around to visit numerous relatives on nearby farms in neighboring counties. This really was "goodbye" to their long-time home on the plains and it was important to touch base with folks they might not see for a long time—or ever again, perhaps. But finally, it was time for the travelers to be on their way. Bill and Ray chased down several of the farm's White Leghorn chickens (no mean feat in and of itself). Then Aunt Mabel unceremoniously wrung their necks, dipped them in boiling water, and plucked them clean. She cut up the lot and fried them like only she seemed able. As a result, Leslie and Bill would snack on the best fried chicken there ever was, their whole trip west.

Early next morning Bill helped out with the farm chores for one last time. He discovered he could still milk a cow pretty well. Then the California-bound travelers were on their way. With Route 66 running right through the farm, getting back on their itinerary was about as handy and simple as it could be: "Drive to the front gate and turn left. Stop when you hit the ocean."

The trip through western Oklahoma and the Texas panhandle went smoothly, but some miles past Tucumcari, New Mexico, ominous noises were heard from the car's engine. Just as they pulled into a filling station to have it checked the motor conked out completely. Fortunately there was a garage with a mechanic on site who was able to quickly diagnose the problem. "The pistons are shot," he said, "and two of them are splintered to bits." He didn't have the equipment to make major repairs, so the engine block had to be taken into Tucumcari. There it would be reground for new pistons.

There were nearby cabins for rent, so Leslie and Bill stayed overnight and most of the next day as their "more than adequate for a trip to California" Plymouth was resurrected. Finally the work was completed and they got the bad news: the cost was $45. Considering all the work involved it was actually a very nominal charge. They knew they had been lucky that a mechanic was even available to make the repairs. But the unexpected outlay still made a very good dent in their total capital.

A detour off Route 66 down to Tucson, Arizona, had been planned from the start. This was to visit the home of the Christian Science practitioner who had worked with Leslie on his tuberculosis back in 1937. She lived there with a temporary boarder named Bonnie Smith†.

Bonnie was a pretty red-head, about Bill's age, and had big, beautiful brown eyes. He wasted no time making his move. Quickly retrieving his guitar from the Plymouth, Bill serenaded her with a song he had recently learned: "I Don't Want to Set the World on Fire." She was quite impressed with this. By the time the Trues hit the road again a budding romance had begun, though at this stage it only amounted to hand-holding on the front porch glider. It would be very different some months later when Bonnie moved back to her home in San Diego to live with her mom and brother. Then she and Bill would become seriously involved, indeed.

On the road again, the Trues made one more detour off Route 66. This time it was to see the Grand Canyon. Neither

Leslie nor Bill had ever been there before and didn't really know what to expect, aside from photographs they'd seen. The road into the canyon area bent in a way that completely concealed the magnificent sight. Then suddenly, coming around a corner, the full massive vista was revealed all at once. It was an awesome sight and completely took their breath away. Neither of the two lifetime flatlanders had ever seen anything like it. Cross-country travel was definitely broadening their horizons.

~ ~ ~

It was only a day later when they made their grand entry into San Diego, California. And what a thrilling experience it was; driving through beautiful Balboa Park with its majestic eucalyptus trees and vast expanse of lawns, then down to the harbor where ships of all kinds filled the scene. There were myriad fishing and commercial vessels, of course, but the Navy ships stole the show. At anchor they packed the harbor as far as the eye could see, all the way out to the Point Loma exit. The vast Pacific lay beyond. Neither of the Trues had ever been near an ocean before. The smell of the salt air was exotic and intoxicating. The hustle and bustle of activity seemed unending. Just as they pulled to the curb at water's edge a formation of Catalina PBYs flew over, with their guttural engines vibrating the very air. This was *nothing* like Omaha, though the two cities were of similar size. This place was ALIVE with activity! Surely it was the land of opportunity as everyone back home had heard.

Consolidated Aircraft was only one of many large manufacturing plants in San Diego. They built B-24 Liberator bombers for the Army, and Catalina flying boats for the Navy and Coast Guard. Leslie's recent training in sheet-metal work would stand him in good stead for employment there. But on the day of their arrival, Consolidated was hiring only skilled toolmakers—an altogether different craft. No matter; Les remained upbeat. There were so many defense plants operating in Southern California that he was sure it would only be a matter of time before he found a lucrative job. So, undaunted, he and Bill drove up the coast to Long Beach, the headquarters of Douglas Aircraft.

Though there was generally a constant need for workers, the timing was bad once more. Again they found disappointment as Douglas would not be hiring till the following week. Les refused to give up, buoyed by the frenetic pace of activity that seemed endemic to the whole region. So once more it was back to San Diego to try their luck. This time they hit pay dirt. Merely a day had passed, and Consolidated was again employing sheet metal workers. The elder True went to work immediately. He and Bill found a small, inexpensive apartment near 18th and Market Streets, and settled into their new environment. They had "arrived."

Bill would not turn 18 until November, so he couldn't go to work at the aircraft plants until then. In the interim, Leslie suggested that he simply walk down Market Street inquiring of the various businesses if they needed a worker. Doing so, he came across the Sanitary Laundry—a sizable operation just a few blocks from their apartment. As an experienced laundryman Bill thought that was a good possibility and asked to see the manager. Sure enough, they had just lost their tumbler operator a few days before. He was hired on the spot.

The pay was 40 cents an hour, *double* his starting rate in Omaha. Already, California was living up to its reputation as the land of milk and honey amidst the Great Depression. Bill still wanted to work at an aircraft plant though, where the starting pay was 60 cents an hour. Toward that end he enrolled in a sheet metal fabrication class, much like the one his father had taken in Nebraska. It was held at the Ford Building in Balboa Park, and would finish in time for his birthday. A job at Consolidated was looking more and more likely in his future.

The tumbler job at the Sanitary Laundry soon became as monotonous as his previous one. But here, at least, the tumbler section was located near the mangles where a number of young women worked. This cast a different, and somewhat better, light on his workday activities. After loading his three tumblers there was often time to stroll over to the mangles and talk to the girls. That helped a great deal in passing the time and it became a regular part of his routine. But the socializing, though pleasant, wasn't always an unmixed blessing.

The laundry was generally a noisy place, where conversation was only practical for two people standing virtually face to face. One of the mangle operators was a good-looking red-head a few years older than Bill. One day, out of the blue, she shouted across the floor, "Hey, are you a cherry?" It was obvious she intended for everyone nearby to hear. And of course he knew what she meant by the question, but was too embarrassed to answer "yes." Several of the girls laughed at his discomfiture.

One of the contracts the laundry had was with an army installation to do their wool blankets. The timing of the tumblers in drying the blankets was tricky compared to regular clothing. Just a minute or two short on the timing and they wouldn't be dry. Yet within a minute or two after that they'd get hot and start smoking. Bill was very careful handling the blankets for the first several weeks. But as the monotony of the work grew, he began to get careless. Two or three times the blankets got too hot and smoked a bit before he could get them out. Then one day he became engrossed talking to one of the pretty Mexican girls. Soon his tumbler load started billowing heavy smoke. He managed to stop the machine before they caught fire, but the laundry manager was out on the floor and saw the incident. The next day Bill was given his final pay check. His career with the Sanitary Laundry had come to a sudden halt.

With his eighteenth birthday only a week or so away, the timing of this ignominy wasn't all that bad. Proof of age was necessary to go to work at Consolidated so Bill sent back to Omaha for his birth certificate. When it came he was disappointed to find that his middle name, Richard, had been left off. Not wanting to take the time to get it corrected, he decided to drop the missing moniker and thus became simply William True. This would continue for the next 57 years. (To celebrate his 75th birthday he legally took his favorite grandfather's name and became William Merit True, II.)

On November 11, 1941,[1] Bill applied for work and became a transport handler at Consolidated Aircraft Corporation. His job was hauling aircraft parts and tools throughout the plant's various buildings. He had hoped to utilize his sheet-metal training, but it was not to be. On the form filled out by the personnel official it said "Youth" in the section titled "Reason for Assignment."

Consolidated was a huge plant, comprised of many buildings. All were bustling with activity as the B-24s and PBYs were built. For a while, Bill found it quite fun pushing his hand cart around to the various sections. He had a front row seat to the spectacle of aircraft manufacture and assembly, and watched with fascination as bare skeletal

---

[1]   See Appendix C, "A Coincidence of Dates."

airframes moved through the various processes to finally roll out to the flight line, ready for test.

Bill had been working at the plant less than a month when a Sunday morning newscast announced that the Japanese had attacked Pearl Harbor. On December 7, he and his dad were driving home from church when the story came over the car radio. Both were stunned. "America is in it now, that's for sure," his dad had exclaimed. After that neither of them spoke as they finished the drive home. The radio droned on with its dire report, but details of the raid were still scant.

Next day the President announced America's formal entry into the war. This had little effect on operations at Consolidated, since the plant had already been operating full-tilt on a three-shift basis. Leslie and Bill both worked days—nine-hours, six days a week. That continued unchanged.

    ಌ   ಌ   ಌ

The transport section of the plant had several motorized carts for moving larger pieces. Bill had hoped to drive one of those, but they were all taken by older workers. There seemed little chance of advancing from his hand cart. As the weeks and then months rolled by, the job became extremely monotonous, rivaling the boredom of his former job at the laundry tumblers.

Bill made the acquaintance of a young man his own age who worked in the paint department. They often passed a few minutes in conversation when Bill's job took him into that area. Soon the two fell into the habit of flipping coins and matching half-dollars. As a result, each made sure he had several 50 cent pieces in his pocket at work.

One day they were tossing coins when one of the plant

17

big-shots rode up on his bicycle. The bike immediately identified him as a honcho: regular employees all had to walk. The man didn't say a word, but they could tell he was displeased by the scowl on his face. He silently wrote down the employee badge numbers of the two, then rode off to attend other officiousness.

Bill didn't know exactly what to make of this, though he strongly suspected it wasn't good. Sure enough, before his shift was over the trouble hit. A big, burly security guard came up to him and grabbed him by the arm. The man was uniformed and wore a badge and a gun. "Come with me," he said gruffly. Next stop was the personnel office where the standard "pink slip" was issued along with all pay owed. Then the guard physically escorted him off the premises, and none too gently. It was quite embarrassing. He'd been fired from jobs before, but the process was usually civil. This felt more like a "bum's rush." Though it was unspoken, the message "Don't come back!" seemed clear enough.

A scant few years before, at the height of America's economic malaise, this would have been more than merely humiliating. It could spell long-term unemployment, and even homelessness. But times had changed and war-production was on the rise—especially in California. Bill shook off the Consolidated rebuff and merely walked down the street to Solar Aircraft. There, an old family friend from Omaha, Bill Schmidt, worked in the personnel office. Within days, young True was once again employed.

Some time later, Schmidt showed Bill a newspaper advertisement. It promised $50 a week for part time work in the evening. Since both of them worked the day shift it sounded like a great opportunity to expand their income. There was to be an evening meeting at an office in a downtown bank building to explain the program. The two aspiring men of means decided to attend.

A spokesman for the Collier Publishing Company began by explaining his firm's intent. "We'll be conducting a massive public relations program here in San Diego. We need representatives to call on selected clientele and explain that effort. Men like you. And when you call you'll be offering these carefully chosen customers, *completely free of charge*, two six-volume sets of books selected from a wide variety of current and classical writers." He briefly paused to evaluate the effect of this on his audience, then went on. "And that's not all. Each customer who signs up will receive, *at no cost whatsoever*, a state-of–the-art, full-color World Atlas, and the internationally renowned Oxford Dictionary."

"Wow!" thought True, on the edge of his seat. "I wonder what we have to sell."

His question was soon answered, as the Collier man demonstrated the exact sales pitch that was to be used.

Ring doorbell. Woman comes to the door. "Good evening, Mrs. Jones, I'm from the San Diego Trust and Savings building, and we're making a special offer to people in your neighborhood this week. Is your husband in?" (Names and addresses would be furnished in order to personalize the presentation, and it was important to always speak with both the husband and wife.)

"As part of a major public relations program the Collier Publishing Company is conducting, you will receive a selection of these handsome volumes absolutely free." (Beautiful enlarged layouts of the many sets of books to be chosen from, and of the atlas and the dictionary, would be displayed on the floor. An ordinary table would be entirely inadequate to handle the display.)

Following an extended discussion of the authors available in the sets of books, and of the world renown of the compilers of the atlas and dictionary, the ultimate and equally attractive part of the program would be presented.

"Mr. and Mrs. Jones, from this list of more than fifty popular magazines (colorful displays of many of the magazines are shown) you may select any two and receive them for three years at a fifty percent discount from the regular news stand price. If you wish to take more than two of these excellent periodicals, I am authorized to allow up to four, with the same fifty percent discount."

"You may indeed wonder how my company can present this astounding subscription opportunity in addition to the free books. But believe me, Collier Publishing has been successful these many decades largely because of just such special offers. And of course, the quality of all our publications has always ensured complete satisfaction by our millions of readers."

When the presentation was concluded several of the attendees, including Bill Schmidt, had misgivings. Most said they'd think it over and respond later. But Bill True was mightily impressed by both the products and potential earnings. Their commission would be five dollars for each successful sale of two subscriptions. "Heck, that's a piece of cake," he thought. "I can probably BEAT that weekly fifty dollars they promised." He signed up on the spot.

Bill's enthusiasm for the Collier program was unbounded. He found himself anxious to get home from work at Solar, change clothes, and get to his designated neighborhoods every night. And with his eagerness came success. Soon he was regularly making 2 or 3 sales per night. Unfortunately, on average only 5 of the deals actually held up per week. The company ran credit checks on all of its potential customers and some were turned down. But still, Bill was pulling in $25 per week—almost as much as he made at Solar. And this was more fun and took a lot fewer hours.

           ☙   ☙   ☙

The work at Solar had been somewhat interesting in the beginning, but soon it, too, became monotonous as the days turned into weeks and the months passed by. His assignment was called "dinging." It consisted of pounding the dents out of manifold exhaust sections after welding. Though more an art than a science, nonetheless it didn't take much genius to be a dinger. Bill was bored.

Meanwhile, the lovely young Bonnie Smith had moved to San Diego to live with her mother. Bill wasted little time in re-lighting their old, brief, flame. The hand-holding they enjoyed in Tucson was soon replaced by heavy petting. And before long, the question of his "cherry" posed months before by the woman at the Sanitary Laundry could be answered with a resounding "No!"

As the summer of 1942 rolled around Bill found his life becoming very full and increasingly "complicated." He was making at least $60 a week between his two jobs. And while the work at Solar was less than stimulating, the six-fold increase in pay from the previous year was darn good. Between financial success, dancing at Pacific Square on weekends, and making out with Bonnie Smith on a regular basis, life wasn't bad. Not bad at all.

Lately the war news had improved from the grim early days when the Japanese had swept everything before them in the Pacific. Even America's allies in Europe were doing better. Bill began to think that the war might end in a not distant future. This was a bothersome idea. He knew he wanted to take some part in the action. But with things going so well in his life there had not seemed to be any rush. At least, not until now.

When he considered what part he might play in the conflict, the Army Air Corps was an appealing possibility. He had watched every day as military planes from all of the branches flew over San Diego. The thought of becoming a pilot gradually developed into an intriguing prospect. Then one day fate threw a wrench into the otherwise well-oiled machinery of his life.

A recent date with Bonnie Smith had ended in a very bitter argument. The cause of the dispute then continued as a source of friction. It concerned a habit she had developed after high school graduation the previous June: smoking cigarettes. Neither Bill nor his dad smoked. In their now staunchly Christian Science household it was not only forbidden, but immoral. Bill made no pretense to hide his strong disapproval. Bonnie promised to quit, but the habit was too much for her. As she continued to light up during subsequent dates, the bloom on the romance was definitely fading.

With his job at the plant increasingly boring, his love life going down hill, and fears rising that he'd "miss out on the whole war," Bill started looking seriously at a change in plans.

A big change.

THE WILD BLUE YONDER
Bill's True Tale

"Off we go, into the wild blue yonder, Riding high, into the sun." The public address system at Solar Aircraft is blaring the Army Air Corps Song during our lunch break. I'm sitting on the pavement and leaning against one of the metal outer walls of the main assembly building eating a sandwich from my brown paper bag. The song is really getting to me. I know every word of it now, and it seems like they play it at least once every shift.

It's July, 1942, and I've been an aircraft worker in San Diego since November of last year. On my eighteenth birthday, Nov. 11, 1941, I went to work for Consolidated Aircraft in the Transport Department. It turned out to be a mighty boring place to work, especially since I didn't get to drive one of the electric cars moving parts and tools between the sprawling buildings of the plant. I'd been assigned to haul smaller items on a hand cart, and frequently had nothing to do. Etched for all time in my memory is the day a big-shot supervisor rode up on his bicycle (having a bicycle clearly identified him as a big shot) and caught another guy and me matching half dollars in the Paint Department. We were fired on the spot, and a guard escorted us out of the plant. What an embarrassment! But I got another job at Solar the next day, so it was small loss.

"Here they come, zooming to meet our thunder, At 'em boys, give 'em the gun." I'm singing the words as I finish off my banana and cupcake. It sure would be neat to be a pilot in the Air Corps, I think, as I stuff the wrappings and banana peel in the sack and jump-shoot a long "two pointer" into the trash container. Walking back to my bench I'm wondering how I could check on becoming a pilot.

My work at Solar is what they call "dinging," and, appropriately enough, the guys who do it are called "dingers." Being assigned as a dinger had sounded pretty good as compared to transport. But it's not really a heck of a lot better, I'm thinking, as I pick up a section of manifold exhaust, hold it against the bucking bar, and start "dinging" the dents out of it with one of the several hammers I use. Solar's primary output is exhaust systems for various aircraft, and dents which occur during the welding process have to be hammered out prior to final assembly.

I've been here at Solar over three months now and my pay is up to 75 cents an hour. Since I'm on the day shift I'm able to also work a part time evening job with Collier Publishing Company selling magazine subscriptions on commission. Sets of books and a very impressive world atlas are a gift package with the subscriptions, and I'm doing very well earning between twenty and thirty dollars a week in commissions. Between my two jobs I'm making up to sixty dollars a week as compared to the ten dollars a week I was making in Omaha just a year ago. Talk about *success*!

It's 4:40 p.m. and I'm riding the bus home after work. I'm thinking about that boring job of dinging as I look at the front page of the San Diego Tribune I bought from the kid at the plant gate. The war seems to be going well for the Allies, and the days when all of the victories were in favor of the Axis are apparently over. There's probably still plenty of time for me to get into the war, but a disturbing idea is starting to niggle my mind nearly every day. "What if the war should end before I get into it?"

The Japanese bombing of Pearl Harbor took place less that four weeks after my eighteenth birthday, and I've never had any doubt that I will play some active role in the war. But there's really no rush. Or *is* there? That niggling thought and a possible doubt keeps recurring.

"Down we dive, spouting our guns from under, With just one hell of a roar." It's 6:55 a.m. and I'm hurrying to get to the time clock at Solar. My shift is starting with a stirring rendition of the Air Corps song, and the guy singing must be an opera star. He's throwing himself into it with relish, and I'm getting chills up my spine. Just before I enter my building a black P-38 Lightning, newest and fastest fighter in the Air Corps, zooms over the plant doing a slow roll. "Man, that could be me," I almost shout aloud.

The morning drags slowly as usual, even though I'm dinging as fast as I can to complete a batch of exhaust sections our lead man said we had to finish before lunch break. The lunch whistle finally blows and I grab my brown bag and head for the public phones over near the drinking fountains. I call information and get the local number of the Army Air Corps. The man who answers gives me the address of their downtown office, and tells me they're open until five p.m.

The afternoon drags even slower than the morning, seeming interminable until at last I hear the shift-end whistle. I almost run to the time clock, and then to the bus stop, since I have only one-half hour to get downtown. There's a bus stop at the downtown plaza where the Air Corps office is located and I don't want to take any chance on getting there after five o'clock.

"What can I do for you?" the very handsome, young, sharply dressed lieutenant asks me as I enter the recruiting office.

"I'd like to find out about becoming an Air Corps Cadet," I reply.

"Well, there is a very rigorous series of tests, both physical and written, that is required," he says, "but at the moment there's a waiting list of candidates. It will be about six months before you can take the tests."

"Do you mean I'd have to wait six months before finding out if I even qualify?" I ask.

"I'm afraid so," he says, "but you're welcome to leave your name and address and we'll notify you when you can come in for the tests."

I leave my name and address, but I'm mighty disappointed as I walk back to the bus stop to continue on home. I don't even feel like cleaning up and selling subscriptions tonight, I think despondently.

∂   ∂   ∂

It's a week later and again I'm waiting very impatiently for the shift-end whistle to blow. Today I'm going by the regular Army recruiting office to see what possibilities might be available other than being a pilot. Six months waiting. Not for me. The war could be over before I even find out whether I'm qualified to be a pilot. I'm remembering when I was a kid and envied the boys whose fathers had been in WW I. I knew my dad had been too young, and I didn't blame him, but my kids are not going to have to envy anybody.

The whistle blows, and again I'm hurrying for the time clock as the song comes on for the first time today. It's the opera guy again, and as I'm heading for the bus stop he sings the concluding line: "We live in fame, go down in flame, There's nothing to stop the Army Air Corps." The chills are still with me as I mount the steps onto the bus.

The sergeant at the recruiting office has been explaining the various possibilities in the regular Army, and I'm not too intrigued by any of them. "Well," he says, after a while, "you probably wouldn't be interested, but we just got the enlistment material on a new kind of outfit, the paratroops. The training is awfully tough, though."

" I did some boxing at the YMCA in Omaha," I answer.

"That would probably stand you in good stead," he says as he goes on to explain the rigorous training they undergo, and about the five parachute jumps to qualify for the silver wings of a paratrooper. I'm getting more than a little intrigued when he pauses and says: "I've not even had time to get it out of the storeroom, but you'd probably like to see something."

He brings out a large, heroic-sized cardboard cutout, in vivid color, of a paratrooper in full regalia prominently displaying jump wings. Bold lettering proclaims: "BECOME A PARATROOPER! WEAR THE SILVER BADGE OF COURAGE!"

"Where do I sign?" I ask.

I'm signed up and about to leave the office when the sergeant says: "By the way, the paratroopers have a song which is sung to the tune of 'The Battle Hymn of the Republic.'

Here's the words if you'd like to take 'em with you."

I know the tune well, and I'm singing the last two lines of the chorus as I walk out of the office: "Gory, gory, what a hell of a way to die, And he ain't gonna jump no more."

After signing his enlistment papers Bill had a week to settle his civilian affairs before reporting to Fort Rosecrans: a coast artillery installation at the end of Point Loma. Winding things up at Solar was simple enough. He said goodbye to his fellow "dingers" with no regrets, although they all had been quite friendly during the few months he was there. His foreman, an older man, showed deep concern when Bill told him he was leaving for the paratroops.

"I read a big write-up about those paratroopers a while back. Boy, you are really in for it. The training alone is a man-killer, and if you get through that, the likelihood of surviving the war is slim to none. What the hell were you thinking about when you signed up? Can you still change your mind?"

"I don't know if I could still get out of it," Bill replied, "but I wouldn't if I could. Some real action is what I'm after in this war, and the paratroops look mighty good from that standpoint. I know people get killed in wars, but I'm not worried. I'll survive this one. My Uncle Ellis was with the artillery in World War I. Fought some pretty big battles, too, and he made it alright. He was my hero as a kid. I want my children to have the same feelings about me."

When it came to leaving his sales job at Collier Publishing, Bill found his leave-taking to be a bit tougher. The regional manager asked him to come in for a personal talk before leaving for the Army. When they met he was lavishly complimentary.

"You were the outstanding performer for us in San Diego. We'd like you to come back to Collier when this war is over. We're a very large company, you know. There are plenty of opportunities for an enthusiastic young man such as yourself."

"Gee, thanks, Mr. Johnson," Bill said. "I like doing this line of work, that's for sure. You can count on me: I'll get in touch as soon as it's all over."

Leaving Bonnie Smith turned out to be *easier* than he expected. The recent arguments had cooled her ardor significantly; their early enchantment with each other had definitely ended. She promised to write while he was in the service, and he pledged the same. But in their hearts, neither thought that would last for long. They were both right.

Bill's mother, her second husband Max, and his little sister Betty Jean, now all lived in the Los Angeles area. The old '33 Plymouth had breathed its last by then, replaced by a relatively new '38. Bill drove it the 150-mile trip up to L.A. to say goodbye. Their reactions were similar to everyone else when he told them of his enlistment in the paratroops.

"There must be lots of interesting jobs in the Army for a bright young man like you," Max observed. "Why'd you go and pick something as dangerous as the paratroops?"

"I don't think I could find anything as exciting as this," Bill replied. "It's the newest thing in the Army. I'll get to be one of the first guys to make it. Sort of like getting in on the ground floor of something big and important."

His mother and sister were clearly fearful for him. Golly, jumping out of planes, and with people on the ground shooting at you? How could anything be more dangerous? But they tried to hide their deep concern and be supportive. Finally, his family had to be satisfied with his promises to be as careful as possible, not take unnecessary chances, and write often. After a single overnight visit, Bill headed back down the road to San Diego and his military future.

డ   డ   డ

YOU'RE IN THE ARMY NOW
Bill's True Tale

"You didn't have to take a day off work to drive me all the way over here to the Fort, Dad."

"No, I suppose not, but I wanted to."

My father is driving me out to Ft. Rosecrans at the end of Point Loma following my final signing of Army enlistment papers last week, including volunteering to be a paratrooper. The recruiting sergeant had worried Dad more than a bit when he told him some of the reasons the paratroops was a tough group. Some second thoughts about his eighteen-year-old son going off to war in such a capacity is probably quite natural, I'm thinking. But I'm also thoroughly savoring the realization that I've finished with that deadly dumb dinging job at Solar Aircraft. Paratroops! Adventure! Wow!

"I'll be knowing the truth about you wherever you are and whatever you're doing," Dad says as we near the fort. "Your safety is in divine mind, Bill, and don't you forget it."

Dad has been a devout Christian Scientist since his recovery from tuberculosis down in Arizona several years ago, and I understand the depth of his beliefs. While I'm not the believer that he is, I'm glad it will help him handle his worries about my welfare.

"I'll sure try to remember that, Dad," I respond as we arrive at the gate entrance to Fort Rosecrans.

I'm out of our recently acquired '38 Plymouth sedan and shaking Dad's hand through his driver-side window. "I'll be sure and write about where I am and what's going on, so don't any of you worry. Adios for now."

"We'll be knowing you're okay, Bill. Bye, Bye."

The olive drab shuttle is taking me from the gate to the main buildings of the fort and I'm observing the well manicured lawns and ship-shape condition of the streets and all the facilities. Not many soldiers about and not much activity as compared to the marine facilities in San Diego where I've seen the boot-camp recruits marching and handling weapons. Then I remember that Fort Rosecrans is a coast artillery installation. Not likely to see much in the way of infantry style marching and drilling.

The supply sergeant has handed me a summer-issue khaki

uniform, an unassembled army cot, and a couple of blankets. "You'll only be here a day or two," he says, "before heading up north to Fort MacArthur. You'll get your main processing and full uniform allowance and other stuff there."

The uniform fits pretty good, but the high top shoes are stiff as boards.

I've spent most of the day just wandering around the fort trying to break in my new shoes, looking at the big guns, and shooting the breeze with a few of the guys. In the afternoon I'm shown the barracks where my cot is to be set up, and I figure I'll take a few minutes and do that.

It's obviously a brand new cot, never been assembled before, and the canvas is like hard leather. There are no directions or instructions on it, and even though I've seen army cots, it's more than a little puzzling as to just how to go about putting one together

I finally figure out that one of the two short sticks goes into each of the channeled ends of the canvas, and then the holes in the end of these sticks go over the protruding dowels on the long-side sticks. The long-side sticks become long-side by folding out on swivel hinges, and they go into the channeled sides of the canvas. I'm starting to make some real headway now, with each of the side sticks folded out and inserted properly, and each of the end sticks set in place. Just one more step will spell victory!

Quite pleased with myself I pick up the remaining end, only to find that the canvas is too short and won't quite reach. Straining to get at least one end in first I finally succeed, figuring that the other end will surely follow. The end remaining, however, is now even farther from its intended dowel. It begins to look like the manufacturer has miscalculated and shorted the canvas by several inches. On reflection I realize that is highly unlikely, and renew my strained efforts to stretch the canvas that last few inches. I'm sprawled down on my side on the floor, pulling one way with my arms and pushing with my feet in the opposite direction with all my might. Holy Jeez, I'm thinkin'. What if I can't put this thing together and I flunk out of the Army even before I have a go at the paratroops? Talk about ignominious failure! I'm gritting my teeth and sweating a bunch but it's moving a little. It's moving a little more! It's moving a little more! It's in! I have a cot! My own personally assembled Army cot!

A guy sticks his head in the door and says "Hey, True, chow in fifteen minutes." Maybe I can get a quick shower before dinner, I'm thinking. Boy, do I need it.

"Did I hear you say you weren't drafted, just volunteered for the Army?" one of the guys asks at the mess table. I'm really enjoying the food after my trying afternoon, especially since everybody had told me Army chow would be lousy. "That's right," I answer, "just got bored with civilian life and thought I'd go for a little adventure."

Another guy at the end of the table says: "Adventure? The Army? Are you kiddin'?"

The sergeant sitting next to me says "This coast artillery set-up is about all the adventure I'm lookin' for. Have you picked any branch you're interested in?"

"Yeah, I volunteered for the paratroops," I respond.

Several voices exclaim: "Paratroops?" and every head turns my way.

Some seconds pass and a fellow on the other side of the table asks: "What does it take to be a paratrooper?"

I'm stumped and don't have any idea how to answer. I guess I could quote the recruiting sergeant and repeat what he'd told my dad and me, but that would sure sound like bragging. And if my dad ever impressed anything on me, it was "never brag."

Another few seconds pass, and the Sergeant says: "Well, I'd reckon it takes about an extra yard of guts."

I'm in the Army now, and my first day passes on about as high a note as I could ask for.

     ∾   ∾   ∾

The bus ride up to Fort MacArthur in San Pedro took about four hours and Bill arrived just in time for noon chow. Following a very good meal he and a number of other new arrivals were assigned to a barracks. Next morning the formal induction processing began. Examinations, both written and physical, were given. Numerous inoculations were received. It was a long day of standing in line and being herded from building to building. Finally it ended with an announcement about what would come next.

They would hold over at Fort MacArthur until enough paratrooper volunteers had accumulated to fill a railroad passenger car. Then they would all be shipped to Georgia where their training would begin. It would probably take a week or so for that many men to be collected. In the meantime, the menial chores of K.P., latrine orderly, and post gardening would be their lot.

Double bunks were the set up in the two story barracks where the new recruits were housed. The young man in the bunk above Bill had been a child actor and played in the "Our Gang" movies. He had a bad case of acne, even worse than Bill's. According to him, that was the reason he couldn't get work in the movies any more. He loved the Australian song "Waltzing Matilda" and sang it often. In a short while, Bill had learned the lyrics and took pleasure in joining his companion, singing with a simulated "down-under" accent.

Bill was assigned to K.P. for the next two days: scrubbing

and washing pots and pans, serving food on the tray line, and peeling what seemed like a million potatoes. These were long, long days.

One night a USO group put on a show for the men. One memorable act featured a song and dance man who had also written some songs. One of his compositions contained the line "Gimme the moonlight, gimme the girl, and leave the rest up to me." His performance got the biggest hand, and after the show Bill was singing the "Gimme the Moonlight" song on his way back to the barracks.

Next day, to his great relief, Bill was taken off K.P. and put on a work detail to perform gardening on the post. He and several other new recruits were marched up a steep hill to where a number of attractive homes were located. The crew spent most of the day weeding, edging and manicuring the lawns of what they later learned were officers' quarters.

"Who the hell do these guys think they are?" Bill groused to a couple of the other men. "By God, I volunteered to be a paratrooper, not the handyman for some fancy pants commissioned officers."

The corporal in charge overheard this and was quick to respond. "Hey you! Shut up or there'll be some work a lot more miserable waiting for you," he said.

Shortly before taps that night Bill checked the barracks bulletin board. Sure enough, there was his name, listed for duty as latrine orderly for the next day. It seemed to him that the famous Army chicken-shit was already getting pretty deep. "I sure hope we get a train load of paratroop volunteers together soon," he thought, as he hit the sack.

Finally, after more than a week of waiting, good news arrived one morning. A passenger car load of new recruits had at last been assembled, and they'd be leaving first thing next day. Their destination was Toccoa, Georgia, a town none of them had ever heard of before.

August 1942, Los Angeles, California. Bill True, brand new soldier in summer khakis about to take train trip to Camp Toccoa, Georgia.

As they loaded onto a Pullman car at Union Station in Los Angeles, the men were told to choose sleeping companions. Two men would be together in a lower berth with one in the upper, for each compartment. During their stay at Fort MacArthur, Bill had gotten to know Bud Edwards from Madera, California, and Les Tindall from a small town farther north. The three of them decided to bunk together. Bill and Bud took the lower with Les above.

The group of twenty prospective paratroopers varied in age from eighteen to twenty-six, and in size from one who was a slight five-feet five to several over six feet. The smallest of the group had his guitar with him. He sang mostly country and western tunes and was quickly dubbed Little Jimmy Dickens, after a popular Grand Ole Opry performer.

Little Jimmy sang a dirty version of an old standard that broke everybody up. The opening verse went like this: "In the shade of the old apple tree, that's where Nelly first showed it to me; Just a little brown spot, she called it her twat, but it looked like a June bug to me." The following verses were even more bawdy. Bill made sure to memorize the lyrics so he could sing and play it when he could send for his own guitar.

The oldest of the group was a handsome Mexican fellow named Fritz Lucero who regaled the younger guys with tales of his prowess as a pimp in East Los Angeles. His jet-black hair and eyes, and Clark Gable-style mustache, were offset by an almost pale complexion that belied his ethnicity. It wasn't a stretch to see how women would be enthralled with him. He described in detail how he'd romance the girls with elegant dinners, dancing, and night club visits to the toniest places. Then would follow passionate love making at his expensive apartment. After they'd fallen head-over-heels for him, he'd say that if they truly loved him, and wanted to prove it, they would go to bed with a good friend of his. After they'd given in the first time, it was easy to turn them into one of his regular girls. Fritz was a smooth talker, that was sure. Though the men were initially skeptical, they finally became true believers in his prowess. Unfortunately, his convincing line of patter wouldn't save him from a humiliating departure from the paratroops just a few short months later.

Little Jimmy had grown up in some hick town in central California near Merced. He'd enlisted along with two other guys from his same neighborhood. Traveling together they were a very tight bunch. One day the three of them got to talking about how tough the paratroop training was going to be and speculating on who would make it through. "I figure most of these other yahoos are gonna wash out," Jimmy was heard to say, referring to the other new recruits in the sleeping car. His friends were quick to chime in. "Yeah, that's for sure," one said. "But we'll be getting' those jump wings in no time," referring to his own small band of compatriots from their non-descript village in the farmland. "Maybe a few of the others will make it, but not many."

Bill True and the rest just listened without comment. At that point, before the "weeding out" process had even begun, it seemed imprudent to speculate on who would or would not succeed. The training was sure to be hard, no doubt. This discretion turned out to be wise. In the end, five of the twenty men on that train failed to win their wings. Little Jimmy and one of his buddies were among them. The wisely cautious True was not.

At their first train stop in Texas several of the men found a liquor store near the station and brought some bottles back. Everybody chipped in on the cost, and the train was hardly out of the station before a party was under way. After a few drinks Little Jimmy got his guitar out and Bill joined him in leading some raucous singing. Some of the other guys also knew a few dirty lyrics and the whole gang loved those. But as the booze started working, Little Jimmy's sentimental nature got the better of him. While he was singing "When I was a lad, and old Shep was a pup" he suddenly burst into tears and became inconsolable. Bill took over on the guitar as the party continued well into the night. The boozing and singing only concluded when even he, as the final holdout, could no longer keep his head up.

It was a hot August in Texas. Their train was diverted frequently, and often stood idle for hours under the roasting sun. With no ventilation or air conditioning of any kind, the windows had to be kept open constantly. This caused a layer of soot to accumulate over everyone and everything, as exhaust from the locomotive rained down. Dirty, sweaty, and uncomfortable, with no chance to get really clean, the complaints were loud and unending. It was by far the most miserable train ride any of them had ever experienced. It gave them a head start on learning to "bitch" about conditions in the Army.

The train was slow and apparently had a low priority among war-time transport. It seemed like every time they got going well it was time to divert onto a siding while other trains passed. The result was a seemingly endless trip through Texas. Each morning the men would wake up, look out the window, and someone would ask the question on everyone's mind: "My God, are we *still* in Texas?" And the answer, morning after morning. would disappointingly be in the affirmative. Then finally came a break.

"We're in Louisiana!" one of the guys shouted from his window as the train pulled into a small station. "I told you we'd get through Texas before this war ends, and by God, I was right." The name on the station sign looked like some French word none of the men had ever heard before, but sure enough it was Louisiana. And it wasn't much longer before they pulled into a real jumping place everyone knew.

"New Orleans!" the conductor shouted. There would be

a six to eight hour layover and they'd have a chance to see a bit of the city. A USO facility with showers was the first stop. The men could clean up, shave, and change uniforms before seeing the sights. A tour of the French Quarter was exciting for all, none of whom had ever been there before. Bill got a big thrill at a Dixieland jazz club, blaring full tilt right in the middle of the afternoon.

Following the tour the men were welcomed back to the USO by several young ladies. They were beautiful and personable and Bill guessed that they were just the sort of young women he had seen frequently on the society pages of the Omaha World Herald. As friendly as they were attractive, the girls danced with the men, talked at length, and joined in board games for more than two hours. In short order Bill was in love with Madeleine, a vivacious brunette who was attending a Catholic college for girls. She gave him her address and they later exchanged a few letters. However, as with so many wartime flirtations, the relationship was not to last and the writing ceased after a few months.

For the remainder of the train ride, from New Orleans all the way to Toccoa, Bill and the others talked about those beautiful southern belles. "Georgia is Deep South too," one said. "We'll probably meet girls like that all the time." Little did they know that the hospitality of the big city could not be matched by a small town in Georgia that was quickly swarming with paratroopers in training.

The California carload of aspiring paratroopers pulled into the small Toccoa railroad station at 2 a.m. on a cool morning in early September, 1942. Trucks were waiting to take them the few miles out of town to their training base. It was called Camp Toombs, named after a famous military hero of long ago. The name would shortly be changed to Camp Toccoa for what seemed obvious reasons.

Upon arriving, the men were unceremoniously unloaded next to a line of tents that were raised beside a road still muddy from the previous day's rain. These would be their barracks for the time being, four men to a tent. They shouldered their duffel bags, shuffled to the five tents they would occupy, and stooped to enter. The floors of the tents were as muddy as the road, and the single bare light bulb lit a dreary domicile indeed. As the men tossed their bags on the cots (the only dry place to put them) their spirits were less than soaring. "Well," Bill mused to his three companions, "we made it this far anyway. And they did warn us that getting to be a paratrooper would be tough."

"Yeah," Les Tindall replied, "but, Holy Mackerel, nobody said we'd have to swim through mud to get to the airplanes!

CHAPTER II

Separating Men From Boys
Camp Toccoa and Currahee Mountain

"Train hard, fight easy."
American proverb

———————

The first full day at Camp Toccoa was inauspicious indeed for the boys from California. In addition to the continuous chilly rain and the miserably muddy condition of their tents, standing endlessly in line for ever more physical examinations was nerve wracking. What they hadn't realized was that the physicals they'd gone through up to that point were merely the basic requirements for general service in the Army. Qualification for the paratroops was something else altogether, and they were only now being measured against those standards. They were all apprehensive, if not downright scared.

Bill was concerned about a childhood hernia operation he'd had, but the examining doc didn't find a problem with it and marked him down as well qualified. Others were not so fortunate. Three of the twenty boys from California saw their paratrooper dreams end as the man with the stethoscope washed them out. Bill thought it was particularly sad when one of the most eager of the group was disqualified for color blindness. The man hadn't even been aware of his problem, and was broken hearted as he packed his bags for transfer to the infantry.

The 506th Parachute Infantry Regiment being formed at

Toccoa was the first of its kind. The men would be trained from the start both in basic infantry skills and the added specializations of paratroops. All existing parachute regiments were different. They consisted of men who had first received infantry basic training, the same as regular troops. Then those who wanted to, volunteered for jump school at Fort Benning, Georgia. After that, each individual was assigned to whatever paratroop unit needed men. Bill's group was among the first to be trained as parachute soldiers from the ground up, and who would all serve together in combat.

Twelve companies would constitute the 506th, as volunteers from all over the country came in. Bill's California contingent found itself assigned to the First Platoon of Company F. Filling out this company would top off the 2nd Battalion. When fully manned, the regiment would consist of three battalions, each with four line companies plus a regimental headquarters unit: total manpower would approach 2,000.

Assignment to a company meant housing in real barracks and, eventually, even paved streets. Each barracks housed sixteen men in double bunks, with windows and doors in the front and rear. Numerous electrical outlets and four overhead lights provided adequate, if not sumptuous, lighting and convenience. Each man had a limited shelf space and floor trunk for storage of uniforms and personal belongings.

Bill True's barracks housed a few of his compatriots from California. But most importantly, the three men who would become his closest buddies throughout the war were assigned there with him: Joe Flick from Pennsylvania; Bob Stone from Massachusetts; and Johnny Jackson from Long Beach, California.

A mess hall large enough to accommodate the 120 enlisted men in each company was located at the end of the company street. Unusual for the Army, the dining was family style. With tables and benches serving ten men each, large serving platters of food were brought from the kitchen to the table by alternating volunteers. "Short stopping" a serving plate to take a portion as it was passed to the man requesting the item was strictly forbidden, as several men unfamiliar with the custom learned early on.

Second helpings on most of the bill of fare were liberally provided, and the man who took the last portion from a platter was obligated to go to the kitchen for the refill. This was usually not a problem except when an especially desirable dessert was provided. Of these there were almost never seconds. The time taken in going to the kitchen could result in a man returning to find a dessert platter with only a tiny portion remaining. Though this was an occasional irritant, the situation never got out of hand. No brawls ever resulted.

The strenuous regimen of physical activity that paratroop training required became apparent immediately. On the very first morning after assignment to F Company, Bill True found himself falling out in the company street at the crack of dawn for vigorous calisthenics. Lt. Tuck led the exercises that morning. After some stretching to loosen up, the group was put through extended and laborious movements. Bill thought Tuck would keep up the "side-straddle-hop" till the whole company would drop in their tracks. It was apparent that the lieutenant was in great physical condition, and he enjoyed showing it.

When most of the company had neared exhaustion the lieutenant asked if anybody would like to come up and lead an exercise. Under the best of circumstances True wouldn't dream of volunteering for such a performance. Few in the company ever did. But Julius Houck immediately stepped forward and offered a special leg exercise he said was designed for skiers. It involved bending and twisting the legs and holding painful positions for an extended time. It was obvious that Houck was trying to outdo Tuck, but the lieutenant was enjoying it and encouraged him to continue. True commented, sotto voce, that Houck was undoubtedly bucking for stripes. "Turning his buddies into contortionists is a hell of a way to go about it, though," he added.

Blue swim trunks and boots were the uniform for calisthenics nearly every morning, and this first day set the pattern. After breakfast the men were allowed a few minutes to make their bunks and straighten up the barracks before forming up again in the company street. Company Commander Lt. Thomas P. Mulvey (shortly to become Captain) told the assembly they would be running up nearby Mt. Currahee that morning. They could expect this to be repeated frequently thereafter as part of their physical training. "It's three miles up and three miles down. We're going to separate the men from the boys," he announced, "so let's see which we have here." That sounded ominous enough to Bill and his buddies, but they had yet to learn just how testing those runs would become.

The first mile and a half of the trail up the mountain rose quite gradually. But then the going got steeper and the last mile was abruptly uphill. What began as a brisk double time had by degrees slowed till a brisk walk was all that could be maintained. Three men had already dropped out, and others were close to sheer exhaustion. Climbing the final mile to the top of Currahee eliminated three more, and left the entire group wondering how they could keep going.

Circling the top of the mountain Mulvey shouted "Cheer

up men, it's all downhill from here on." Breaking into a brisk double time once more he led the column back down the trail. True, Joe Flick, Bob Stone and Johnny Jackson were at the rear of the formation and had already noticed the accordion effect that occurs in such movements. Following elements of a column gradually lose ground and fall behind, and then have to scramble to catch up again. In catching up they tend to bunch together and then have to slow down to get back to normal intervals.

Flick voiced the feelings of all of the men in the rear: "It looks to me like it's a heck of lot easier to run up front where you set your own pace. Back here we're either all jammed up and have to slow down, or run like hell to catch up."

"Yeah," True said, "next time let's hope 1st Platoon leads the way and we can try to maneuver our squad as close to the front as possible."

That first Mt. Currahee run took slightly over an hour, and ten of the men didn't make it all the way. All of those would eventually wash out, three of them leaving that same day. Others would follow their lead before basic training ended. Allowed time was gradually tightened as training continued, and the last run before leaving Toccoa for Fort Benning at the end of November took under fifty minutes.

The company was given the luxury of a fifteen minute break after the Currahee jaunt before falling out for close order drill. Almost none of the men had previous experience in any kind of marching. Even learning to properly "right face," "left face," and "about face," took a bit of time. They wouldn't get their rifles for a few weeks, but they could learn the fundamentals of marching into left and right turns, by columns and by flanks, while waiting. Adding the "manual of arms" when the rifles came would round them into a sharp marching and drilling unit.

Fall 1942, Camp Toccoa, Georgia. Bill True in blue swim trunks and Army shoes, uniform for nearly half the time during basic training as they engaged in extensive physical exercise including (a) running Mt. Currahee (three miles up and three miles down in about 50 minutes); (b) running the demanding obstacle course; (c) tossing logs; (d) double-timing everywhere, and (e) etc., etc.

After their initial drill there was nearly an hour left before lunch break. The company double-timed to a hillside just beyond the barracks area for a lecture from the company Executive Officer, Lt. Carl B. MacDowell. "Military Courtesy" and the "Ten General Orders for Guard Duty" were the topics he discussed, and he stressed that when an enlisted man saluted an officer, it simply amounted to courtesy for the uniform. Everyone just "knew" that a private in the paratroops was the equivalent of a commissioned officer in any other branch, but military courtesy called for the salute.

Written copies of the guard duty orders were distributed and the men were instructed to memorize them during the next several days. An officer or one of the cadre sergeants could ask a man to recite one of the General Orders at any time, and an incorrect response would result in an extra KP or Latrine Orderly assignment. Lt. MacDowell lightened the occasion by telling the story, probably apocryphal, about a private who was court-martialed for looking into a bedroom window as an officer's wife undressed. The soldier was acquitted, defending his actions with the 1st General Order: "To walk my post in a military manner keeping always on the alert and observing everything that takes place within sight or hearing."

An entire hour and a half break for lunch was a welcome respite and most of the men managed a half-hour nap before falling out for a full afternoon of activity. This relaxation was a good thing. After lunch began the first of daily intensive training aimed at real paratroop work.

Fall 1942, Camp Toccoa, Georgia. Bill True wearing regular fatigue uniform and both a main and reserve parachute, standing beside a mock-up plane door that they practiced exiting from for hours at a time.

First up was practice jumps from ground level mock planes as the men wore simulated parachutes. These planes were modeled after the C-47, an Army modification of the civilian DC-3. The men formed groups of 16, which were expected to be a typical full load of paratroopers in any single aircraft. The official term for this assemblage was a "stick" of jumpers.

They learned that the first command in preparing to jump was to "Stand up and hook up!" This order meant to rise from their bucket seats and hook the parachute's static line to the cable running overhead through the center of the cabin.

The next order would be a check of each man's rigging and static line by the man behind him. A slap on the back would indicate that all was okay. Then came the command to "Sound off for equipment check!" In countdown order each man in the stick would shout "Sixteen okay!," "Fifteen okay!," "Fourteen okay!," indicating that they were ready to exit the aircraft.

Other commands and actions led to the final act of jumping from the plane door, which was located on the port (left) side, aft. In reality this was more like "stepping" out the door, but with a very specific and choreographed move. With his left foot planted at the edge of the doorway, the jumper swung his right leg out and pivoted to the left as he fell into space.

In an actual jump this put his back to both the prop wash and the forward movement of the aircraft. His weight would then automatically drop him safely below the tail section while the plane passed above. As the force of the wind carried him rearward, his fall would pull the static line which was still connected to the cable inside the plane. At the end of its travel, the line ripped off a protective cover to deploy the chute, and then the line snapped free.

When a jump was done properly it would result in a relatively gentle acceleration, at least until the canopy opened and filled with air. As each man left the practice airplane he shouted slowly, "One thousand, two thousand, three thousand!" This was to measure the time before the shock was felt of the parachute opening. If no shock had occurred by the count of three thousand, it was time to pull the manual rip-cord on the emergency chute.

After several "jumps" the company double-timed to a large athletic field a half mile from the barracks for more parachute practicing. There, a five-foot high platform was set up, surrounded by thirty-foot tall wooden upright beams. From these, simulated parachute risers and harnesses were suspended. Strapping into the harness and jumping off the platform, each man received directions from Lt. Brierre on how to manipulate the risers to minimize oscillation, turn his back into the wind, and take other measures to minimize the danger of injury on landing.

Nearby was another piece of parachute simulation that was a bit more of a challenge, both physically and mentally. It was a thirty-five foot high wooden tower. From this the men would jump wearing a parachute-type harness attached by risers to a pulley. The pulley rode on a fifty-foot long cable that ran from the tower top to the ground. The goal here was learning to "roll" when hitting the ground, and this took some practice and effort. More than a few men suffered minor injuries in the process. The leap from the mock-up didn't equal an actual jump from a plane, of course, but the drop did produce a sickening stomach wrench. Landing on the ground wasn't as hard as a real hit either, but it helped in teaching the men how to roll with the momentum.

All these practice procedures were repeated nearly every day at Toccoa. By the time the regiment arrived at Ft.

Benning in early December to make real jumps from real planes, the entire process was automatic with no thought required.

When their first parachute simulations were finally over, there was still more activity to come. A quick double-time back to the hillside near the barracks put them in place for lectures from the officers on various aspects of infantry life. At least the shift away from hard physical activities to more "intellectual" pursuits was a welcome relief. Lt. Colt discussed basic tactics and introduced the fundamental rule for action in combat: "Do *something*, even if it's wrong!" (In later times Flick and True would corrupt this into what became almost a motto for their own squad: "Do something, even if it's right!")

Next Lt. Tuck talked about map reading, and demonstrated the use of a compass in crossing unfamiliar terrain. His knowledge of the subject was thorough and obvious. First was a lesson in "striking an azimuth." Then came perhaps an even more important skill: how to "get reoriented" when lost. Navigation on the battlefield was covered at great length.

Nearly an hour remained before evening chow on their first full day at Camp Toccoa. Not to waste any opportunity for training, the men were ordered to assemble on the company street for yet further close order drill. Tired as they were, and with only their earlier brief exposure to the subject, precision and timing on the various movements had already improved. There was still a long way to go to achieve the perfection of crack troops. But they had begun.

As they returned from the mess hall, night closed in on a *very* tired bunch of trainees. To a man, they fell onto their bunks with grateful sighs that a long, long day had finally ended.

Fall 1942, Camp Toccoa, Georgia. Bill True wearing swim trunks and shoes as he traverses monkey bars over water on the obstacle course.

త్   త్   త్

On their second day at Toccoa, a new challenge awaited Bill and his fellow volunteers. At the southern edge of the athletic field was an obstacle course which the men could see from the parachute simulation area. This had not been run the day before, in lieu of the Currahee climb. But in the future, on any day when they didn't go up the mountain, this would be the alternative.

The course started at the top of a precipitous rise and ran 75 yards steeply downhill, with numerous obstacles to be clambered over and through along the way. At the bottom there was a fifty-foot-wide, shallow-water moat which had to be traversed by swinging across hand over hand on monkey bars. Numerous trainees got a thorough soaking in their first attempts to cross.

Once past the moat, another fifty yards of painful obstructions awaited them: rope swings over ditches, crawling through tunnels, the hazardous inclined "pipe ladder" and other challenges. The worst was a fifteen-foot tall log wall, which required climbing hand over hand by sheer strength. Though these obstacles ran mostly on level ground, they led to a final leg straight back up the hill. By the time the troops had regained the top, everyone was in a state of utter exhaustion.

Now the men knew intimately the face of their principle challenge at Toccoa: physical conditioning. Every day it would be either the mountain or the course. "Men" would make it, while the "boys" would gradually fall aside. But grueling as the obstacle course was, it never induced the sheer, moaning dread that was the cruelty of Currahee Mountain. "Currahee" is an Indian word meaning "he who stands alone" and it became the official motto of the 506th. It was a fitting slogan.

ও   ও   ও

Early rising at reveille every morning took some getting used to for most of the men, but the battalion bugler was a professional musician with a bent for improvisation. Soon they became curious with anticipation as to what he'd be blowing each day. This took some edge off the misery of rising at the crack of dawn.

"Policing" the company street and general barracks area each day was a common ritual. True wondered at the use of the word policing to describe what was simply "trash collection" to him, but he learned to accept Army lingo, whatever it's origin. The same cadre sergeant usually supervised this process, and his favored order to begin was, "All I want to see is assholes and elbows."

The same man often admonished his charges to "field strip" their cigarette butts, meaning essentially to dismantle them in a way that left no evidence. This not only would leave no trail for an enemy to follow, but would make the "policing" of the company streets a lot easier. The instruction held little import for Bill, since he did not yet smoke. That would soon change.

The American tobacco companies were patriotically eager to "comfort" soldiers in the field by providing them with free smokes. Of course, the creation of an entire generation of loyal customers was probably not far behind that sentiment in their motivations. As a result, free packs of cigarettes were liberally distributed to virtually anyone who wanted them. Once, on an overnight field problem, Bill was tossed a pack of Lucky Strikes, and that was all it took. With tobacco almost free in the Army PX, and actually included in every "K" and "C" ration, he quickly developed a habit that took him nearly 20 years to break. His father would *not* be pleased.

In addition to strange new official Army lingo, Bill True was introduced to the use of profanity far exceeding anything he'd known before. He was used to the f— word, of course, but not its monotonous use as a common adjective to describe anything or anyone derisively. "This f—ing chow is slop," or "those f—ing cooks couldn't boil eggs." But what really shocked him, the term that he never heard with anything but revulsion, was "mother-f—r." Some of the southern boys seemed to use it nearly as often as the simple f— word, and so casually that it became apparent that they didn't even think of it as anything other than normal polite conversation. For some, the habitual profanity would become troublesome when they were allowed their first leaves home to see family and friends. It just wouldn't do at the dinner table to forget your place, and ask your mother to "pass the f—ing peas!"

☙   ☙   ☙

Bill's later deep friendship with Johnny Jackson could not have been predicted by either of them when they met. Back at Fort MacArthur, the two Californians had gotten off to a bad start. True was naturally shy and reserved. This was seen by Johnny as somehow superior or "uppity," and thereafter he seemed to take every opportunity to criticize and needle his fellow recruit. By the time they got to Toccoa the relationship was approaching genuine animosity.

Once F Company had settled into something of a routine, it became normal for regular barracks inspections to be held. An item always addressed was the proper making up of bunks. Each had to be smartly dressed, with the top blanket so taught that a quarter would bounce off it. This inspection was a group responsibility. A failure on any single count would lead to punishment or loss of privileges for everyone in the barracks.

One morning, just before inspection, Johnny Jackson walked calmly over to True's bunk and suddenly flopped down on it, intentionally rumpling it. This was hostile and overtly physical—a definite escalation of their conflict.

Bill knew he couldn't just let it ride. He immediately walked to Johnny's bunk and did the same, sprawling on the blanket and snarling it in a mess. With that, the battle was joined.

Johnny gave a shout and lunged across the barracks at Bill, taking a huge swing at his jaw. True dodged the blow, which landed on his shoulder instead, and threw a left jab at Johnny's chin in return. Now the others quickly jumped in. It would go hard on everyone if the inspecting officer came in to find not an orderly and well-kept barracks, but a sloppy brawl in progress. The combatants were forcibly separated and each sullenly re-made his own bunk with a scowl.

The barracks passed inspection, no thanks to the two Californians, who kept to themselves for the remainder of the morning. But then, after lunch, Bill got a real surprise. Johnny came over to his bunk, offered his hand in a friendly shake, and actually apologized. Both the hand and apology were readily accepted and the two buried the hatchet at once and forever. After that a friendship grew that eventually surpassed even that of many blood brothers.

At Toccoa, each day came to routinely include extensive physical exertions: either the Mt. Currahee or obstacle course runs, plus additional calisthenics and other forms of strength development. Then one of the regimental officers happened to read about a "log tossing" maneuver Canadian commandos used for conditioning. Well, anything those Canucks could do, the Airborne could do better! So one morning the 506 men found the athletic field littered with logs.

Each log was ten feet long with a diameter of eight to ten inches. These would be lifted by eight men, four on each side, and tossed as high as possible. Catching the log as it fell back the men would place it on the ground again, then pick it up and repeat the full maneuver. Each step in the process was performed on command by one of the lieutenants. The exercise continued till the men could barely lift the logs.

This was repeated on numerous subsequent days. On one of the early log rolling drills Joe Flick muttered to True, "The lieutenant knows the commands by heart, but you sure as hell don't see any *officers* tossing these damn things!"

৯৭   ৯৭   ৯৭

Field maneuvers were often held in the afternoons. This required marches into the Georgia hills to find terrain appropriate for the various infantry problems. Generally speaking, these were long and boring. In his youth, Bill and his dad had sung songs together to entertain themselves during their bachelor years. They took turns with either melody or harmony, and now it seemed natural for Bill to sing with the rhythm of a marching column. So one day, all on his own, True let out with a familiar tune. Soon nearly all of the men in his 3rd Squad, and many of the others in the 1st Platoon, joined in. After that it became natural for the men to sing as entertainment to pass the miles. "The Battle Hymn of the Republic," especially, lent itself to a marching cadence, and numerous parodies were applied to that tune.

One grasshopper hopped upon
    another grasshopper's back,
One grasshopper hopped upon
    another grasshopper's back,
One grasshopper hopped upon
    another grasshopper's back,
As we go marching on.

They were only playing leap frog,
They were only playing leap frog,
They were only playing leap frog.
As one grasshopper hopped upon
    another grasshopper's back.

Friday night marches became part of the weekly regimen, beginning with the first week of training. Full pack, with no canteen and no breaks on the entire march was S.O.P. (standard operating procedure). The length varied, beginning at about ten miles their first time out. After that, a mile or two was added each week, with little other variation. Fortunately, coffee and doughnuts always awaited them on their return, hot and freshly made by the company cooks. It was the one bright spot in an otherwise arduous routine.

By the sixth Friday night march the distance was up to nearly twenty miles. The men were becoming hardened by all of their physical conditioning, but twenty miles with no breaks and nothing to drink was still a daunting challenge. Fatigue was only exceeded by the cotton-spitting dryness of every mouth. Toward the end of this particular trek the route crossed a small stream. The men had been warned never to drink from any of the creeks they encountered, for health reasons. Beyond that, trying to sneak a drink would be a major disciplinary infraction. But on this night, as one of the cadre sergeants was wading through the stream he suddenly stumbled and fell. His face went into the water, and it seemed to all who saw him that he took longer than needed to stand and resume the march. Lt. Tuck, in particular, observed this delay with obvious interest. Nothing was said at the time, and no official explanation was ever offered. But that sergeant was shipped out to the regular infantry the very next day. The significance of this was not lost on anyone in camp.

THE FIRST PLATOON SINGERS
Bill's True Tale

I've been here at Camp Toccoa for nearly two months now, assigned to 1st Platoon, Company F, 2nd Battalion, 506th Parachute Infantry Regiment. The 3rd Battalion, last to be formed in the regiment, now also has its full complement of men and officers, and the entire regiment is fully engaged in a tough routine of basic infantry and paratrooper training.

A lot of good men washed out of W Company where we all were initially assigned while undergoing testing and stringent physical examinations. I really felt sorry for Al Sprague who came with me and the others on the train from California. The most eager volunteer for the paratroops I'd met yet, he flunked out for color blindness. He was crushed and it scared me that the docs might find out about my hernia operation as a kid and wash me out, too. Luckily I passed.

We've just returned to barracks after a brisk march of six or seven miles back to camp following some field maneuvers that took up most of the day. "Dude Boy" Stone says "Hey,

Bill, have you heard that the 2nd and 3rd Platoon guys are starting to call us the Singers? The First Platoon Singers. How do you like that?"

"Well, I've been called a lot worse things than that, Dude," I reply. "They're probably just jealous of our outstanding musical abilities and wish they could match us." I'm remembering the last thing we were singing as we marched back into camp today. We sing a lot of stuff to the tune of "The Battle Hymn of the Republic."

"Is everybody happy?" cried the sergeant looking up
Our hero bravely answered "yes"
    and then they stood him up
He jumped right out into the blast
    his static line unhooked
And he ain't gonna jump no more

Gory, gory, what a helluva way to die
Gory, gory, what a helluva way to die
Gory, gory, what a helluva way to die
And he ain't gonna jump no more

"I think you're right, Bill, they're just envious and would love to have our operatic talents," Dude says as we grab our towels and soap and head for the showers. "The main thing they're missing, though, is how some singing on the march helps pass the time and shorten the miles."

It's after chow and some of us are down at the PX having a few cokes and shooting the breeze. Johnny Jackson, Joe Flick, Dude and I are at a table together when a 2nd Platoon guy hollers over and says "How about some entertainment for the fighting platoons from our First Platoon Singers?"

Dude is always the fastest among us with the comeback

so he hollers "When somebody puts a little green on the table we'll be glad to sing for our many fans. Otherwise, our only free performances are on the road where your song requests will be given every consideration."

"That ought to slow loudmouth Barnes down for a bit," Flick, says.

"It might if that dummy could even recognize a put down when he heard it," I observe. "But he probably thinks we were flattered by his stupid remark."

"You know it's been some time, Dude, since you've recounted your recollections from that play 'Tobacco Road' that you saw in New York," Johnny suggests. Joe and I second his request.

"Okay, guys," Dude agrees. "You remember it's about this hillbilly Lester family that has a somewhat backward son they call Dude Boy, and a good-looking daughter, Ellie Mae, who vamps simple-minded share-croppers out of their rutabagas."

"Well, throughout the play Dude Boy is forever bouncing a ball off the side of the house, and Jeeter Lester, the father, keeps hollering out 'Dude Boy, stop a bouncin' that ball off'n them clapper boards.'" The rest of us have never seen the play, but we know that with Dude's mimicry ability we're hearing the authentic Broadway Jeeter Lester.

Dude knows that he's been stuck with his nickname not out of any lack of smarts, but because of his rendition of that line and our real affection for him. A nickname in the military may occasionally be bestowed for other reasons, but it's usually a sign of respect and affection, and that's certainly true with Robert S. "Dude Boy" Stone.

"How about when Jeeter lures Luv into the yard so Ellie Mae can hustle him out of his sack of vegetables?" Joe suggests.

"Yeah, well, Luv is walking past the Lester place and

Jeeter is leaning on the pitiful remains of a picket fence when he calls out 'Luv, whatcha got in that there croaker sack, rutabagas maybe?"'

I'm laughing as I'm reminded of another of Jeeter's lines about rutabagas and ask Dude to do it as well.

"Jeeter is looking out across a vista that obviously includes a lot more land than just his little farm (on which he does precious little farming anyway) and he's waxing philosophical as he talks about what he's going to do some time in the future. 'Some day I'm gonna plow up aaallll that land and plant it all in rutabagas. Yes sir, some day [and now he's sweeping his arm all across the sky] 'I'm gonna plow up aaallll that land as fur as the eye can see and I'm gonna plant it all in rutabagas.'"

Dude is really getting into it now, and guys at other tables are listening and laughing too, as Johnny suggests that he do some of his President Roosevelt stuff.

Dude stands up for this one, enunciating slowly and dramatically. "I hate wahr! Eleanor hates wahr! Our little Scotty Fala hates wahr!"

Some of the guys who've not heard Dude do this bit are splitting a gut. As many times as I've heard it I can't stop laughing either. I swear I think if FDR heard himself mimicked so well, especially by a soldier who's not a professional comedian, he'd get a big kick out of it, too.

"Do another FDR!" somebody from another platoon calls over.

Again with drama and drawn out phrasing: "I will not send our boys ovehseas this yeah...or next yeah...or any other yeah."

Dude sits down and we all give him a round of applause.

It occurs to me that that last FDR line will be ironically funny, big time, sometime in the future when the 506th ships out for some destination that will be "oveh" the seas for sure.

"We run Currahee tomorrow," someone mentions loudly, and there is general moaning. The three-mile up and three-mile down run that we make on Mount Currahee every other morning has become a frightful chore for everyone. We have a monster of an obstacle course, and engage in various other forms of tortuous exercise every day as well, but nothing matches the mountain in dread.

Chairs are loudly scraping away from tables throughout the PX as everyone knows a good night's sleep is especially important for Mount Currahee mornings. Nevertheless Dude, Joe, Johnny and I decide to add to our reputation as The First Platoon Singers by harmonizing on "Show Me the Way to Go Home."

> Show me the way to go home,
> I'm tired and I want to go to bed,
> I had a little drink about an hour ago,
> And it went right to my head,
> Wherever I may roam,
> Over land or sea or foam,
> You can always hear me singin' this song,
> Show me the way to go home.

Promotions to PFC were posted the same Saturday the cadre sergeant left. But as the men read down the list there had obviously been an error. Bill was disappointed not to be promoted, but that wasn't the worst part. Ray Ott *was*, and everyone in camp knew that was wrong. Ray barely made it through much of the exercises and was considered to be a good candidate for washing out altogether. Yet Otto May, one of the older guys and an excellent soldier, had been *left off!* Who the hell did that!? It looked like somebody had been a little hasty and careless with the typewriter. Did they get "Ott" and "Otto" confused? Sure looked like it.

BILL TRUE F COMPANY
BY CHRISTENSON

Postwar drawing of Bill True in jump suit and holding a guitar. The drawing is by Burton "Chris" Christenson of E Company ("Band of Brothers"). Chris could sing a great tenor harmony, and he and Bill (on guitar) did a lot of singing together at postwar reunions.

Though never acknowledged by the officers, this and other errors were corrected the following week. Otto May did make PFC, and to their great pleasure so did Bill True and Joe Flick. Julius Houck was promoted to Corporal at the same time; one of the first of the raw recruits to attain non-com status. No one was surprised at this. His aggressive behavior from the time of their first calisthenics had marked him as a strong leader.

The duties of a Corporal included serving as Charge of Quarters: "CQ" for short. This involved manning the company headquarters office at night and waking the men in the morning. Corporal Houck learned to relish making his wake up calls. Throwing open the barracks door with a crash, he would shout, "Drop your cocks, and grab your socks!" Though this was mildly amusing at first, True soon found it irritating and became glad that Houck didn't get CQ very often.

Gordon Mather was also among the first group to be promoted to Corporal. No one in the 1st Platoon was surprised by this and most were pleased. Gordon was one of the best soldiers in the outfit. He hailed from Indiana, but had spent some time in Africa working in diamond mines. He was in his early twenties—older than most of the other guys—and a natural leader. The men readily accepted his supervision. Everyone got a kick from his tales of working with crews in the mines. He often entertained the squad with his deep-voiced imitation of native workers there, tossing out such phrases as "Bwana Makooba," and "Poonjohnny." Nobody knew what these meant, but it didn't matter. They always got a laugh.

Bill True was extremely pleased to make PFC since it meant official recognition that he was a good soldier. He had no aspirations for non-com status, since responsibility for the conduct and discipline of men older than himself was well beyond his level of self confidence. But he took pride in doing a good job and being known as an asset to the company.

      ∾   ∾   ∾

One day the men were herded into a large tent for a lecture and "demonstration" by the battalion doctor. It was on a subject which was not exactly new, but the extent and detail now presented were a step up from before. The subject: VD.

"I suppose you guys have heard the smart-ass expression that 'any man who won't f..., won't fight,'" said the doc. "Well that's bullshit, but this isn't: 'Any man who has a dose of venereal disease sure as hell *can't* fight!' I'm not here to give you any lectures on abstinence. I'm here to tell you how to protect yourselves."

Bill True remembered his introduction to the subject during his brief stay at Fort MacArthur. Especially vivid was the memory of a film all the new recruits had been shown. It depicted the horrors of VD in graphic and gruesome detail. One poor victim had a horribly disfigured face and he could only talk in a hoarse whisper as the disease ravaged his body. It made Bill's skin crawl just to think of that image.

"Always, *always* use a rubber, men!" the doc continued. "But that's only a beginning! You'll be issued a 'pro-kit' every time you go on any pass or furlough. I can't over-emphasize how important it is to use *everything in the kit*. Here's what you've got to do to protect yourselves."

Then the doctor opened up the pro-kit and gave a detailed explanation of its contents and use. Besides the standard rubber prophylactic, which all the men were familiar

66

with, there were two small tubes of medicine. The first was an antibiotic cream for internal use: it was to be squeezed into the end of the penis and massaged up the urethra by hand. "You'll have to work at it a bit," he said, "but it's important to get that stuff way up in there."

Next was a medicinal cream for external use. It was to be smeared all over the penis and the testicles. This seemed like a lot of trouble to endure, just to get safely laid. Some of the guys asked dumb questions about having to use the whole routine, but the doctor was adamant. "The only way to completely protect yourself is to do everything I've said—no exceptions. I know you'll all want to go home clean and healthy, so *don't take any chances!*"

True to its word, the Army issued pro-kits to the men liberally throughout their entire enlistments. It was a remarkably enlightened and positive step to keep soldiers hale and hearty for combat. Contrary to popular notion, military leaders *are* capable of learning important lessons. This one had come from hard experience going all the way back to the Civil War, when blue-nosed Victorian attitudes disallowed even the mention of "social diseases" in polite company. At its peak, the epidemic of syphilis had disabled nearly a third of the Army of the Potomac. Armies engaged in the global conflict of the 1940s could not allow such reckless disregard for health.

                ❧   ❧   ❧

Up to this point the men at Toccoa had not trained with actual weapons. The camp didn't even have a firing range. And in any event, their brand new M-1 Garand rifles were still on back-order. Instead, the recruits had used broomsticks to practice drilling.

Finally, after weeks of anticipation, all that changed. The new rifles arrived and were greeted with great delight. Fresh from the factory, they were still covered with a thick coating of cosmolene, so the first task was to disassemble and clean them thoroughly. First Sergeant Willie Morris demonstrated how to take them apart. His first admonition was that the militarily correct term for the weapon was not "rifle" but "piece." "Calling it a rifle is permissible, but not really correct. And you must never *ever* refer to it as a 'gun'," he said. "Your piece will be your best friend in the combat to come. Take care of it accordingly and treat it like your first love."

This was sound advice, and the M-1 was worthy of such respect. Adopted by the U.S. military in 1936, it was the brain child of a genuine genius: John Cantius Garand. It was the only semi-automatic weapon used by common soldiers of *any* army in World War II. It could empty its 8-round clip of .30-06 ammunition as fast as the soldier could repeatedly pull the trigger. Installing a fresh clip took only a second. When supplied in the field with a full bandolier of ammo, the American soldier wielded impressive firepower. By contrast, German soldiers had to rack the bolt separately for each round on a slow, 5-shot rifle whose basic design dated from the previous century.

The M-1 was powerful and extremely accurate. It weighed in at a hefty 11 pounds when fully loaded, but was well-balanced and easy to shoot, with excellent sights and an effective range of over 400 yards. Lt. Gen. George S. Patton once remarked, "In my opinion, the M-1 rifle is the greatest battle implement ever devised."

Continuing his instruction, Sgt. Morris taught his men the nomenclature of all the parts in their piece—trigger housing group, barrel, receiver group, stock group—and how to assemble and disassemble it blindfolded. Each man was ordered to memorize the serial number of his piece and, as with the Guard Duty General Orders, be ready to count it off when questioned. Extra KP and Latrine Orderly assignments were the standard punishment for nearly all transgressions; forgotten serial numbers were no exception.

With the arrival of the new rifles, close order drills were quickly supplemented with the "manual of arms." Learning to "order arms," "shoulder arms," and "port arms," came relatively easy. The choreography for "inspection arms" was a bit more tricky, however.

Formal inspection of arms always occurred during a strict stand to attention. If the man had his piece at the right shoulder arms position, the drilling officer would first give the command to "Or–der…h'arms." At this the man would ground his piece on his right side. Next the drilling officer would bark the instruction "Inspec–tion…h'arms," and the man would sharply snap his piece to the port arm position before his chest. While holding it with the right hand alone he would then quickly look down, throw the bolt open and lock it with the left.

At this point the inspecting officer would step forward and raise his arms to take the piece. Before the officer's hands reached the rifle, however, the soldier was to quickly release it and drop his hands to his side. The inspector would then grasp and raise the rifle into the air and peer through the muzzle to check the bore. Woe unto him whose piece was not spotlessly clean! Having finished, the inspecting officer would hand the piece back, then side-step to the next man in the rank.

Receiving his inspected rifle back with the bolt still open, the soldier would firmly grasp it with his left hand. While depressing the clip spring with his right thumb, he would simultaneously hold the bolt open with the heel of his right hand. Releasing the bolt and removing his thumb at the same split second permitted the bolt to safely slam closed. This was the delicate part of the process since the bolt spring was very strong, with a fast action. Any delay in removing the thumb completely out of the clip area would result in a very pained digit or, in the worst case, a trip to medical.

It was presumed by all that Lt. Tuck had attended some kind of military school or academy before entering the army. He had a unique manner of rifle inspection that was really spectacular. As a soldier would drop his piece for the inspection, Tuck would grab it with one hand, whirl it like a propeller a few times, toss it to the other hand in an almost invisible motion, and with a final flourish throw the rifle to the raised position for peering through the bore. After watching this performance a few times True got the feeling that Tuck would have appreciated some applause.

Since there was no rifle range at Camp Toccoa, only dry-run practice firing took place there. Lt. Freeling Colt generally led these instructions. In his slow but pleasant southern drawl he emphasized "squeeeeezing" the trigger. This helped make the dullness of dry firing palatable. As the sight of the M-1 was zeroed in on the target, a "sloooow" squeeze by the trigger finger, rather than a quick snap or jerk, was constantly touted as the only way to become a real marksman. This was repeated so often that Bill True began having dreams of squeeeezing an M-1 trigger.

Now that they had their rifles for practice it was time to learn a secondary, but important, skill: use of the optional attached bayonet. Lt. Havorka was leader of the 2nd Platoon, and he instructed the whole company in bayonet. He, himself, had trained under a German veteran of WW I, and had adapted a German accent in barking out some of his commands. One of his favorites was "Schlapp dat piece." This was an order to smack the rifle soundly with the left hand in order to loosen the bayonet from the bones of an enemy that had just been skewered. Havorka's bayonet drill was extremely arduous. He would make each man extend his rifle fully out and hold it by just the right arm for what seemed an interminable length of time. "You're doughboys, men," he'd shout. "American doughboys, and your strong arms will smash your enemy." Every man in the company breathed a sigh of relief each time bayonet drill ended, and all were thankful that it wasn't held every day.

In addition to intensive training on the M-1, everyone got some general experience with the .30 caliber machine gun, the 60 mm mortar, and the Thompson .45 caliber sub-machine gun. Again, this was all "dry-fire" simulation. Throwing dummy hand grenades to get the feel for distance and accuracy was also part of the regimen.

First and second gunners on the machine guns, and the mortar crews, got special in-depth training on those weapons. True was assigned to a mortar squad with Joe Flick as acting squad leader. Together with Bob Stone and Johnny Jackson they spent many hours learning to estimate distances, how to set the mortar up rapidly, and how to adjust its elevation and direction for accurate fire. But they still had not fired a single weapon!

৵   ৵   ৵

Every Saturday called for a full dress inspection of the barracks plus a review and parade of the entire regiment on the athletic field. There was no band, but recorded marches were broadcast over the loudspeaker as each company passed in review before the Regimental Commander, Colonel Robert Sink. For Bill True these became memorable occasions. A martial fervor, which he never knew he had, seemed to well up within him as they stepped with precision to the stirring airs of John Phillip Souza. Performing manual of arms with their rifles while in full marching order seemed to him the ultimate in military accomplishment and recognition.

After Saturday afternoon parade the men generally were given the remainder of the weekend off. Some of the guys visited larger cities such as Gainesville, and a few even got as far as Atlanta. But True never ventured beyond the nearby town of Toccoa. He and Les Tindall attended church in town on occasion, hoping to be invited home for dinner by families with beautiful daughters. It never worked out though, and they finally just gave it up in favor of a restful Sunday in camp. That made for an easy day of just laying around the barracks, browsing at the PX, reading and writing letters home. It also meant having extra food and desserts at chow time, since so many of the others were missing. Bill found this to be a nifty way to end a strenuous week. Some real rest in preparation for an early Monday morning start was just the ticket. It was sure to be followed by yet another week of arduous effort, probably more demanding than the last. Staying put and taking it easy seemed a very sensible thing to do.

శ   శ   శ

Finally one morning, F Company was loaded onto trucks for the trip to Clemson College and the first firing of their Garands at the Camp Croft range. It was a real "acid test" for the prospective infantrymen. Platoons, companies, and even battalions were all in fierce competition to produce the highest number of qualified "experts," "sharpshooters," and "marksmen." Those who qualified expert were promised three-day passes. Weeks of dry-fire practice now had to evolve into real-world skills at bulls-eye target shooting with live ammunition.

There were no quarters for the men to stay overnight at the college so they pitched their pup tents, all in neat rows, for an outside bivouac of three days. A small river ran near the firing range. Although the men were warned to stay away from it, nearly all managed to slip in for a dip or two during their stay. The cooks set up a field kitchen and served meals nearly as hearty as back in camp, so the lack of barracks proved to be little more than a minor inconvenience.

This would be the real introduction to how their new M-1s behaved. Setting of sights, and zeroing them in was necessary. Every piece received meticulous care: set those sights firm; blacken them with burnt cork until glare was totally eliminated. But the men had to take turns performing the mundane tasks of "operating" the range as well, so the very first order of business was learning how to work the targets.

Paper targets were mounted on frames which could be raised above ground level from the safety of a deep trench, where the operators stood for safety. After lifting a target into place, the man at the firing line was given time to shoot. Then the target would be lowered into the trench and evaluated. Different markers would be raised to show the shooter how well he did, ranging from a bull's eye five, to lesser scores. If the soldier missed entirely, a red flag was waved in the air in front of the target. This became known as "Maggie's Drawers," and was a sign of failure. Everyone feared this ignominy, plainly visible to all others on the range, but it happened plenty in the first live-fire exercises.

Once the men had settled into the task of real shooting, training officers conducted a check of each man to see if the critical "squeeze, don't jerk the trigger" had sunk in. Assuming a prone position with his rifle, the man would look away as an officer placed either a live round or a spent cartridge in the chamber. With a live round it wasn't possible to be sure whether a man flinched or not. The punishing kick of the .30-06 ammunition would always jar him. Thus it was necessary for the trainer to first put in a couple of real rounds for the man to fire, getting him accustomed to the powerful jolt of the rifle. Then the trainer would surreptitiously slip in a spent cartridge. It was always comically apparent when a man jerked on a dead cartridge: only a "click" sounded and no recoil was felt. Even the offender would usually join in the laughter.

In his youth, Bill had fired a 20 gauge shotgun a few times—pretty light stuff compared with what he now held in his hands. In fact, most of his gun experience had been even milder: a .22 caliber rifle that had no recoil whatsoever. Yet with only this limited experience, he found he had little difficulty in squeezing smoothly on the trigger. He did make the common mistake, however, of putting his cheek bone too close to the rear sight when the first round was fired. The tremendous kick of the piece gave him a painful bruise that would last for some time. Many of the troopers sported the same trophy of that initial shooting of the M-1.

True quickly learned the intricacies of using the Garand's leather sling to advantage. When done properly this lent tremendous stability and, hence, accuracy to the shooting. In his first "rapid fire prone" sequence Bill put fifteen of sixteen rounds in the bulls eye with the other round just outside. It was a very satisfying experience, but sadly his overall score just missed the mark for "expert." The much-coveted three-day pass had just slipped through his trigger finger.

Other men fared worse. Bob Carlson†, who was minimally adept at most of the skills required of an infantryman, never got over flinching as he pulled the trigger of his rifle. In nearly every firing sequence at Clemson, he got red flags for complete misses and became known as the "King of Maggie's Drawers."

❧   ❧   ❧

Soon after the return from Clemson a Mini-Olympics was arranged; a regiment-wide test of physical fitness. That meant a genuinely grueling test of endurance among men who had spent many weeks concentrating nearly every waking hour on developing exactly that. Ten men from each of the twelve companies were chosen for the competition. Bill True and Dude Stone were among those representing F Company. The all-day event was set for Friday. Men not competing would continue with their regular training activities.

The contestants each took part in ten events, with time representing the score for several. In the case of push-ups, chin-ups, and the like, the number of "reps" achieved was the determining factor.

Bill won his heat in the 100 yard dash, but was beaten by Lou Truax, of D Company, on the obstacle course. Lou was smaller and slighter of build, but as they turned up the hill for the killing grind of the uphill finish, Bill was flabbergasted at the ease with which Lou passed him.

The "mile run" covered part of the Currahee Mountain trail but circled back before the cruelest ascent began. True stayed close to the two leaders. They were both from companies in the 1st Battalion and had been in front from the start. Thinking to make his move at the half-mile mark, instead they started to pull away and just seemed to keep on going. By the three-quarter mile, one of them was 100 yards ahead and the other about 50. Bill had heard about it, but never before experienced the "second wind" that guys talked about in the longer distance sports. But right then, almost like magic, it kicked in for him. With almost embarrassing ease he overtook the erstwhile second placer, and passed him smooth as melting butter. Then damn if he didn't almost take the whole race, crossing the finish line a mere 3 seconds behind the winner!

Next was the awkward-looking and technically grueling 50-yard "Duck Walk." True led his heat for most of the way and at the end figured he was a sure winner. But then suddenly he felt a tap on his shoulder by one of the officers officiating the event. "Disqualified!" the man said. Bill was at first baffled by the pronouncement. But then the lieutenant told him, "You weren't down in a full duck walk, so you're out."

It was a bitter disappointment to receive a zero score in the event, especially since F Company was doing very well and might even take first place. Dude Stone and two of the other men had won or placed well in most of their events. True feared that his negative showing on the Duck Walk would scratch their chances for sure.

The final scores for the Mini-Olympics were posted the following day, Saturday. Company F had finished in third place. Although disappointed in the overall scores, Bill did some math in his head and was consoled somewhat. Even if he had come in first on the Duck Walk, the results would have been the same.

November 11, 1942, was True's nineteenth birthday, and his mother had sent him a ruby ring inscribed "Mother to Bill, 11/11/42" which was handsome beyond anything he'd ever had in the way of jewelry. It would remain on his hand throughout the war and eventually be passed, somewhat chipped and scratched, to his eldest son who prized it beyond measure. But for now, Bill was proud to wear it as Co. F traveled by truck the short distance to Seneca, South Carolina, to march in an Armistice Day Parade.

Some of the officers had already been to Ft. Benning and had earned their wings. As part of the festivities, these men performed a demonstration jump for the folks of Seneca.

After the parade ended, Johnny Jackson and Bill True took a walk on their own up the main street. On their way they happened to notice two teen-aged girls and a gray haired woman leaning out of a second story window. Always eager for female companionship they said hi to the girls, received a friendly response, and stopped to chat awhile. The guys introduced themselves, then the girls also gave their names and seemed interested in striking up an acquaintance.

Johnny invited the ladies to come down and join them for a walk. Perhaps they could lead the way to a local ice cream parlor. At first, the girls just giggled and made excuses. But then, after a few minutes of small talk, they disappeared from the window and seconds later emerged from a nearby door.

As it turned out, a drug store with soda fountain was just two blocks down the street. There, the four new friends enjoyed hot fudge sundaes and banana splits as they got to know each other. The girls were first cousins; seventeen and eighteen years old, respectively. The older woman who had been in the window with them was their maternal grandmother. Finishing their ice cream, Bill asked what had made the girls change their minds and come down for a walk.

The older one, who had somehow become Bill's "date," answered for them both. "Grandma told us to get down there right now and be friendly with those nice soldier boys who marched in that parade for you." Her lilting southern accent was charming. Bill managed two trips back to Seneca for dates with his new girl, but the affair never advanced beyond a modest good night kiss. His hoped for South Carolina romance never blossomed.

Meanwhile, back at Toccoa, field maneuvers (officially known as "tactical problems") continued throughout the month of November. These occurred at least once a week, each requiring longer and harder marches to remote terrain in the forest. This would be followed by rugged and aggressive combat simulations. Mock-ups of enemy strongholds were vigorously attacked, and imaginary enemy soldiers mercilessly slaughtered with no quarter shown. After several hours of exhausting endeavors came another hard march back to camp, just in time for evening chow. By this time in their training, the first platoon had fallen into a regular habit of singing as they walked along. But it was always more vigorous on the way out than on the way home.

One night, after a particularly tiring day of simulated fighting and killing, True suddenly awoke at midnight with an urgent need for a bowel movement. As he walked quickly toward the latrine, trying hard to "hold it in," he passed several men coming and going on the same path. Arriving, he found every stool occupied plus a line of men standing and waiting their turn—none too patiently, either. Bill had always felt that he had an exceptionally strong stomach, but on this occasion his need would not permit delay. He took off at a brisk pace for the next company's facility. All the crappers were available there and he breathed a grateful sigh of relief as he seated himself at the nearest one and let go.

Next day it was found that all of F Company, to a man, had caught the "green apple quick trot" at the same time. The cause of this sudden diarrhea attack was never conclusively proven, but speculation pointed to careless washing and rinsing of utensils by the company cooks. It was well known that G.I. soap was strong enough to shine up a rusty horseshoe, so the theory of "soap in the pots" became the accepted answer. In any event, the men later heard that Captain Mulvey had given severe ultimatums to the cooks. There was never a repetition of the debacle.

ॐ   ॐ   ॐ

In all their field problems thus far, the men had been restricted to one canteen of water. This led to speculation that the regiment was preparing to fight in the Sahara Desert, or some similar arid place. As November wore down it was announced that there was to be a final, three-day and two-night field exercise. One canteen would again be the order of the day. But this time there were dark rumors of some new and grisly elements to be added, increasing the reality of combat simulations. No one knew exactly what these might be, but apprehension was rife.

On November 25th Bill True wrote home about his expectations as follows:

"I guess I'd better hurry up and write a letter or I won't get a chance to this week. Tomorrow morning we're starting on a three-day problem and I guess it's going to be pretty tough…We're going to have simulated air attacks and gas attacks and everything to make it as realistic as possible, including sleeping on the very cold ground. It's really starting to get cold down here too, so I guess we're going to really freeze…"

The company scuttlebutt was right on target. In addition to the usual maneuvers, a night assault on a heavily defended dam redoubt was mounted. The attacking troopers advanced by crawling under low strung wires, while live machine gun bullets cracked and whizzed just inches over their heads. This was frightening enough, but matters were made worse by what they found themselves crawling *through*. The exercise became infamous later, known simply as the "Hawg Innards Problem." A local slaughterhouse had provided the army with fresh guts and entrails from animals they had butchered. These were spread liberally on the ground so that each man had to slither through them, becoming smeared with the slimy, bloody goo. It was a revolting and truly terrifying experience which none would ever forget. Bill True couldn't imagine the reality of actual combat being worse—at any rate that was his heartfelt prayer.

The hog guts maneuver was a special exercise enjoyed by the 2nd Battalion alone. It took place over Thanksgiving, while the rest of the regiment was relishing traditional turkey and trimmings. Instead, Companies D, E, F and 2nd Battalion Headquarters were introduced to C rations in the field. These meals in cans were despised by some of the men but oddly, True found himself almost enjoying them—especially the mulligan stew-like dinner ration.

The three-day exercise was taxing, well beyond anything the men had yet experienced, both physically and emotionally. When it was over they were given the unusual luxury of a full weekend off. This was the first time in three months that Bill and his buddies had enjoyed both a Saturday and Sunday free from training. It was a fortunate and appropriate respite. At the crack of dawn on Monday morning the battalion found itself on the march in full field gear, carrying all weapons.

Their destination was Atlanta—118 miles away.

Training in the U.S.A.

Colonel Sink had recently read about a record march made by Japanese soldiers, somewhere in Malaysia. He became determined that men of the 506th should crack that record. The walk to Atlanta was farther than the Japs had made, and completing it in three days would shatter the enemy's mark.

This would be the crowning achievement of their days at

Toccoa, most of which were spent building toward the marvelous feat of endurance they now undertook. After parading triumphantly through Atlanta, the troops would board trains for Fort Benning, where their final parachute training, including jumps from actual planes, would occur.

The men were of good cheer as they set out and True's platoon was soon into its marching songs. About mid-morning a cold rain set in, however, and by noon the rustic dirt road they were traveling had become a quagmire. The gooey Georgia mud pulled at their feet and made the march a miserable effort. By late afternoon Bill was counting the minutes and seconds between their hourly ten-minute breaks. Despite the cold, and rain, and sloppy ground, he found that his weariness allowed nine and a half minutes of actual sleep out of the ten-minute break time.

It was well past dark when the first day's march ended. They had covered forty miles: a solid start. But with almost eighty miles still to go that was little comfort, as they searched for dry patches to pitch their pup tents. Finally it stopped raining, and that was good. However, with that the temperature dropped and a frigid wind began to blow. It looked to be a cold night indeed.

Full field kitchens could not be set up in time for a hot meal, so sandwiches were the night's fare. The troops wolfed their food and washed it down with hot coffee, then everyone collapsed for the night. While they slept the cooks scrambled to set up proper kitchens.

True and Johnny Jackson shared a pup tent, and they both made the mistake of removing the wet boots from their bone-tired feet. That night the temperature dropped below freezing. Bill and Johnny realized their error first thing next morning. Their boots were frozen stiff. It was all they could do to work the leather soft enough to put them on their still-sore feet. Each of them vowed he wouldn't even think about removing those boots again until they reached Atlanta.

The cooks put out a hot breakfast to help get the second day started. Even so, the 2nd Battalion of the 506th wasn't the merry crew that had set out twenty-four hours before. Thankfully it didn't rain that day, but the accumulating miles were starting to take their toll. As the afternoon wore on a few of the older guys needed rides in either the cooks' truck or the accompanying ambulance. At least a good hot meal greeted them that night as they bivouacked on dry ground after another day's hard forty miles. It froze again before morning, but that night True and Jackson wisely slept with their boots on.

By the early evening of the third day a few more of the older men (those in their late twenties and early thirties) were getting occasional rides in the truck or ambulance. But all of the young guys in Bill True's barracks at Toccoa made it the full distance to their destination: the grounds at Oglethorpe University where they camped for the night on the outskirts of Atlanta. True, Flick, Jackson, Stone, Tom Alley and Bud Edwards all reflected on some of the first words spoken at Toccoa: "We're going to separate the men from the boys." It looked to them like the boys were the *last* to be "separated." At least on this occasion.

After they'd set up their pup tents and had another hot supper, an announcement was made. Anyone who wanted a truck ride into nearby Atlanta for a "night on the town" was welcome to go. In the last few miles of the march True had not been able to think of anything but hitting the sack. Most of the guys were of a similar mind. But with this news, suddenly attitudes changed and a miraculous burst of energy somehow materialized. Soon there was a mad scramble to shave, clean up and head for town.

As they got off the truck in Atlanta, Jackson and True spotted a Turkish Bath. Without hesitation they made it their first stop. In addition to the steam baths there was a masseur on duty and both men took the full treatment. The massage included a good rub down of the feet, and Bill counted that as the most delicious feeling he'd had since losing his virginity with Bonnie Smith in San Diego.

Rising from the massage table, Johnny and Bill both realized that their feet were so tender they could hardly stand. And when they tried to put their jump boots on they found that their feet had swollen at least two sizes beyond normal. Donning their footwear was almost as difficult as the time they had with the frozen leather on the march, even after pulling out the laces as loose as could be! The two hobbled to a nearby speakeasy which had been recommended by the masseur. After downing a couple of boilermakers each (a shot of whiskey with a beer chaser) they were much too beat for a real night on the town. All they wanted to see was a truck headed back to the bivouac.

Following a leisurely breakfast and clean up of the camp area next morning, the battalion formed up for the triumphant march into Atlanta. The high point would be a scheduled trip down Peachtree Street where a large turnout of citizens was expected. Many of the men were still near exhaustion, however, and there were lingering doubts they could present a really sharp image to the populace.

As the battalion neared the starting point of the parade they were met by four high school marching bands, one for each of the companies. The one assigned to F Company struck up a stirring march, in somewhat quicker time than their Saturday parades at Toccoa had been. Considering the fatigue of every man present, this might have posed a problem. But then another miracle occurred. It was as if every trooper had suddenly been transformed by some genie's magic elixir. The excitement in the air was palpable; the energy fairly bursting at the seams.

Bill True felt shivers of excitement, and immediately forgot his sore feet and tired muscles as he fell into the rapid cadence of the band. He quickly asked Dude Stone if he could carry the mortar for him, but Dude declined. The machine gunners in the other squads, who had happily let others relieve them of their heavy weapons on the march, also decided their guns weren't such a load after all. The martial music made all of the men feel heroic, and the applause of the people on the sidewalks was exhilarating beyond words.

Every newspaper in Atlanta covered the parade in their afternoon editions, with banner headlines and front page photos. The papers came out before the train left for Fort Benning, so True and his buddies had a chance to read about themselves before boarding. Bill got a kick out of a somewhat contradictory quote attributed to Col. Sink regarding the record march: "Not a man fell out; and when they fell, they fell face forward."

The train ride to Fort Benning roused eager anticipation in the men as they knew they were approaching their supreme objective: five live jumps and their silver parachute wings. Bill True's mind was flooded as well with memories of the tough basic training they had just completed. He knew that whatever transpired henceforth, Camp Toccoa would always be his first home in the Army. He was already feeling a touch of homesickness.

CHAPTER III

The Silver Badge of Courage
From Fort Benning to Overseas on the Samaria

"The aim of military training is not just to prepare men for battle, but to make them long for it."
                              Louis Simpson

———————

Fort Benning was a disappointment. After their arduous training at Toccoa the men of F Company eagerly anticipated this supreme objective where silver wings awaited them. Expectations ran high. Finding their spartan quarters far less inviting than what they had just left was a real let-down. And the barren, almost desolate look of their assigned area, ominously dubbed "the Frying Pan," added to the disillusionment.

Flimsy wooden framed barracks lined two sides of a dusty unpaved company street, with the kitchen and mess hall at one end and the latrine at the other. A commodious post exchange with juke box and barber shop was not distant, however, and that somewhat mitigated the depressing atmosphere.

At Benning, standard jump training for all troops had previously consisted of four weekly stages designated A, B, C and D. Stage A was primarily physical training, concentrating on fitness and conditioning. But the 506 men had already received three months of extremely rigorous experience in that. The cadre sergeants in charge of A-phase soon learned to their embarrassment that calisthenics were completely

87

unnecessary for their new charges. An instructor would start out on a long double-time run of several miles only to find his trainees leading him, running backwards, and taunting sarcastically, "is that as fast as you can go?" A-stage was waved, if only to save the dignity of the instructors.

December 1942, studio photo of Bill True in full uniform taken in Columbus, Georgia, after their arrival at Fort Benning, but before they made their five qualifying jumps.

Stage B included practice for parachute maneuvering while hanging from harnesses, plus landing and rolling after jumps from 10-foot platforms. Leaps from both a ground level mock plane, and another one 40 feet high were repeated endlessly. Descent by cable from the 40-foot mock-up provided further experience in proper technique for a safe landing. Most of this was pretty "old hat" for the Toccoa men, but soon there began new and intensely "interesting" subjects. First among these was parachute packing. The men would pack their own chutes for their five qualifying jumps. Bill True was not alone in paying very close attention to these instructions.

"Flash Gordon" was the name bestowed upon one of the training instructors. He was assigned to work B-stage, which included basic parachute skills but also leaned heavily on physical training. For him it was a most appropriate assignment. He had the build and conditioning of a Mr. America, and the nickname came from his resemblance to the handsome movie star Buster Crabbe. Good looking, blond, blue eyed, and six-foot-two: he could do almost numberless pushups with either arm singly. Yet despite his own obvious physical prowess, he was impressed with the men from Toccoa. They were in far better shape than the average trainees he'd seen before. To a man they could breeze through fifty pushups without even breathing hard. Seeing this, he was inclined to treat them with a bit more respect than was his custom.

Stage C began with practice in collapsing a billowing parachute blown by the propeller of an airplane engine. This was designed to prepare the men for landing on terrain in high surface winds. The troopers took turns strapping into an opened chute that was then blown into action by the powerful blast of a C-47 prop. Invariably this would drag the man almost uncontrollably over the rough ground. He would then have to pull frantically at the risers which would spill air out of the canopy and collapse it, allowing him to release the harness. Naturally the incentive was strong to bring this painful ride to as rapid a conclusion as possible. Most of the men became competent after only a few bumpy trips across the sandy Georgia earth. On his third try, True was checked off as qualified and sighed with relief. His second session had been a tough one, leaving him with a sore butt as a reminder.

Four daylight jumps from 250-foot towers were scheduled for each of the men during the week of Stage C. There were four suspension arms projecting from the top of the tower framework, so four men could be lifted and released at the same time. It was more of a "drop" than a jump. The soldier was strapped into a parachute harness already attached to the circle of metal rings on the tower arm, then raised to the top. At a signal from the ground instructor, the parachute was released. The seemingly endless lessons in parachute maneuver and manipulation were now greatly appreciated as the men "slipped" their chutes away from the iron frame of the tower with ease.

Little Jimmie Dickens, who had been on the train with Bill True from California to Camp Toccoa, made the first of the tower drops, but was mysteriously missing from the company formation next morning. Acrophobia was the culprit. The 250-foot height had proved to be more than he could handle, and Captain Mulvey had arranged his immediate transfer out of the regiment. The march from Toccoa to Atlanta had finished off one of Jimmie's hometown buddies as well. Thus their predictions as to which of them would win their wings had been grossly amiss.

JUMP WINGS AND BLOUSED BOOTS
Bill's True Tale

"Slip right! Slip right!" The tower instructor on the ground is hollering at me. I've just been dropped from the suspension arm for the one jump we'll make at night, and apparently I'm drifting toward the tower. Grabbing my right risers I pull like crazy, spilling air from my chute on that side and hoping I'll slip away from the iron grid work of the 250 foot structure. It's so dark I can't make out the tower, nor can I see the ground, but I must have done what was called for because the yelling has stopped and I'm floating free.

The ground is a real sharp surprise as I slam down much harder than on any of the several day drops we made from the towers. My feet must not have hit the ground together because the pain in my left heel is excruciating. It feels like it's broken. Scrambling to my feet I hobble out of the jump area carrying my chute and praying that no one will notice the way I'm dragging my left foot.

Two of our F Company men were injured on the day drops from the towers. They're expected to fully recover and make their qualifying jumps sometime later, but they won't graduate from jump school and get their wings with the rest of the company. All of us feel really sorry for them and are hoping against hope nothing like that will happen to us. Has it just happened to me?

It's next morning and I've awakened with an awful ache in my left foot. None of the instructors or officers became aware of my incapacity last night, and I was hoping the pain would be better today. It may be worse. We're scheduled to make our first real jump this morning though, and "By God, I'm not going to miss it!"

All of the guys are very sympathetic, and Johnny and

Dude and Joe are going to help me conceal any limp or hobble I can't avoid. I could hardly get the boot off my foot last night, and getting it back on this morning figures to be no picnic. The laces are as loose as it's possible to get them as I start to ease my foot into the boot. The pain in the heel when any pressure is applied is teeth-clenching, and I stop to catch my breath. Johnny is watching and suggests I use some powder on the heel of my sock to make it slip better.

The powder helps a lot. I'm fully dressed, but a close look would reveal a very loosely laced left boot. By walking on my left toes I'm able to minimize the pain, and after a little practice walking around the barracks it would take serious scrutiny to detect my problem. If any of our lieutenants discover my injury, I know my jumps will be delayed for some time, so I'll have to put on a smooth performance.

Even double-timing I'm able to pretty well conceal my problem, and we've arrived at the packing shed to pick up the parachutes for our first jump. Last week we had packed all five of the chutes we'll use for our qualifying jumps. Learning to pack a parachute was a bit complicated, and I had paid decidedly close attention to our instructors. Deliberately laying out the suspension lines and the chute panels on the long tables got my strictest scrutiny, and I carefully secured them with the lead shot bags as other components were assembled. The need to keep a precise count of shot bags was noted repeatedly, to be sure that none were left in the chute as it was folded and stowed in the pack tray. All of the instructions were intended to minimize parachute malfunction, and I took every one of them to heart. Packing our own chutes was meant to give us confidence in making our first jumps, and I was determined to have no doubts in that regard.

We're boarding our C-47 as the pilot revs the engines.

Our first jump. My knees have gone weak, my mouth is cotton-dry, and my stomach is a churning maelstrom as I climb up the several steps. Avoiding putting weight on my left heel is actually a welcome distraction. I'm ninth in the stick and shuffle up the aisle to flop down on my designated bucket seat.

We've been airborne for several minutes now, and have flown what seemed to be a couple of complete circles. Through the open door I can see below me how Fort Benning stretches out and covers a really substantial area. The Chattahoochee River has passed beneath us a couple of times when the jump master startles me as he shouts "Stand up and hook up!" We rise and form a tight single line facing aft. My fingers are all thumbs as I fumble with my static line buckle, but I finally manage to get it open and hooked onto the overhead cable.

"Sound off for equipment check!" We all check the guy in front of us to be sure he's hooked up and that his chute straps and fasteners look okay. I give number eight a reassuring slap on the back and receive one myself. Starting from the end of the line the sound off is made with "Sixteen okay!" "Fifteen okay!"… "Nine okay!" I'm able to choke out as the count continues down to one.

A red light over the door goes on and we hear a loud "Close up and stand in the door!"

I can't see the door, but the drill is for the first man to place his left foot across the door sill, place his hands outside the door on either side, and look at the horizon. I hear the shouted "Go!" that sends the first trooper out, and the line begins to move.

Next thing I know, my chute is open and I see others above and below me, but all I can remember after that first loud "Go!" is a dark numbness and a drop into emptiness with my stomach coming up to my throat. "I've made my first jump! I've made my first jump!" I'm totally elated as I float down, and even remember to work my risers and stop my oscillations.

The ground is rising fast when I remember my heel and just hope I don't damage it further. I'm lucky as I land in a somewhat soft grassy area which takes some of the impact. I've come down on both feet but tumble forward absorbing much of the fall throughout my body. The heel hurts bad, that's for sure, but I'm able to gather my chute and walk back to the nearest truck with pretty much the same gait I've been using.

∾   ∾   ∾

We made our second jump yesterday, and my heel problem still hasn't caught the attention of any of our officers. Our third jump is this afternoon, and I'm getting more and more confident that I'll get through all five without being discovered.

We've boarded our plane and it turns out that I'll be jumping number one today. The jump master had asked who would like to jump first, and I volunteered. While my second jump was still plenty scary, I wasn't so terrified as to black out like I did on the first one. Today I'm jumping at the head of the stick, and that will be an interesting experience. Johnny is right behind me, and Dude and Joe are both in this stick, too.

The jump master has just yelled "Close up and stand in the door!" and here I am. Right foot back and left foot over the door sill, hands on both outer sides of the door, eyes on the horizon, and the wind whipping my face. It seems like I've held this pose for a long time when suddenly I feel a slap on the butt and hear a loud "Go!" As I step out the door I make a half-left turn and hold my legs tight together and my arms close to my body. The emptiness meets me and engulfs me and my stomach leaps into my throat, but this time I'm acutely aware and I wait for the opening shock. The prop blast on my back gives a mighty thrust to my drop and within seconds the sharp yank of my fully opened canopy violently jerks me into an upright position. I reach for my risers and feel the utter elation of knowing I'm one jump closer to those coveted parachute wings.

అ   అ   అ

We're walking out to the plane for our fifth jump. The qualifier. My heel still hurts, but it may be getting better. I'm really smooth at covering up any limp now, and not an officer has noticed anything. We'll be full fledged paratroopers with wings on our chest and boot-bloused pants that *no one* can criticize after today. We've been blousing our pants over our boots ever since basic training back at Toccoa, but old timers at Benning were critical of the practice when we arrived. We were the first regiment ever to train from scratch as paratroopers, though, and felt no compunction in adapting the elite practice of pants-tucked boots. Just let some smart-ass cadre instructor make wise cracks about us after *this* jump!

అ   అ   అ

It's Christmas Day, 1942, and my injured heel is quickly becoming a distant memory. This morning we have our wing-pinning ceremonies. Our company commander, Captain Mulvey, will do the pinning, and while he's been real hard on us for the past four months, he'll be Santa Claus today. The company is at attention in full dress uniform and the Captain has just stepped in front of me to pin the wings on my blouse. As he does so and we salute each other my heart is beating like a voodoo drum and I can hardly breathe.

I'm remembering the Army Recruiting Office in San Diego back in August. The heroic-sized paratrooper cutout in full regalia with the big message across his body: "WEAR THE SILVER BADGE OF COURAGE!" I'm wearing it, and am I proud!

ॐ   ॐ   ॐ

Following the wing pinning ceremonies a bountiful Christmas dinner was provided for the entire 2nd Battalion. Printed menus contained both the roster of men and officers in each of the four companies as well as the list of luxurious food items on the bill of fare.

It was a momentous occasion—and not simply because of the sumptuous fare, though it was far-and-away the best they'd yet enjoyed. This represented the culmination of their dreams. They were now full-fledged paratroopers who would soon be going home, proudly wearing their new wings. After four long months of hard work and demanding requirements, family and friends would admire their accomplishment.

Every element of the meal was savored. Bill was sure that each course tasted even better than the last. It seemed the finest meal he'd ever had, and that was saying something. Both his mother and his Aunt Mary enjoyed vaunted reputations for culinary skills. But this time, it looked like the battalion cooks had even outdone those masterly chefs.

A few nights later Captain Mulvey threw a beer party for the company in their mess hall. The giddy bunch drank their 3.2 beer like there was no tomorrow. Until his term in the service, Bill True hadn't consumed enough alcohol to really feel it since childhood, when his "drinking Uncle Elvin" would pay nieces and nephews a quarter each to take a slug out of his pint bottle of bourbon. Bill made up for lost time that night though, as he downed glass after glass. Even the lightly spirited brew soon had him reeling.

Mulvey was hitting the beer pretty hard, too, and a couple of the officers had brought bottles of Georgia moonshine which they shared around. Then the F Company commander did something he had never done before. Surprising everyone, he climbed up on a table and began to speak. His words were only slightly slurred as he began pronouncing in stentorian terms the heroic destiny of his men, all of whom were drunkenly gathered around him. "Whether future battle foes turn out to be German or Jap, or better yet both, they'll learn to dread the awful slaughter carried out by you Currahee Geronimos," he announced. "Blood will run and guts will spill, no quarter given! Those rotten sons-of-bitches are gonna pay!!!"

Similar words went on for some time until, thoroughly drunk, his speech rose in volume to a final crescendo and he hurled a fateful challenge to the assembly. Pointing to the mess hall entrance he shouted, "And any man who doesn't think he can handle our kind of killing can walk out that door right now!"

Mulvey paused, now wavering on his feet atop the table, having loquaciously "run out of gas." Incapable of further utterance—at least any that made sense—he waited dumbly for someone else to say something. The uncomfortable silence continued until finally Bill True spoke up and announced, in his own thoroughly beer-addled mutter, "Heck, I couldn't possibly make it all the way to that door."

That was it. The tension broke as Mulvey became the first to burst into laughter. Their captain was happy to let the lighter note end his speech as the party went on till the beer ran out. Eventually everyone either lurched back to barracks or simply passed out in place.

The cooks were not pleased when breakfast time rolled around only to find a pile of comatose troopers, fully dressed and reeking of alcohol, unconscious on their serving tables.

అ   అ   అ

In reward for their remarkable achievements, ten-day furloughs were granted to the entire company. Unfortunately for the West Coast men this did not include travel time. Air fare was too expensive for Bill True and the others, and a train ride took four days each way. That left only two days remaining for the home visit. Consequently, some of the Californians, including Johnny Jackson, elected to spend their furlough in Georgia or surrounding states. But True, Les Tindall and Bud Edwards chose the train trip. On the way west, all agreed that there would probably be minimal repercussions if they got back to Fort Benning a few days late. They would learn to their chagrin that such was not the case.

Bill True returned to a home in San Diego significantly changed since he had left the previous August. His sister Betty Jean had come back to live with her dad, who in the meantime had taken a second wife: Hazel Pillsbury. Hazel and her two children Dona and Duane had been friends of the family in Omaha. Les True sent for them shortly after Bill entered the Army. He also purchased a home in the Normal Heights area, which was reasonably convenient to his job at Consolidated Aircraft.

This newly formed family welcomed their paratrooper son home with open arms, and he noticed immediately the blue star proudly displayed in a front window. A blue star signified a home that had someone serving in the military. A gold star meant that a loved one had served and died.

January 1943, San Diego, California. Bill True home on leave posing in jump jacket with wings in front yard of family home at 4774 E. Mt. View Drive.

The next days were filled with picnics and visits to new places Bill had never seen before enlisting. Popcorn, root beer, and board games occupied most evenings spent with family and friends.

January 1943, San Diego, California. Bill True home on leave, sporting his new paratrooper wings, posed with sister Betty Jean True in front of Hoover High School.

Bill had one date with Bonnie Smith, his hot romance of the previous spring. The ardor they shared had cooled even before his entry to the service, but it was now painfully obvious that it had fully expired. Bonnie insisted that they spend the evening in the apartment she shared with her mother and little brother, both of whom were present. The most exciting part of the evening was a game of pick-up-sticks which Bonnie won. Bill said an early goodnight in the full knowledge that the affair had ended.

☙   ☙   ☙

The train ride back to Columbus, Georgia, took the same four long days as the journey home. Bill arrived at Fort Benning on the fourteenth day of his ten-day furlough and was told to report immediately to Captain Mulvey. His excuse of "late trains" and other travel impediments fell on deaf ears. Absent-Without-Leave (AWOL) was a serious offense and the Army meant to treat it as such. For his reckless disregard for orders, Bill would receive a four-part punishment: (1) loss of his P.F.C. stripe; (2) a fine of two month's jump pay; (3) restriction to the Fort for a month; and (4) walking the company street carrying a machine gun and tripod four hours every night for a week.

Leaving Mulvey's office chastised and embarrassed, Bill ran into Joe Flick. According to Joe, only a handful of men had gotten back from furlough on time, most of them mistakenly figuring on impunity due to their exalted position as full-fledged paratroopers. Quite a few hadn't made it YET. True got first hand evidence of the number of transgressors as he had lots of company on his four hours' nightly servitude, trudging back and forth in front of the barracks. Compounding his misery, a drenching rain fell nearly every night, turning the unpaved street into a muddy morass.

☙   ☙   ☙

Field maneuvers began even before all of the men had returned from furlough. Overnight tactical problems not seen since Toccoa were again instituted on a weekly basis. The men soon learned that becoming full-fledged paratroopers had done little to ease life's burdens. Long marches into the countryside became commonplace to conduct mock warfare. Other days were filled with strenuous calisthenics, close order drills, manual of arms practice, and a multitude of class instructions on infantry operations.

About this time Bill learned in a letter from his Aunt Bessie (one of his mother's older sisters) that his cousin Harold Burke was in OCS at Fort Benning. Harold was three and a half years older than Bill, and they had played together some as children. He didn't think any more about it and hadn't even considered trying to look up his cousin. Then one day someone in the barracks shouted "Ten-shun." Bill looked up and was surprised to see Harold standing there.

Military courtesy was stressed in the 506th, and entry of any officer into a barracks required someone to announce his presence by calling everyone to attention. As a brand new 2nd Lieutenant, Harold was embarrassed by the recognition and waved it off. He hadn't yet learned that the proper response of an officer was a loudly announced "At ease!"

The two cousins had a good time catching up on family doings, and Harold confessed that he hoped to become a paratrooper himself. His wife Judy was with him on the post, though. Harold wasn't sure he could convince her that jumping out of airplanes was a good idea, and his mother was certain to object as well. Later, Bill got together with Harold and Judy for a short visit at their quarters on the post. He eventually learned his cousin had finished the war with an infantry unit in the Pacific.

☙   ☙   ☙

One night after a particularly grueling field problem the men in True's barracks decided to have a beer party. Payday was still a week off, but everyone chipped in with what money they had, and enough was collected to buy a hefty stock of low-priced PX beer.

A few rounds was enough to get everyone into a festive mood. Bill started the singing and as the alcohol began to really kick in, got to dancing a shuffle his Uncle Elvin had taught him as a kid. It was a burlesque-like shuffle step with a rhythmic motion of legs and hips that suggested erotic doings. Hoots and laughter rewarded Bill's performance, and soon everyone was doing some version of the sexy dance.

As the evening wore on and the beer consumption mounted, True began singing bawdy songs and dirty limericks. Lou "Slinky" Cioni was from Chicago. He was forever touting the merits of his home hockey team, the Chicago Black Hawks, but seemed never interested in singing. So everyone was surprised when he burst out with a Chicago song that was ready-made for raunchy improvisation. One time through the simple lyrics and tune and the whole bunch joined in.

I used to work in Chicago, in a department store,
I used to work in Chicago, I did but I don't anymore.
A lady came in and asked for a coat,
I asked her what kind she'd adore,
Fox she want, fox she got.
I don't work there anymore.

In following lyrics, the lady kept coming in and asking for everything from screws to hockey pucks to whatever suggestive item a drunken bunch of troopers could come up with. They were still inventing wildly improbable items for the lady to request when the CQ for the day, Sergeant Malley, stuck his head in the barrack's door and warned them to knock it off. "Shut up, goddamit! They can hear you guys clear down to the end of the company street," he said, "and *some* folks are trying to sleep."

The beer supply was nearly exhausted, anyway, as the revelers retired to their bunks. Most fell quickly to sleep wearing field uniforms, boots and all.

                                   æ   æ   æ

All of the men of F Company had gotten back from furlough within a week of the due date except for Bill True's fellow Californian, Fritz Lucero. Fritz was nearly three weeks late and became targeted to serve as an example. Every company in the regiment had at least a few men who were AWOL a week or more, and one man from each company was selected to receive an unusual discipline. Fritz was among those slated for the worst: official "drumming out," with full military ceremonial dishonors.

The event was scheduled. Bill and his buddies had heard that this was a traditional British ritual, intended to administer a humiliating punishment for the offender, with the added purpose of delivering a loud message to the observers.

The entire regiment was assembled in full dress uniform to witness the mortifying penalty. As each man's name was called, he stepped forward from the ranks and was escorted to the center of the assembly field by an armed officer. They marched front and center to the slow beat of a drummer, and as the drum roll continued, the man's wings and all insignia were literally and forcibly ripped from his uniform. He was made to de-blouse his pant legs from his boots and leave the field destined, all knew, for the regular infantry. Ugh! What disgrace!

True felt stomach tremors as each man was dealt with, but when Fritz Lucero received the treatment, Bill almost threw up. This was a man with whom he had shared the long and arduous basic training at Camp Toccoa. Fritz had walked every mile of the march from Toccoa to Atlanta, and had made the five qualifying jumps to become a paratrooper. To see him now so utterly shamed was deeply tragic.

Most of the men shared the feeling that the "Drumming Out" ceremony was too much. They also knew, however, that everyone would think long and hard before stretching any pass or furlough in the future.

    ~p   ~p   ~p

Fort Benning sat astride the Chattahoochee river which formed the border between Georgia and Alabama. At the end of January, 1943, the regiment moved from the Frying Pan area across the river to the "-bama" side. This was a major improvement. First class barracks with latrines and showers in-house were provided. The well-appointed mess hall had a juke box. Even KP duty there wasn't the dreaded assignment it had been, as a man could listen or sing along with "Brazil," "Tangerine," or "That Old Black Magic" while scrubbing the pots and pans.

F Company made its sixth jump soon after the move, this time carrying rifles. First platoon had a new lieutenant, Frank McFadden in charge, and he had watched from the ground with binoculars as True's 3rd squad exited their plane. He later chided Bill and Johnny Jackson for a sloppy jump. In their rush to empty the plane as fast as possible, Johnny had gone a bit past the door and had to back up. By the time he'd recovered and was stepping out, Bill was ready to jump and the two of them had jammed up, exiting together. It was an amateurish mistake, unworthy of qualified paratroopers.

ॐ   ॐ   ॐ

All the men had received instructions on the use of gas masks from earliest basic training days, but they had never used them in actual gas exposure. They now got that opportunity: a tear-gas chamber had been set up that could handle a full squad of troopers all at once.

Joe Flick had just sewed on his buck sergeant stripes and was no longer just acting squad leader. When their turn came he led his men into the chamber and gave the order to don masks. Before the men could get the masks fully in place the tear-gas was turned on, and they got a taste of what nasty stuff it was. The purpose of the drill was to emphasize the importance of getting the gas mask on in a hurry, as well as to give the men a taste of the horrible nature of a gas attack. Later Joe Flick, Johnny Jackson, Dude Stone and Bill True all agreed that getting gassed would be a really lousy way to go out. "Better a nice fast bullet or artillery blast" was the general consensus.

Overnight field problems became routine again, usually beginning in the afternoon and extending till next morning. One night Flick and his squad got separated from the rest of the platoon and ended up lost. Wandering in the woods they heard a banjo and some singing in the distance. They followed the sound and came upon a secluded cabin nestled among the trees with several people on the porch making the music. Not knowing where the rest of the platoon and the company were maneuvering anyway, they decided to stop and listen for a while. Approaching closer, Bill recognized a tune: "When My Blue Moon Turns to Gold Again," sung with skillful harmony by several voices. He had learned the words from the mess hall juke box and joined in, much to the pleasure of the folks on the porch. Soon all were rapt in song, the military field problem long forgotten.

Hours later, finally noting the passage of time, Flick announced that they'd better start looking for the rest of the outfit. Heading in what they thought was the most likely direction they walked for more than an hour, but came across nothing but woods and silence. Joe was now using his compass but didn't know how far or in which direction they'd traveled before getting lost. Several more hours of stumbling around in the woods accomplished nothing but mounting exhaustion.

"Why don't we rest a while, Joe?" True finally asked. "We don't know if we're getting closer or just going the wrong way anyhow."

Jackson, Stone, and the rest of the men echoed the sentiment, and Flick agreed they should take a breather. Soon what started as a "break" turned into sound sleep as everyone sprawled out on the forest floor for a nap.

Stone was the first to wake up as dawn crept into the woods. He shook everyone else awake. "Damn, I guess we all fell asleep on that break, Joe," he said. "We'd better get going or you're gonna be in big trouble."

"Yeah, that new Lt. McFadden may be a hard case," Joe replied. "Let's just hope we can find some landmark soon to tell us where we are."

Fortunately the squad soon came across a road, clearly marked on the map, and headed for home. It took them more than two hours to get back and they realized they had really wandered far afield. Flick told the men to return to their barracks while he reported to Company Headquarters.

Joe slipped back into the barracks in just a few minutes. "It's just as well I didn't sew these stripes on all my uniforms. I'm Private Joe Flick again. Oh, and Bill, Lt. McFadden wants to see you in the office, too."

"You're acting squad leader, True," the lieutenant announced as soon as Bill entered the headquarters office. "Flick tried to give me some cock and bull story about getting lost and trying all night to find the platoon. You guys all got some shuteye while the rest of the men were working their butts off on the problem, didn't you? I don't like goof-offs. Show me you can handle that squad or I'll find someone else."

"Yes, sir," True replied, saluted, and returned to the barracks.

"He made me acting squad leader," Bill announced when he got back. "I don't think I want to be responsible for you guys, but I guess I'm stuck with it for now."

Johnny Jackson and Dude Stone said that was okay with them, and even Joe agreed it was fine. Since the four of them had been close from the very beginning of basic training, which one of them was squad leader didn't really matter. As things turned out, the acting squad leader designation would pass back and forth between Flick and True more than once in the months to come. And neither was up to disciplining the men he had trained with since earliest days.

ꙮ   ꙮ   ꙮ

March, 1943, found the 506th on the move again. This time they were heading for Camp Mackall, North Carolina, a new camp constructed specifically to accommodate airborne troops. A huge airfield was provided with extensive runways, equipped to handle day and night regiment-sized jumps and glider operations. It had been named for the first paratrooper killed in action in World War II, Pvt. John T. Mackall. He had been lost on a mission with the 82nd Airborne in North Africa.

The barracks were as comfortable as those on the Alabama side at Fort Benning, and the setting amidst pine trees was almost idyllic. Large, well furnished mess halls with juke boxes were provided. Memories of the lean facilities in the Frying Pan at Benning gave the whole setup an almost luxurious air.

Spring 1943, Camp Mackall, North Carolina. Three of us from the 3rd Squad, 1st Platoon, of F Company, with our 60 mm mortar. Bill True and Johnny Jackson manning the mortar, and Bob "Dude Boy" Stone feigning his demise.

A day jump was scheduled early on, with yet more weapons and equipment to be carried. Besides rifles, the machine gun and mortar squads would jump with those weapons and ammunition for them. In Bill True's mortar squad one man took the mortar tube and bipod itself, another would take the base plate, and the others would all carry several of the 60 mm rounds. This was all in addition to bandoliers of clips for their rifles, hand grenades, entrenching tools, gas masks, and other essentials. They were being prepared for the massive load a combat jump called for when more than 100 pounds of parachute, arms, and paraphernalia would be strapped on.

The jump went well, considering the great addition of items carried. Some of the men with the greatest loads lost a few articles at the opening shock of the parachute, but it was a learning experience and they would do better next time.

Field problems in the woods surrounding the camp soon became an almost daily affair, with two- and three-day overnight maneuvers interspersed. These exercises were getting ever more strenuous with less and less time for sleep at night. The officers said a typical paratrooper mission would consist of a sudden assault with intense and sustained action for two to three days before being relieved. True got the feeling that the current training objective was to build to a three-day action with no sleep at all.

THOSE JAPANESE AND GERMANESE
Bill's True Tale

It's Saturday afternoon and Johnny Jackson and I are in Charlotte, N.C., on our first weekend pass since the outfit arrived in Camp Mackall, N.C. Though North Carolina is dry, everyone knows that hotel bellhops in the big city can get a bottle for you most any time, and feminine companionship can be arranged through them as well.

In spite of this reasonable availability of the two most essential ingredients of a successful outing, Johnny and I have decided to cross over the nearby state border into Rock Hill, S.C. South Carolina sells packaged liquor at state-run stores and you can take the booze into restaurants and get set-ups for mixed drinks. "Whitey" Swafford, in the Second Platoon, had told me about this just last week, and he also said any cab driver in Rock Hill could get you to a cat house.

It's a short bus ride over to Rock Hill, and just outside the bus station stand a couple of taxis. We approach one of them and ask the driver if he knows of any available girls. He says "Sure, jump in," and we take off. He explains that there has been a recent police crackdown, and the girls can only entertain us as we drive around in the taxi. If that's okay with us he'll drive out to a house and we can pick a girl to go for a ride with us.

It sounds a bit weird to Johnny and me, but we agree it's at least something different, so we go for it.

We've just pulled up to a large two-storied house about a mile out of town and the driver jumps out and says "I'll be right back." He's only in the house a minute or two and comes back out the front door followed shortly by three scantily clad women. They wouldn't be described as raving beauties by even the least discerning half-drunk trooper, and Johnny and I are cold sober. I'm struck by the range of their ages from the youngest who can't be more than seventeen or eighteen, to the oldest who *might* be under fifty. The old one reminds me of a line from a Gilbert and Sullivan operetta, "She could easily pass for forty-three, in the dusk with the light behind her." And this one's facing a bright Carolina sun.

Johnny and I confer briefly and quickly decide the young one is our only choice, as she is also closest to a possible description of pretty among the three. The other two women head back for the house as Johnny opens the back door of the cab for our selected companion. He turns and says "Shall we flip for first go?" I agree, Johnny wins the toss, and we're off and running.

The taxi is just an open sedan with no glass partition between the front and back, but the driver and I try to provide a little privacy as we engage in our own conversation. We're driving farther out into the country and a discussion of the progress of the farm crops constitutes our primary subject.

After a fairly short time, probably less than ten minutes it seems to me, Johnny tells us he's finished and the driver pulls over and stops. We make the switch and are again driving down the road.

I tell the girl my name is Bill and ask hers. She quickly says Sally Belle, and wastes no time in helping me get my pants down. She watches as I put on a rubber, and neither of us is interested in a kiss as I initiate our "romantic" encounter. I take even less time than Johnny.

We're back in Rock Hill and the driver has just thanked us as we each give him a ten dollar bill. Together with the ten dollars we each gave Sally Belle we've already spent twenty bucks apiece. That's less than half of our monthly paratrooper bonus though, so what's to worry.

The taxi driver tells us where the nearest package liquor store is located and we're headed that way when we run into Don Davis from our own First Platoon. Don has also heard about the attractions in Rock Hill so we join forces to head on down for some booze.

We've still got a block or two to go to the liquor store when a school bus stops at the corner where we're about to cross. Don waves at the lady driver and motions for her to open the door for him. She does and he yells "I was a school bus driver back in Ohio for two years." She invites us aboard and we pile into the bus which is about half full of kids that she's apparently dropping at their homes.

The driver's name is Ellen, and she is having a good time talking to the three paratroopers. The kids seem to be getting a kick out of us, too. As she continues to drop kids off along her route, and finally drops the last one, Don talks her into letting him drive the bus. Don is having a big time driving, and it's apparent that he knows what he's doing as he moves smoothly through the gears.

"I have to get the bus back to our terminal before long," Ellen says, "but tell me where you fellows were headed, Don, and I'll take you." She knows where the liquor store is, and as we arrive there she tells us how much she and the children have enjoyed having us with them. "All of us are mighty proud of our service men, and I'll be praying for the paratroopers I met today," she concludes as the three of us step down from her bus.

The prices for liquor are quite reasonable, and we each buy a fifth. Probably more than we need for tonight, I'm thinking, but we'll have some for the ride back to Mackall tomorrow. We ask, and the liquor store clerk tells us where the nearest restaurant is that can furnish the set ups.

The restaurant is modern and nicely furnished with both a counter and numerous tables. We take a table near the counter where several men and a couple of women are sitting, and we're soon flying low. A middle-aged couple located nearest to us at the counter ask us about our experiences as paratroopers. We're more than happy to explain our exploits to them, and as the drinks remind us of more and more spectacular details of jumping out of planes and miraculous landings, I'm aware that some fiction is creeping into our accounts.

My own stories have moved overseas to combat now and I'm detailing some of the methods by which we paratroopers will be exterminating those Japanese and Germanese. The first time I make the mispronunciation I start to correct myself. Then it occurs to me that it's pretty damn clever anyway, so I continue to use it repeatedly. "When we get through with those Japanese and Germanese, they're gonna wish to hell they'd never heard of those Americanese, I'll tell ya that, right now." Wow, I'm thinking, I can stick that "ese" on a lotta stuff and sound like one helluva guy.

A big policeman just came in. A really big policeman. Real tall and he must weigh at least two fifty. He's talking to the guy by the cash register who seems to be pointing in our direction. He's probably telling the cop about the wonderful paratroopers who've been entertaining the customers, so I decide to saunter over and tell the policeman personally something about us. I stumble a little on the way across the room, don't actually fall down or anything though, and on the way I remember the big BUY WAR BONDS signs I'd seen around town earlier in the day.

"Shay, oshifer," I blurt out. Quickly realizing that I've slurred that a bit I start over. "Officer," I say, as I proceed very carefully, "are you buying plenty of war bonds so my paratrooper buddies and I can go overseas and start killing those Japanese and Germanese?" It sounds to me like I got that out real good, so I continue. "Us Americanese paratroopers will be happy to go over there and kill those Japanese and Germanese if you cops will just keep buying enough war bonds."

Maybe it's the booze, but the officer does not seem very friendly. In fact, there seems to be a downright frown on his face as he turns on his heel and walks out. Johnny and Don have now taken up the Japanese and Germanese theme and are trying to put it to song. Johnny can't carry a tune in a basket, but I think their effort is admirable. Leading the singing for the platoon is my bag, of course, so I soon have them singing about those Japanese and Germanese a bit more melodiously.

The door to the restaurant opens loudly as five or six policemen come charging in. The big one to whom I've been hustling war bonds stalks over to our table and announces loudly "You drunks are under arrest and you're coming to jail right now!" He grabs me by the collar and the seat of the pants and starts pushing me towards the door. The other cops are also manhandling Johnny and Don out of the place.

The cop has me by the belt in the back of my pants and he is one strong son of a gun. He keeps lifting me along as we head down the street and I think my feet are hitting the ground about every other step. I'm rather enjoying the whole thing by now, he hasn't hit me or anything, and the jail must be close since we're apparently going to walk there.

We're in the jail now and they're booking us for drunk and disorderly and some other stuff, too, it sounds like, but Johnny and Don and I are all pretty happy and upbeat about the whole thing. Luckily we're a trio of happy drunks or things could have been pretty messy back in that restaurant. I'm thinking how fortunate we all are, including the policemen, that Jess Orosco of our platoon wasn't with us. It would have taken the five or six cops to handle that wild Indian alone, and by the time the three of us had joined in with him, the restaurant would have ended up a disaster area. Jess had already been part of such calamitous doings two or three times, and his reputation is known regiment wide.

All three of us sleep pretty good. It's the morning after, and the cops are ready to get us out of there. The fines we have to pay coincidentally add up to just the amount we have, and we're put out on the street with only some loose change remaining in our pockets.

"How the hell are we going to get back to camp without the money to even pay bus fare?" Johnny moans as we walk in the direction of what we assume is the bus station. Don reassures us and tells about the several times he's sponged off the bus operators and gotten free rides.

Sure enough, Don has soft-soaped the manager at the bus station regarding our plight, leaving out some details I'm sure, and we have tickets back to Charlotte including transfers to Fayetteville. Johnny and I are mightily impressed. The platoon has long known of Don's many household talents, including cooking, sewing, pressing, barbering, and the like (all for a price, of course), but this is something beyond. "Don is one mighty resourceful fellow," I'm thinking, "and our platoon is lucky indeed to have his quick wit aboard as we approach the combat that awaits us."

෨   ෨   ෨

In a letter Bill True wrote home in March, 1943, was the following:

"We've got a wildcat for a mascot in the battalion now. There is a farmer near here who has a little zoo and he had a couple of wildcats, among other things. The colonel thought he'd like one for a mascot so he offered a 3-day pass and $10 to anyone who would swipe one of them. One of the sergeants in our company took him up on it and we now have it in a cage out in back of the barracks. They're going to try to jump the cat like that dog you've read about. I sure don't want to be the one to throw him out."

Here's the story behind this episode:

While at Camp Mackall the 2nd Battalion Commander, Colonel Strayer, had heard rumors that other outfits were "jumping dogs." Well, he couldn't let the 506th be bested, or even equaled, so he decided to one-up them by jumping a wildcat. Thus it was officially announced that anyone who acquired one for him would get a 3-day pass and $10.

Sergeant Don Replogle and "Studs" Malley got roaring drunk one night in town and on the way back, discovered a roadside "zoo," owned and operated by a local farmer. This zoo happened to have a bobcat in a cage, and it seemed just the ticket for Col. Strayer's plans. Their first thought was to "throw a raincoat over it and take it back," but after approaching the cage closely and seeing the cat's wild and angry demeanor, they changed the plan. He was three times the size of a large house cat and growling and spitting very aggressively. This was, indeed, a "wild" cat.

Not to be stymied, Replogle and Malley decided to steal the cat and its entire cage, intact. But the contraption was too big to fit in the cab they had hired. So they opened the trunk, and rolled down the back windows on each side of the car. The cage fit part way into the trunk but hung out. They both rode, standing on the back bumper, holding on to the cab window frames for balance and gripping the cage so it wouldn't slide out and fall in the street. Thus they returned to camp, where the MP at the gate cheerfully waved them through.

As soon as Replogle and Malley got inside the gate they drove straight to Col. Strayer's personal quarters. It was 2 a.m., but they rang the bell and woke him up anyway. He was tired, and appeared inebriated (though not as drunk as they), and asked what they wanted. "Here's your wildcat, sir!" they both slurred happily, offering sloppy salutes. Strayer had them put the cat, cage and all, in the middle of his living room.

Then true to his word, both men received $10 and a 3-day pass.

Next day the owner came to the camp to ask if any paratroopers had stolen his cat (not an unreasonable suspicion) and was told "absolutely not." He went away disappointed and clearly distrustful of the Army. And the men of the 506th soon found that acquiring a wildcat, and getting him to qualify for parachute wings, were two entirely different challenges.

The parachute riggers were happy to make a chute harness, boots, and other rigging for the bobcat. But as one might expect, this four-legged trooper was reluctant to try them on. No problem. A quick trip to medical produced a bottle of chloroform which they quickly used to knock the animal out. They then dressed him in paratrooper rigging and waited for him to wake up.

Upon awakening the cat was none too pleased. He was also strong and had sharp claws and teeth. Within minutes he had torn the parachute harness to ribbons. He never did get to jump. But Gus Patruno was given the duty (pleasant as it turned out) of feeding and "training" the cat, which meant that at any given time on a field maneuver he might be excused by the Colonel to "go back and feed my wildcat." This order was invariably met with a cheerful "Yes, sir!" and a snappy salute from Gus.

The cat became a mascot for the Battalion the entire time they were at Camp Mackall. When the 506th shipped out, they passed it along to the next unit arriving, to see what they could do with it.

A rope climb had been set up in the woods near the 1st Platoon barracks and Bill True and some of the men started competing among themselves, just for fun. Bill worked at it and got to be quite fast: faster than anyone in his barracks. Word spread that he thought he was best in the company, so guys started dropping by to challenge him. Several men from the other platoons came by to try their luck, but none could beat his time.

True hadn't intended to become the center of a competition, but he did anyway, and it went on for several days. Finally Orel Lev, a small, wiry man from the 2nd Platoon, came by. Men in his platoon had bets going that he could beat Bill, so there was more than passing interest in this match. Lev turned out to be the company champion and he easily won by a full two seconds.

Spring 1943, Camp Mackall, North Carolina. Some thirteen of us from our barracks posing in rear of barracks. Left-to-right, Front: Steve Pustola. Kneeling: Doug Roth, Louis Cioni, Bob Vogel, Gordon Mather, Cliff Valleries. Standing: George Fink, Bill True, Alvin Wilson, Johnny Jackson, Ken Stewart, Leslie Tindall.

A regimental newsletter was started in March with the fitting cover designation "PARA-DICE." An insignia for the regiment had already been designed which displayed a pair of dice showing a five and a six up. With an O running through the dice, and featuring a screaming eagle in flight with a parachute canopy behind, the representation of the 506th Parachute Infantry Regiment was cleverly presented.

The first issue of "PARA-DICE" included the results of a regimental contest to see who had the prettiest wives and sweethearts. Bill True had recently received a picture from his cousin Eula Friend in Omaha and submitted it for the competition. Eula was a real beauty. She had sent him a photograph of herself that Look Magazine had featured in 1942 under the heading "Most Beautiful College Girls of 1941." She was included in the final group of "lookers" in the Para-Dice contest, and Bill was thus among the prize winners. His award: a luxury weekend in Charlotte.

The next newsletter issue carried a story about those weekend doings, which culminated at a gala ballroom dance where "...some twenty-five of Charlotte's loveliest Victory Belles greeted the men of the sky..." True's date for the evening was a college coed named Louise Moore. She was gorgeous, charming, and a feather in his arms as they danced. He was instantly smitten, and when the clock reached midnight and the lady chaperones announced the conclusion of the dance, he hastened to get her address. Visions of future weekends in her company eased the pain of her parting words, "Good night, Bill True."

Bill wrote to Louise on his first day back at camp, and tried to keep the tone at a sophisticated level. She was a senior at Queens College, at least a year or two older than he, and it seemed important to make a good impression with his writing. He couldn't resist getting at least a bit romantic, however. He described how the line from Maurice Chevalier's song "Every little breeze seems to whisper Louise" was constantly running through his head. Louise answered his letter but it contained the sad news that she had a very close boyfriend who had just gone overseas. Bill wondered for a bit why she hadn't told him the night of the dance. Then he realized she had been graciously entertaining a young soldier far from home, and probably didn't think it necessary or appropriate.

ॐ   ॐ   ॐ

Days on the firing range were always greatly preferable to field problems with their long, fast marches and exhausting attacks on simulated enemy strongholds. The two- and three-day field maneuvers were worst of all, with sparse field rations of food and cold nights sleeping on the ground.

In a letter home Bill discussed time on the firing range:

"We were out on the range today, zeroing our rifles in and firing the practice course. Tomorrow we're going on a combat range that is supposed to be a humdinger. They've been working on it quite a while—there's supposed to be all kinds of surprise targets, barbed wire, machine guns firing (pointed at us) and stuff like that. Better be hittin the hay."

The "humdinger" was all of that. For the second time in their training the men were subjected to live machine gun fire crackling close over their heads as they crawled on their bellies under barbed wire strung low to the ground. New this time, however, was house to house close combat action with surprise targets springing up at any time. Even more unusual, the men would be using the famous Thompson sub-machine gun.

The Thompson had been around since its use by soldiers

in World War I, where it was nicknamed "the trench sweeper." Later, in the 1920s and '30s, it was a favorite of criminals such as "Machine-Gun Kelly" as well as other gangsters, and was a regular weapon of the FBI. It fired the standard .45 caliber ACP cartridge, originally designed by John Browning for his legendary pistol. But unlike the ubiquitous .45 handgun, the Thompson could put out a tremendous amount of lead in a big hurry, firing in fully-automatic mode. This ability lent it both a fearsome reputation to the foe, and a challenge to its user.

Virtually every weapon creates recoil when fired. It causes the gun to move backward, and the muzzle generally to rise, according to Newton's laws of physics. With the semi-automatic M-1 rifle, a soldier accounted for this by taking time to lower his gun and re-aim before firing a second or third round. But the fully-automatic Thompson kept cycling and firing bullets repeatedly as long as a finger pressed the trigger. Each individual round kicked the weapon back and the muzzle upward a little more, with no time to recover. The result was that a long string of fire caused the shooter to almost lose control, and end up firing nearly straight up in the air. Thus the needed skill was to release the trigger so quickly as to get off only a few well-aimed rounds—ideally two or three at a time.

Armed with a sub-Thompson, each man was put through the close-combat course with an officer instructor following closely and evaluating him. True's first test was to kick open a door and charge into a room in which there might be an enemy. As he burst through and leaped into the room, sure enough a German soldier popped up in front of him. Remarkably, Bill somehow managed to fire a single round into the middle of his chest. This was impressive skill indeed, and the instructor told him so.

The remainder of the course consisted of dodging down a street with unexpected explosions occurring at various intervals. Enemy soldiers aiming weapons suddenly appeared in windows and around corners. Bill was able to limit his firing to short bursts as required, but his aim was not as precise as it had been in the very close quarters of the first room. Nevertheless he managed to ultimately dispatch each of his enemies and was given a good overall score on the exercise.

Now the men were introduced to new weapons. All troops learned the rudiments of handling them, even though specialists would be trained to use them on a regular basis. They included the bazooka, the BAR (Browning Automatic Rifle), and the M-1 carbine. Extensive time was spent on the carbine since it would be a fairly common weapon, especially among officers and some of the non-coms. It fired a .30 caliber bullet but didn't pack the punch of the M-1's .30-'06 cartridge. The weapon itself was also shorter and lighter than the M-1, but unsuitable for long-range targets. It's recoil wasn't as punishing, and it's reduced weight made it less burdensome to lug over long marches.

True found the carbine much to his liking and became quite proficient with it. In addition to the firing positions usual for the M-1 rifle, a squatting stance was practiced with the smaller weapon. A man would assume that position with his left and right elbows resting on his knees. This provided substantial support for a steady aim, and with its lesser recoil, a rapid fire could be accurately placed.

On one of the "rapid fire squatting" sessions True fired a perfect score, and word of this soon reached Captain Mulvey. The Captain had quickly mastered the carbine himself, and fired a perfect score in the "rapid fire standing" sequence. He challenged Bill to a competition in the prone position in which a friendly one-dollar bet was waged. Officers and men alike were intrigued with the match and gathered to watch the two competitors: one the company commander, and the other a mere PFC. Both men fired an almost perfect score, but missed the silhouette with one shot. The bet was thus a standoff, and the company resumed routine firing range work. But for the moment, at least, a mutual respect and comradely bond had been forged between Bill and his superior officer.

In a subsequent letter home Bill wrote about this day on the range as follows.

"We were out on the range last week and fired our new carbines. They're a new type especially designed for paratroops. When they're folded they look like a pop gun. They're pretty hard to fire accurately 'cause the sights aren't very adjustable and you have to allow Kentucky windage and elevation. Mine was in good shape though—and I didn't have to do as much of that as most of the guys. My score was second highest in the company..."

ॐ   ॐ   ॐ

A regimental review with a battalion-sized jump was arranged for a group of visiting dignitaries which included President Roosevelt himself. Several high ranking Army officers and a number of civilian luminaries as well were to be present for the doings.

The 1st Battalion was selected to make the jump, with the 2nd and 3rd to pass in review. Excellent weather prevailed on the appointed day, no wind, so the parachute drop at a fairly high altitude would be impressively visible. The two marching battalions, clad in their full dress uniforms, passed in review stepping smartly to a John Philip Sousa march. As they held their ranks waiting for the jumpers to arrive, the first echelon of the C-47s appeared in the distance.

Unknown to any of the observers, and certainly not to those up on the reviewing stand, several men in the 1st Battalion had planned a comic stunt as part of their jump. Robert Flory was one of this group, and he had drawn the short straw which meant he would be the one to release a full roll of toilet paper on the way down.

Flory's stick was in the 4th serial of planes, and he tells his story as follows:

"As we made our approach, I could see hundreds of civilians and the other two battalions, plus the reviewing stand watching us...we emptied the plane in under 12 seconds...I slipped the roll of toilet paper out of my jump suit pocket and holding it by the end, I released the roll...I thought the roll would never stop unwinding. When it did, the toilet paper...started twisting and turning like a giant snake. At about 500 feet, my heart practically stopped beating. That cursed toilet paper was festooning all over the occupants of the reviewing stand! I tried desperately to slip away from the stand, but I landed directly in front, not 30 feet from it. As I rolled over to get out of my harness, I glanced up. There stood our President, literally swallowed by toilet paper, and grinning like a Cheshire cat with that cigarette holder pointed up at a rakish angle! Colonel Sink was directly behind him and laughing like it was the funniest thing he had ever seen."

Rather than being disciplined, as Flory fully expected when the toilet paper wound its way into the reviewing stand, he received a three-day pass.

A large tree back of the 1ˢᵗ Platoon barracks located near the rope climb became a favorite for knife throw practice. One balmy evening after an unusually easy day of mostly classroom instructions, Whitey Swafford from 2ⁿᵈ Platoon was heaving his bayonet at the tree. One of his throws ricocheted off and stuck hanging in Bill True's leg, as he was standing nearby. Bill removed the bayonet from his leg and handed it to Swafford, expecting at least something of an apology. Instead, Whitey offered only a very embarrassed smile.

Spring 1943, Camp Mackall, North Carolina. Group of us informally dressed at the rear of our barracks. Left to right: Steve Pustola, Ken Stewart, Gordon Mather (probably—that would be a characteristic pose), Cliff Valliers, Bill True, Lou Cioni (barely visible), Linus Brown, and Otto May.

Swafford was a heavily-built man weighing nearly 200 pounds, and was a Golden Glove champion boxer before the war. He had been on the regimental boxing team since its founding at Camp Toccoa, and clearly took real pleasure in hitting people. True recalled a time when one of the sergeants had called Whitey down for breaking into the chow line at Fort Benning. The sergeant soon found himself stretched out cold on the ground. Bill was more than willing to accept Whitey's sheepish grin as sincere regret.

At a USO dance a few nights later Swafford did render a more practical apology. Bill had danced several numbers with the same girl, and each time someone tried to cut in he would graciously give the girl her choice of partners. In every instance the girl had indicated she wanted to continue dancing with True, but one trooper became quite insistent and bothersome. As he was once more turned down he grabbed Bill by the shoulder and spun him around. From out of nowhere Whitey Swafford suddenly appeared and delivered a roundhouse haymaker to the man's chin. As the fellow slid on his back across the floor, True continued dancing without further interruption.

ᔑ   ᔑ   ᔑ

Cliff Valleries, a 1st Platoon man in Bill True's barracks, had a wife back in Massachusetts who was planning to come down for a weekend visit with her husband. She had an unmarried girl friend who would be coming with her, so Cliff suggested Bill could be her date when they arrived. The foursome met at the bus station in Rockingham, with an overnight visit to Charlotte scheduled.

On the bus ride to Charlotte, Bill got some singing going and was surprised and pleased to find that Theresa Montagna had both a fine voice and handled a nifty harmony. Theresa knew the lyrics to everything Bill initiated, as the two crooned together on "The Bells Are Ringing," "Shine On Harvest Moon," and numerous other hits of the era.

Theresa took a separate room for herself when they

registered at the hotel, but True was still hopeful that intimate relations might work out. After a late dinner and a number of rum and Coca Colas, shared in the married couple's room, Bill suggested that it was getting a bit late. Theresa agreed. When they got to her room she asked if he'd like to come in for a few minutes. True figured he was about to score.

They did some light smooching sitting on the edge of her bed, and eventually were lying down. Passionate French kisses ensued and Bill moved his hand up under her dress to advance his cause to the next level. Pushing his hand away she hastened to tell him she just didn't go "all the way" with a man. She thought Bill was a fine fellow and she liked him a lot, but he certainly wouldn't respect her in the morning if they went the distance.

Bill used all the persuasion he could think of to convince her that his respect for her could only rise with intimacy between them. After a few more deep kisses he reminded her that he was going to war. Tender memories of their passionate moments would give him courage on the battlefield.

A quotation he'd learned from Doug Roth and Bill Tucker came to him and he thought it was worth a try. "You know, Theresa, some very wise philosophers have thought about life and what it means and what makes it all worthwhile, and I'd like to quote one of them for you. 'It is better to drink life for one flaming hour and to reel across the sun, than to sip pale years and cower before oblivion.'"

"That's sort of the byword for paratroopers too, you know," he added. "You wouldn't want to return home after this weekend and figure you could have been drinking life and reeling with Bill True instead of sipping pale hours, would you?"

Unfortunately for him, Theresa Montagna recognized

bullshit when she heard it. She remained a "good girl" to the end of the evening. True finally gave up and returned to his room with an ache between his legs—a serious case of the "stonies."

Cliff Valleries got involved with a North Carolina woman shortly after this visit from his wife. One day, while writing letters to the two of them, he accidentally mixed the envelopes which naturally resulted in simultaneous estrangement from both. Unlucky in more than just love, Cliff would later suffer several serious broken bones on a practice jump and be transferred out of the 506th.

ʘ ʘ ʘ

One day True got word by mail that his favorite grandma, Nannie Dorcas Rowland True, had died in Oklahoma. His dad had gone back for her services and wrote about it. Bill remembered his days as a child visiting his grandparents' home in El Reno. Nannie was a sweet little lady who always cried when the visits ended. Bill would never forget her singing the many verses of "Billy Boy" to him as she bustled about her modest kitchen. It was sad news that she was gone.

Not long after this, Don Replogle and Bill True got an overnight pass into Rockingham one weekend, and happened to walk by a bookstore. In the front window was an ad for the book "God's Little Acre." True had heard that there was some pretty sexy stuff in it so he stopped to buy. The young woman behind the counter made several suggestive remarks about the work, which convinced Bill that his expectations were on the mark. Everyone in the barracks managed to read it in coming days, and Bill got the nickname "TyTy" from a lecherous character in the book. In it, Ty Ty used the phrase "those rising beauties" to describe a daughter-in-law's chest.

True thought the words had a neat ring to them. By the time he'd used the phrase a few times himself, his nickname was applied and lasted throughout the war.

The evening of the bookstore purchase, Don and Bill attended a USO dance where both men tried to pick up dates to take home. Don was a few years older than Bill, good looking, and dressed impeccably. Even so, he bombed out on the beauty he was trying to land. Bill settled for a much plainer girl but succeeded in convincing her to let him take her home. She lived more than a mile from the dance hall. During the walk home he mused to himself that all his effort had "better pay off." They did some light petting on her porch swing, but it was soon apparent that this was as far as anything would go. True gave up shortly and trudged all the way back to the hotel.

Don was still up reading "God's Little Acre" when Bill returned to their room. "Did you make out?" he asked as Bill entered.

"Yeah, ya doggone right I did," Bill lied. Going into the bathroom he made a big show of applying a full prophylactic treatment to himself. In coming days he would feel sheepish about going through such a ritual just to convince a buddy that he had made a sexual conquest. But "Hey, a guy has a reputation to uphold, right?" he told himself.

ॐ   ॐ   ॐ

In a letter home True wrote the following.

"I just got back from a 3-day problem today and there were 3 letters from you all waiting for me. I really enjoyed them, too. The problem was pretty much of a stickler at times. For about the first 32 hours we only got about 2 or 3 hours of sleep altogether. The problem started with a regimental jump. That's the first time the whole regiment has ever jumped together. I made a pretty good jump although I landed real hard. I jumped number 13 which is the first time I've ever been so far back. They say a person never gets used to jumping but I think that's a lot of bunk cause I know they're certainly getting easier for me. We had a nice long 45-minute ride and everybody had a good time. We were all up and down the aisle, in the cockpit, sticking our heads out the door and just generally having a good time. All during the problem our re-supply and chow was dropped to us from the planes. Yesterday one of the riggers was pushing out the chow 'chutes when he fell out himself. They always wear free chutes but the plane was only about 250 feet high and it looked like he was a cooked goose. He really acted fast though and I guess he was about 75 feet or so from the ground when his chute was full opened. He had a swell landing but you should have seen how he was shaking."

On one of the nights during this field problem True's squad had a difficult compass assignment that took them through something much like an Everglades swamp in Florida. Thick masses of vines and swamp growths of all types had to be traversed. As they approached a clearing they came across a house on stilts with lamplight shining through the windows. A fiddle could be heard and as they got closer they could see people sitting on the porch and hear them singing. They passed on without stopping to join, as they had done that night in the Alabama woods. But Bill heard a chorus line often enough to remember it. "I don't feel at home in this world anymore." In that previous time in 'bama they had gotten lost. This time, Lt. McFadden was gratified with the successful completion of their mission and complimented the entire squad on a job well done.

❧   ❧   ❧

In another letter home about this time True wrote.

"Getting kinda lax on my writing aren't I? No really good excuses but we have been working pretty hard. Three-day problems, Thursday, Friday, and Saturday are definitely a habit now. We haven't missed any since over a month ago and they're getting rougher all the time. Each week we spend more time on the problems with less sleep each time. I guess they're trying to work us up to a point where we can just about stay up three days straight."

❧   ❧   ❧

One Saturday Johnny Jackson, Dude Stone, and Bill True got midnight passes together into Hamlet, North Carolina. Jackson had met Sylvia Smith at a dance there, and they had dated once after that. She told him to bring a buddy or two with him next time he came to town. She had several friends who'd like to meet a paratrooper from Camp Mackall. He called her and arranged for a triple date that night.

There would be no trucks leaving the camp for Hamlet for several hours after their passes started, so the three buddies decided to hitchhike into town. There seemed to be literally no traffic until finally a soldier driving a dark blue late model Chevrolet sedan came by and offered to take them into town for $5 each. They all felt that was an awful lot of money for the relatively short trip, but the driver was adamant and insisted that was his standard price. Besides, he told them, it would be the fastest ride into town they'd ever had and would find it worth the money.

Anxious to get there quickly the trio reluctantly agreed to his price, and forked over the money. They weren't exactly happy, however, and Dude Stone in particular was really steaming. As soon as they were in the car the driver spun the wheels taking off, and shortly they were traveling 65 miles an hour.

True was more than a little edgy going that fast down a narrow gravel road, but Dude was determined to bug the driver. "Is that as fast as this crate will go?" he demanded. "I thought you said we'd get a fast drive into town."

Jackson and True were both nervously eyeing the speedometer as it rose from 70 to 75 mph, but Dude wouldn't settle for that. "My old maid aunt back in Orange, Massachusetts drives faster than this going to church Sunday morning. If you can't get any real speed out of this heap, we're gonna want some money back."

Perspiration began appearing on the driver's upper lip, but he responded to Dude's challenge as the speedometer crept over 80. Bill soon found it hard to swallow, and seeing Johnny's ashen face he knew his own rising panic was shared. "Maybe this is fast enough," Bill whispered to Dude, hoping he'd finally lay off the guy.

Dude shook off the suggestion and continued his needling. The driver got the speed up to 85, but that was either as fast as the car would go, or he'd reached the limit of his own daring. When they finally slowed down pulling into Hamlet, Johnny and Bill both heaved sighs of relief and were grateful to be in one piece. Dude, however, couldn't resist a parting shot as they got out of the car. "You're lucky we're nice guys," he told the driver. "We could easily demand our money back after your promise of a fast ride into town."

Bill's date was seventeen-year old Jeannie Bryan. She had wavy light brown hair, with hints of auburn, that fell to her shoulders. A dimpled smile enhanced facial features that might have graced Helen of Troy. Height a little short of average, and a trim figure bordering on slight, she suggested to Bill the lines from Stephen Foster's song "I dream of Jeannie with the light brown hair... floating like a vapor on the soft summer air."

True had had blind dates before, but he knew no one would ever top this one arranged for him by Sylvia Smith of Hamlet, North Carolina. Jeannie became the only girl he would be with before going overseas a few months later. They saw the movie "Hello, Frisco, Hello" starring Alice Faye and John Payne on a subsequent date. The lyrics Alice sang "You'll never know just how much I love you" became *their song*, and would be mentioned frequently in future letters to each other.

Mrs. Smith, Sylvia's mother, became a wonderful friend to both Johnny and Bill. When they had overnight passes they could sleep on the lounges on her enclosed front porch, and then wake up to a hearty southern breakfast in the morning. She frequently loaned the family car to Bill so he could drive over to get Jeannie, whose home was on the edge of town. And on more than one occasion she gave the boys money when they were short of cash to take the girls out. A year and a half later Johnny would come home to marry Sylvia following a serious shrapnel wound suffered from an artillery tree-burst at Bastogne.

One day without preamble or warning, fifteen men were suddenly transferred out of F Company. They were part of a total contingent of 150 from the regiment. The men who were *not* selected for culling out breathed a collective sigh of relief. Nearly everyone had been with the 506th since basic training at Camp Toccoa, the better part of a year now, and any thought of having to leave the unit was truly painful. But it was made clear that this was in no way a punishment for infractions of discipline. They would fill up regiments in the 82nd Airborne Division, and soon see real combat in North Africa.

Bill Tucker had been with the 1st Platoon of F Company from the start and was one of those slated to leave. He was heartbroken and appealed the decision to Captain Mulvey. But apparently the company executive officer, Lt. Carl McDowell, had made the selection and remained adamant that he go.

True learned that there was a bad "history" between the two men, starting from their first days together. McDowell was only a high school graduate, while Tucker had spent a year attending Harvard. He had made the mistake of bragging about this to the lieutenant, and it caused a resentment that afterward never waned. Now Tucker was openly sorry he hadn't tried a bit harder to mollify his superior officer.

ॐ   ॐ   ॐ

A stop and go train ride at the beginning of June transported the 506th to Sturgis, Kentucky, for the beginning of extended maneuvers. The 101st Airborne Division had been assigned to the "Blue Army" for a huge mock war, shooting blanks at another American unit designated "Red Army." This game included the largest airborne exercise yet staged. Ranging from Kentucky and Indiana all the way into Tennessee, the actions were meant to provide the closest thing to real warfare that the troops had yet experienced. Bill True and his buddies thought the real aim was to provide practice for the higher ranking officers in maneuvering large units. Everyone at the squad, platoon, and even company level, had already learned most everything they could, short of actual combat.

The 2nd Battalion made their jump early in the action and True wrote home about it in the following words:

"It was a pretty good jump although they did unload us all over the woods. I was sure surprised when I saw all those trees under me but I managed to slip into a little clearing. Even then I barely missed a barbed wire fence and my chute did tangle in it. They told us we made the lowest battalion jump ever made in the U.S. and also landed in the smallest area. The reds (our enemy) were evidently expecting us cause they were shooting all over the place. I got in back of one of them and held my rifle right over his head and fired. He nearly jumped out of his shoes."

Now long night marches ranged through overgrown backwoods and over steep hills and mountainous terrain. It became routine to trudge through swamps and slash through matted underbrush to gain tactical advantage over the Red Army units. Rough as the maneuvers became, however, they never exceeded the physical demands the men of the 506th had already endured at Toccoa. Mt. Currahee still reigned supreme.

F Company made a second jump during the mock war. This time Bill True barely missed crashing into a farmer's rock wall. In maneuvering to avoid it, however, his landing was awkward and he seriously injured his right knee. Barely able to hobble to the planned assembly area, he was evacuated to one of the field hospitals that had been set up as part of the simulated war conditions.

His leg was placed in a full cast and he missed some of the subsequent war games. There were a large number of injured soldiers in the hospital, but Bill was the only paratrooper. Days were long and boring in the hot tents, and the doctors tried to find ways to occupy the men. One day one of them asked Bill if he'd mind telling an assembly of the other patients about his experiences. True knew that soldiers in general were a bit in awe of paratroopers, but he'd never done any public speaking and was somewhat apprehensive about giving such a talk. He nevertheless agreed to it and was pleasantly surprised by the experience. He found himself speaking quite freely about the hard training and the frightening aspects of his first jumps. The admiration of his listeners, as evidenced by their attention and frequent questions, was gratifying. And the respect and deference shown to him afterwards became a source of continuing satisfaction and pride.

One of True's letters home at this time included:

"They've got me in a hospital right now with... a torn cartilage in my knee... We made our 11th jump... and I didn't land the way I've been taught. Someone gets hurt on most every jump... This has been quite a maneuver from what I've been able to hear. I guess most of the paratroops are wiped out by now but they sure messed up things while they were going. They just brought another guy in from our platoon and he said ours was the only platoon left in the battalion."

                                                      ॐ   ॐ   ॐ

When Bill returned to his outfit he was on light duty for a short time but was soon back into full action. One night an extremely arduous exercise took place. The company was ordered to carry boats up and down through thickets and wild growths of underbrush for what seemed like miles before reaching a river. Slipping and scrambling down the steep banks, followed by noisy splashes into the water, did not make for a quiet crossing. What was supposed to be a surprise commando-type raid unintentionally alerted the "enemy." By the time they had clambered up the slippery banks on the other side, their intended victims had quietly left the area.

One of the things the men grew to hate most about these simulated war games was the repetitive order to "dig in" at every halt. Whether for a short break or an extended stay in one spot, the standing order was the same. The men instinctively knew this would be standard procedure when real combat came, but chopping into the hard Tennessee clay with their entrenching tools at every stop seemed a stupid waste of energy. This was especially so when an hour of strenuous digging would suddenly be interrupted by the command to "Fill 'em up, we're moving out."

Chiggers were another constant irritation. Sleeping on the ground night after night gave these pests every opportunity to plague the troops who soon found themselves scratching their skin raw. Some relief finally came with the issuance of a strong bug-repellent powder, but not till many of the men had developed serious rashes.

On one of the missions the 506th found itself not far from Nashville, Tennessee. At Camp Mackall, True had begun teaching Dude Stone how to play a few chords on the guitar. With that in mind he now told of his admiration for Roy Acuff and the present close proximity to the Grand Ole Opry. A visit to see and hear Roy perform would be wonderful and seemed possible. They tried desperately to wangle a pass into the city, but of course no one got passes during active maneuvers. Many years after the war, when the 101st Airborne Association held its annual reunion in Nashville, Bill was finally able to get to the Grand Ole Opry and actually meet Roy Acuff. As True described that fruitless attempt in 1943, Roy said he *did* remember the time of the big Army maneuvers and was only sorry it took Bill so long to get to the Opry.

The 506th concluded their maneuvers at Camp Breckinridge, Kentucky in late July. Then some of the men started to get furloughs, and it was announced that the regiment would soon be heading for Fort Bragg, North Carolina. This was not far from Camp Mackall and Bill True looked forward to seeing his girl, Jeannie Bryan, in Hamlet again.

ɤ   ɤ   ɤ

Another slow train ride took the 506th to Fort Bragg. There Bill found the best barracks he had experienced since Fort MacArthur. It was a welcome greeting after the grueling field maneuvers and the bare accommodations at Sturgis and Breckenridge. Normal training schedules were resumed, but now began a major re-outfitting, with new uniforms, supplies and equipment. This was a tip-off that the regiment was preparing to ship overseas. Speculation was rampant as to which direction they'd be headed—east or west—but no one at the company level knew for sure which.

At this time the first platoon got a new leader. Lt. Robert Brewer, a tall man from California, was well-liked. He willingly participated in physical competitions with the enlisted men and was the winner of most. During a quarter-mile sprint, however, True passed him in the closing yards and the lieutenant was surprised. More than a good sport about it, he congratulated Bill and was always warm toward him thereafter.

In this period Captain Mulvey initiated some special manual of arms drills which called for performance of surprise commands quickly and precisely. Those who failed a movement perfectly, or were slow in responding, were "eliminated" from the exercise. Bill enjoyed the competition involved in manipulating the rifle. He practiced on his own a bit, became quite good at it, and on one occasion he was the last to be culled out—only eliminated due to a slight delay in performing "Rifle Salute!" Perhaps a bit slow to catch on, True finally got the idea that his apparent superiority might very well be due to wiser men who didn't enjoy such efforts, eliminating themselves on purpose.

TIT-FOR-TAT or "ALL'S WELL THAT ENDS WELL"
Bill's True Tale

We're at Fort Bragg, North Carolina, and headed overseas almost anytime. That has been quite apparent ever since we got back from Tennessee Maneuvers and they started issuing us new equipment, uniforms and various other combat gear. We're still not sure which way we'll be going, east or west, and a few bets have been placed on both directions.

Johnny is going into Hamlet tonight to see Sylvia, but since Jeanie is not available, I'm going to give Fayetteville a lookover. Neither Johnny nor I have been to this nearer and much larger town since we're both pretty much in love with our Hamlet girls. I'll certainly not be looking for any female companionship on this venture, but I'll have a few beers and check out some of the joints the guys have been talking about.

Fayetteville sure has a lot more bars and saloons and night spots than tiny Hamlet, and having a beer in as many as I can cover in an evening has got me several sheets to the wind. I didn't find anything particularly unique about any of them, in spite of some tall tales from several of the guys, so as the time to get back to Bragg approaches I'm ready to go.

The bus back to the base is loaded, and even the aisles are jammed with airborne troopers. I'm standing fairly near the back and feeling grateful that the ride back to Bragg is not a long one.

About six or seven feet in front of me is an artillery trooper--in the fairly dim bus-light I am still able to see the red piping on his cap as distinct from our infantry blue--who catches my eye and gives me one really dirty look.

What the heck was that all about, I'm thinking? I don't recall encountering him in any of the night spots, or as we were loading on the bus. I glance at him again, and still fixing the dirty look he says in a loud and menacing tone "Fuck You!"

Now I am really non-plussed, but I know I can't allow the insult to go unanswered. So calling on my quick-witted repartee I reply "Well, Fuck You, Too!"

"I'm going to kick your ass clean up between your shoulders when this bus stops!" he readily responds.

Has he had a recent beef with someone from the infantry, or do I possibly resemble someone who's given him a bad time? Recovering a bit from my initial surprise, I think I do a bit better with my reply this time when I say: "The day a piss-ant artilleryman gives an infantryman's ass anything but a kiss will be a long time coming!"

I've had a chance to study the guy some by this time, and notice that he's blond, pretty well built, and about as good looking as Whitey Swafford of my F Company. The guys around us are starting to get interested in our dispute, and are obviously looking forward to witnessing a hell of a scrap when the bus unloads.

Holy Crap, I'm thinking. I sure as hell hope he only looks like Whitey, who was Light-Heavyweight Golden Glove Champion of the State of Indiana before joining the paratroops. He seems to be only about my size though, Middleweight at best, so he shouldn't have much, if any, size advantage on me.

"By the time I've dragged your miserable infantryman's ass from the Post Gate to the C-47 macadam air strip you'll wish you'd never seen an artilleryman!" He's yelling now.

I had done a fair amount of boxing at the YMCA back when I was sixteen and seventeen, but my last flat-out fisticuffs had been at age 12. Hustling the Omaha World Herald on the southeast corner of 18th and Farnum Streets at the time, I'd had a to-do with the boy hustling the competing Hearst newspaper, the Omaha Bee News. That tussle had come about in a dispute over two cents.

Two cents was not an insignificant amount at the time, since my average earnings for the three-hour stint from three P.M. after school, till six P.M., averaged ten to twelve cents. As hustlers we bought our papers for one and ¾ cents, sold them for three cents, pocketing the one and ¼ cent profit. Selling eight to ten papers an evening was about average for my poor corner, although some of the older boys had better spots and could make as much as twenty-five to thirty cents.

My Uncle Olin Trotter, my mother's younger brother, in playing and sparring with me as a very small youngster had taught me how to use the left jab. I had used it to very good advantage in the two-cent fight, and had so bloodied my opponent that I'd felt sorry for him and let him have the money.

"Your ass is what will be dragging when I finish stomping the living crap out of you," I yell back. I'm going to hit that guy with a stiff left jab first thing off the bus, I'm thinking, and then kick him in the balls before he's even got both feet well planted on the ground.

"No goddamned fucking sonofabitch infantryman is ever going to stomp anything but his own pussy-livered feet when a real artillery soldier marches by," he screams at me.

I'd been complimented on my very fast and firm left jab by several people at the Y in Omaha. But the one trainer or coach had been too busy with his older Golden Glove contenders to spend time teaching me how to use my right effectively. Consequently, being matched several times with boys who could use both hands, I had led a rather short and inglorious career as a boxer.

I was remembering that aspect of my background as my looming encounter came closer and closer. His last diatribe had seemed somehow over the top. How to top something already "over the top" was a challenge certainly, but I had to at least have a go at it.

"The day that I can't take the likes of you and plaster your sad ass with one hand tied behind me, will be the day Poland China Pigs are flying and Holstein Cows are ice skating in hell."

The bus is now pulling into the unloading area and guys are starting to pour out. My erstwhile verbal opponent is walking down the exit steps just in front of me and I realize I'm only moments away from giving this yahoo the stiffest left jab I could muster. However, to my amazement the guy just keeps walking, heading for the Artillery barracks. For the briefest second I'm disappointed to be cheated out of the glory of humbling him, but I am quite satisfied to turn and start walking in the other direction towards the Infantry area.

And about now I realize that I am more than simply satisfied. I'm damn proud that I broke even on my "tit-for-tat" verbal exchange with the Artilleryman. And even better,

I'm happy that he and I agreed to forego fisticuffs, and to settle for the Shakespearean phrase that "all's well that ends well."

❧   ❧   ❧

There were more signals that their time states-side was about to end. Ten-day furloughs now were granted to all the units, in turns. Early in August Bill's platoon was given theirs, the last in the company to get them. He vividly remembered the eight-day train trip to get home the previous January, and the punishment meted out to those who returned late. With that in mind, True decided to spend some savings and fly the round trip to California.

There were no discounts for military personnel and the cost to fly Delta was $350. This was pricey indeed. But the expected joy of a family reunion, combined with the painful memory of Fritz Lucero's drumming out, seemed to make the expense a wise one.

Several Californians including Bill, Len Hicks and Les Tindall got tickets together, and all lamented the lack of any "servicemen's discount." To make matters worse, on the trip which left from Raleigh, North Carolina, they got bounced off in Jackson, Mississippi. Civilians with priorities apparently took precedence, and the troopers' seats were needed for these "more important" people. Len Hicks was especially miffed at this. He expressed the feelings of all in extremely purple language, telling the airline folks just what he thought of their priority system.

The troopers got bounced from scheduled flights more than once on their trip out west. But despite this, True was home in less than 24 hours and was glad to have flown. He spent several busy and fun days with his now-extended family in San Diego. They took lots of photos around the Mountain View Drive home and scenic spots throughout San Diego and environs. An especially memorable afternoon was spent at the Cove in La Jolla with a picnic, swimming in the surf, and just plain lazy sunbathing.

Bill's mother and step-father lived in Inglewood at this time, about 150 miles north of San Diego, so he caught a bus there to spend a day with them before heading back to North Carolina. While there he told his mom about the special girl, Jeannie, back in Hamlet. It sure would be nice to take her something special on his return. Next day, his mother took him to a nearby jewelry store and helped pick out a nice gift.

August 1943, San Diego, California. Bill True home on leave shortly before going overseas. Posing with family, left to right, step-siblings Duane and Dona Pillsbury, stepmother Hazel Pillsbury True, sister Betty Jean True, Bill, and father Leslie Arthur True.

The plane trip back to Raleigh, North Carolina, was both memorable and incongruously terrifying. The aircraft was a DC-3: civilian version of the same plane from which Bill had parachuted so many times. But on his training jumps the circumstances were decidedly different. Each of those hops had been of short duration, since the object was not to actually "travel" somewhere but merely get in the air over an appropriately clear field and jump out. Training flights were invariably made at low altitude, and purposely in calm weather. Even more to the point, Bill had always been wearing two parachutes: a main pack and a reserve. Except for these two civilian flights on furlough he had never even been *in* a plane without the security of those two 'chutes.

Now things were different. Somewhere over the Midwest the DC-3 hit stormy weather. Soon the plane began violently dropping and bucking wildly all over the sky. True was totally traumatized, even more than on his first parachute jump. There seemed to be no letup to the storm, and soon it was hard to believe they'd make it through intact. Nearing the point of abject panic, he felt he would have gladly leaped from the plane even without a chute. Their eventual safe landing in Raleigh was welcomed with an emotional relief Bill True would never forget. Only his first combat jump in Normandy would ever rival the sheer horror of this cross-country flight.

Shortly after True's return from furlough the 506th held a dress parade and inspection, with formal ceremonies attaching the regiment to the 101st Airborne Division. Speeches were given by General William C. Lee, division commander, and by Colonel Sink, regimental commander. Even the governor of North Carolina was on hand to commemorate the occasion. Their talks were congratulatory and brief, much to the relief of the assembled troops. No one in the 1st Platoon knew much about the 101st yet, but the

Screaming Eagle patch looked mighty good on their left shoulders. The general consensus was that after adding the 506 to its ranks, the 101st was probably the best airborne division in the world.

Not long after this ceremony, close inspections of all uniforms, equipment, supplies and weapons began. Much of this was newly issued. Trips to the firing range were made to be certain of weapon reliability and proper "sighting in." It became obvious that the regiment would be moving out shortly. The only uncertainties were the exact day of departure and the final destination.

"We're boarding trains tomorrow," Captain Mulvey announced one morning, "and the company photo will be taken at 1600 hours today. Wear jump suits and try to look handsome and dashing," he added.

Bill True hadn't gotten into Hamlet to see Jeannie Bryan since his return from furlough, and dreaded the thought of shipping out without seeing her one more time. Johnny Jackson also wanted to see Sylvia Smith again. They agreed to ask the captain for a pass to town that afternoon and evening. Mulvey reminded them they'd miss out on the company photo if they took off, but both insisted on seeing their girls for the last time. It took some convincing, but finally the captain relented, and the two of them rushed to clean up and get into their dress uniforms. Years later they would regret missing that company photo. As it turned out, nearly a dozen men did the same, and most lived to have similar feelings.

True was almost immediately sorry for his decision. His trip into Hamlet proved useless. Jeannie and her mother had taken the train that afternoon to visit a close relative who had taken suddenly ill. The balance of the wartime romance between Jeannie and Bill would consist entirely of the written word.

ॐ   ॐ   ॐ

Soon after the train left the station next morning it was clear that they were heading northeast. This meant an undoubted final destination in Europe. It was shortly confirmed when Lt. Brewer told the platoon they were on their way to Camp Shanks in New York.

Bill took his guitar with him on the train. It required little encouragement to get some singing started. One of the recent tunes Bill had learned at the Fort Bragg PX was "Lay That Pistol Down, Babe." Everyone could join in on the chorus:

Lay that pistol down, Babe, lay that pistol down,
Pistol Packin' Mama, lay that pistol down.

As expected, someone had smuggled a jug of white lightning aboard. Just a few shots of that around and the Pistol Packin' Mama song was hitting high volume.

I was drinkin' beer in a cabaret, and was I havin' fun,
Till one night she caught me right, and now I'm on the run.

Oh, lay that pistol down, Babe, lay that pistol down,
Pistol packin' Mama, lay that pistol down.

She kicked out my windshield, she hit me over the head,
She cussed and cried, and swore I'd lied, and wished that I was dead.

Oh, lay that pistol down, Babe, lay that pistol down,
Pistol packin' Mama, lay that pistol down.

The train made numerous stops along the way, usually just long enough to drop off and board passengers. Bill was in the same car with his dubious friend, Whitey Swafford. Everyone was bored with the ride. The windows of the car were open to allow passengers a little fresh air and to lean out and talk to passersby on the platforms. As they pulled out of one of the stations, Whitey startled everyone with yet another example of his pugilistic bent. A total stranger stood next to the train, apparently waiting to board his own. Without warning, Whitey leaned out the car window and for no apparent reason swung a huge right-hand haymaker, landing it squarely on the man's jaw. As the hapless stranger fell backward and slid across the platform, Bill was reminded of the soldier at the USO dance. Swafford had a decidedly sadistic streak. Good or bad, this would probably serve him well once he found himself in combat with *real* enemies.

☙　　☙　　☙

Camp Shanks was located up the Hudson River from New York City, and became the regiment's home for the following week. Most of the men had never been to New York and they were all hoping for at least short passes into the city. None were forthcoming, however. Security regarding overseas-bound troops was given as the reason.

Boring days were now filled with repeated inspections. Worse still were the innumerable inoculations for more diseases than Bill True thought ever existed. The tedium was so great that even working KP helped to pass the time, and became almost welcome. There was a well stocked PX with a juke box to occupy the evenings. "I'm Gonna Buy a Paper Doll" was a hit song by the Mills Brothers and Bill soon learned the lyrics and worked out the chords on his guitar.

Early on the morning of September 6, the men were told to pack their barracks bags and fall out to board a ferry for the trip to New York Harbor. Their assigned ship was an English passenger vessel formerly of the Cunard line: HMS *Samaria*. Like many others, she had been converted for troop transport and awaited the men of the 506th at Pier 90, North River, New York. On their way to its pier they happened to pass the famous (or was it now infamous?) French ship *Normandie*, which lay burned and capsized in the harbor. Newspapers had made much of the tragic demise of this noble liner.

The *Normandie* was launched in 1932, unquestionably the finest luxury passenger ship of its time. After 139 Atlantic crossings, including five record-breaking speed runs, she happened to be moored in New York harbor on the day that France fell to the Nazis in June of 1940. Since she was in U.S. waters, the Coast Guard "took her into custody" and shortly after the Japanese attack on Pearl Harbor, the United States officially confiscated her as a prize of war. Intending to convert her for troop transport, welders were re-cutting her innards when an errant spark lighted a bale of life jackets below deck. Subsequent mistakes on the part of the crew led to uncontrollable fires, and eventually the great ship heeled on its port side and sank in the harbor. It was an inglorious end to a majestic piece of maritime history.

But that was then and this was now. After arriving at their New York debarkation, the men of Fox Company enjoyed coffee and doughnuts provided by Red Cross ladies as they waited dock side to board their ship, the *Samaria*. Then carrying their heavily loaded barracks bags and rifles, the men walked up a long steep gangplank, and were checked off and given bunk assignments. There would be more than twice the usual number of troops on board. Two men were assigned to each bunk. They were expected to each alternate with one night below in the bunk and the next sleeping up on the outside open deck.

It took several hours for everyone to board. Finally the ship lifted anchor and tiny tugboats pulled it from the dock to guide it through the harbor. Passing the Statue of Liberty, Bill True was moved to reflect on events of the past year. It had been by far the most interesting, exciting, and, of course the hardest year of his life. And now he was sailing away from America to unknown adventures in foreign lands. A strange mixture of emotions new to his experience swept over him.

&ep;   &ep;   &ep;

The bunks below deck consisted of canvas spread between iron rods, and were stacked four high. With barely headroom enough for a man to slide into them they were uninviting at best. Bill spent the first night in his assigned bunk and that was enough to convince him of its drawbacks. The remainder of his nights were spent on deck. Bedding down with his blankets far aft on the ship, he found the rising and falling motion enjoyable and slept far better than he had deep in the ship's hold.

Breakfast their first morning was a foreboding harbinger of the fare that awaited the men for the remainder of the voyage. Boiled fish and tomatoes was served with coffee that tasted like dirty dish rags had been left in the pot. Many of the men were so disgusted with this "official" food, they dumped the whole mess into the garbage. Some lived on candy bars and peanuts for the rest of the trip.

The mess hall itself was on the bottom deck of the ship, and the iron steps leading to it wound in small circles down through the intervening levels. Strong and extremely unpleasant cooking odors wafted up the stairs. Many a soldier started in line intending to force himself to eat whatever was provided, then suddenly found himself upchucking whatever was already in his belly. As the floor gradually became slickly awash in vomit, the combination of its odor and those provided from the galley made certain that only the strongest of stomachs would make it all the way to chow.

Only two meals a day were served, and it took several hours for the line to wind down the stairs to the mess. Bill True had fortunately thought to bring several paperback books to read on the trip, and that helped him endure the long waits. He lined up for every meal and ate at least part of what was served. His buddies marveled at the iron lining of his digestive system, but never fathomed how he could stifle his taste buds so completely.

The cramped quarters, combined with less than plentiful air circulation, made personal hygiene a real issue. A cold shower in salt water was the only way to get a sweaty body less odorous, and fresh water for drinking was limited to a few hours each day. After just a few days, air in the quarters below deck became very foul. True found this to be further reason for staying topside as much as possible.

Wearing life jackets was required at all times, and lifeboat drills were frequent. Regular physical exercise was very limited, and while some organized calisthenics were attempted, this was soon discontinued as logistically impractical. Assembly for company roster and occasional rifle inspections were conducted, more to pass the time than for any other purpose.

For sheer entertainment, crap games and poker sessions

were constantly in session somewhere on the ship. Anyone craving action could always find an outlet. True noticed one sharp gambler running a house blackjack deal, but cutting the odds in his favor by not allowing either "double downs" or "splits." Bill had learned the probabilities and odds on the game of "Twenty-one" from his drinking (and gambling) Uncle Elvin, and could see that this sharpie figured to clean up big on the voyage. True took his business elsewhere.

The *Samaria* was part of a large convoy, with other nearby ships visible at most times. Occasionally they sighted one of the Navy's destroyers passing on the horizon, which added interest to the trip. And it seemed they were continuously zigging and zagging. Once there was even a U-boat scare. The men never learned whether or not a German submarine had actually gotten close, but the alarm was enough to confirm that they were indeed headed for a real war.

Finally, on September 15, 1943, the *Samaria* docked in Liverpool, England. The 506th had landed in Europe, and the men were more than happy to debark and conclude their less than luxurious trip across the Atlantic. Further hard months of training in the drizzly, foggy fields of England would precede their first actual combat. But they had come a long way... and they were ready.

CHAPTER IV

Thatch Roofs and Warm Beer
England: the run-up to D-Day

"Overpaid, overfed, oversexed, and over here."
Anonymous British complaint regarding U.S. soldiers

"Underpaid, underfed, undersexed, and under Eisenhower."
American response

No cheering throngs or brass bands lined the docks at Liverpool to welcome the 506th, but friendly stevedores waved genially to the arriving American soldiers. A train ride took them south to Wiltshire County where they boarded trucks for their final destination. The severity of blackout restrictions brought it home to the men that England was a country at war, and that they were getting closer to a personal involvement in that war.

F Company was billeted in the village of Aldbourne, 80 miles west of London and some ten miles from the next larger town of Swindon. It was late at night when the trucks let the men off. This left them more than a mile to walk, carrying their heavy duffel bags. Finally arriving at their double-bunked, 16-man Quonset huts they were more than ready to hit the sack.

Such was not to be, however, as they were led to a haystack in a field well outside the village. There they were told to fill their mattress covers. Summers on his uncle's farm in Oklahoma had taught Bill True that hay could compress into a rather solid mass, so he was careful to stuff his cover as full as possible. Some of his city buddies learned this lesson the hard way, to their own discomfort. Next day they all trekked back to the haystack for a "refill" of their bedding.

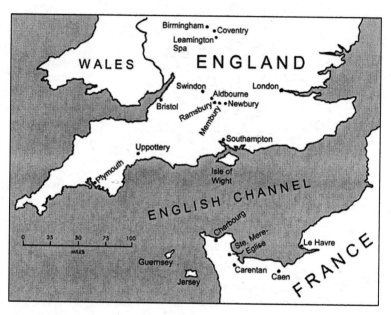

Training in England

Bill's first letter home on September 17th described the new setting: "The barracks are certainly different from any we've ever had. They're made of corrugated iron just arched over a floor. And what a stove. About as big around as a plate and two feet high. The camp is almost in the middle of a very picturesque village."

The battalion mess hall was some distance from F Company's area, and the route went past several civilian homes. On the way to breakfast the first morning True had been impressed with Aldbourne's cobblestone paths and quaint cottages covered with thatch roofs. Remembering childhood books with fairy-tale pictures, he thought nostalgically that these dwellings could very well be "once upon a time" houses. Little Red Riding Hood might come out at any moment with a basket of goodies on her arm for Grandma.

There were a total of eight F Company huts spread out on two sides of a large open area where company formations were held. This also served as an athletic field, and was used for company-sized close order drills. One side of the field housed the latrine. It had no running water and consisted of the usual outhouse openings cut into wooden benches. There were large thirty gallon buckets under the seats, and the weekly visit of the collection truck was noted by the locals with, "'Ere comes the 'oney bucket lorry."

Like the mess hall, the building which housed showers and sinks for shaving was a battalion facility, and was also situated deeper into the village. The daily trip for ablutions thus provided further glimpses of town, including the green and the five public houses. The American soldiers quickly acquired a taste for warm beer dispensed by British pubs. An ancient medieval church and burial ground, dating from the 12th century, looked down on the center of the village. It reminded the men that they were in a country far older than their own. In point of fact, Aldbourne was a well-established community 300 years before William the Conqueror was born.

Army higher-ups were sensitive to the possibility of friction between American soldiers and the conservative British villagers with whom they were in such close proximity. This prompted extensive orientation sessions for the men. In their first few weeks the troopers attended classes where English customs and manners were explained in detail. This educational effort was amply rewarded. No significant alterations occurred in the village the entire time the 506th spent there. The same could not be said of the large nearby city of Swindon, nor certainly of London. But the Currahee men clearly made a distinction between their affectionate "village home" and the metropolitan areas.

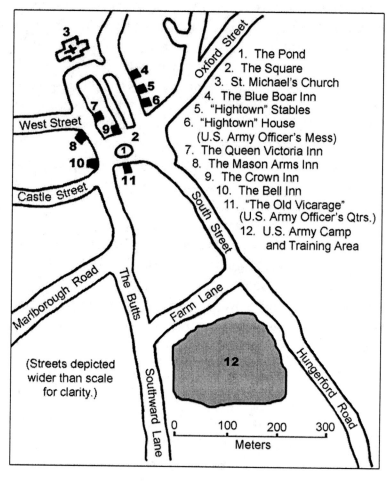

Aldbourne, Wiltshire, September 1944. Source material courtesy of Cecil Newton and the Aldbourne Civic Society.

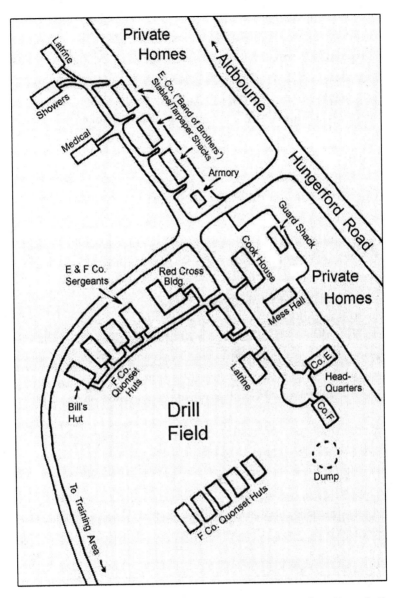

U.S. Army Camp, 101st A/B, 506th PIR, Companies E and F, Aldbourne, Wiltshire. Source material courtesy of Cecil Newton and Burton Christenson.

Food rationing was a real fact of life in England. It was distinctly different from the comparatively mild limitations Bill's family wrote of back in the U.S. Most of the everyday food items in Britain were powdered or dehydrated including milk, eggs, and fruit. And Spam seemed to be the meat staple for both military and civilian populations alike. True was lucky to find Spam very much to his taste, but he never grew to tolerate the powdered eggs and milk very well.

The powdered milk reminded him of a childhood experience in Omaha. In the mid-thirties, when his dad was hospitalized for tuberculosis, the family had gone on public relief. During one visit to the welfare office, his mother took Bill and his younger sister Betty Jean along. Both children were embarrassed when their mother started pounding on the counter and demanding more powdered milk. "I'm not leaving here until I have enough for my kids," she'd shouted as Bill and his sister cringed. Both of them hated the chalky-tasting stuff anyway, and secretly hoped no more would be provided. He couldn't recall the outcome of that argument, but the memory of Bill's embarrassment was very clear to him.

Full scale training activities began in earnest after the first two weeks in England. Overnight field maneuvers involved simulated attacks across plowed fields and over the Wiltshire hills. These were followed by long marches back to camp. Nearly continuous classes in infantry tactics, map reading, first aid, communications, and chemical warfare were interspersed with close order drill and combat exercises. Long forced hikes of up to 25 miles with full combat packs were reminiscent of the arduous night marches at Toccoa.

On the positive side, weekend passes into Swindon were freely offered, partly to prevent exhaustion of the beer supply at the local Aldbourne pubs. There was a large Red Cross facility in Swindon where frequent dances were held, and the 506 men learned of it early on. Bill could do a bit of jitterbugging, but he found the English girls to be highly skilled and enthusiastic on the dance floor. He met one particularly attractive young woman and danced with her several times on his first pass into town. She was ecstatic over American swing. When he asked if he could make a date with her for a future dance she said "Sorry, I'm only dancing with you tonight because my regular Yank couldn't make it. He can *really* jitterbug." True was quite disappointed to bomb out on this first encounter with an English female.

SOLDIER'S PARADISE
Bill's True Tale

We've been in England more than a month now and they're really laying the hard maneuvers on us. It seems like we've spent endless hours tramping up and down these Wiltshire hills attacking imaginary German lines and fortifications of all kinds from dawn to dusk, and occasionally through the night. My 20th birthday last week was celebrated chasing simulated SS Troops over hill and dale. Right now I'm enjoying the almost unheard-of luxury of getting both Saturday and Sunday off. But it will be short lived. We're merely resting up for the next attack sequence, which will include a jump and three hard days in the field.

Some guys from the Second Platoon have challenged us to a touch football game in the quad and I'm playing right end for our First Platoon team. We've got the ball and I'm going out for a long pass from Joe Flick who throws a good spiral. I'm racing full steam down the field, the ball is in the air, I leap high to reach the somewhat overthrown ball, miss it, and come down hard on my right arm.

The pain is unreal and so intense that I feel like I'm going to pass out. Johnny Jackson says: "You look like hell, Ty Ty—you'd better check in with the medics." He helps me over to the battalion doctor's quarters where the doc looks at me and tries out my arm. I yell like I've been bayoneted! "Okay, it's most likely broken so we'll have to send you to the hospital in Swindon for X-rays," he tells me. "If you've got a fracture they'll cast it and you'll probably be there a few days."

I notice right off that the nurse assistant to the doc in Swindon is a real looker. The X-ray has shown that I have a definite fracture, and they're about to put me to sleep to set the arm and apply a cast. The nurse slips a needle into my arm and says count slowly to ten. "One... two... three... four... five... sixxx... seeeveeen... zzzz.

I'm awake and I'm feeling just great—like maybe I've had about three quick boilermakers and I'm floating on air. "Lieutenant, you are absolutely gorgeous," I affectionately announce to the nurse, and then remember that she's an officer. But I'm on cloud nine with nothing to lose, so I go ahead and tell her I'm in love with her. "The pentathol has really got you going," she laughs, as she directs a couple of male attendants to wheel me out to the ward.

After a couple of days at the hospital they tell me I'm being transferred to a convalescent hospital up in Warwickshire. Apparently the policy is that a line soldier in any infantry outfit can't return to his unit until he's able to take on full duties. In my case that means until the cast comes off and I have some therapy. It appears that I'll be stuck with this soft hospital life for at least a few weeks. With that really stringent training and the obnoxious field exercises going on back at Aldbourne I feel sort of like Br'er Rabbit being thrown into the briar patch by Br'er Fox and Br'er Bear.

The convalescent hospital is out in the country a ways, and about equally distant from Coventry, Leamington Spa, and the village of Kenilworth. Our duties are very light: a bit of barracks clean up, some minor kitchen duties, and passes into town every night. Wow! This is the life!!

There are no other military facilities close to any of our three nearby towns, and after a pass or two into each of them we find that the girls are more than a little lonesome for some male companionship. I've struck up a quick friendship with an infantryman from South Carolina named Terry Anders. We arrived the same day and he's here with a shoulder separation suffered in a practice beach landing. We have a lot of interests in common, including families with quite uncommon religious beliefs. His folks are big-time foot washers, while mine are fully into Christian Science. Neither of us is an enthusiastic adherent of such familial leanings, however.

The two of us catch the bus into town together one night and we meet a pair of sisters in Leamington Spa right off. Terry is ruggedly handsome and pretty smooth with the girls. He ends up with the better-looking sister although mine, named Beryl, isn't a bad looker herself. Beryl is a bit overweight, however, and I think of the somewhat unfortunate connotation of her name, one that I've never encountered before. We date them a couple of times, but quickly look around for friendlier types since neither of them goes in for serious male/female relations.

On an especially auspicious evening Terry and I run across a good-looking brunette and an even better-looking blond who live in Coventry, but are in Leamington Spa on this occasion to see a movie. Luckily, I tie in with the blond, Alice Johnson†, and the four of us take in the movie and a late supper. Alice is a tall girl, probably five seven or eight, with enticingly ample breasts that I was able to tentatively explore during the movie. When we leave the restaurant the two couples break up and Alice and I enjoy a truly romantic and ultimately erotic interlude in a nearby graveyard. A comfortable layer of leaves located between imposing stone markers makes for the most unique sexual setting I've yet experienced. Terry also scores with his brunette and we know we've now hit pay dirt.

Alice and I don't have an exclusive dating arrangement, however, and one night in Leamington Spa I meet Martha Brown† from Kenilworth. She is a distinct contrast from Alice, slight and dark, but equally attractive and alluring. We have some fish and chips and hit it off pretty well so she invites me to come and see her in her town sometime. The next night I'm in Kenilworth, and since I don't have to be back at the hospital for any duties in the morning I spend the whole night with Martha. When she wakes me next morning to bring my breakfast in bed I feel like I'm in a soldier's dream world. After this idyllic night and the surprising morning she loans me her bicycle so I can ride the few miles back and forth from the hospital any time I get free.

One night after visiting a couple of pubs in Kenilworth, and buying "winner's beers" for my various dart competitors, Martha and I take a walk past the Kenilworth Castle. It's a real medieval castle that I hope to visit some time. She's telling me about her brother who's in the army and has this terrific job as "batman" for an officer. I know that a batman is really just a personal servant so I tell her that in the American army such an individual would be held in disdain and we'd refer to him as a "dog robber." Martha is quite nonplussed over such scorn for a respectable assignment in the British Army, so I acknowledge her attitude and simply chalk it up to the English acceptance of their class system.

I have a kitchen assignment first thing in the morning so I'm riding Martha's bike back to the hospital. The night is as black as the bottom of a West Virginia coal mine and I'm afraid I'll hit a rut or a pothole or something along the way. The luck of this charmed life I'm leading holds, though, and I get back expeditiously and even have some sack time before my kitchen duties.

I've been up here in this Garden of Eden well over a month now, and every week the doc examines each of us to see if we're ready to go back to our outfits. My cast came off last week, and I know I'll have some mixed emotions about my next review by the doctor. I've exchanged a few letters with Joe, Dude and Johnny back in Aldbourne and they're still enduring some really tough training exercises. There's a bit of guilt between what they're doing and this "Life of Reilly" I'm leading. But should I really insist on getting back there as soon as possible? I've mulled it over at length and decided I'll let the doctor make the decision for me, rather than pushing it one way or the other. Let him use his professional judgment about what's best. That's fair enough, isn't it?

"How does that arm feel, soldier?" the doctor is asking me. "Well, it feels pretty good, sir," I respond, "but do you think the cast has been off long enough for me to return to full duty?"

Checking my medical record the doctor says: "I see it's only been off about a week, so a couple more weeks with some additional physical therapy will be in order. Who's next?" the doc asks as he dismisses me. "I can live with that,"

I think to myself. It's a professional resolution to my personal doubts and misgivings.

Sunday afternoon finds Martha and me standing at the bus stop in Kenilworth to go into Leamington Spa to see a movie she's heard about. The bus comes from Coventry, and as it picks us up and we walk to the rear for seats, who do we pass but Alice Johnson. She looks at me with a slight smile but doesn't say anything and neither do I. This is one uncomfortable bus ride I'm thinking, but nothing untoward happens as Martha and Alice are obviously unacquainted.

Hoping my luck is still holding, I call Alice a couple of days later and she agrees to meet me for a date that night. Neither of us make any mention of Sunday's encounter, and Alice shows me around some of the badly bombed areas of Coventry that I've not seen before. We spend the evening pub hopping and singing some of the bawdy English songs of the war days.

Alice and I are getting pretty sentimental as the evening wears on, and between kisses she says: "Let's exchange remembrance notes. Let's take one of your Yankee bills, tear it in two, and write each other a note." I've still got a few American one dollar bills, so we tear one of them and she writes on her half to give me: "Forget me not, Alice Johnson." Reading her note, I respond by writing on my half to give her: "I'll remember you, Bill True."

Alice is a truly passionate and loving girl, and she takes me to a nearby park. It's a cold night in late December, so I remove my heavy army overcoat and spread it on a grassy area for her. We express our loving affections for each other both verbally and physically as I wonder if anyone else in the world could be as contented and happy as I am at this enchanted moment.

ॐ ॐ ॐ

"Hey, True, the captain wants to see you in his office." It's one of the non-coms working as Charge of Quarters out of the C.O.'s office. Officers in charge of the hospital come and go since they're also patients like the rest of us. The last one was a lieutenant. I haven't met this one yet.

Saluting smartly I bark: "P.F.C. William True reporting, sir." I figure it can't hurt to be very militarily correct with this captain, at least until I find out what's on his mind,

"Sheila Bradley† of Leamington Spa just called and said a William True of this hospital has put her in a family way. She demands that you make an honorable woman of her immediately or she's seeing a barrister." The captain wears a very stern demeanor.

"Sheila Bradley?" I blurt in amazement. "I just met her two nights ago. We did it all right, but it was standing up in a doorway, and I used a rubber. If she's pregnant I guarantee it's by some other guy and not by me." I'm getting pretty vociferous by now, and am about to raise the volume of my protestations even further when I notice the captain is starting to smile.

"Don't worry, True. I know the family, and I've dated and laid her sister several times. The two of them are just a tad above street walkers. Forget it. I'll call her and tell her to kiss off."

Whew! That was some kind of a scare. I probably deserve it for cheating on Martha and Alice like that. But I wasn't looking for anything but a couple of pints of 'alf and 'alf when that Bradley broad vamped me. "Dadgummit," as my dad might say, "I gotta be more careful in the future."

Two days later, the Sheila Bradley affair is suddenly and finally moot.

"Well, True, I think you're ready to return to duty. What do you think?" It's the doc talking at what I expect will be my last weekly review.

"Yes sir, I think I'm ready," I reply. My conscience is going to be pretty clear, I'm thinking, when I head off down Aldbourne way to reunite with my buddies. I've had the better part of two months of a soldier's paradise; but then, maybe I deserved it. Who's to say?

Aldbourne, Wiltshire - October 3, 1979. Bill True standing in the village square at the Crown Inn. The spire of St. Michael's Church (12ᵗʰ Century) is visible in the distance at the north end of town.

Bill's same bunk awaited him in Aldbourne on his return from the extended convalescence in Warwickshire. A new man had replaced Cliff Valleries, who had been seriously injured in a training jump, but otherwise things were just as he'd left them two months before. Cliff had landed in a tree on a practice drop during a three-day maneuver. When the chute collapsed, he fell through the branches breaking both legs and his back. The battalion doctor told the men that Valleries had bought a sure ticket out of the war.

Now Christmas packages started to arrive from home. They contained mostly cookies, candy and other goodies to eat. True got a gift each from his folks, his Aunt Mary, and the family of his high school girl friend Virginia Lightfoot. His parents had sent an ocarina, socks, and caramel popcorn, plus a silver bracelet with parachute wings and his name engraved. In return, Bill wired $100 home for purchase of Christmas gifts on his behalf, and some English and ETO (European Theater of Operations) greeting cards.

The intense training schedule had not eased during True's absence, and his soft time in convalescence now left him physically unprepared for the tough regimen ahead. Long marches and charges through mud and thickets seemed significantly more strenuous, and the all-night problems seemed even colder than the freezing march to Atlanta he had endured more than a year before. The English weather had turned frigid with the onset of winter, so this wasn't just his imagination.

The tiny pot bellied stove in each Quonset hut burned wood. It provided only minimal heat, at best. One day, "Rebel" Adams and Russ Schwenk in the 3rd Platoon spotted some coal piled at the side of the road on their way to Swindon. True, Jackson, Stone and Flick decided to take a hike there and gather the wherewithal for some real warmth in their hut. Emptying their barracks bags to use as sacks, they headed out for the coal. Along the way they passed other F Company men coming back with their own sacks full.

Obviously, others had gotten the jump on them, but there was still a bit of coal left, and they quickly finished it off.

For a couple of days this minor crime paid off with a stove that put out some real heat. The coal, however, had been intended for battalion officers' quarters. When it turned up missing, a search for the culprits was soon under way. Ashes left by the coal were very different from the normal wood fuel, so the investigation soon identified the guilty Quonset huts. Telltale evidence was found in six of the eight F Company huts, and all the residents received the same punishment: hauling coal by *handfuls* to the homes where it was originally intended. This took most of a weekend and brought loud complaints from the innocents. But Flick admonished the protesters: "Quit your bitching! You guys enjoyed the heat as much as any of us."

The "purloined coal" incident was only one of many attempts to ease the burden of barracks life. One Sunday morning as they were heading for chow, Jackson and True began conspiring on a way to sleep late once in a while. Sunday breakfasts were an informal affair with service from seven to ten A.M. They decided to alternate with one going to chow and bringing breakfast back for the other. The following Sunday they tried the scheme and it worked well. From that time until the Normandy invasion, if neither was on pass into town, one or the other got to sleep until ten o'clock and be served breakfast in bed. What luxury!

❧   ❧   ❧

Another three-day field problem was scheduled, with a night jump set to start it off. The truck ride to the airfield was boisterously lighthearted, since a three day pass for everyone was a promised reward. The cheerful atmosphere continued as the men strapped into their chutes and boarded the planes. Bill's stick had just taken their seats when the pilot came out of the cockpit to announce a new feature of the C-47s. "We now have an alarm system in the event of any mechanical problem such as engine failure. If you hear this buzzer," he said, waving to a crewman up front, "get the hell out as fast as you can because it means I've got a problem." An earsplitting buzzer went off and everyone jumped. "I certainly don't expect to have to use it tonight, but that's the signal if something should happen."

"We've never had any kind of a problem," Dude Stone said as the pilot went back up front. "Getting shook up by that damn alarm would probably be the worst that could happen anyway."

It was still daylight when the planes took off and started maneuvering into formation. Since the jump itself wasn't scheduled for at least another hour, most of the men took off their chutes so they could wander around the plane in comfort, look out the door, and just enjoy the ride. Dude was the first to doff his chute, tossing it into the aisle in back. Others soon followed suit. True was one of the few who kept his chute securely fastened. Ever since his harrowing experience on the flight back from home furlough the previous summer, the very thought of sitting in an airplane without a chute was unnerving.

It was still not quite dark when True noticed a slight change in vibrations of the bucket seat beneath him. Shortly after that, suddenly the "trouble alarm" went off, startling everyone. A mad scramble for parachutes ensued. Bill was mighty happy he had not removed his chute, as the jumpmaster frantically shouted for everyone to "Hook up NOW!!!" While others strapped into their harnesses, Bill fumbled to open his static line clasp and get it snapped on the cable. All of the routine commands that normally precede a jump were bypassed as the jumpmaster screamed "Let's go!" and went out the door.

As True approached the door he saw Dude Stone just starting to put his arms into his main shoulder straps. His parachute had been on the bottom of the pile and he'd just waited while the others grabbed theirs and strapped them on. As Bill exited the door he could see they were not as high as usual. Worse yet, they were directly over a thickly wooded area. After jumping out, he tried to steer his chute toward a clearing but came down directly into a large leafy tree. Closing his legs tightly he got lucky, slipping through the branches with his canopy catching a limb and gently lowering him to the ground. He hung there with his feet slightly off the ground in the softest landing he'd yet experienced.

They learned later from the pilot that one of the two engines had failed. The plane had quickly lost altitude from twelve hundred feet to less than five hundred when the last trooper exited.

Dude Stone was that last man. He had just time enough to put his arms through the shoulder harness of his main chute, snap the reserve to that, and jump, pulling the manual ripcord of the reserve. When he related this story, everyone was amazed that the opening shock hadn't jerked him right out of his rig. The primary holding straps and the snaps of the main harness were all open. Only by clasping his hands together and holding frantically tight was he able to keep from falling out.

As a result of this mishap, True's stick had landed far from the planned drop zone and missed most of the three-day problem. They didn't miss out on the three day passes promised to everyone, however, and men from F Company took full advantage, heading out for various parts of the country. Most went to London, including True's squad and almost the entire 1st Platoon.

On their first night in London Tom Alley, Jesse Orosco and E. B. Wallace had a run in with some British paratroopers. Altercations with other branches of the American army, especially tankers, were not unusual for men of the 506th. These dated from earliest times in Columbus, Georgia. But brawling with soldiers of other nations was something new.

Tom, Jesse and E. B. had just exited a pub and were walking down a darkened sidewalk when they heard heavy footsteps approaching from the opposite direction. It was a group of British soldiers. The narrow sidewalk was barely wide enough to accommodate two abreast, so it was evident that someone would have to step into the street for the groups to pass. All paratroopers, whatever their nationality, were unaccustomed to giving way to any non-jumpers. The inevitable occurred.

In truth, neither Tom nor E. B. were inclined to go out of their way for a fight. Not so with Jesse. When he'd had a few belts his temper was short fused, and F Company men had long since learned to respect his exceptional strength and quick fists. Jesse threw one of the Britishers into the middle of the street, and knocked another one down with a right roundhouse to the jaw. The third was happy to avoid Jesse by helping his comrades to their feet. Alley and Wallace had not had to throw a punch, and managed to convince Orosco that getting to another pub was more important than continuing the scrap.

Bill True was duly impressed with the international flavor

of London. In Leicester and Trafalgar Squares, Hyde Park, and, of course, Piccadilly Circus, he marveled at the display of colorful uniforms from around the globe. Australia, New Zealand, South Africa, France, Poland, Belgium, Holland and others were all represented by smartly uniformed military personnel.

True was now accustomed to the friendly attitude of people in Aldbourne and Swindon, but was a bit surprised that folks in cosmopolitan London were just as amiable. The bobbies, especially, seemed to go out of their way to befriend American soldiers. Bill got a kick out of the details offered whenever he asked directions. These were followed inevitably by the standard phrase "You cawn't miss it, Yank."

❧   ❧   ❧

All the men in the company returned from pass on time except for one man: Private Ivar B. Odegaard of the 1st Platoon. For more than a month, morning company muster would follow the same pattern. Sergeant Don Replogle would stand to attention and report with a snappy salute: "All present and accounted for, sir, except Odegaard."

Strangely, when "Odie" finally did make it back he received no punishment and simply returned to routine training duties. His buddies were shocked by this, and dogged him for an explanation. He was reluctant at first, but finally told them the story on condition that every man swear not to "rat him out."

While on leave in London he met a woman who had a fabulous apartment. Her husband was an officer in the British Army who had been killed in Africa. She obviously found something in Odegaard to like, as she immediately invited him to share the apartment with her. Odie figured she would have kept him throughout the whole war, but he started feeling guilty after a month or so. Knowing he would be in serious trouble without an awfully good explanation for his absence, he struck on an idea: amnesia. Before the war Ivar had spent two college years majoring in psychology, and figured he might just get away with this lie.

Saying his farewells to the lovely woman whom he'd shacked up with for almost six weeks, Odie hitched a ride out into the country—the moors he called it. There he rolled in the dirt, scratched his face, and ripped a few tears in his uniform. Hitching another ride into the nearest town he found an MP station where he claimed he had just regained consciousness out on the moors. The Army doctors were naturally skeptical. But after repeated interviews by a battery of psychiatrists, the story remained intact: he just couldn't remember anything from the time he arrived in London until he woke up out on the moors. How such a patently cock-and-bull story ever convinced *anyone* was a source of continuing amazement for his buddies.

æ   æ   æ

Training continued, and with it came the usual ups and downs of Army life. For years, Bill had been plagued off and on by sinus headaches. The increasingly cold, damp English weather was gradually bringing this chronic problem to an acute stage. On some days his throbbing pain could only be endured by sitting in his Quonset hut huddled near the stove, with his forehead close to the heat. Finally, the battalion doctor sent him to an Army specialist at a clinic near Swindon.

The specialist quickly diagnosed the problem, saying, "We'll just have to flush your sinuses out." With that, he and his nurse assistant inserted tubes into Bill's nostrils and started pumping liquids through. Bill was shocked at the incredible gunk and goo that came gushing out of his nose and mouth. But amazingly, his pounding headache *immediately* disappeared! The pain never returned, and thereafter he found himself, somewhat incongruously, grateful to the dank English weather for forcing him to correct the problem.

Joe Flick had always been something of an artist. One day he got some paint and brushes from company supplies, and really showed off his talent. There was a famous pinup photo of Betty Grable at the time, and one of the troopers had pasted it up in his locker. Shot from behind, it showed her wearing a bathing suit, looking backward over her shoulder. Joe used that as a model to paint his version: a life size portrait on the Quonset front door, with one arm raised as if she were knocking to get in. Betty's derriere wasn't one whit sexier than that of Joe's woman. Better yet, his was nude. From the distance of the drill field, it sure looked like a naked woman was trying to get into the hut. Joe got a lot of admiring compliments on his artistry.

About this time someone at headquarters got the idea of short-term swapping some of the men between a British paratroop outfit and the 506th, to give each side the benefit of another perspective. The concept was something like that of "foreign exchange students" in college. Several of the Englishmen were assigned to F Company, and two of them ended up in Bill True's Quonset hut. They were very impressed with the nude at the door, but found most of the American training rather similar to their own. The weapons were different, of course, but an infantryman's function was pretty standardized. England and the United States could have permanently traded many of their soldiers with little effective loss.

The Americans were impressed with one aspect of British paratroops: they made all of their jumps with only a main chute and no reserve. In all of F Company only Dude Stone had ever actually used his backup parachute, but it was a psychological prop that meant a lot to nearly everyone.

The Tommies tagged along with Bill and his buddies on a two-day field problem. They had no difficulty adapting to the way the 506 men maneuvered and deployed, carrying out their mock attacks. The toughest part for them was going without the traditional English tea break, which seemed to be a higher priority than any military necessity. They made this complaint loud and clear.

While marching back to camp after this problem, the men passed a farm where a group of Italian POWs had been put to work. Friendly greetings with such prisoners was common among the Americans. After all, the Yanks had no beef with these guys any more, and certainly nothing to fear from them. This chance meeting followed the pattern, and Bill True wrote home about it:

"There are several Mexicans in the outfit and they can talk to the Italian prisoners of war around here. There are a lot of them working on the farms and every time we go by someone always hollers 'Paisan' and the Italians really start rattling off. I was talking to one of them (that is we were talking at each other) and somehow he asked me where I was from and I told him California. He really went into ecstasies about 'Sana Franaceesco' and said 'Caleefornia and Etalee ara veery seemilar.'"

The Brits seemed a bit surprised, even shocked, at the friendliness of this exchange between the Americans and the

Italians. This doubtless reflected a fundamental disparity in the attitudes of the two allies. "Cultural differences" like this, and the sorely missed "tea time," were clearly more significant than any practical distinctions between the paratroopers.

∾   ∾   ∾

One day Tom Alley told Bill about a girl he'd met up in Birmingham. She had an older sister who'd like to date a paratrooper.

"Yeah? How *much* older?" True asked, his suspicions immediately aroused.

"Well, my girl is about 19 or 20, and her sister Doris† is probably 10 years older. But she'd be a young 30 though, that's for sure. She's a pretty good looker and I know you can handle an older woman, Ty Ty."

Bill smelled the faint odor of "sales job" coming from Tom, but what the heck. He'd heard that mature women could really turn a guy on. Alley said he'd call and set it up for the following Saturday, and the two agreed to put in for the necessary overnight passes.

The train ride to Birmingham took almost as long as the one to London. Alley and True rode in a car with disconnected compartments that opened directly out onto the station platforms. This seemed so strange compared to American trains, with their center aisles connecting all of the passenger cars together. Along the way they met various traveling companions, as people got on and off at station stops. The trip itself became a journey of interest, independent of their final destination. Finally, they arrived at Birmingham early on Saturday evening.

Ann Middleton† was Tom's girl—a pretty brunette nearly as tall as he. She looked like she might be even younger than the 19 or 20 reported earlier. Bill's date, Doris, was all of 30 as expected, but she was a very attractive blond, indeed. Even better, she was immediately friendly as were many women Bill had met in England.

The two couples took in a British movie, which Bill found as uninteresting as most English films he'd seen. That was probably just as well. It allowed him to devote full attention to Doris's physical attributes, which she was very willing to share with him. Soon his hands were extremely busy indeed. She was even more amorous than Alice Johnson of Coventry, whom he had dated when he was stationed in the convalescent hospital months before. And it was good that their seats were in the upper balcony, where none of the other patrons seemed to pay any attention to their romancing.

After the movies the foursome found a pub where they had several pints to wash down their fish and chips. Ann and Doris both had engaging personalities and enjoyed hearing about the boys' adventures in the paratroops, and life in the United States.

It was a short taxi ride to the girls' apartment where Tom and Ann immediately retired to the one bedroom. Meanwhile Bill and Doris relaxed on the living room sofa. Doris lived up to all the stories Bill had heard about the passions of older women. He was more than happy that Tom had talked him into the venture. After their lovemaking, Doris made a pallet for Bill to sleep on that was quite comfortable. He soon fell into a satisfied post-coital sleep.

On the train trip back to Swindon on Sunday, Tom remarked emphatically that Ann had the softest lips of any woman he'd ever kissed. "I don't know about soft lips," Bill replied, "but her big sister sure provided all the romance I could ask for. We'll have to get up here to Birmingham again soon." And so they did, more than once.

ಶಿ   ಶಿ   ಶಿ

As winter finally began to loosen its grip on the English countryside, the 506th was selected to make a demonstration jump for numerous high-ranking military officials and dignitaries. The 1st Battalion would pass in review and stand inspection, while the 2nd and 3rd Battalions would make the jump. Bill True described it in a letter home on March 25, 1944:

"I've never seen so many chutes in the air at once before. I didn't see any of the lead planes jump and when I went out it was just a sea of parachutes below. It really surprised me at first. We had a pretty famous audience to watch the jump. General Eisenhower, Churchill, and a lot of other big shots, both civilian and military, were there. Churchill gave his speech before we jumped so we didn't get to hear that but he and the others drove through our assembly area to inspect the positions and we all got to see them. They said Churchill got so excited during the jump he forgot to light his cigar."

For a week before this demonstration jump the men had practiced assembling and taking up defensive positions following their mock parachute invasion. All went very smoothly on the day of the celebrity jump, and Bill True's mortar squad got to see Eisenhower and Churchill up close. Bill noted that Churchill had regained his composure and was busily smoking his cigar when he and Ike passed by their positions, mere yards away.

ಶಿ   ಶಿ   ಶಿ

Stringent weekly inspections were made of the Quonset huts by company officers, and occasionally by someone from Battalion Headquarters. Preparation for these required meticulous cleaning of the quarters top-to-bottom, and by precision arrangement of equipment and uniforms in a military manner. Failure to pass inspection could result in denial of weekend passes for all sixteen men. When that happened, whatever trooper had been careless of the rules was in for a serious drubbing by his buddies.

One day word came down that an officer from Regimental Headquarters would conduct the Saturday inspection. This was unusual and made it even more important than passing muster with the battalion mucky-mucks. Now the pressure was really on. As the major and an aide entered Bill True's hut, Joe Flick shouted the mandatory "Ten-hut!" and everyone snapped to attention. All, that is, except Johnny Jackson. He was so nervous that he fell backwards into his own footlocker, widely scattering the carefully arranged contents all over the barracks floor. It was a terrible mess. Johnny scrambled to rearrange things and try to salvage at least *some* dignity and military decorum from the debacle. The major only gave a small smile and announced the usual "At ease!" as he began the inspection tour.

As it happened, a nearby neighborhood lady had been doing their laundry for some of the men from the time of their first arrival in Aldbourne. She kept a beautiful and lovingly tended flower garden. The night before this inspection her daughter had delivered the laundry, and brought along some of the spring blooms from the garden as well. True scrounged a glass pitcher from the mess hall to serve as a vase, and put the flowers on the small table in the center of the hut. Spotting the blossoms, the major's smile became even broader. "I'm pleased to see that you men have brought an unusual element of refinement to your quarters," he said. Following a very cursory inspection he departed, and all was well with the world.

Later that day, in a letter to his folks, Bill mentioned the incident as follows:

"Our little laundry girl brought us some pussy willows and flowers last night when she brought the laundry. They were on the table this morning and I think helped us pass inspection."

❧   ❧   ❧

OLGA FROM THE VOLGA
Bill's True Tale

Replogle and I have forty-eight hour passes starting in the morning, and we've decided to go to London. "Rep" is now our platoon sergeant, and while we both date our time back to basic at Toccoa, and went on pass together occasionally in those earlier days, he's been mostly aloof since achieving staff sergeant rank. I'm thus a bit surprised that we're linked for this outing. Still mighty glad to be going, though.

We're in the orderly room signing out for our passes and picking up our rubbers and pro kits. "You guys be careful now," First Sergeant Morris says as he hands our VD protection materials to us. "Have a good time, but be damned careful, hear?"

"You can count on that, Sarge," Rep replies. "I'll see that True does likewise," he adds.

As we head for the trucks to take us into Swindon where we'll catch the train to London, Rep says "That's a pretty rumpled shirt you're wearing, Bill. Let's stop by my hut so you can change to a decent one before we go."

Replogle is a few years older than I am and has always been a sharp dresser so his opinion on my appearance is convincing. "I washed this stuff yesterday," I say, "but didn't have time to have Davis iron it." Don Davis is our "jack of all trades" who irons, sews, barbers and does sundry household tasks—all for a price, of course.

I've changed into one of Rep's shirts and he's given me an extra to stow in my bag along with some socks, underwear and toilet articles, and we're away to London.

We've been pub hopping ever since we got to London and have now found ourselves in a rather upscale establishment that is interestingly located downstairs in a kind-of semi basement. Rep and I have been sitting on stools at the bar and have gotten rather friendly with the bartender who seems quite interested in talking to a couple of Yanks. Referring to people who are always griping about war-time conditions the bartender mentions the expression "the grass is always greener," and I refer to Americans who always want "egg in their beer."

We then get into a discussion of what an egg would taste like in beer, and Rep and I both say we wish we could try it so we'd then be able to tell people if the phrase made any sense. The bartender happens to have a fresh egg (rare though they are in wartime England), and agrees to mix it up in a pint of 'alf and 'alf for us.

Well, it tastes just terrible. "Rep" and I and the bartender all agree that we have wasted a perfectly good egg. A couple of other patrons take a sip as well, and the opinion is unanimous, "egg in your beer," ain't what it's cracked up to be.

I've been noticing a couple of very pretty, stylishly dressed young women sitting at a table half way across the room. Unless I'm mistaken, they've been getting a kick out of our doings at the bar, so I ask the bartender if he thinks we might offer to buy the ladies a drink. He immediately walks over to their table, converses a moment, comes back and says

"You Yanks are in luck. Not only can you order them a drink, you're invited to join them."

The girls are in their early twenties, I'm guessing, and from the level of their conversation they've had considerable education. Turns out they've both recently graduated from university, and may be going on to graduate study. They also do volunteer war work and are happy to meet and talk with a couple of Yank paratroopers.

Sara and Rose will be pleased to have dinner with us after drinks, and both of them suggest that the restaurant we're already in is first rate. I'm getting encouraged big-time about later all-night possibilities with the ladies, and I can see Rep is becoming enthused as well. Rep may be the best-looking man in F Company, and his maturity and smooth-talking ability, which are well beyond mine, have my hopes flying high.

The dinner is excellent, and I'm pleased no end that I seem to be holding up my end of the conversation very well. We've talked about the progress of the war, England's courage and endurance in holding out till America got into it, and when the war will end and what the future holds for all of us.

Rep and I have both been lighting up between courses, and as we finish dessert and again take out our cigarettes Sara says "You boys really do smoke too much."

"Yes, indeed you do," Rose echoes. "You're very sweet boys, but heavy smoking can only do you harm."

The girls' concern for our health is not unexpected as I recall the references during dinner to possible medical school for both of them. Although talk about smoking and health is not where the two Yanks want to focus, neither Rep nor I have gotten specific about our expectations after dinner. Trying to get the conversation pointed in a purposeful direction I mention that we probably smoke a lot more with drinks and food than in other settings, and we'd sure like to engage in some healthy exercise at a dance or similar activity after dinner.

There has yet been no apparent pairing up between the two girls and us during the evening; just the four of us as a genial group. But Rose speaks rather directly to me as she says "Oh, Bill, I hope we haven't misled you, but Sara and I both have beaus in the army. They're abroad in Italy now."

Sara quickly adds "We've so enjoyed the evening with you. You're the first Yanks we've spent any real time with, and it's easy to see why so many English girls are charmed by you. But we'll have to be leaving for home soon."

We've just put the girls in a taxi and exchanged condolences on our unsuccessful enterprise as we head for another pub. We've not far to go, and as we push open the black-out door it's apparent from the smoke and smell and noise and rousing music that this joint will contain no female college graduates who are aspiring doctors—and here come a couple of Yanks who'll be grateful for that.

Rep and I have downed several pints and joined in a number of rowdy songs when someone starts a chorus of "Roll Me Over In The Clover." Next to "God Save The King" this must be damn near the British National Anthem, I think as I join in.

Roll me over, in the clover,
Roll me over, lay me down, and do it again.

Oh this is number three, and 'is 'and is on me knee,
Roll me over, lay me down and do it again,
Roll me over, in the clover,
Roll me over, lay me down and do it again.

I am six sheets to the wind, and Rep is surely right with me, when we finally stagger out of the pub at some wee-in-the-morning hour. All I can think of is someplace to lie down and go to sleep and I remember that there are bunk set-ups in some of the underground subway stations. We finally find a stairway down to an underground station (did it say Charing Cross?) and we're in luck as it's one with the bunks. I flop on one and am gone.

"Not exactly the Waldorf-Astoria," I announce to Rep next morning as we wake to the bustle of busy people rushing through a subway station for a multitude of destinations. "But I slept pretty well, all things considered, and I see we were fortunate enough to hang on to our mini-duffels through all of last night's action. Where do you suppose we could get a shower and shave?"

"Sergeant Morris mentioned a Red Cross building where we actually could have bunked for the night. They're sure to have showers and stuff, too. It shouldn't be hard to find."

We find the Red Cross building, get cleaned up and change underwear, shirts and socks, feel real good again. Then there's a monstrous breakfast in Piccadilly Circus. We pub-hop the afternoon away and are now in some kind of cafeteria-deli sort of place with all kinds of English specialties. Bubble and squeak, bangers and squeeze, toad in the hole, and other "exotic" dishes are listed in large lettering above the counters. Rep and I are trying to figure out what the different stuff is and what we might like when I notice a couple of fairly young women come in. They're maybe mid to late twenties and not bad lookers. They glance over at us and give a little smile which we take as a clear invitation.

Turns out they're Russians (Russkees, is sort of how they said it), and they don't speak a lot more English than Rep and I speak Russian. Between hand signals and pointing and head motions and a bit of English we communicate reasonably well though. It's understood that we've invited Olga and Svetlana to dinner, and they've agreed to help us pick out what we'd like to eat.

I think what I'm eating is the bubble and squeak, which is just mashed potatoes and cabbage anyway, but it isn't bad. After dinner the girls go pub crawling with us for a few hours and we get to communicating better and better. It looks like Olga and I have paired up, and I'm remembering the old song that includes a line about Olga from the Volga.

As the hour grows late I hand signal and head nod and make sleeping noises and finally make it clear to the girls that Rep and I don't have a place to sleep. "Nyet problemski," Olga says, or some similarly reassuring words, and Svetlana uses some seductive body motions that clearly indicate we'll be sleeping with the girls themselves.

"That Joe Stalin may be a son-of-a-bitch," Rep says aside to me, "but I'm sure glad the Russians are on our side."

The girls' apartment is up three long flights of stairs, and it isn't much, to put it kindly. The entire place consists of a tiny kitchen and an even smaller bedroom with a standard-size double bed that virtually fills the room. The bathroom is down the hall some distance.

The Russians and Americans are really close allies tonight as the four of us pile into that one bed to engage in some intimate international relations.

Perhaps not unexpectedly, I'm not sleeping soundly, and it doesn't seem like anyone else is either. Between our full encounters, two or three at most, Olga and I are both tossing and turning quite a bit. On several occasions I notice that Rep's girl is pressing her bottom against my hand. Taking her actions in the friendly manner in which I presume they're intended, I respond with some affectionate pats and squeezes as any red-blooded American paratrooper would be wont to do. This is not only fun, but it's ego building as well. After all, Rep is a handsome and dashing fellow, and to have Svetlana as well as Olga cottoning up to me is pretty terrific.

Next morning after some toast and tea, Rep and I are on our way. We've been walking for a while, neither of us talking, when he suddenly turns and says "You know, Bill, that Olga of yours seemed to be patting and rubbing my butt half the night."

Knowing that Olga had been on the outside of the bed on our side, and suddenly realizing that Rep's girl had to have been on the outside also, it becomes very clear whose bottom I had enjoyed toying with throughout the night. "No kidding?" I choke out a response.

Now I'm thinking, "Damn, that Rep has a nice bottom. But he's sure as hell never going to learn it from me!"

We continue walking in silence for some time when I decide to see how much money I've got and find my wallet empty. "Hey, Rep," I say, "I may not have had much left, but they cleaned out my wallet."

He checks his pockets. His money's gone too, but he says "Oh well, I know I didn't have much left either so why don't we just forget it." Not wanting to walk clear back to that dingy apartment myself, I agree and we check it off as a learning experience.

It's back to the Red Cross Building to get a small loan for train fare back to camp. Some guys only think of the Red Cross as being good for some occasional coffee and doughnuts, but more than once they've really come through when a soldier is completely down and out. I've become a real fan and plan to make some substantial donations when this war is over and I'm in the bucks.

"Well, Olga," I'm thinking philosophically as Rep and I

board the train for Swindon, "I know it was well short of true love, and you even clipped me for a few shillings. Nevertheless, memories of my Olga from the Volga will always be pretty nice at that."

∾   ∾   ∾

Standing in the chow line for lunch one day, True heard a man from another company loudly exclaim, "That Goddamn Weiner!" Captain Weiner was the mess officer for the 2nd Battalion, and was frequently the butt of disparaging remarks from the men over the dull monotony of their fare. On this occasion, however, the Captain happened to be nearby. Hearing the remark, he spotted the man and yelled "What did you say, soldier?"

The guy was either a quick thinker or, as Bill later speculated, the whole episode may have been something of a setup. The offender earnestly responded: "I said, 'Those Goddamn *wieners* for dinner again!'" The captain slowly looked the soldier up and down with a very jaundiced eye. He wasn't buying this crapola, but it was certain that everybody in the line would gladly back their buddy up. Finally, the mess officer just stalked off without another word.

One day, unexpectedly, three men from the 1st Platoon were transferred to other companies in the battalion. They had all been with the platoon from earliest times at Toccoa and would be sorely missed by the others. For a time, the story behind this remained a mystery. Then True learned that the transfers were *by request*. All three had developed personal beefs with their own platoon sergeant, Don Replogle. Captain Mulvey became convinced of the need for change, and granted their appeals to leave Fox Company.

Les Tyndall went to Dog Company, Lou Cioni went to 2nd

Battalion Headquarters, and Dave Webster went to Easy Company, later of "Band of Brothers" fame. Cioni and Tyndall were friendly and easy going and would have little difficulty adjusting to their new units. Webster tended to be somewhat standoffish, however, and would doubtless take a bit of time to get tight with his new companions.

Bill remembered Dave from earliest days at Toccoa when they were both assigned to the same barracks. Webster had never been unfriendly or hostile to any of the men, but he was always a bit aloof and only slowly warmed to others. True's clearest picture of him would always be the way he meticulously donned pajamas every night when in barracks, while the rest of the men slept in their skivvy shorts or in the raw. Dave endured a good deal of ribbing for this before everyone finally accepted it as a minor idiosyncrasy. Eventually, nearly all came to admire Webster's determined habits and character—even those who had originally been most critical. Bill was quite sure that he himself would never have had the guts to wear those PJs in the face of humiliating criticism.

Lou Cioni survived the war and eventually returned to Chicago and resumed rooting for his beloved Blackhawks. Les Tyndall was killed on the D-Day jump. Dave Webster survived the rigors of combat but in 1961 lost his life in a fatal boating accident. The True and Webster families had grown close in the several years just preceding that tragic event. Dave's widow, Barbara, became a famous fine artist and remained in contact with Bill through all the years that followed.

Hard training continued with many three-day field problems, as spring blossomed in Wiltshire. The men came to appreciate the beauty of their surroundings as everything turned green, and the well-tended flower gardens of their Aldbourne neighbors burst forth in riotous colors. In a letter home on April 16, 1944, Bill True noted the weather change as follows. "Just got back from a three-day problem. It wasn't nearly so bad sleeping out as it was last winter."

Though it might have seemed impossible, the month of May brought even more intense training in the field. Now maneuvers included jumps whose purpose was to integrate airborne units with other groups: ground forces, the army air corps, and naval operations. These exercises were primarily held to give high level officers some experience commanding troops and coordinating their movements. Proper harmonizing of all forces involved in the invasion was critical. These large-scale simulations would provide vital training for the top ranks.

While the purpose may have been training for the higher-ups, it was just the usual drudgery for the rank-and-file soldiers. They trudged through great expanses of English countryside, clambered under and over countless barbed wire fences, and slogged across fields sometimes ankle deep in mud, to attack simulated enemy strongholds. But this was more than just old stuff. It was painful repetition piled on top of even *more* painful repetition. Many of those at the basic troop level longed for actual combat, if only as a welcome change. It couldn't be worse than this!

Marching back to camp after one of the most rigorous of these field problems, Bill True made an ill-conceived bet with Johnny Jackson. The challenge hurled was that Johnny couldn't spell the name of Joe Flick's hometown: Bala Cynwyd, PA. The unwisely-chosen stakes were an artifact of the incredible fatigue both men felt on the long march. Johnny won the bet and Bill wrote home about it:

"I pretty near knocked myself out yesterday because of a silly bet. I lost and had to carry Jackson about 2 miles back to camp. Is he *heavy*. I don't think I'll ever make another bet."

An occasional weekend respite from the rigorous field activities occurred during May. Dude Stone and Bill True got a Saturday pass and made the most of it.

ও   ও   ও

GETTING HIGH IN BRISTOL
Bill's True Tale

Dude and I have a one-day pass to Bristol. We've not been there before but some of the guys have, and they say it's a pretty good town. We have to be back by midnight so London is out, and nothing special is cooking in Swindon. Heading someplace different sounds good.

As a matter of fact, I've been thinking of getting down to Bristol for some time now. My favorite book as a kid (I must have read it ten times or more) was "Treasure Island," and Bristol was the port Jim Hawkins sailed from on the Hispaniola for his great adventure. My adventure too, because I could open the book at any point and I was Jim himself. Whether I was crouched in the apple barrel overhearing Long John Silver plot his piracy, or later in the stockade with Captain Smollett, Squire Trelawney, and others of the loyal crew planning our defense, those were heroic times for me.

The train ride from Swindon seems slow and longer than we expected, but we arrive in Bristol in the early afternoon. Dude and I have talked some about visiting the harbor area before we get into some serious beer drinking, so that's where we head first off.

"I know the docks won't look anything like my memory pictures from 'Treasure Island', Dude, but I'd really like to see them," I say as we walk from the train station.

"Nothing stays the same," Dude says, "but there figures to be plenty of pubs in that area anyway so we got nothing to lose."

I'm even more disappointed than I expected to be, since all of the modern ships and shipping technology bear absolutely no resemblance to the port Robert Louis Stevenson pictured for me. No tall ships, and not a schooner or sail-borne frigate in sight. But in my imagination I can see that peg-legged sailor with the patch over his eye and a parrot on his shoulder clumping along the dock.

Dude was right though, and we head for the nearest pub named "The Blue Boar." It's a fairly sizable place as pubs go, with a bar at least thirty feet long, six or eight tables and chairs, and a large fireplace. We take a table next to the fireplace and a buxom young girl brings our pints of 'alf and 'alf.

We've had several pints when we get on the subject of English money: a sore point all of us have complained about at one time or another. "This pence and shilling and pound and quid crap is really silly compared to our dollars and cents," Dude says. "How the hell do you suppose they came up with such a system?"

"Beats me, but it's weird for sure," I reply. "Some of these coins they call 'apenny, and tuppence, and thrupnebit and stuff like that is crazy, too," I continue as I empty my pockets and put all of my money on the table.

We've consumed a few more pints when I ask the counter girl to change one of my pound notes into thrupnebits. (It is kind of fun just saying "thrupnebit" at that.) "Oh, I say,

Yank, we may not have that many thrupnebits, but I can give you different coins for your quid," she responds.

"Okay," I say, "just give me some of all the different kinds you've got then."

"Me, too," Dude says and hands her a five pound note.

"Do you really want all coins for this fiver, Yank?" the girl asks.

"Sure," Dude tells her, "we're gonna have a game."

"See that silver mug in the fireplace, Ty Ty," he says to me. "Let's see how many coins we can toss into it from here."

We've been tossing coins at the mug for about fifteen minutes, even getting a few in, when I finally run out. Dude pushes some of his over to me, and we continue tossing for a while before we tire of the game.

"Shall we pick up the coins we didn't get in the mug?" I ask as we scoop the rest of the money on the table into our pockets. "Or should we just leave it as a tip for the girl?"

"Let's leave it for her," Dude says. "She can probably use the money, and I like the friendly way she called us Yank."

We've walked several blocks when we pass a movie theatre. Dude stops to look at the billing and I join him. It's an English movie and I notice it features sexy dancing girls wearing almost no costumes.

"Why don't we give this a try?" I ask, as Dude is already walking toward the ticket booth.

A ticket-taker hands us our stubs, points to some stairs, and we head up. We come to a landing, but notice there are stairs continuing on up, so we keep going. Another landing and more stairs and we're still climbing. We're getting a kick out of this now, but we finally run out of stairs and come up against a heavy-looking door with a big red "Emergency Exit" sign on it.

We push open the door and find ourselves out on the

roof. "Hey, this is neat," I'm thinking as we head for what looks to be the front of the theater. There's a low parapet at the front of the building, about a foot wide, and Dude is up on it walking with arms out as if he were on a tight wire. I join him, but adopt a more cautious attitude as I notice we're up at least four or five stories.

"Hey, let's have another game with this dumb Limey money," Dude says. "See if you can hit the top of one of those cabs driving by. No fair hitting any car that's parked, it's got to be moving."

"Okay," I answer, and start tossing at the passing cars. I'm pretty sure I hit at least one, but most of the coins are landing in the street, and I notice a couple of cyclists have stopped and are picking up the money.

We're having a darned good time but notice that traffic has stopped and people are pointing up at us. Suddenly, a guy comes charging out of the roof door (I figure it's the theater manager) and starts hollering at us. As he gets closer he calms a bit, lowers his voice, and tells us we'd better come down and leave the theater or we may get arrested.

Dude says he's hungry anyway and we ought to get out of there and have some fish and chips, so we accompany the manager down to the theatre entrance. As we're about to leave the premises Dude says to him: "We didn't get to see the show and we want our money back!"

The guy is only too happy to refund our admission fee and get rid of us. My one regret is that we didn't get to see those dancing girls in the skimpy garb. Of course it would have been great to see the old Hispaniola at anchor in the Bristol harbor, too.

On board the train heading back to camp, at least in my mind's eye, I do get to see that old schooner under full sail. She's off with the morning tide out of Bristol, and again I feel an eleven-year-old's excitement at the prospect of great adventure in the search for pirate treasure.

During the merry month of May in England, the weather again turned nasty. True's mortar squad was bored one rainy Sunday. They took the afternoon to employ their in-house barber, Don Davis, to give them Mohawk haircuts, which seemed to be the "in thing" with paratroopers at the time. In a letter home on May 17th Bill wrote about it:

"Our spring weather is very unspringy again. It's been raining again (or yet) and it's pretty cold, too. You should see our mortar squad with our new hair cuts. Johnny, Dude, Joe and I all got a skin job with a small tuft in front. Johnny looks pretty good with a spit curl in front but I got the feeling I look like 'The Angel.'" (The Angel was a grotesquely ugly professional wrestler in the U.S. at the time.)

Their unsightly haircuts didn't discourage Bill True and Johnny Jackson from getting into Swindon one last time before they left for the marshalling area to prepare for the big jump into France. One of their favorite Swindon haunts since arrival in England had been a pub in the Great Western Hotel. Located just across the street from the railroad station, it was convenient, and attracted a goodly crowd who loved to sing the bawdy English ballads.

It was here that Bill had met Gwen Stack. They attended several of the Red Cross dances over the months, went roller skating a time or two at the rink downtown, and took in some movies. After the last showing of any film, everyone in the house stood and sang the English national anthem. Bill quickly learned the words to "God Save the King." He always sang it as vigorously and patriotically as anyone in the theater.

No serious romance ever developed with Gwen, but they had good times together and shared a number of common interests. She was crazy about the Mills Brothers, who Bill liked as well, and he even tried to imitate their style with his guitar and personal rendition of their big hit at the time: "Paper Doll." He and Gwen also enjoyed singing another of their popular numbers: "I'll Be Around."

So it was quite natural for Jackson and True to head for the Great Western pub on what they expected would be their final visit. There they ran into another 1st Platoon man, Irwin Napierelski, who was with his girl friend and her mother. "Nappy's" serious involvement with the girl was known, but the mother now informed Bill and Johnny that her daughter and their friend were to be married at the earliest possible date. She went on to berate American soldiers in general who were always chasing "hussies," and hoped that Bill and Johnny would try to find "nice girls" like her daughter.

Jackson and True's last night in Swindon ended on a great note. For once, the fish-and-chips place next to their Aldbourne truck pick-up point had a plentiful supply. Too often the fish had been exhausted before time to head back to camp. But when it was available, the vinegar-sprinkled meal in the newspaper cone made the ride to Aldbourne a distinct pleasure.

"How did you like those cracks Nappy's future mother-in-law made about the way we chase these Swindon hussies?" Johnny asked on the ride home.

"Some of them may be hussies, all right," Bill replied, "but chasing them figures to be much more fun and a hell of a lot safer than getting permanently hooked by a so-called nice girl."

❧   ❧   ❧

On May 31, 1944, Fox Company packed up their gear and marched through Aldbourne to waiting trucks. These would take them to Uppottery Airfield: their marshalling area for the invasion of France. Some of the men would never see their lovely British village again—or, in truth, any other. The ultimate ordeal for which they had trained for nearly two years was about to begin.

CHAPTER V

Invasion
"The Cow Spoke French"

"It's a gift to face one's own mortality when young."
Anonymous

"This is it!" Gradually the same thought entered the minds of everyone in the marshalling area, till it was far past cliché and had become a sobering and universal truth.

By the afternoon of June 4, everyone knew that the invasion was days, or maybe even just hours, away. A sudden increase in security had sharply increased the feeling around camp. Troopers were strictly forbidden from discussing the mission with non-combat personnel such as MPs, cooks, orderlies and the like. At last a series of "final briefings" were convened. Bill True joined his comrades to get the real story of what was about to happen.

The location of the drop was well known to all the jumpers by then, including detailed assignments and objectives for each element of the division, down to the level of individual squads. The men had been poring over sand tables for days, memorizing plans. Now the actual hour of the mission was announced: at midnight tonight both the 82nd and 101st Airborne Divisions would begin dropping over France. The men were given final reminders and some good old-fashioned Knute Rockne pep talk.

The enemy they faced was ruthless, battle-hardened, and skilled. Germany would treat all paratroops on their territory

199

as spies, to be shot summarily on the spot—no mercy. Therefore our troops would treat them the same way.

Success of the invasion was desperately important to the allied cause; so vital that no chance could be left for it to fail. There would be no time to take and hold prisoners in the first 24 hours of the landing. The obvious implication of this was not lost on the men, and it was reinforced strongly by their leaders: kill every German you see, whenever and wherever you see them. No exceptions.

Early June 1944, marshalling area at Uppottery Airfield, shortly before D-Day. Part of the 1st Platoon, F Company, poses. Left to right, first row: Alvin W. Wilson, John E. Jackson, Joseph S. Flick, William True; second row: Erwin Napierelski, Robert F. Stone, Donald H. Replogle, Joseph R. Droogan, Ken Stewart; third row: Douglas G. Roth, Nicholas J. Cortese, Jesse G. Orosco, Ivar B. Odegaarde.

Officers were not to be saluted on D-Day, nor even "sirred." There would be no firearms used during the night for fear of shooting each other in the dark. Bayonets and trench knives were the only weapons allowed. The password, "Flash" and response, "Thunder," plus use of the toy crickets they had been given, were the primary means of identifying friendly forces. Injured American troops would be given whatever first aid was practical, but they must be left behind and not carried to aid stations, since that would slow down the able-bodied troops and might prevent them from achieving their objectives: clearing the causeways and exits behind Utah Beach.

Colonel Bob Sink, Regimental Commander of the 506th, finished the last briefing to his troops on an upbeat note: The Allied Expeditionary Force had assembled the most massive, lethal body of men and machinery the world had ever seen and was about to throw the lot of it at Hitler's Fortress Europe. Hundreds of bombers would devastate the beach areas before any troops landed. Naval gunfire would destroy the German shore batteries. Thousands of surface vessels would bring massive numbers of men ashore to stamp out Nazism forever. And leading the whole operation would be the most highly skilled, trained, dedicated, elite troops in all of history: the 506th Parachute Infantry Regiment, and the rest of the 101st Airborne Division. His final words: "I just feel sorry as hell for those poor German bastards when YOU get there!" It drew a laugh, and put a lump in more than one trooper's throat. And it did its job. The men were convinced more than ever that they were indeed the best in the world. They were ready.

When the briefings were concluded the soldiers made their way to hangars where the regimental parachute riggers had their equipment waiting for them. Everyone made a careful inspection of the harness and rigging, reserve and main chutes, and related paraphernalia. Then each man stuffed these into canvass storage bags and wrote his name on the outside. They would be moved by truck and be waiting at the planes when the order was given to pack and board for the flight to France.

ॐ   ॐ   ॐ

The same afternoon 1st Lt. Harold Wayne King, a C-47 pilot, also received his briefing about the invasion. He would be flying the plane he had come to call affectionately "Old Army #849," the ship he'd picked up—factory new—in Fort Wayne, Indiana, and would pilot throughout the war. In the cabin he would be carrying the men of stick #76.

Everyone knew generally what was coming, but the sheer magnitude of the operation was staggering. Its details came as a complete revelation to most of the air crewmen. After the mechanics of the mission had been neatly laid out, including take-off sequence, route, rendezvous points, etc., Wayne recalled that his mind seemed to "spin out" over the numbers being thrown at them. There would be 1400 transport planes (mostly C-47 Dakotas), in waves of 81 ships, each wave 5 minutes apart. These would drop some 18,000 paratroopers onto the Cherbourg peninsula. At 0630 the amphibious landings would begin. They planned to put 100,000 men ashore by noon, and 1,000,000 on the continent within 24 hours.

The briefing personnel made a strong point of the fact that 13,000 surface vessels would be crossing the channel below, and these should be viewed as a potential threat to the flight crews. A narrow corridor had been laid out for the planes, and any that strayed outside it would be subject to "friendly fire" from allied gunners who were sure to be nervous and trigger happy. Navigation was critical. It was a sobering thought.

The first wave of paratroops was scheduled to drop at midnight, with the last wave coming about an hour and a half later. Doing some quick calculations, Wayne realized that he'd be going in near the end of the airborne operation. Unless the Germans were completely oblivious, which seemed highly unlikely, they would be busy throwing everything they could at the planes and troops overhead by the time King got there. What he did *not* know was that the town of Ste. Mère-Eglise, where he would eventually drop his troops, was the headquarters for a full company of anti-aircraft emplacements. Nearby was a variety of regimental supply echelons, to give them plenty of ammo. In this instance, late arrival into combat would not be an advantage.

Lieutenant King's briefing ended with an unsettling announcement. A messenger brought news that the weather was turning sour over the drop zone and there would be at least a 24-hour delay. The air crews would now have lots of time to think about the mission ahead, laid out in such grim and full detail. Anxiety would have its chance to grow.

       ॐ   ॐ   ॐ

Before the evening meal, while the paratroopers were relaxing in the company tents, word was also passed to them that the invasion had been postponed. The news brought mixed feelings for most. True remembers being somewhat relieved that "at least we're not going in tonight." But everyone also knew that this only put off the inevitable, probably for 24 hours at most. They were left hanging in an emotional no-man's land, with lots of time to wait and think. Tomorrow they would again go through the wrenching process of mental preparation for their first combat—an experience that some would surely not survive.

Supper was the usual good fare of late: real meat, mashed

potatoes with gravy, unlimited coffee, and ice cream for dessert. It was delicious. But the mood had changed in the camp. After eating there would be few card games, or other entertainment as the men waited for lights out. Many took some time to write home.

Next morning the troopers awoke to a day of uncertainty. Chances were good that they'd be dropping into France sometime that night, but even this was not assured. Having nothing else to do, they spent the day repeating preparations for combat: checking, cleaning, and oiling weapons, inventorying equipment and supplies, and sharpening knives. Always the sharpening of knives. It seemed that everyone had a morbid fascination with honing every blade to the point that even a dry shave would be comfortable.

Each paratrooper was issued three blades. The trench knife was strapped to the leg, for easy access. This was his primary killing knife, if needed in hand-to-hand combat. It was supposed to be the weapon of choice during the night of the invasion, though no one took seriously the admonition to "withhold firing weapons 'til day break." Next was the bayonet, which fitted onto the muzzle of the standard M-1 rifle. It was carried in a pouch inside and under all the equipment strapped to each soldier. It wouldn't be immediately available on landing, but was there just in case. And last was the "jump knife." This was a switch-blade, with black simulated stag-horn handle. The blade swung out from the side. The knife was stored in a pocket high on the jump suit near the neck. It would be readily available in case the jumper was tangled in shroud lines, or trees, and had to cut his way out of his chute in a hurry. All the blades had received careful attention and were honed to a razor's edge. Now, on June 5, with little else for the men to do, they got even more time at the whetstone.

After lunch, Bill True was lying on his cot, killing time by reading a novel, when Tom Alley popped his head in.

"Did you hear about Bishop?" he asked. Edgar Bishop was another trooper in F Company and was known to True, though not well.

"No, what?"

"At lunch they caught him blabbing to the cooks about the jump, and flashing his French money. He's in a tent down the way, gettin' the crap beat out of him. Whole company's invited to beat on him—but only one hit each. They say it might even be Mulvey that OK'd it. Can't shoot him, can't court-martial him, so..."

"Jeez, did you go?" True asked.

"Yeah, but I wish I hadn't. Bishop was in the middle of the circle just taking it with his hands at his sides. When I got there he already looked pretty bad. A few of the guys from 3rd platoon—you know, that one mean ass little group—*they* sure got in on it. And you know Swafford had to be there, too. He came up and Bishop said, 'Go ahead, Whitey, I deserve it'. Then Whitey laid a haymaker right to the face with all he had. Bishop nearly flipped. Never saw a man just let himself be hit like that, blood flyin' everywhere... made me want to puke."

"Goddam. Is he OK to jump tonight?"

"Don't look like it to me. I didn't see him get up. More'n likely he'll be in the hospital. You goin' down there?"

"Shit no. Can't the Army figure out a better way than that to put out discipline? Our own guy!" Bill was more than a little sickened at the idea. He was also glad he didn't actually see the beating—that would have been too much to take. He thought, "This high security stuff is gettin' awful deep!"

Some time later, supply personnel began distributing burnt cork and grease paint around the tents. The men used it to blacken their faces and hands, and some chose to imitate Indian war paint, for added ferocity. They looked like a huge pack of soiled chimney sweeps when they went through the chow line around 5 p.m. for their last meal in England. After eating, the chaplains held worship services in various locations throughout the camp. Attendance was estimated at "generally high." Then finally, word was passed: "Get ready. Trucks will be at the company areas in half an hour to haul everyone to the planes."

In early evening, on the tarmac at the airstrip, hundreds of C-47s stood waiting. They looked different than before. Three large white stripes had been painted on their wings and fuselage, just in the last day or so. Someone said this was to be sure they weren't confused with enemy aircraft and shot down by our own troops, which had happened to the 82nd Airborne in Sicily.

The planes were a military version of the civilian DC-3, used by the Army primarily for cargo and troop transport. They were twin-engine tail-draggers that had two cargo doors, port side aft, which swung outward from the middle like those on a barn. These could not be opened in flight. The forward door would be pushed closed by the slip-stream, while the rear door, if cracked, would catch the wind and be torn off its hinges, possibly striking the tail of the plane as it left. For this mission the rear door had been unbolted and completely removed. The hinges and other sharp edges around the opening were then carefully taped to prevent anything from snagging as the men jumped from the aircraft. The open doorway would provide almost the only view the soldiers in back would have on their way to France.

Lieutenant Wayne King had borrowed a jeep and was driving down the ramp toward his plane to make last minute preparations. Suddenly, before reaching the ship, a very pale-faced officer of the day flagged him down excitedly, waving his arms in the air. "Hey, didn't you hear the guards yelling?!!" he said, breathlessly.

"No, why?" King replied.

"I just came around a corner and saw one drawing a bead on you with his rifle! I had to knock it out of his hands before he killed you!! You overran his post, fella, and these guys are in no mood to relax security right about now."

Wayne felt the awful truth of this in his gut. He recalled the surprise of how quickly the "atmosphere" at Uppottery had changed in the last few days. Some of the larger buildings had suddenly become surrounded by huge entanglements of barbed wire, and the engineers had even built watch towers with mounted machine guns at the corners of the yards. Clearly the Army was expecting to house a large number of POWs in the very near future. The sight of these stockades had sent a chill down many a spine, something that King now was feeling with a vengeance. He had nearly lost his life to friendly forces before ever flying his first combat mission over Europe.

That evening the Supreme Allied Commander, Gen. Dwight D. Eisenhower, paid a personal visit to the troops of the 101st, assembling at the airstrips. It was a compassionate move and revealed the sincere anguish Ike felt sending these men into battle. Air Marshall Leigh-Mallory had predicted that casualties among the paratroops would run as high as 75% and Eisenhower stated openly that this caused him to be "deeply concerned." Had the invasion failed he would have been haunted forever with the responsibility for nearly 20,000 useless American deaths.

Famous photo of General Eisenhower talking to 101st men just before they take off for the D-Day jump.

Though symbolic in nature—he couldn't possibly shake the hand of every man in the division—Ike's gesture was heartfelt and very moving to the men. Many years later, when asked what was the high point of his military career, Ike replied that "...the greatest moment was when I got the word that the 82nd and 101st Airborne Divisions had landed and gone into action on the Cherbourg Peninsula." For the men with whom Bill True had shared a Quonset hut in the previous months, Leigh-Mallory's prediction would prove overly optimistic.

True, Jackson, Flick, Stone and the others of stick #76 were let off at the airfield near Dakota #849. Their chutes and all the equipment they would carry were waiting for them. The troopers were dressed in their usual garb, but there was a difference. Over the cotton underwear, woolen long johns, and olive drab shirt and pants (ODs), they had donned jump suits that were impregnated with a chemical that was supposed to ward off poison gas, in case the Germans used it. This made the suits sticky to the touch, and they had an odd odor. It was an unpleasant addition to the burdens they

June 5, 1944, approximately 10 p.m. Bill True's jump stick is on the plane and waiting for take-off. Right side, front to back: Capt. Thomas P. Mulvey (company commander), Sgt. Julius A. Houck, PFC Robert F. Stone, Pvt. John E. Jackson, Sgt. Joseph S. Flick, PFC William True, T/5 Loy O. Rasmussen, and standing, Marvin F. Crawford. Left side, front to back (some are not visible): Mario J. (Gus) Patruno, unknown, Jack D. Dickerson, Joseph G. Chapelle, and standing, Sgt. Donald H. Replogle. Next to Replogle is 2nd Lt. Tommy Waldman, AAF navigator, and then 1st Lt. Harold Wayne King, AAF pilot.

now took on as they started strapping and securing equipment to themselves for the jump. They were far more heavily loaded than for any previous flight and had to be assisted up the steps into the plane.

Finally, the ponderously heavy troopers were all in their assigned bucket seats. As the cabin lights went out they heard the familiar whine, cough, and guttural growl as #1 engine roared to life. Everyone could feel the vibration through the hard metal beneath them. Engine #2 started up and the plane began to taxi into take-off position, in the long line of other C-47s already moving. Then the engines screamed to full throttle, main wheel brakes locked, and suddenly the thrust of take-off could be felt, pushing everyone aft. As they gained speed the tail lifted and the cabin became horizontal. Then they were airborne, and the rolling green countryside swept past the open cabin door. It was nearly 11:30 p.m., but with war-time double daylight savings the sky was still light in the gathering dusk of a lovely summer's day.

❧　　❧　　❧

The flight was an unusually long one for a parachute drop—much longer than any training mission. Hundreds of planes had to group in a "V of Vs" formation and this took time. The men in back were mostly quiet. It may have been the airsickness pills, or simply the grave nature of the situation, causing each man to become quietly lost in his own thoughts. There was no singing or horsing around as on all the other jumps they'd made. Some of the men even dozed off. A crewman passed among the troops handing out candy. True remembers a feeling of "unreality" about it.

Meanwhile, the atmosphere in the cockpit was anything but calm.

June 5, 1944, approximately 10 p.m. Crew of the plane that flew Bill True's stick to Normandy. Left to right: Lt. Frank P. DeFelitta, co-pilot; Lt. Tommy Waldman, navigator; Lt. Harold Wayne King, pilot; Sgt. Jerome Sterling, radio operator; Sgt. Vincent "Zeke" Zielinski, crew chief.

Dakota #849, and the others in her flight, were scheduled to rendezvous at a precise time near Southampton but arrived a few minutes early. This meant the pilots had to fly "S" patterns to kill time, which created a wild "accordion" effect, nearly throwing the group out of control. For a few minutes Wayne worried that they wouldn't make it to the Channel at all.

Finally in formation, they headed out on the precisely specified corridor toward France. Navigators and pilots alike remembered the admonition not to stray over friendly ships below for fear of getting shot out of the sky. Then the signal was flashed for all planes to extinguish external lights.

The first leg of the flight from England was south, designed deliberately to confuse the enemy into thinking the invasion would take place on the Brest peninsula in Brittany. Then there was a massive left turn to the east—not an easy maneuver with so many planes flying practically wing-tip to wing-tip. It took all their skill and concentration not to loosen up and at the same time avoid mid-air collisions. No sooner had they recovered from the turn, and were still some 30 miles out from landfall, than there came a terrifying shock. Unpredicted by the meteorologists, a fog bank lay straight in their path. As they flew into the misty shroud, suddenly it was as if a huge bucket of white paint had been splashed on the windshield. Within seconds every pilot was on instruments, with no visual horizon to guide him. The danger of mid-air collisions was now extremely high, and the air crews fought off panic as they tried to keep together and on course.

Struggling to stay in formation, barely able to see the planes around him, Wayne watched in growing fear as their airspeed dropped steadily, falling below 100 MPH and approaching stall. He suspected that the flight leader had developed vertigo, the terrible dizziness and spinning sensation pilots sometimes get when they lose their orientation. Breaking the strict rule of radio silence, Wayne called the lead plane to "wake him up." This worked, but only too well. Soon they had overcompensated and were flying at more than 200 MPH, making it impossible for the ships in back to keep up with the group. The planes were like a string of beads, trying desperately to stay together. But stretched beyond its limits, the string had broken.

"The hell with this," thought King. Frightened of the immense body of ships laying ahead, and knowing he couldn't hold his assigned slot in the formation, he peeled out, descending, and prayed that the path below was clear. They would have to find their own way to the drop zone.

Other pilots in other planes had made the same decision.

Now the navigator, 2nd Lt. Tommy Waldman, became the most critical member of the crew. His orders: analyze the map for a topography reading and report an altitude that would clear the highest point of their flight path by 200 feet. The ship's engineer, T/Sgt Victor Zielinski, was told to stand lookout at the astrodome, in the navigator's compartment, and give a sharp kick to the pilot's back if he saw any planes dropping down on them from above. The flight crew was on triple alert for impending shadows in the sightless muck.

Then just as quickly as it had ambushed them, the fog evaporated and they were in the clear. From out of nowhere a C-47 sliced underneath the nose, 50 feet below. Another Dakota dropped down, crossing their course 200 feet ahead. Confusion became the order of the day. Ahead the coast of France appeared, and there in all its horrific reality, World War II rose up to greet them with waves of flak and bullets.

As they crossed the coastline, #849 was quickly awash in a sea of gunfire, explosions, and burning aircraft. They ploughed through this for what seemed an eternity. King watched as two planes in front drove straight into a nearly solid curtain of tracers and anti-aircraft bursts. Mentally, he urged the pilots to evade, but that ran the risk of mid-air collision and was against orders, so the young aviators stayed on course. One was hit, sparks flying out the top of the cockpit. He did a wingover and went into a diving turn. Wayne's co-pilot, Frank DeFelitta, gave a running account as the stricken ship made a one-eighty and went down: "It looks like he's going to make it. He's got his landing lights on." But then there was a huge explosion and fire ball. The pilot had not yet jumped his troopers. The plane was full when it hit the ground, killing all aboard. It was stick #66, Easy Company guys including the C.O., Tom Meehan.

Now in front of them appeared an amazing sight. King

could see hundreds, no, thousands of parachutes in the sky. It looked like the entire 101st Airborne Division was being dropped in the same location. Though the plan had called for a 600 foot altitude, he descended to 300 feet, the absolute minimum, thinking, "Better not let those guys hang in the sky catching machine gun fire any longer than necessary." Conscious of airspeed he throttled back, more so on the left engine to reduce prop wash for the jumpers. Lost, and terrified for himself and the men in back, he said to DeFelitta, "I don't know what this is apt to do to their scheduled plan, but at least they'll have one helluva lot of company right here."

He hit the jump light switch. Immediately after that he felt the change in weight and trim of the plane as each individual paratrooper left with his massive load of arms.

NORMANDY RUN
Bill's True Tale

This is my 17th ride in a C-47, but this time it's eerily silent here in the darkness. None of the joking, cajoling or singing that was part of our field practice and war maneuver jumps. This time WE'RE GOING TO WAR! Dude Stone is uncharacteristically quiet, as are Gus Patruno and the other jokers who could always be counted on for wise cracks and smart-aleck commentary on life as a paratrooper. And I sure don't feel like starting some singing as has come to be my role in the platoon.

The rhythmic beat of the motors is the only sound other than the occasional click of a cigarette lighter as another nervous trooper lights up. I do hear some low murmurs though as the long minutes become an hour, and then two. Are some of the guys praying? It's been a long time... but maybe I should recite the Scientific Statement of Being I learned as a kid in Sunday School at the Christian Science Church. Under my breath I begin: "There is no life, truth, nor intelligence in matter, all is infinite mind and its infinite manifestation ..."

Suddenly there is a loud explosion and the bright flash of red and orange colors appears just outside the door of the plane. Tracer bullets are also sweeping the sky next to us and our C-47 dives to start evasive maneuvers. The violent drop and jarring motions of the plane have us clinging to our metal bucket seats, and now there is no question of whether anyone is praying. More than one trooper is voicing "Hail Mary, full of grace..."

The light from the German artillery and tracer bullets outside the plane door is steady bright now, and I'm sure our tail is on fire. Shrapnel striking the ship sounds like rocks rattling on a tin roof. My thoughts are a jumble of terror, but one surprising idea is dominant: "Those people down on the ground are trying to kill me. Me! Bill True! Personally." And the possibility that they might succeed is becoming very apparent.

The red signal light above the cabin door finally comes on and Captain Mulvey shouts: "Stand up and hook up!" I'm thinking: "Oh yes, please, please, faster, faster." From both sides of the plane we lurch to our feet and meld into our jump order like a pack of shuffled cards. We snap our parachute static lines to the overhead cable and check the equipment of the man in front of us and give him an OKAY slap on the rear. The "Sound off for equipment check!" is an extremely hurried affair, but the few seconds seem an eternity as we bounce and jerk violently, clinging with desperation to the static line for balance. The green light flashes at last and the captain shouts "Go!" as he leaps out the door. In spite of the excessive weight of our equipment and ammunition, our training for rapid exit, coupled with our violent dread, makes for a fast-moving jump.

"The cow spoke French..." Photographed in the Summer of 2002 by a French friend, Thierry Ferey, who is standing on the spot Bill True probably landed at 1:20 a.m. on 6 June 1944—and local cows stand in for the one Bill met that morning (perhaps descendants?).

As I exit the door the display of artillery fire and tracer bullets fills the entire sky. My chute opening is more violent than normal, but not unexpected in view of our great weight. I spot a fire on the ground and assume at first that it's the Pathfinders signal for our assembly point. It's not, and as I hit the ground much quicker than usual, I realize that we've jumped very low and probably far from our intended landing area.

It's a bright moonlit night, 1:20 a.m., and I'm in the middle of a farm field next to a Normandy cow with big eyes, a welcome sight indeed. I mutter something to her as I scramble from my harness, but she does not respond. Again I observe the criss-crossing of tracer bullets up and down the lines of parachutes from following planes. I'm in Normandy and at war.

৵   ৵   ৵

Bill True was never so scared, or so relieved to get out of a plane. As he dove out the door he could see a fire off to his left on the ground below. "Probably a pathfinder signal," he thought. Others made the same assumption and all were wrong. It was a house fire in the town of Ste. Mère Eglise, completely unrelated to the invasion. Unknowingly, they were miles from their intended drop zone.

Though it seemed an eternity in the air, in fact this was the fastest descent Bill ever made. The 18 feet of static line played out quickly as he plummeted with all the excess weight. When he reached its end the cover tore off his chute, the canopy pulled out by its apex and popped open. After just a single oscillation he landed hard in a pasture surrounded by hedgerows. Nearby, clearly visible by the light of the full moon, was a Normandy cow with huge udders and big soulful eyes. She was placidly chewing her cud and totally unconcerned with the dramatic events unfolding around her. The sense of "unreality" True had felt on the ride from England remained. He was several hundred yards due east of Ste. Mère-Eglise, behind German lines, and lost.

In the sky above, Dakota #849 was not on fire as the troopers had feared. More danger lay ahead as she made her way back to the coast, but the crew would arrive in England safely. Their ordeal was nearly over for now, while that of the ground troops was just beginning.

In the pasture, True realized he was out in the open and

vulnerable—easily seen by any German troops which might be lurking. He struggled to get out of his chute. First the two buckles of the reserve, then the belly band, then the main harness. Looking up, he saw the sky filled with parachutes from horizon to horizon. Streams of machine gun tracers raked the lines of dangling paratroopers as they floated to earth. The sight made his stomach churn. Glancing in the direction of the cow he softly muttered a heartfelt "You're beautiful."

She did not respond. The cow spoke French.

Freed of his chute at last, Bill grabbed the canvas case with his M-1 in it and made double time for the relative safety of the nearest hedgerow. At that moment he didn't even have a gun with which to defend himself. His rifle was in three pieces, and it would take several precious seconds to assemble. Suddenly he saw a shadow moving down the row directly toward him.

"Oh, shit, a German!" he thought. "Get the rifle together! Quick! No time! No time!" He made up his mind that at the last instant he would simply throw the unassembled gun into the face of his foe, reach for the trench knife strapped to his leg, and attack the Kraut in hand to hand combat. Then he heard it: "Click, Clack." The sound of a toy cricket. Where was his? Not where he could reach it in time to respond. Damn! The password, what was it? Then he remembered. "Flash," he half-whispered, half-spoke—just loud enough for the cricketeer to hear. "Thunder," came the correct response. Thank God!

It was Johnny Jackson, who had leaped through the cargo door just ahead of him. But for the sound of a child's toy, Bill True had very nearly attacked and killed his best friend.

"You land OK?" Bill asked.

"Yeah, I guess. Kinda hard, though. Awfully low drop."

"Yeah. What do we do now?"

They both instinctively looked up. The sky was still filled with planes and parachutes, and the aircraft were all going the same direction. If the operation had gone off anything like the plan, then the planes had to be generally heading east. But a better guide was tucked in each man's pocket.

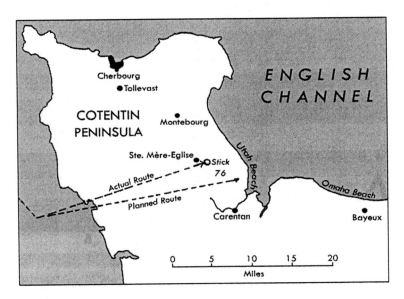

Route of Stick 76

"Where's my compass?" Johnny asked, digging in his jumpsuit. "We gotta find the other guys and start headin' for the beach." True took the scarf from around his neck: on it was printed a map of the invasion area, an important item included in the invasion kit given to all the troopers. They started to form a plan. Now at least each man was not alone. They assembled their rifles and headed out toward what they thought was the direction of their objective: the town of Pouppeville and the Exit #1 causeway leading inland from Utah Beach.

True and Jackson had been lucky. One stick of men from their platoon had landed in the town of Ste. Mère-Eglise itself. Richard Buchter was killed by German troops right in the town square. Another, Bill Hale was riddled with machine gun fire as he floated to the ground. He was found dead, hanging in a tree the next morning by Jesse Orosco. As Jesse tried to cut him down, a German machine gun opened up and drove him away.

Walter Hult and Ray Kermode had also been killed on the jump. Tom Alley barely avoided landing in the burning structure Bill had seen as he exited his plane. Don "Pedro" Davis had landed in the middle of town and pulled off a minor miracle. With German soldiers all around him all he could think to do was "play possum," which he did with apparently consummate skill. The enemy soldiers found him, kicked him, even rolled him over, but were convinced. They left him for dead and he escaped the town. Sadly, it was only a reprieve as he was killed days later in the massive German counterattack at Carentan.

ຈົ   ຈົ   ຈົ

Gradually, True and Jackson were joined by others of the 506th in their march to the causeway. First was Dude Stone, who had jumped with them. Then came others. Eventually they began to resemble a real fighting unit, with non-coms and even an officer or two, though it was a real hash of companies and units represented. They found a road, which led them to signposts that fixed their location. That told them how far off course they had been dropped. It also gave them the exact direction to Utah Beach, and then they had both a purpose and a direction to travel.

Most of the night was spent picking up additional

troopers while moving to the beach, but there was occasional sporadic action. Several times the men received small arms fire coming from hedgerows. Ignoring orders not to shoot ("Remember men, use only bayonets and knives"), they returned fire. Having no clear targets, however, the troopers were doubtful that they had done much damage to the enemy.

Once, they passed a farm house where someone said they thought Germans had been seen entering. The soldiers fired randomly at this for awhile, but there was no response, so they moved on.

Not long after setting out, Johnny Jackson started having trouble with his knees. He had landed very hard, and with all the extra weight, had suffered sprains. Soon he had ditched the mortar tube, his assignment on the jump, and needed help from Dude Stone just to make his way down the road. Leaning on his fellow trooper the progress was slow, which made it officially against orders on the invasion night. But buddies are buddies, and the men had been together since training days at Toccoa. Besides, they knew the drop zone had been missed by miles and the plan was already off track. The overall group kept moving, however it was starting to spread out and break apart.

True discarded the mortar base plate, useless now that the tube was gone. He took on the role of "middle man." The guys ahead gradually got to be some 40 to 50 yards out, while Johnny Jackson and Dude were about a similar distance behind. Bill took turns alternately yelling at the men in front to slow down a bit and urging Johnny and Dude to hurry up. It seemed to him critically important that he and Dude and Johnny not get separated from the main body. A large force of soldiers could defend itself far better than a group of only three guys, especially with one of them incapacitated. Increasingly, this looked like a losing proposition as the men in front were not inclined to slow down, in accordance with their orders. Then luck intervened as they ran into a make-shift aid station. Johnny was dropped off, and the others continued their journey. But True would later feel guilty. Whatever intellectual justification there might be for the role he had played as "middle man," he knew he'd always regret not going back to help Johnny and Dude speed up.

Soon after this, rounding a bend in the road, they came across a pile of corpses at the side. Getting closer, everyone could see that they were German soldiers. The bodies were in a depression, or ditch, at the side of the roadway. It was apparent from their position that these men had been lined up and executed. True remembered the admonition that "we can't waste time marching prisoners around during the night of the invasion." He felt numb. Not saddened, or sympathetic, or angry. These were the enemy. More than anything else, he felt glad that it wasn't him or his comrades lying bullet-riddled in the dirt. But he was also relieved that it had not been his lot to make this happen.

Things remained fairly quiet for a time—just sporadic shooting from and at the surrounding hedgerows; nothing very concentrated or serious. After their harrowing flight and jump into enemy territory a few scattered, stray bullets didn't seem all that terrifying. Then up ahead, the men could see that a real fire fight was under way. A group of E Company men, augmented by some of True's buddies in F Co., had engaged a battery of four 105mm German gun emplacements. These were aimed directly at Utah Beach still out of sight in the distance, and they were a serious threat to the men landing ashore. It was vital that they be taken out.

Julius Houck and Len Hicks, both F Company men, were among those who volunteered for a piece of this action. The Germans had been routed from #1 and #2 guns, and the barrels had been spiked with grenades. Now the third was under attack by the paratroopers. Len and Julius crept up close enough to fire at the defending troops directly. The two Americans were lying in a depression, side by side, as they planned their next move. There was very little cover. Hicks was ready to fire his M-1, while Houck would throw a grenade. Len told Houck, "Be careful, they may be tossing some back at us and we're pretty exposed here."

Hicks fired and the German soldier he'd aimed at went down. But Houck raised up to throw his grenade, completely exposing himself just at the time a burst of machine gun fire was heard. He was struck multiple times in the chest by the burp gun and went down instantly. Later, Hicks recalled that the fatal injuries were all internal. According to him, "There wasn't enough blood showing to even soak a cigarette paper."

Fifty yards back, True and the others had observed this action. Bill saw vividly how Julius seemed to be taking unnecessary chances, overly aggressive in exposing himself. Then he saw him fall and knew immediately that he was dead.

Though by now Bill had seen more than one dead body, this was the first time he had actually witnessed the act of someone being killed. Julius Houck was a friend, going way back to training at Camp Toccoa, and had led the men in much of their calisthenics and other physical training. Seeing him die caused sudden but unexpected emotions. There was sadness, of course. But this was the heat of battle and men who are engaged in action have no time to mourn—that happens later. There was also the selfish thought that, "At least it wasn't me." More than anything else was the need to move on. There were objectives to be taken and little time to dwell on the death of a fallen comrade. One of the non-coms passed the word: "They've got this handled. Let's move out!" The group resumed their march toward their planned objectives behind Utah Beach.

It was well after dawn when they came to an area with water on either side of the road. This was foretold in their briefings; that the Germans would flood the fields behind the invasion beaches to ward off a paratroop assault. The effort had met with some success. Many troopers were dropped here and had drowned under the weight of their own equipment. Now, standing on the causeway of Exit #1 leading up from Utah Beach, True and his cohorts watched as a column of Americans marched up from the shore to meet them.

While still some distance away, True called out to the man in the lead: "Hey Mac, what outfit is that?" It was a casual, friendly greeting to friendly troops, and the answer was just as cordial: "Fourth Infantry, son, movin' inland." When the two groups passed, True saw a star on each collar of the man he had addressed. Later he learned that there was one general officer who had landed in the first attack waves and marched ashore at Utah. It was Brig. Gen. Theodore Roosevelt, Jr., grandson of President Teddy, who had begged for the privilege of being first on the beach. Bill sheepishly recalled that he, a lowly PFC, had called the man "Mac."

By most accounts the Allied airborne drop had been something of a mess. Almost none of the 101st Division

224

elements had landed anywhere near their planned objectives. All the time they had spent poring over sand tables and planning their attacks in minute detail were largely for naught. But the troops used their intelligence, ingenuity, and perseverance to make the best of the situation, and it had worked. The Germans were even more confused than they, and never knew where or even what they really faced. This was a significant factor in the relatively light casualties incurred at Utah, compared to the terrible carnage at Omaha Beach.

Ahead of Bill and his friends lay the bloody battle for Carentan and weeks of withering hedge-row fighting. But for now, at least, they had survived their first harrowing ordeal of combat.

They were at war.

CHAPTER VI

Rat Killin'
The Normandy Campaign

"War loses a great deal of its romance after a soldier sees his first battle."

John Singleton Mosby

The last time in human history that a cross-channel invasion had succeeded was the Battle of Hastings in 1066. Initial reports on June 6, 1944 did not suggest that a repeat was assured. But though the Allied airborne operations had been marred by mis-drops and general confusion, their positive effect on the invasion was substantial. American paratroops were scattered over the Cotentin Peninsula in such a way that the German commanders could not determine either their numbers or import. With the "Fuhrer Principle" dominating their actions, the enemy could make no decisive movements until ordered from the ranks above. And Hitler was asleep, left blissfully ignorant of the invasion by subordinates who had learned through harsh experience not to disturb his rest.

In contrast to the Germans, American soldiers had been trained to be not only confident in their own judgment, but assertive in the face of confusion. Bill True and his comrades knew they had missed their intended drop zone, but it made no difference in their will to reach the goal: achieve the beach and take the causeway exits leading in from the sea. Thousands of other soldiers, brothers-in-arms now queasy riding Channel swells, would need that support or might be tossed back into the waves by German defenses.

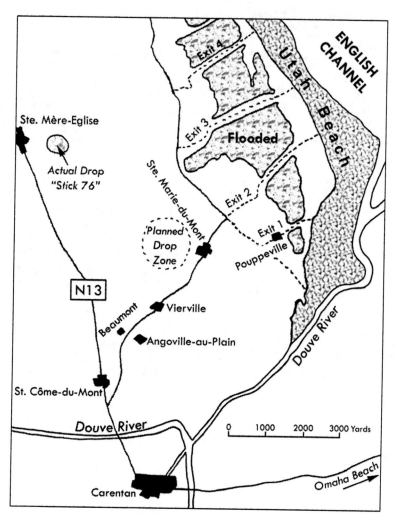

506th PIR Invasion Theater – Early Normandy Campaign

And so they came together—first in small, mixed-rank bunches, and later in groups that looked more like properly organized units. Throughout the night and following day, men of the 101st Division filtered north and east toward Utah Beach. Some saw significant action on their way, while others merely marched with determination toward their target.

One of the phrases Bill True remembered from his childhood days in Omaha, Nebraska, was, "Time to get on with your rat killin'." His dad had learned it as a boy reared in the Oklahoma Territory. It meant "get to work on your chores." Whether it was shining the family shoes on Sunday, or weeding the garden and mowing the lawn on Saturday, or clearing and washing the supper dishes any night of the week, when his dad said, "Time to get on with your rat killin'," Bill knew it was serious work time.

Probably few American soldiers in Normandy would have recognized that salty phrase from the western frontier, but Bill remembered it, and he knew just how apt it was to the task set before him and his buddies. Digging foxholes and moving aggressively through the Normandy hedgerows was serious rat killin'. Bill knew that if Leslie Arthur True were the platoon lieutenant, that admonition would be getting considerable usage right about now.

By late afternoon of June 6, over half of Fox Company, 506th PIR, had assembled at Pouppeville to receive further instructions from Capt. Mulvey. They were ordered inland one mile to take the small village of Ste. Marie-du-Mont.

Bill and Dude Stone found themselves on a country road with 50-60 others, representing all the ranks up to captain. Now heading west they encountered little enemy resistance as they marched, but there was serious activity going on overhead.

"What was that?" Dude said, looking up. True followed his gaze and saw something new to his experience. It was hard to make out but looked like a quick, perhaps metallic flash in the sky heading in from the beach. This was accompanied by a strange "rushing" sound, something like a rocket. He'd never heard anything like it before. "Damned if I know," he said.

"Navy," said a trooper behind them. "Them's the *big* guns, off the battleships and such out in the Channel. You don't ever want to be in a place where *that* shit is landing!"

They knew the truth of this at gut level. Fourteen-inch guns off the dreadnought USS *Texas*, cruising just off the beach, could launch a 1500 lb. shell twenty-eight miles inland, with enough accuracy to hit a football field. The Texas was joined by other battleships and cruisers, and together they gave a serious pounding to German positions all across the invasion map. True and Stone were standing mid-way in the shells' trajectory: so far away that they heard neither the firing of the gun, nor the explosion of the shell's impact. But merely the sound of such massive artillery streaking overhead was awesome, sending shivers down their spines. Somebody or someplace inland was going to get a real shellacking and True was indeed glad not to be where the gigantic shells were landing.

           ❧   ❧   ❧

No one really knew what to expect at Ste. Marie-du-Mont. The only weaponry the troopers had was a sizable cache of small arms—no artillery or armored vehicles of any kind had joined them yet. But if they were worried, none showed it. And their confidence served them well. The German force, whatever it was in the little hamlet, had not much stomach for a real fire fight. With only rifles, light machine guns, and hand grenades, Fox Company moved into the town as the enemy moved out; the Americans took it with relatively few casualties. Lt. Freeling Colt of the third platoon was one exception, killed as he entered the town. Universally liked by the troops, his loss was a sore one.

It had now been almost 24 hours since their assembly at the airstrips in England, and the men had gone much longer than that without sleep. It was time to set up a defensive perimeter and dig in for the night. Stone and True teamed up to excavate a two-man foxhole right next to a fancy country mansion just outside town.

As night fell the temperature dropped fast, and soon Ty-Ty and Dude were shivering in their hole. The ground was hard, too, even worse than the Army cots they'd gotten used to in the marshalling area. With no immediate combat action to worry about, attention turned toward their own physical comfort. "Hey Ty-Ty. Let's check that house over there. Looks deserted. Maybe we can get some coats or blankets, or something," said Stone.

The house was indeed abandoned; most likely the vacation home of a rich family, and only occupied part of the year. Stone and True had no trouble gaining entrance, and few compunctions about garnering supplies "on loan for the duration." In the cellar Dude was pleased to find an entire case-load of Calvados, the delicious Normandy liquor made from apples. And in an upstairs bedroom, True discovered a whole closet full of elegant silk bed comforters. The pair quickly made off with the booty and soon were ensconced in their now-snug foxhole with soft down blankets and a little liquid cheer. If only the Germans would leave them alone for the night, even taking two-hour turns at "watch" wouldn't be so hard to endure. The comforters were warm, and thick enough to cushion even a hardscrabble dirt hole. The effeminate lace ruffles didn't bother their masculine sensibilities in the least.

❧   ❧   ❧

June 7 dawned cold and gray. Now the troopers would learn first-hand what it meant to *live* in the field of battle, with meager logistical support. First order of business: breakfast.

The men had jumped into France carrying three days' worth of K-rations. Each ration held three compact containers labeled "breakfast," "dinner," and "supper," though many recipients found the distinction between them to be more semantic than substantive. Bill unwrapped the breakfast box and this is what he found: one small can of unidentifiable meat, biscuits wrapped in cellophane, a compressed cereal bar, powdered instant coffee, a fruit bar, gum, and sugar tablets. There was also a can opener, a wooden spoon, one tiny package of toilet paper, and a miniature box of four Fleetwood cigarettes with matches. If he had mistakenly opened a "supper," the principle difference would have been inclusion of a powdered lemonade-like drink. In time this became universally considered undrinkable by the troops. Some thought it might have found good use stripping paint.

"Fleetwood" cigarettes were one of several brands packed in K-rations. "Chelsea's" were another. It was said they were American made, but they weren't like any of the regular store-brands—Camels and others that everyone remembered. Fleetwoods in particular tasted bad, burned hot, and held an ash like a cigar. A man could watch one burn all the way to his fingers without the ash falling off. It was a constant source of amazement.

The meat, biscuits, and fruit bar were palatable, if not fancy fare. At least they filled the void in a man's stomach. But it was clear that a steady diet of K's would get old quick.

In actual fact, the K-ration itself had been carefully designed with a very specific mission: to support airborne and other assault troops for a maximum of three days, in conditions where field kitchens could not be established. The rations had to be compact, lightweight, nourishing, and as tasty as possible given the other restrictions. This was not easily accomplished, but the Army knew that if food isn't appetizing, people won't eat it until they have to. By then their fighting ability will suffer for lack of sustenance. And though often denigrated, the K-ration was a triumph of compromises that kept men fit for fighting, at least in the short term.

ॐ　　　ॐ　　　ॐ

The night of June 6-7 had been a quiet one. Their first combat objectives having been met the day before, the troops were ready for whatever would come next. Word came down to begin moving further west and south, deeper into the peninsula. Everyone knew that eventually they must take and hold Carentan, a sizable town at the intersection of major highways linking Utah and Omaha Beaches with the interior. But there was plenty of territory, and presumably plenty of Germans, to face in between. Breakfast being over, they fell in for a march of several miles. For Stone, True, Flick and the others, the immediate goal on June 7 became the town of Vierville and beyond that to set up a defensive perimeter in the area of St. Come-du-Mont.

Stone looked True over, especially the gear hanging on his standard web belt. "You still got your gas mask!? What the hell for?"

Each soldier had been issued a bulky, awkward canister-type gas mask as a matter of course. No one knew what weapons the Germans might employ, and Supreme Command wanted to cover all contingencies. But the masks were clumsy affairs, and banged against the leg as a soldier walked. Most of the troops didn't think gas attacks would be part of the action, since there had been no evidence of it so far in previous fights. It became common to simply throw the device into a nearby ditch, to make the march more comfortable.

Bill True was ever the cautious one. "Yeah, I figure it can't hurt to have it. Never know what those German bastards might do out here. I'd rather be prepared," he said.

"Suit yourself," was the reply. Later, Stone would have cause to sheepishly recall this conversation.

Passing through the Normandy countryside, they now had time to closely view and consider the famous "hedgerow" terrain which would be their battleground. It was well-suited for defensive actions, which the Germans would fully exploit.

For centuries, farmers had built hedgerows to define land holdings, keep in cattle, and generally protect their fields. The enclosures were often irregular in shape and varied greatly in size. A typical hedgerow was made of a dirt embankment anywhere from two to six feet high, and often wide enough for a road on top. The crown would be planted with a variety of large bushes and trees. These made excellent barriers behind which a defender could hide, protected, while firing at an advancing enemy. Anyone who dared to charge across the open field between rows would be extremely vulnerable to machine gun and mortar fire. Thus in June of 1944 each pasture and field became its own separate battleground, to be taken or held independently of the others.

Open areas which were large enough to support glider landings had been salted with a variety of obstacles to discourage just such an operation. To one side of the road True saw a field covered with stout wooden poles sticking out of the earth at angles. These were the infamous "Rommel's Asparagus" which did so much damage. Here was stark evidence of its deadliness. Several gliders had landed, probably on D-Day morning, and been completely destroyed. Torn and splintered wings and fuselages were scattered and smashed like broken toys. It was hard to imagine how anyone aboard could have survived. Not for the last time, True thought himself lucky to have been a parachutist: better a quick and terrifying jump than a crash-landing in a darkened aircraft!

Not far into their day's march, the captain decided to send out a reconnaissance patrol and asked for volunteers. They were to simply move out ahead of the main body of troops, make a big circle of about 2 miles, and report back any enemy activity; no fire fights, just bring back information. Joe Flick was eager: "I'll go, and so will True," he said. So Flick the zealot, and True the "volunteer," joined three men from 2nd platoon: Privates Olanie and Casey, and Sergeant Frank Griffin. The five marched off while the others took a break.

Griffin took the lead and, with True and Flick bringing up the rear, they moved in single file 25 or 30 feet apart along a road that topped a hedgerow, watching carefully for signs of enemy presence. Suddenly True spotted three German soldiers to his left, in a field perhaps 40 or 50 yards away. One of them was pointing a pistol at the lead men in the patrol, who were as yet unaware of the danger. Bill calmly but quickly raised his M-1, flicking off the safety as his sights came to bear on the enemy, and squeezed off a round. This action was completely automatic, just like shooting at paper targets on the rifle range back at Camp Mackall. He was surprised to feel almost no emotion whatever. Yet for the first time he had actually fired a weapon at a real, live person he could see. Two years of physical training and mental conditioning had given him the will and ability to do the job required.

But his shot was wide, and a second pull of the trigger produced only an audible "click": his rifle had jammed and failed to chamber the next round.

With shots fired, now the alarm was raised. In the split second it took to clear his weapon, Bill saw his buddies all shooting. The German pistoleer hit the ground, riddled with bullets. His two companions disappeared in the tall grass of the field; the danger wasn't over yet. But Captain Mulvey's orders had been "strictly reconnaissance," meaning that if and when the enemy was spotted, this patrol was to return. Since that had now happened the troopers turned back the way they came, to report their findings. The two Germans in the grass would be dealt with another time.

Earlier, the patrol had passed a field containing ammunition packs, most likely dropped by parachute the day before. They contained .30 caliber cartridge belts in sealed cans, and would be vital for the machine gun squads. Bill True remembered seeing it. "Hey, guys, let's pick that stuff up. Somebody's gonna need it," he said.

"Yeah, you're right," said the sergeant. "You stay up here and keep a close watch for those two Krauts, in case they followed us."

While the other four moved down the embankment, True stood on the other side of the hedge atop the row, looking back along the road they had just traveled. Brush and trees now formed a curtain between him and his comrades collecting bundles in the field behind. Then a very odd thing occurred. A little black dog came trotting, all alone, from the very place the patrol had just left. "That's strange," Bill thought. "Dogs don't just go for walks in the countryside all by themselves." He was immediately suspicious. Sure enough, next came not two, but three German soldiers.

The enemy were some 60 or 70 yards away. Bill knew that if he yelled at his buddies it would alert the Germans as well. He decided on action instead. One or two fast shots would alert his friends, and might wreak some useful damage as well. He aimed and fired. The three soldiers immediately vanished into the hedgerow as the American paratroopers rushed back to join the fray.

Joe Flick was first to reach the road, scrambling up the dirt incline. "Where are they?" he asked excitedly, poking his head through the brush.

Bill pointed. "Over there," he whispered as he crouched near the cover of the hedge.

Within limits, paratroopers were given some discretion in the choice of personal weapons they carried. The M-1 rifle was True's favorite and he always felt confident with it. Joe, on the other hand, was a flashy sort of guy, and his natural choice was the Thompson submachine gun. Now he put it to flamboyant use. Charging out of cover, standing up straight in the middle of the road, Joe sprayed automatic fire in the general direction he thought the Germans had gone. Shooting from the hip, a rapid stream of empty shell casings flew from his weapon like angry hornets launched from a rock-struck hive. Bill watched this "movie-like" scene from cover and despite the seriousness of events, had to suppress a chuckle. He thought to himself, "Goddam, he looks like John Wayne holding off a whole army! He can't even *see* the sons of bitches, but he sure is having fun!"

The enemy soldiers never did reappear and after the excitement had died down, each man on the patrol picked up a can of ammo and resumed the march.

They had nearly reached the rest of the company when a strange sight greeted them. Galloping down the road was a snow-white horse. It's bareback rider was an American soldier with full field pack and helmet, waving his rifle in the air. When he got close enough they could hear him shouting, "Yeee-Hawww"! and obviously having himself a grand time. It was Mario "Gus" Patruno, of their own third platoon. As he pulled the reins up to a sudden halt in front of them, Flick shouted, "Hey, where'd you get *that*?"

"Damnedest thing," Mario replied. "I was going down the road yesterday morning, and off to the side was this huge barn, maybe 80 foot long. In the pasture outside was a big group of German cavalry horses, and there weren't nobody else around. Didn't see no saddles, but that was a fine lot of horse flesh, and I *know* horses. Figured if I'm gonna steal one, it oughta be pure white. So I grabbed a bridle, and cut this one out of the herd."

"What ya gonna do with him?"

"Ride him, what else! The captain'll prob'ly make me give it up pretty soon anyway. But in the mean time this is just like back home." And with that he wheeled his mount, dug his combat boots into the horse's flanks, and galloped off, again waving his rifle in the air and shouting, "Yeee-Hawww!" Flick just shook his head, picked up his ammo can, and resumed the march, with the others just as bemused.

They never did find out what, if any, importance there was to the information gathered on their patrol. Presumably, any scrap of solid data about the enemy would be useful to *someone*. But soldiers in the field get quickly used to acting on orders without really knowing the big picture. Now that the company was back together, it was time to head out for Vierville.

First battalion of the 506th had been given the honor of leading this movement. Later, as Fox Company and the rest of second battalion followed, they could see that their compatriots had run into fairly serious resistance. Dead soldiers of both armies became an increasingly common sight as True and the rest approached town. In the central square at the intersection of two highways an American lay face down, obviously bled out. Though they had seen dead men before, the sight was sobering to the men moving through the now-quiet village. Bill noticed a German machine gun emplacement, abandoned in a hedgerow just outside town as they were leaving to the south.

Benjamin Stoney was the dead man at the crossroads, and he was personally known to some in Fox Co. The story soon spread that he had been shot by two very young German soldiers manning a machine gun—kids, really. It was the gun True had seen. The German boys had surrendered to the American force right after Stoney was killed.

"Goddam it! Why couldn't they surrender BEFORE shooting!" was the general feeling among the troops. It seemed such a useless waste.

෨   ෨   ෨

By late afternoon, the second battalion of the 506th was in the area of Angoville-au-Plain. Here they learned the details of the fight that first battalion had encountered. German troops had put up fierce resistance at Vierville, then beyond at Beaumont, and finally had stopped the American advance altogether at St. Come-du-Mont. The exhausted paratroopers had been ordered to fall back while plans were laid to try again next day. Meanwhile, Fox Company was told to dig in where they were and set defenses for the night.

Overnight on June 7-8, the American commanders huddled and reorganized their forces for a major assault at 0445 next morning. By now an Allied beachhead had been established at the coast, and heavy armament was pouring ashore, becoming a welcome addition to the light weaponry of the paratroops. Tanks and artillery would play a pivotal role in the plan.

    ∾   ∾   ∾

As dawn broke, True and the rest of Fox Company moved out to take position in reserve protecting the flank, west of St-Come-du-Mont, while other units attacked directly from the north. For more than two days now the enemy had launched determined, but largely uncoordinated counterattacks against invading Allied troops. The Germans still lacked commitment and decisive action from the High Command, and field units were becoming disarrayed. In the middle of the afternoon, June 8, two American battalions moved into the town expecting a serious fight. Instead they found that the enemy had begun to withdraw. Later that day, reconnaissance patrols reported the town deserted.

Nearing St. Come-du-Mont, Stone, Flick, and True saw further evidence of first battalion's earlier struggle. Dead soldiers lay in fields and roads leading into town. Decaying cows, bloated and reeking with swarms of flies, dotted the countryside. At a corner in the south end of town they encountered a burned-out American tank, its dead commander hanging from the turret. For the second time in recent days Bill was thankful to be a paratrooper. Tanks seemed like steel traps. Not that he didn't want to have some Shermans on his side in a serious fire fight, of course. But it was best not to be *inside* one when it really hit the fan.

As the day ended, the men got their first chance since the invasion to communicate with loved ones at home. Provision was made for each soldier to send a telegram home via Western Union. Bill True knew that by now his family would have read about the invasion. He didn't have time or space for more than a few words, and he wanted most of all to relieve their worries. This is what he wrote:

HI Y'ALL DOING FINE
BILL TRUE

☙   ☙   ☙

On D-Day plus two, Wayne King found himself again piloting Old Army #849 into Normandy, but this time it was a re-supply mission. Two miles inland from Exit #4, engineers had leveled the forest and put in a steel-mat runway along side a medical tent city. Coming in for a landing, the crew beheld an amazing sight—trucks, tanks, and heavy construction equipment swarmed over the area like a stomped-on ant-hill. The invasion area was not yet secure, but it looked to Wayne like that would be only a matter of time with all the materiel pouring ashore.

After touchdown, Lt. King met to confer with the supply major outside his headquarters tent while the plane was unloaded. Suddenly, from out of a hedgerow to their left emerged a young, lone paratrooper who appeared to be in shock. When asked what had happened, he only muttered,

"He shot 'em all."

Wayne and the major both knew something bad had happened, and slowly they drew the story out. Finally it became clear. The young soldier and his company commander were escorting a group of 30-odd German prisoners along a road when they came upon an awful sight: Nazi soldiers had strung up an American paratrooper by his heels and slit his throat execution-style. When the officer saw this he had gone crazy and machine-gunned all the prisoners on the spot, to the shock of his companion. Shaken to the core, the trooper now was escorted to the medical station for assistance, desperately in need of solace from any source available.

No sooner had this episode ended than another drama played itself out, this time in the sky overhead. Flying low, seemingly from out of nowhere, came two P-51 Mustangs, followed in hot pursuit by two German Me 109s. Engine screaming, the lead Mustang was suddenly hit hard and went down in a fiery explosion perhaps a mile away. The 109s peeled off and left the scene, while the remaining P-51 sputtered, smoke billowing from the engine cowling. Somehow the pilot managed to turn the plane and attempt a landing, but there simply wasn't room. His plane bellied-into a field of tree stumps next to the steel runway, and slid to a stop while the trees tore off the wings and stabilizers. Amazingly, when it was over the pilot stood up, in a now-completely stripped canopy, climbed out and walked straight up to Wayne and the supply major. "You going back to England in that Dakota?" he asked, out of breath.

"Soon as we're unloaded, yeah," Wayne replied.

"Good, you can give me a lift. I'm gettin' me another plane and comin' back to *kill* that son-of-a-bitch!"

Wayne could only gape in awe.

242

❧   ❧   ❧

By D+3, dead bodies on the battlefield were becoming a problem. This was anticipated by the Army. An obvious fact of war is that there will be corpses to deal with—both your own and those of the enemy. Rotting flesh is a health hazard to all. And the continuous sight of human carrion does not have a positive effect on the morale of fighting troops. Consequently, battlefield morticians in the Graves Registration section of the Quartermaster Corps had come into Normandy as early as the afternoon of June 6.

Sergeant Elbert Legg of the 82nd Airborne Division was among them. He established the first temporary cemetery at Blosville, just south of Ste. Mère-Eglise, and immediately began processing the dead: making positive identification, safeguarding personal effects, etc. Soon others did the same. Each division was assigned one platoon of 36 men for this purpose. But they couldn't do the job alone and it became policy for a unit to "police its own area" for corpses.

In the middle of a day's march, one squad from Fox Company, 506th, was assigned a grim task: search surrounding fields and carry the dead they found to the side of the road for disposal. Graves Registration would take care of the rest. So Bill True found himself joining others in the first of several details he would encounter along these lines.

It was a warm day. Sweeping through a field of tall grass they passed bloated cows and horses rotting in the sun. These had become an increasingly common sight. But then the troopers came across a number of German soldiers. Dead, bloody, flyblown, their stench was nearly overwhelming. And the color of exposed flesh—the pallor of death—was a sickening sight. One by one the paratroopers took them by the arms and feet and carried the bodies to the side of the road to pile them up. Bill could see that most of them had been young and hearty soldiers, worthy foes. Though he felt only disgust for the German government, these were merely foot soldiers fighting for their country, as he was. He always felt respect for the adversary.

Soon the detail came to what looked like the remains of an aid station. There were packages and other materiel with red crosses on them scattered about. The site had apparently taken a direct hit from either artillery or heavy mortar fire, because the destruction was terrible. Not bodies, but *parts* of bodies lay strewn around the area; arms, legs; heads and torsos torn asunder. Bill had seen dead men before, but this was the first time he had to actually touch and handle them in *pieces*. Revolting as it was, at least these were enemy, and not Americans. He knew all too well that sooner or later he would also have to deal with that.

                      ☙   ☙   ☙

June 10 found Fox Company still heading south. There had been sporadic action all along their way so far, but nothing very serious—just a sniper once in awhile or brief exchange with an enemy patrol.

Moving through an open field, the men found remains of what had been German defensive positions. Whatever action had taken place was long over, and it looked like some heavy artillery had been the deciding factor. Bill came across a large foxhole containing three of the German dead. His first impulse, and that of most every American soldier, was to check the bodies for pistols. The famed Luger was the greatest prize, of course, but any sidearm was desirable.

No pistols.

Next he looked in the knapsack of the man who appeared least mangled. Never knew what you might find that could be useful. Inside were a can of good German black bread and a tube of soft, ripened cheese. These proved to be delicious and a welcome change from K-rations. But he found another prize as well: a large Hohner harmonica. Engraved on its side were the words, "Der Gute Kammerad"—the good friend. Bill had been taught to play by his father years before. A little music during lulls could be a very comforting balm to the spirit. He thought, "It wasn't necessarily such a good friend to you, fellow, but it may be for me." He put it in his pocket and moved on.

Carentan was the largest town in the southern Cotentin Peninsula. It lay on the N13, a major highway linking Cherbourg in the north with Caen in the east, and running parallel to all the invasion beaches. Taking the city would ensure linkup of the Americans at Utah and Omaha, and provide a launching point for the push deep into enemy territory south. Generals Eisenhower and Bradley both knew they must soon seize Carentan to make the invasion stick. The very outcome of the war stood in the balance.

Thus the period of June 9 through 11 had become a time of preparation for Fox Company. Serious fire fights were less common. Reconnaissance patrols were frequent. The last of the stragglers from mis-drops on D-Day wandered in to rejoin their units. And the general activity was that of gradually moving south, re-grouping, and putting resources in place around the Carentan perimeter to further its capture.

NIGHT PATROL
Bill's True Tale

"You dummy!" I'm thinkin' to myself. "Lettin' Lieutenant Tuck hear you talkin' Kraut to Joe Flick: 'Hander hoch! Kommin zee mit mir!'" I don't get to go on enough patrols, do I? Gotta show off my smart-ass linguistics. Damn!.

I'm crawling along next to this Normandy hedgerow. Ever since Joe thought he saw something ahead we've been on our hands and knees creeping along. Never thought I'd spend such long night hours covering so little ground. Fortunately, or unfortunately, depending on your point of view I guess, Joe was wrong. But we're still down crawling. No Germans so far, just some Normandy cows peacefully grazing and chewing their cuds.

"Holy Christ, but it's dark," I say silently to myself for the umpteenth time. Just hope we don't run into any Krauts layin' low out here in these fields or behind a hedgerow waitin' for some dumb bastards like us to come stumblin' into 'em. Wouldn't that be somethin'? "Entire American paratroop patrol captured by heroic German soldiers in battle for Normandy." There's a headline for some Nazi propaganda.

FREEZE! It's suddenly bright as high noon on a sunny ski slope as a flare bursts above us. The training command to "FREEZE!" and make like a statue hits my mind, and I do just that. Joe is frozen too, not wanting to make any motion by turning to see what the other guys are doing. I pray that they remember our training as well. This is our first exposure to a night-time flare experience in combat, and it is terrifying. Our best hope is that it's an American flare by some unit that didn't know we'd be out here tonight; otherwise we're dreading the distinctive sound of the German machine gun. Luckily we're still on our hands and knees making less of a silhouette, and thus also close to the ground if the frightful brrrrrp of the rapid-fire Kraut guns open up.

Each slowly passing second seems an eternity as the silence remains unbroken. We're okay—we're okay—I'm prayerfully thinking as the flare finally flickers down and out, returning the blessed darkness.

We hold a brief, hushed parlay and conclude that it was probably some flare-happy GI who has hopefully been castigated for the unauthorized daylight. Lt. Tuck says "Okay, let's go," and we move on.

I think back to how the whole thing came down this morning. Joe and I were shootin' the shit about the lousy fruit bar in the breakfast K-Ration and drinkin' coffee. Joe whipped out his copy of the handy little German guide to useful phrases, said "Hander hoch," and I hadda shoot right back with "Kommin zee mit mir." It's practically all I know. Almost my complete damn German vocabulary, except for asking where's the toilet. We had all learned that in both French and German.

And so who came walking up just at that very second? First Lt. Andrew H. Tuck, the Third, that's who. (The "f...in" Third when he wasn't in earshot.) He of the military school, gung ho, spit and polish.

"Hey, Flick, True," he'd said. "You guys sound more like Krauts than Fritz himself. I need somebody on point for a reconnaissance patrol tonight. It'd be good to bring back a prisoner, too. Guys talkin' German like you two are just the ticket. Which one wants to come?"

I looked over at Joe. Joe looked back at me. Hell. Seemed like we'd both been on patrol damn near every day since the jump. But a night patrol? It's unsettling and weird enough being way out in front of your lines in daylight. But it's got to be even more frightening in the dark, I'm thinking.

Joe and I both took a look at Lt. Tuck., then looked at each other again. Then we both chorused at the same time "Okay, I'll go."

"Hey that's great," Tuck said. "I can use you both."

Joe Droogan, our platoon medic, had been standing around, silently watching this exchange. After Lt. Tuck left, Joe almost fell down laughing.

"What's so damn funny?" I asked.

"I knew soon as Tuck asked which of you wanted to go you'd both end up on patrol."

"Yeah, well," Flick had said, "it was probably that bastardized German song you taught us back in England that got us into this mess anyway. I hope Tuck brings you along tonight, too. It'd serve you right."

I wasn't really in a singing mood, but maybe just to get my mind off of the coming night, I broke into the first verse of Droogan's song.

Mine hond on mineself, und vass ist dass here?
Dass ist mine schvett boxer (head), schhool teacher dear.
Schvett boxer, vicky, vacky, voo, dass vass ich leaarn in
    schhool.

Both Joes had joined in by then and the second verse continued.

Mine hond on mineself, und vass ist dass here?
Dass ist mine schnoot bloozer (nose), schhool teacher
    dear.
Schvett boxer, schnoot bloozer, vicky, vacky, voo, dass
    wass ich leaarn in schhool.

Mine hond on mineself, und vass ist dass here?
Dass ist mine schinnvisker (chin), schhool teacher dear,.
Schvett boxer, schnoot bloozer, schinnvisker, vicky, vacky,
    voo, dass vass ich leaarn in schhool.

Mine hond on mineself, und vass ist dass here?
Dass ist mine schvannstucker (penis), schhool teacher
    dear,
Schvett   boxer,   schnoot   bloozer,   schinnvisker,
    schvannstucker, vicky, vacky, voo, dass vass ich leaarn
    in schhool.

As usual, the last verse about the schvannstucker was
sung with extra vigor and vibrato.

I wonder how much longer Lt. Tuck's gonna want to keep
wandering around out here in the boonies. It's blacker than
midnight on a coal barge, and crawling along I put one hand
right into a big, wet pile of cow flop a ways back. I'm still
trying to rub it off. Because of the darkness and the need for
silence all seven of us have had to stay much closer together
than normal just to keep from losing contact. We're all
doubtless enjoying the same wonderful aroma.

At last we're back walking again, trying our damnedest to
keep quiet. Flick's in front, I'm next, with the Lt. bringing up
the rear, occasionally whispering word up the line as to
direction. We've surely covered several miles of the fields and
woods in front of our lines, even with crawling some of the
time. I can't even see the face of my watch, but it's got to be
at least two or three hours since we headed out.

"Pssst, TyTy." It's Joe Droogan, who ended up
volunteering for the patrol after all. He's been right behind
me the last hour or so. "Tuck says this is enough. We're
headin' back."

I "pssst" Flick and give him the word. On the way back Joe says "Goddammit, TyTy! With all that crawlin' around tonight, especially after that pile of cowshit we slithered into, I was half wishin' we'd get to use our Kraut stuff. Maybe bring back a Fritz or two."

I say to Joe, "Yeah, uh huh. Well, you can keep the German and I'll stick to French. Some time I want to try 'Voulez-vous couchez avec moi' on some French mademoiselle, and just hope *she* surrenders. That would beat the hell out of taking a Kraut prisoner any day."

ᔥ   ᔥ   ᔥ

By the morning of Sunday, June 11, Fox Company was bivouacked south of the Douve River. It was a day of rest and recuperation. Field kitchens were set up and the men received hot meals. Religious services were held. Captain Mulvey made an informal inspection of the troops and when he got to True he paused.

"Looks like you could use a shave there, fellah."

For foot soldiers, maintaining personal hygiene in the field is not an easy thing to do, but it *is* an important factor in overall morale. Mulvey was merely doing his job, in a friendly way. By now, though, the troops had been through some fairly harrowing times, had gotten to know each other under very stressful conditions, and were in a mood to take liberties that would have been inappropriate before Normandy. Pfc. True, in a cocky mood, answered back, "Camouflage, Captain. This way the Germans can't see me."

Mulvey suppressed a chuckle. "Yeah, right. Let's shave it off anyway, OK?"

"Yes, sir!" was the reply, no sarcasm in his voice. But Bill thought his new growth was starting to look pretty good—

red in color and coming in nicely now after nearly a week of benign neglect. Using his standard issue safety razor, with water heated in his linerless helmet, he gazed into the polished tin mirror and made up his mind: the goatee would stay. Thereafter neither Mulvey, nor any other officer, criticized him as long as the rest of his face looked like he had been paying attention to it. His new beard would prove to be an identifying feature not just in Normandy, but to at least one young woman working the streets of Piccadilly Circus, upon his return to England.

There was also time to write letters home, and Bill did so. It became a hallmark of all his correspondence to be brief, and transmit few details, while reassuring everyone that he was alive and well. Later this was not always easy. His father in particular pumped him at length for all the gory facts he could get. But the development of "V-Mail" helped Bill in this regard.

Every soldier and sailor who ever served has learned the importance of mail from home. The Allied Supreme Command certainly knew its positive effect on morale. But tons of paper moving back and forth overseas was a logistical problem. Most shipping space had to be reserved for getting men and war materiel to Europe in the quickest way. As a result, a specialized form of letter was developed for the troops: V-Mail.

A paper form was used to write a V-Mail letter. It was one page long, with a limited space to write on, and only one side could be used. The soldier filled in the address, and added his message in the body of the letter. It then went to a specialized facility where it was photographed, reduced in size, and shipped to the United States as a negative. Once there, the negative was printed on paper and delivered via the Post Office to the addressee. Loved ones at home received an envelope approximately 4.5" x 3.75," marked on the outside "WAR & NAVY DEPARTMENTS—Official Business." The envelope also stated "Penalty for private use to avoid payment of postage: $300." Inside was the letter itself, or more accurately, a small photographic copy of the original.

The paucity of writing space made it impossible to say more than a few words in any one letter. This worked well for Bill. Never big on writing, he nevertheless wanted as many letters in return as he could get. V-Mail let him faithfully correspond, without consuming lots of time or effort.

On June 11 he wrote the following and sent it off:

"Dear dad mom and kids,

"Bon Jour. Comment alley vous? Am I fluent with my French or am I? I haven't received a very good impression of France as yet. It's too much like England with all the rain, etc. However I'm doing fine and dandy. This is Sunday and I went to Church this afternoon. I'd like to read the paper you'r (sic) reading today and find out what's going on over here.

"Say dad, this is the only V-mail I can get so I wish you'd drop a line to Aunt Mary and Jeannie and tell them I'm doing O.K. Jeannie's address is Miss Jean Bryan, P.O. Box. 427, Hamlet, N.C. Well I guess I'd better say Au Revoir for now.

"Love, Bill"

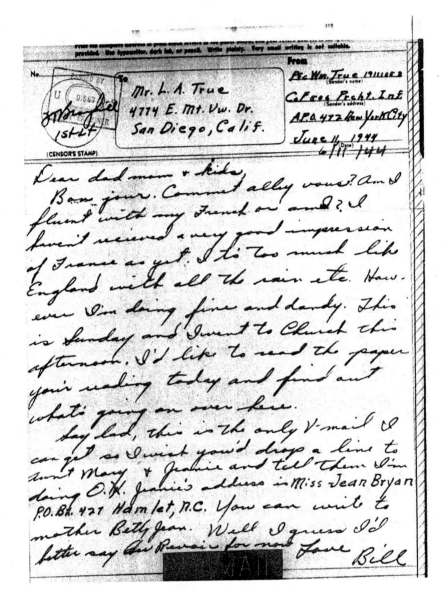

June 11, 1944 V-mail from somewhere in Normandy, France.

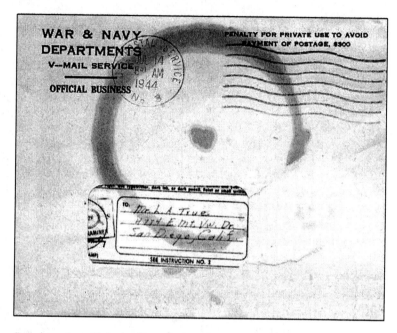

Envelope in which the V-mail shown on the previous page was sent after being processed in the States. Note the cancellation, "U.S. Postal Service No. 3, 8:30 AM, Jul 14, 1944," just over a month after the letter was written.

At mid-day, True joined the others for a hot lunch at a hastily set-up field kitchen. The food was good—some of it from captured German rations. Near the end of the meal an excited trooper ran up, breathless, with scary news:

"Hey guys, I just heard the Germans are using gas bombs! Find your masks, quick!"

This caused quite a stir. Most of the men, like Dude Stone, had earlier discarded their cumbersome masks. Now a number of the troopers quickly finished eating and left, to scrounge for protection against this terrifying menace. Bill noticed that Stone left with the others. Pfc. True, ever the cautious one, allowed the slightest smile to cross his face and calmly continued eating. He *knew* where his mask was.

The rumor turned out to be false.

                   ꝏ   ꝏ   ꝏ

Though unaware of details at the time, the men of the 506th were now part of a master plan to shortly capture the town of Carentan. Their bivouac west of the city had nearly completed its encirclement by other units, many of which had already been engaged in heavy fighting. Having been granted a day or so of rest and recuperation, the regiment was chosen to lead the final push into town in a pincer movement coordinated with the 327th glider unit.

At 2100 hours on June 11, General Taylor, commander of the 101st Airborne Division, met with Colonel Sink at his Command Post and issued the final orders. The 506th would move south-east to Hill 30, link up with the 501st to surround the city, then drive directly north into the heart of Carentan. The attack was scheduled for 0500 next morning.

Bill True, and others of Fox Company, led out at the scheduled time along the main road into town. They met machine gun fire, but it was merely harassing, and no other serious resistance was encountered. Other elements of the second battalion, which followed, had a tougher time. German artillery had zeroed their guns on the main road intersection out of the city, and Easy Company took several casualties as they advanced. But heavy action in previous days had apparently convinced the Germans to concede Carentan for the time being. Around 0700, Fox Company met up with glidermen from the 327th, moving down from the north. The pincers closed and Carentan was theirs. All that was left was a house-to-house search, confirming that the enemy was gone.

Bill and the rest of his squad was assigned to search

buildings surrounding a main square. At the center was a monument to World War I veterans. Around the square were a hotel, some shops, and other commercial buildings. Searching these was a new, and at first, scary task. No one knew what they might find. But a thorough search was essential to make sure all resistance had been eliminated.

Moving door to door, rifles at the ready and hand grenades in easy reach, the troopers moved through. Occasionally force was needed to enter, other times they merely walked in cautiously. But early on it became apparent that the Germans had left. Gradually the soldiers relaxed, and the clearing of the town became more routine and calm. By 1000 hours Carentan was declared officially secure. Colonel Strayer of the 506th, 2nd Battalion, and Colonel Allen of 3rd, 327th, met in town and immediately found a wine shop. A bottle was opened and shared in celebration of the victory.

∂   ∂   ∂

The fall of Carentan to the Screaming Eagles was the most significant Normandy conquest to date. Although the Omaha and Utah beachheads had technically been linked two days before, the line of troops between them was still thin. And the only good network of roads and rail lines in the area ran through this important hub. Division headquarters knew that it was vital to hold the city, and also that a major German counterattack could be anticipated—probably from the south-west. On the afternoon of June 12, the 506th got orders to push out the defensive line in that direction. Stone, Flick, True, and the others moved down the main highway toward Douville and near its outskirts, they dug in.

Some regimental units began to encounter German resistance, portending the fight to come. However, Fox

Company found itself in an area that, temporarily at least, was quiet. After completing his foxhole, True wandered back to the platoon command post to chat with others and see "what's up." Stone was there too. "Guess we're out of the mortar business, huh?" Dude said, remembering Jackson and his crippling D-Day march which left the mortar tube in a ditch.

"Yeah, I guess we're just riflemen for now," True observed. Though technically part of a mortar squad, he was armed only with his M-1 and a handful of grenades. If any action were to take place, these weapons would have to do. But the army would certainly find alternative and necessary tasks for everyone in the days to come.

Returning to his foxhole, Bill found an unsettling sight. Sitting squarely in the middle of it was a rat. A *large* rat. And it gave him the "willies." Ever since his boyhood days delivering newspapers to the tenements in Omaha, Nebraska, he had had a morbid fear and loathing of the vermin. Once, he had even encountered a menacing pack which appeared ready to attack him. They scattered at loud shouts, but the memory was vivid and powerful.

Ordinarily, a soldier in combat is loath to fire his weapon except when shooting at an enemy. Shots fired immediately alert everyone nearby that some action is taking place, and a false alarm is extremely undesirable. But True wasn't thinking about that. Without hesitation he aimed his rifle and fired in genuine hatred. The high powered bullet made quick, but messy work of the creature and Bill felt an involuntary shudder rack his bones. The thought crossed his mind that it may have been the only enemy he had killed in the war so far. He abandoned the hole rather than clean up the remains.

Shouted questions from nearby foxholes were answered with reassurances as Bill, cursing, began digging once more.

Everyone again settled down into their defensive positions.

Next came an unexpected experience. Traveling down the road was a horse-drawn cart. A farmer, the family patriarch, was at the reins. Next to him was his wife and in back were several young children. As he approached Bill's position the farmer stopped, got out, and unashamedly urinated by the side of the road. He then calmly climbed back to the driver's seat and continued on.

By civilian standards in America this was shocking, and True reacted with a typical American's disapproval. "Jeez," he thought, "right in front of his wife and daughters and everybody. Don't these people have any shame!?" This was the first, but certainly not the last time, that Bill would encounter the "European" attitude toward natural body functions. It was something that he finally accepted, but could never fully adopt for himself.

ತಿ   ತಿ   ತಿ

Not long before midnight, June 12, regimental commanders met in Carentan to assess the situation and make plans. German activity in the south-west had convinced them an attack was coming, and that was the logical sector from which to expect it. Together, Colonel Sink and the others came up with a strategy: with the 506th as right flank, and 501st on the left, they would drive outward from Carentan, extend the Allied front, and hopefully beat the enemy to the punch before they could mount a real offensive. Artillery would begin a softening-up barrage at 0430 next morning, with the infantry moving out at 0500. But what the American leaders could only surmise was indeed fact: the enemy planned an attack in the opposite direction, at the same location, and at almost exactly the same time.

Carentan, France, June 6, 1994. Bill True in the town square on a 50th anniversary tour, with the World War I (and now World War II) monument that stood there when his squad searched the buildings around the square after taking the city in June 1944. A photo of the monument as it appeared at the time was published in the July 3, 1944, edition of *Life* magazine.

Chapter VI – Rat Killin'

Fox Company moved out on schedule, but it soon became obvious that something was amiss. First harassing, then later more serious machine gun fire was encountered. They began to see enemy troops and armored vehicles in the distance passing them and moving in the opposite direction, toward Carentan. The fighting became more furious and confusion mounted. Soon True and others of the first platoon, Fox Company, found themselves in the fiercest fire fight they had yet seen, and it was only beginning.

Stretched out along a hedgerow, the troopers faced a line of German infantry some 200 yards away, in the area of a small rise. The hedgerow was a stout one: five to six feet of sloped earthen berm, topped by light shrub and occasional trees. The berm made a formidable defense, as the men lay prone and protected against it's rearward slope, their eyes just peering over the top to see the enemy in the distance.

Having discarded their mortar on D-Day, Bill's squad found themselves filling in wherever needed, with him working as second gunner on a .30 cal. air-cooled light machine gun. The weapon's tripod just topped the berm. Ray Aebischer, the first gunner, would do the shooting while Bill crouched on the left side, feeding belts of ammunition from a can: 250 rounds to each, tracers every 5th cartridge. Ten feet to their right was Joe Flick and next to him Dude Stone. Fifteen or twenty feet down the row to their left was a small tree and on the other side of it Johnny Supco and Don Davis took up rifle positions. As they readied for the fight, German gun fire cut the leaves just over their heads, bullets ripping through the hedge.

Ray peered into the distance and spotted 5 or 6 soldiers crawling up an embankment. "Here we go!" he shouted to be heard over the rising commotion, and racked his bolt to chamber the first round.

"You sure those are Germans and not *our* guys?" True asked. Ever since nearly attacking Johnny Jackson on the D-Day jump he'd been leery of "friendly fire" accidents. The thought of killing American troops scared him almost as much as combat itself, and he felt a little queasy at the possibility.

"Damn right they're German, I can see their helmets. Look where they are. We don't have anybody out that far!" shouted Ray. He began firing. True fed the belt.

Ray was an expert gunner. It was the reason he, out of the 12-man squad, was the #1 trigger man. Firing short bursts of 5 or 6 rounds, he smoothly stitched the ground up and down the slope 200 yards away. One by one, as the stream of bullets reached them, the soldiers stopped moving. No sooner was the last man killed than solid proof arrived that they were surely Germans. An enemy tank appeared above the rise where they had been scrambling to get away from Aebischer's onslaught. It immediately began firing at the Americans' hedgerow.

High-velocity rifles, as well as big guns such as the 88mm on German tanks, fire projectiles that travel much faster than the speed of sound. Hollywood movies have convinced most people that they will hear the report—the "bang"—of a gun before the bullet reaches them, but this is not so. Supco, Davis, Stone, True and the rest could tell when the tank had fired not by its sound, but by the flash of light at the muzzle. They instantly ducked behind the protection of the berm as the shell exploded in front of them. It was followed by a series of shots, and the volley was soon joined by that of other tanks coming over the rise. Fox Company was in real trouble.

Rifles and light machine guns do little damage to tanks, but having nothing better, the troops shot back as opportunity allowed in between the canon fire. Muzzle flash—duck behind the row. BOOM! Red-hot shrapnel tore the air, making a "whizzing" sound, as dirt and debris rained down on them. Pop up, fire a few rounds, then another muzzle flash—drop behind the row. BOOM! Another shower of dirt and deadly metal shards. And though the earthen berm that protected them was substantial, it was no match for a sustained barrage. Soon casualties began to mount. To his right, Bill heard Dude Stone cry out in agony as shrapnel tore open his left calf. Droogan soon found him and bound the wound, trying desperately to stanch the bleeding before too much was lost.

The German tanker was experienced and battle-hardened and knew the tricks of his trade. Now he sent a round into the branches of the tree to Bill's left. This "tree burst" caused the shell to explode above the ground, spreading its blast and shrapnel over a far greater distance, and past obstacles that otherwise would block its effect. The sound was deafening and everyone was dazed for an instant or two before they could recover. Davis and Supco did not recover. Concussion from the blast immediately above had killed them instantly.

Soon, even though they had stood their ground, the troopers knew the defensive line could probably not be held unless the German tanks were stopped.

A soldier came down the row with new orders. "Fall back to the next hedgerow!"

Fall back? Retreat? Though they'd never heard such a command before, there was no sense of panic. It was just another order like any other: "spread out, go left, head right, do this or that." But the men would have to cross an open field between hedgerows, and that in itself was risky. Bill joined Joe Flick at Dude Stone's position in the hedge. Stone had received a field dressing for his wound and a styrette of morphine to dull the pain, but was alert and conscious. "Dude, come on, we'll help you back," said True.

"No. You guys go on. I'm real slowed up—don't want to cross that open ground like this. I'll be OK here."

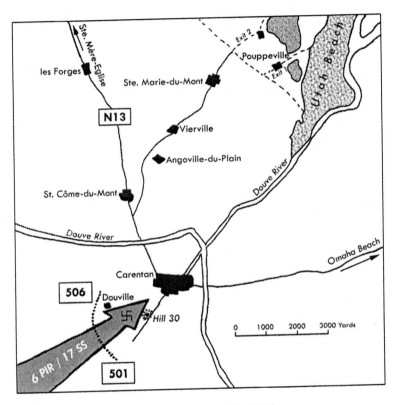

German Counterattack, Carentan, June 13, 1944

Under the circumstances this wasn't an entirely irrational decision, and it was his to make. Dude Boy Stone was older than the other two, and always had an air of confidence that was compelling. He was cool as a cucumber, brave and resourceful, and even Flick as squad leader looked up to him, seldom arguing with anything he said. With Dude adamant about staying, True and Flick left him in place and fell back. Dodging hails of machine gun fire, they reached the safety of the next hedgerow, and the first man they came to was Sergeant Gordon Mather.

"Where's Stone? I saw him get hit!" said Mather.

True and Flick explained what Dude had said. At the time, the decision to leave him had made sense, but now it began to appear questionable.

"Goddammit! You should have *made* him come with you!"

Gordon was generally considered one of the best, if not *the* best, soldier in the company. His condemnation of their action cut deep. Guilt began to rise.

Later, during a lull in the action, Stone was helped back by Doug Roth, a man from Fox Company Headquarters. Both True and Flick breathed heartfelt thanks that their brief lapse of judgment at the forward hedgerow had not led to disaster. Dude would be back to fight by their side in future battles.

ཉ   ཉ   ཉ

The battle raged throughout the afternoon as the Germans mounted a skillful and massive counterattack to re-occupy Carentan. Fox Company had taken the worst of the tank barrage and, even though forced to withdraw, acquitted themselves well. Ultimately the battle WAS decided by armored vehicles but it was the Americans, and not the Germans who prevailed. At 3 p.m. the troopers heard the first rumblings of big, beautiful Shermans. It was the 2nd Armored Division, and the tanks were followed by waves of infantry, fresh from landing and ready for their first serious combat. Though action would continue for another day, the German counterattack on Carentan was broken. Linkup of

Utah and Omaha beaches was at last secure. By the afternoon of June 14, Fox Company was relaxing in town, and lining up at the local wine shops for some much-needed "attitude adjustment."

For the next two weeks, the men of Fox Company continued to hold their defensive position south-west of Carentan. There was little real action but plenty of patrols and, especially, outpost duty. It was stressful to march several hours on patrol, never knowing what might be encountered, but standing outpost seemed to many an even more onerous duty.

OUTPOST
Bill's True Tale

"Come on, TyTy, we got outpost duty again tonight, and it'll be dark in another hour." It's Joe Flick, buck sergeant and squad leader of the third squad. He's talking to me, the last member of his squad left to lead.

It's late June, 1944, and it's been about three weeks since we jumped into Nazi-occupied Normandy. Three weeks that were supposed to be three days. All of our training, preparation, equipment, supplies, and ammunition for the D-Day invasion had been predicated on a swift assault that would be intense for seventy-two hours, following which we would return to England to prepare for another mission. The classic use of paratroopers.

So much for the classics.

"Again, for Christ's sake? Have we turned into some kind of expert outposters?" I'm shaving with cold water in my wash basin helmet as I answer Joe. Damn! There goes another razor snag, and I'm bleeding like my jugular's been slit. The bloody face staring at me in the crimped tin mirror adds no cheer to my thoughts of the coming night.

"I argued my ass off," Joe replies, "but some of the third platoon are going on patrol in another sector, and I don't know what the hell the second is doing. At least Lt. Tuck says we can take two guys from the first squad with us so it won't be just you and me like last time."

Our ranks are really thinning out. Even though the 506th hasn't made any offensive moves for the last week or so, defense of shifting fronts takes its toll as well. Joe and I were comparing notes just yesterday. Of the sixteen men bunking in our Quonset hut in England, six have now been killed and seven wounded. Lousy odds.

I'm thinking of night patrols as well as other outpost assignments during the last three weeks. Don't know which I dread most. We've lost men on patrols and none from overrun outposts. But at least patrols don't last all night and you're always on the move.

"Tuck told me G-2 expects the Krauts to hit somewhere on the 506 front tonight," Joe says, squatting on his helmet and lighting up a Fleetwood. What lousy cigarettes. They hold an ash for an inch and a half, and taste like a mixture of rotten rope and bull shit. Whoever makes 'em must've gotten to the K-Ration people 'cause they're in every damn box. "And if the Krauts come in on us, we're supposed to make enough racket and throw so much lead we can convince 'em, at least for a while, that our outpost is the main line. Sound like fun?"

"Oh, hell yes, a regular blast," I answer. "Can we get George and Linus and their machine gun from the First Squad?"

"Yeah, I pushed Tuck real hard to give us the best

machine gun team, and one of them will also have a sub-Thompson. I'll have my sub too, and you can bring the BAR. We'll have enough automatic stuff to create a real fuss."

"Listen, Joe, I'm not lookin' forward to this one damn bit," I say. "Tuck's been after us like a duck on a June bug ever since he found out we learned those few words in Kraut. He knows damn well our being able to say 'Hander hoch,' and 'Kummin zee mit mir,' ain't gonna make a f...in' bit o' difference on outpost."

"That's for damn sure," Joe says. "I may bitch so loud the C.O. hears it if Tuck doesn't spread the shit details around a little better from now on. But tonight's a done deal. I'll go get George and Linus geared up."

∂   ∂   ∂

I've finished oiling and checking out the BAR, and have all the ammo I want to carry for 200 yards or so. Some of the jaw-breaking chocolate we jumped with and a couple of K-Ration fruit bars may suffice for chewing during the long night hours. I'm hoping to hell it'll be long quiet hours. Images of the alternative churn my gut.

It's nearly dark as the four of us head out for a hedgerow and small strip of trees about 175 to 200 yards to our front. We're walking slow and silent and pausing every fifteen or twenty yards to listen and look around. We finally reach the hedgerow. It's now blacker than Coaly's ass, as some of the boys from the Pennsylvania coal mine area are wont to say, and a cold drizzle has started.

Joe sets George and Linus up near the right edge of the trees, and he and I find a spot about twenty-five yards to their left.

The drizzle turns to downpour, and back to drizzle again.

Phantom Germans bending and trotting with their burp guns at the ready fade in and out of the wet blackness. Shadowy sounds of Kraut boots silently stalking seem to intensify and then diminish as the rain shifts between drips and deluge.

"Did you see that? Did you hear something?" Whispered exchanges between Joe and me have yet to confirm real enemies before us. I slip over to check with George and Linus. Same thing. Lots of fearful images and fancied sounds—even some smells, but nothing real. That's what four tired troopers on outpost are praying, anyway.

A long, long, long night. I'm shaking my head and kicking my ankles to stay alert. Dead tired and soddenly sleepy, with my life perhaps at stake in staying awake. A memory I'll take to the grave—hopefully a distant time from tonight.

"Christ Almighty, TyTy, don't snore so goddamn loud," Joe hisses at me.

"Sorry Joe, I'll watch it," I answer. My head had jerked and awakened me just before Joe spoke—I'd have sworn I'd been alertly peering into the dark.

The night is slowly receding as slight slivers of light pierce the thinning rain clouds. Dawn builds as bright shafts of sunlight paint delicious yellows and oranges and reds across the sky. Last night is gone—it's today—we're still here—one more time, we're still here.

Joe and I head over to George and Linus. Their smiles are like Christmas morning and a new red bicycle. "Hey, Joe, TyTy, we did it. How about that? The Krauts must have heard we were out here, and knew they'd better not attack," Linus exults.

"You damn well betcha," Joe answers. "Let's give 'em a burst or two so they'll know they used good judgment."

Linus and George are laughing excitedly as they level their machine gun and let fire. Bang! No burst, just one bang.

George cocks and fires again. Bang! Just one round. A third and fourth time, same thing.

"Must have been that all night rain," Joe says. "Give us a burst with your BAR, TyTy. That'll wake people up."

"Sure enough," I say. I set my bipod, aim at the enemy, and lay on the trigger. Bang! I cock and squeeze again. Bang! Again and again I get off one round.

"Well, for Christ's sake! Linus, let's at least let 'em hear some chatter from our subs," Joe says, as he faces out and fires. Bang! Joe is crestfallen as he repeatedly fires one round at a time. Linus, too. Not one of the automatic weapons will fire more than a shot at a time.

The four of us silently exchange long looks of bewilderment, wonder, and awe.

❧ ❧ ❧

We're back in the platoon command post and Lt. Tuck asks how things went.

"No sweat," Joe replies.

"That's great!" Tuck exclaims. "How'd you guys like to take it on again tonight then? Captain Mulvey wants all the patrol and outpost duty to be volunteer from now on."

"Maybe some other time," the four of us chorus. Oh yeah, I'm thinking. When pigs fly, when they're ice skating in that hot place down below, and when officers are all gentlemen—that's when I volunteer.

❧ ❧ ❧

On June 27 the VII Corps had finally taken complete control of the city of Cherbourg at the north end of the peninsula. At about the same time, elements of the 101st began moving in that direction for the assignment that would complete their campaign in Normandy.

True and Flick fell in for a day's march and somewhere along the way they managed to snag a copy of "Stars and Stripes." This was an important means of information, and of boosted morale, that troops eagerly sought. But when Joe read the lead story his jaw dropped and he let out a string of cuss words that was vehement, even by paratroop standards:

"Goddamn it, look at this! Says here the f...in' RANGERS captured Carentan!! Hell, they weren't even in our sector! Can ya beat that?"

True was philosophical.

"Hey, *we* know what happened at Carentan, and so does the Army. Don't let it get ya down. In fact, it's so wrong I almost want to laugh." But he didn't laugh. Instead, as he often did, Bill chose to sing, and Flick joined in as they danced a little jig, marching down the road. To the tune of "Skip to My Lou," they began, "Rangers took Carentan two by two, Rangers took Carentan two by two, Rangers took Carentan two by two, Skip to my Lou my darlin'"... Soon the rest of the platoon had joined in, and spirits were high once again.

Rangers took Carentan... what a joke!

By 2100 on June 29 all elements of the Screaming Eagle Division were together in one place, which hadn't happened since D-Day. It was in the town and surrounding area of Tollevast, 4 miles south of Cherbourg. Their remaining mission was to hold defensive positions covering the northern third of the peninsula, from a line running east and west through Montebourg. From then until mid July the men saw increasingly less of patrol and outpost duty. Finally, on July 10, relief began to arrive. True and the rest of Fox Company were replaced on the line with brand-new, green troops, whose awe of their combat-proven brethren was quite apparent. The paratroopers were now the elite, tested soldiers who had proved that Germans were not the supermen their leaders had described. At the foxholes along a hedgerow, the new replacements took their places with a little apprehension, though all was quiet. Slightly swaggering, True and his buddies boarded trucks for the trip to a bivouac area behind Utah Beach.

Next day Captain Mulvey assembled his troops at the boarding ramp of the LST that would take them back to England, and commenced calling the roll: last name by Mulvey, answered by each man calling out his first name, serial number, and rank.

"Flick…"

Answer.

"Lovell…"

Answer.

"True…"

Answer: "William, 19111058, Ranking PFC."

Mulvey just laughed at the joke—as if "ranking PFC" *meant* anything! But others shouted in good natured derision. "Bullshit!" came from Zerby, who actually had been PFC longer than True. They were safe and headed back to England for a good rest, and nothing would dampen their spirits that day.

The ride across the channel was a peaceful one. When they arrived, each man returned to the Quonset hut in which he had lived before the invasion. Each Quonset had housed 16 men. True looked around and counted heads of those who had returned unscathed from Normandy.

Including himself, there were three.

CHAPTER VII

Long Drills and Short-Arm Inspections
The Lull Between Storms

> "All quiet on the Potomac tonight,
> No sound save the rush of the river,
> While soft falls the dew on the face of the dead—
> The picket's off duty forever."
> Ethel Lynn Beers
> 'The Picket Guard,' 1861

———————

Getting back to Aldbourne, England, was almost like going home. It had been F Company's Army home for nearly nine months; to this point, the longest they'd been in one spot yet. The familiar drill field and Quonset huts seemed welcoming indeed after the long days and weeks fighting through Normandy's hedgerows.

Entering their hut at the far end of the camp Bill True, Joe Flick and George Lovell realized that they were the only three unscathed survivors out of the sixteen who lived there just six weeks before. Johnny Jackson had received knee injuries on the Normandy jump and was evacuated early on. Now healed, he was waiting for them on their return from France. But four men in a barracks meant for sixteen leaves lots of lonesome space.

"Guess I'll take my old bunk," True said, just to break the deafening silence that all the vacant bunks declared.

"Yeah, that's what I did," Jackson added. "Are you guys all that are coming?"

Johnny hadn't received any word of F Company

casualties. Flick gave him the bad news. "Yep, we're it. Hopefully two or three of the guys that just got wounded will get back sometime—I sure as hell hope Dude gets back before long—but six of the guys won't be joining us, ever."

Bill filled Johnny in on the details of the Normandy campaign as Company F saw it. There was a lot to tell. Later, the two of them decided on a walk to the mess hall just to kill some time and see what the cooks were brewing up. Passing the hut that served as their recreation room, they ran into Norm Davis. Norm's brother Don had been a long-time member of F Company and had jumped with them in France. Norm was with an engineering outfit stationed near Swindon. His unit had not gone across to Normandy yet, but he'd heard the rumors that the 506th was returning today from their first combat campaign. He was naturally anxious for word of his brother.

"Hey Johnny, TyTy, great to see you guys," Norm greeted them cheerfully. "Where's Don?"

Don "Pedro" Davis had bunked in the same Quonset hut with True and the others before the invasion. Of the original 16 men who shared those quarters, six had been killed in action. Tragically, Don was one of them. Jackson and True were now stunned to realize that they would have to break the sad news to his brother. After a pained silence of several seconds Bill managed to mutter "Gosh, Norm, I'm afraid Don isn't coming back." He didn't elaborate.

Norm appeared to take the news in stride. Small talk ensued about the various actions in Normandy. Finally, Davis said he'd like to talk with others of the 1st Platoon, and headed off for the company huts, seemingly in good spirits.

True was completely nonplussed. Continuing their walk to the mess hall he said to Johnny, "Man, I've never had to tell anyone about the death of a close relative. Guess I didn't get the story across too well, huh?"

"Yeah," said Johnny, and his voice just trailed off. "You know, I'll never forget that great time you and I had with Don back in Rock Hill. He was one hellova talented guy, and this outfit is really gonna miss him."

"That's for sure," Bill replied. "God, I'm feeling worse now than I did the day Don was killed."

It was a common enough reaction among men who had just tasted combat, and True was feeling it in spades. In the heat and fury of battle there is little time to mourn the dead. The job at hand takes first priority, and sorrowful emotions seem to automatically get put on hold, only surfacing much later. But now, facing the brother of his fallen friend, Bill got a big helping of guilt and sorrow all at once. It would not be the last, or even most powerful, dose. That would come some 50 years hence as he laid flowers at headstones of friends he'd known and loved as brothers in arms.

Later, as they returned from chow, True and Jackson passed by Gordon Mather's hut. Through the open door they could see that almost the entire surviving remains of the 1st Platoon had collected there. Entering, they saw Norm Davis seated on a bunk. There were tears in his eyes as Gordon explained quietly but directly how Don had died during the German counterattack outside Carentan.

Hearing this, Bill was now certain that Norm had misunderstood his earlier words, thinking his brother was merely injured and wouldn't be coming back *right away*. Mather, the best soldier in the platoon, was older and wiser than Bill. Gordon knew what the others would only learn through bitter experience: really bad news, such as a death in the family, must be conveyed clearly and succinctly to be heard. Denial is the first line of defense for a grievously wounded soul. It was a painful lesson for all.

~   ~   ~

The next morning, their first back at Aldbourne, started as a most happy day. Sergeant Willie Morris announced that seven-day furloughs were being granted to every man in the company, and the line up for back pay would begin at 1000 hours.

The rush to clean up, lay out dress uniforms and polish jump boots to a brilliant shine was on. Even the overload on the hot water didn't slow things down. Cold showers and shaves were happily endured as the laughing troopers prepared to blow off a long accumulation of pent up steam.

Most of the men planned to go to London, although a few were bound for Scotland and various cities around the island. Someone had told Tom Alley that Edinburgh was a jumping town, and that's where he, E.B. Wallace, Linus Brown and Otto May were headed. But Johnny Jackson and Bill True decided on London. They had both been there before, and they knew that it was the place where wine, women and song were readily at hand.

A truck into Swindon and the train to London got the two of them into Paddington Station well before nightfall. Catching the tube to Piccadilly Circus, they were ready for their first night of celebration.

As they walked down the heavily trafficked center of Piccadilly they passed an attractive young woman who called out to Bill in an enticing voice "Hi there, Ginger."

True was still wearing the goatee he had grown in Normandy. It was quite red in color, and from this he got the connection with her greeting. The woman was good looking and smartly dressed, but it was obvious that she was a "lady of the evening." Johnny and Bill had already decided that on this trip they would not stoop to engaging professionals for female companionship. They just returned the "Hi" and continued on their way.

At the counter of a below-street-level restaurant, Johnny was waiting for his fish and chips when he noticed a pair of women at a nearby table. With friendly smiles the two kept glancing his way. Soon he and Bill were carrying their food and pints of half and half over to the girls. Johnny asked if he and Bill might join them.

"We'd be delighted," one of them quickly responded as Johnny sat down across from her. Her companion smiled at Bill and gestured to the seat next to Johnny. They were in their mid-twenties and neither of the women were raving beauties. But they were nicely dressed and, on second look, weren't all *that* bad looking. The troopers were satisfied they had chosen wisely for their first dates in town.

Brief introductions were made all around, followed by mundane small talk. Gwen and Stella were their names. When the preliminaries were out of the way, the women asked if maybe the Yanks would like to go dancing. Johnny had been to Covent Gardens on a previous trip to London, and knew the way. It was a popular dance hall, usually crowded with servicemen and their girls. All agreed that another round of half and half would be good before leaving. It was then that the boys learned how well their new companions could hold their liquor. A jigger of gin seemed appropriate to go with the beer. That was followed by two more, and the foursome left their restaurant well lubricated and eager for the athleticism of a jitterbug dance floor.

It quickly became apparent that both Gwen and Stella could not only drink their share, they were very good dancers as well. Bill and Johnny were barely able to keep up with them. The guys could do a bit of jitterbugging, sort of, but the women had obviously done a lot. They could and did swing with the best of the Yank soldiers on the floor. Soon the paratroopers were exhausted and ready to find another form of entertainment. But the girls were still up for more partying... and drinking.

So to their astonishment, the guys found themselves escorting the women to yet another watering hole. In a nearby pub they joined a raucous crowd singing bawdy English songs. The foursome joined in, singing and drinking with gusto. But there were other agendas on the table, at least in the minds of the soldiers. Finally, during the third round of gin and beers Bill broached the subject of the night's lodging. Apparently speaking for them both, Stella allowed as how there was a hotel in the neighborhood where the cost of rooms wasn't "too dear." Bill was delighted to see Gwen, his date, nod agreement with a sly smile. So that was it! The boys knew now that the goal posts were in sight and they were about to score. It was a good thing. Much more drinking and they'd have trouble even *finding* the uprights. So off they went.

The hotel wasn't exactly the Astor, but it seemed to be clean and the beds were comfortable. The couples took two adjacent rooms.

Bill and Gwen wasted little time getting down to business. She was good in bed, though not spectacular and her techniques definitely got the job done. Naturally True wore a rubber. But since she wasn't a "professional" he skipped using the full pro-kit that all the soldiers carried. "What the hell, she's just a fun girl out for a good time like me," he thought. "What's the harm?"

When they were finished with their post-coital cigarettes, Gwen began what seemed to be a novel, even strange ritual. As Bill lay on his stomach she began sliding her hands lightly across his back, cooing softly. "Oh, here's a blackhead, dearie. Mind if I just pop it for you?" Bill had no objection, though it seemed an odd thing for a woman to do. Soon she was going over his entire back and chest, intently clearing his skin of blemishes. It reminded him of how the monkeys in the San Diego Zoo conducted their grooming rituals. He had never experienced this kind of attention before, but she was taking such delight with every squeeze that he began enjoying it too. Gwen was still murmuring "Ooh, 'ere's another one, luv," when Bill drifted off to sleep.

After an early breakfast next morning the girls thanked the men for a lovely evening, and explained that they had to get to their jobs. "We're working girls, you know, and we're 'elping out in the war effort," Stella explained.

When they'd left, Johnny and Bill got to speculating on the kind of work they might be doing. "Well, they didn't charge us for sleeping with them," Johnny offered. "But I wouldn't be surprised if they sometimes make a few bucks that way."

"Yeah," Bill said, "they were sure an easy score. Maybe sleeping with lonely Yanks on occasion is how they're 'elpin' out in the war effort. I'll bet they're not working on a production line at a munitions factory."

Later that morning the two ran into Vince Ochipinti who'd been to an American movie the night before. "You guys have to see it! It's called 'Up In Arms,' and there's a guy named Danny Kaye in it. He's funny as hell!"

In the next few days they *did* get to see the movie. Both agreed it was a great comedy. And they also took a city tour which Bill knew he should do. That way he could write home about something constructive he'd done in London. The trip included a visit to the Tower of London, St. Paul's Cathedral, Hyde Park, and other famous landmarks. Ordinarily he would have thought this was pretty boring stuff—kind of like "paying his dues." But surprisingly, he found it was an enjoyable change of pace from their continual bar-hopping. Afterward, Bill sent a picture postcard of the Houses of Parliament home to his dad on which he wrote: "You and your Toastmasters should be over here in Hyde Park. A soap box is all you need and you can talk all night. They do it too."

❧   ❧   ❧

On the morning of their fourth day in London, Bill was startled and chagrined to find that urination was painful. A yellow discharge confirmed the bad news. He headed for the American Red Cross building in Piccadilly Circus that also housed a prophylactic station. The soldier technician on duty took a sample of the discharge and soon confirmed that Bill indeed had gonorrhea—a humiliating "dose of the clap."

The technician interviewed him about his sexual encounters. This was a standard part of the Army's V.D. Control Program. Bill told all he knew about Gwen, and the details of their encounter. She was the only woman he'd had sex with. The tech just shook his head. He was obviously less than sympathetic. "Hey, man, you know rubbers alone aren't enough to stop that stuff! Get smart next time, alright?" This was more than a little embarrassing. The standard pro kit included a potent antibiotic cream that was very effective. How many times had he been told that? True asked himself

After the necessary paperwork was processed, one of the pro station techs brought a jeep around and drove Bill to a hospital in another part of London, where he was admitted. There was a whole ward of soldiers there, all with the same medical problem. Minutes after arriving, True received the first of many penicillin shots: the latest answer to gonorrhea.

On his second day in the hospital Bill got into an argument with one of the nurses. At question was the issue of rape: civilian women attacked by soldiers. True maintained that Americans generally treated all civilians with respect, even though there were obviously exceptions. But the Germans, Russians, Japanese, all were known to abuse their captive populations. The nurse stoutly maintained that all men are alike, really just pigs in uniform. Nothing would convince her that soldiers of foreign armies were any worse than Americans. Bill concluded that working on a V.D. ward may have colored her judgment. There was no point in continuing the dispute.

Following the third day of Bill's stay and just before he was to be discharged from the hospital, they showed a Bing Crosby movie for the troops. "Going My Way" was the usual, highly entertaining Crosby film. But True thought this particular one had a message. He didn't know if any of the others on the ward noticed. In it Bing sang a top hit song that won the Academy Award that year. The tag line of the whole piece advised everyone that "you can be better than you are—you could be swinging on a star." Had someone up in headquarters decided these men needed some moral guidance? Who knew? But it sure seemed right on target for this group of guys.

After they returned from furlough the men of Fox Company were switched around in their Quonset hut assignments. No reason was given for the change, but the troops all knew it was to minimize the psychological impact of losing buddies they'd bunked with before Normandy. A trickle of replacements began arriving, soon becoming a flood. This, too, helped the company to move on. And with the new replacements came the inevitable heavy training regimen. Overnight problems as well as daylight field maneuvers became common, in part to bring the incoming officers up to speed. But the exercises also helped teach the new recruits at squad level how to function as a team with the seasoned combat veterans.

Whenever they weren't involved in field problems, the men spent most of their time at the firing range. Everyone was included; riflemen, machine gunners, bazooka crews, and other specialists. In addition, new and sophisticated explosives were introduced, along with tactics for their use. One of these utilized a primer detonation cord that was very precise. True and Flick got to arguing over who could time their explosions best, down to the split second. On a bet, True lost and had to make up Joe's bed for a week.

Despite the constant activity, in most ways it was a period of calm which led Bill back into his Sunday routine of writing home. As was his habit, his V-Mail letters were always brief, speaking mostly of the weather, training activities and passes into town. No mention was ever made of his brief hospital stay in London, of course. And he had always been vague about his Normandy combat experiences. His dad continued to press him for details about those actions, but True was determined not to worry his folks. Whenever he spoke at all of such things he kept to generalities such as "a little shooting, and a lot of dodging."

A letter home written on August 6th, 1944 was fairly typical and contained the following comment about the mustache and goatee Bill had grown in Normandy. "I'm still cultivating my mustache although I had to get rid of the beard. It's [the mustache] getting out where I can twist the ends now, and really looking sharp. They call 'em R.A.F. mustaches over here."

In their sparse free time the men listened to the Armed

Forces Network radio broadcasts for news and entertainment. It aired from early morning till late every night. For his part, True began following a singing contest between Bing Crosby and Frank Sinatra. It was a real musical duel. Songs by each of the crooners would be played and then the listeners were asked to write in and say which man sounded best. Bill was surprised when he found himself liking Sinatra better. Crosby had always been a great favorite with him from early childhood days. His mother was an avid fan and had played Bing's records frequently. It felt a bit disloyal to prefer Sinatra, but his opinion was supported by the soldiers, who voted strongly in favor of Frank. In the end, Sinatra won.

By contrast, listening to German radio occasionally provided real laughs as Axis Sally and Lord Haw Haw broadcast their crude propaganda. It was always especially fun when Bill's own division and regiment would be named, along with dire predictions of what the German soldiers would do to them upon their return to the continent. Such was morale among the troops that these segments brought guffaws of laughter, instead of the intended dismay.

Sally always leaned on the sentimental side. In dulcet, sympathetic tones she bemoaned the fate of the poor American soldiers so far from home, forgotten and abandoned by their countrymen who enjoyed the good life back in the states. "Your wives and sweethearts are sleeping with all the 4-F profiteers. And here you are fighting and dying for them. What a shame." You could almost see the fake tears welling up in her eyes.

Bill had to smile at the preposterous notion. He was certain Jeannie Bryan, his 17-year old sweetheart in North Carolina, would never betray him like that. But on reflection, he feared that some of the older men in the company might

283

be vulnerable to this psychological attack. The married guys in particular seemed to show signs of doubt as Sally cooed her poison over the airwaves. But overall the German effort to demoralize the troops was a complete bust, at least as far as the 101st Airborne was concerned.

❧   ❧   ❧

One day Tom Alley burst into True's Quonset hut with hot news from company headquarters. "You guys hear the latest?!! Mulvey just got relieved as company commander. Not only that, Willie Morris isn't top kick any more. *He's* been busted to *buck private*. They both get shipped out today!"

"What the hell's that all about?" asked Flick, with stunned disbelief.

"I don't know anything official. But it sounds like something to do with our company fallback at Carentan. They say maybe the captain didn't clear it with Battalion before he ordered us to drop back to that second hedgerow."

"Yeah, I remember that did seem a little strange at the time," True said. "The Krauts were kickin' us good in that counterattack, no doubt about it. But it looked to me like we were holdin' our own—even if it was just our small arms against their tanks. Going backwards was sure a new experience for F Company!"

"That's what I thought, too," Joe Flick added. "But I figured it was just some tactic to re-group, or do somethin' else."

"Well whatever it is, I'll tell you this," Alley said. "There ain't nothin' fair about poor Willie getting busted while the captain gets to keep his rank!"

"Yeah, that's right!" Flick almost shouted. "Goddam! If anybody takes the heat it should be the f...in' company commander, not the sergeant!"

"That's just like the Army," True said. "The officers get the gravy while the enlisteds get the shaft! Who're we getting as replacements?"

"Lieutenant Tuck is acting company commander for now," Tom said. "Don't know who's gonna be first sergeant."

"Shit!" Joe exclaimed as he slammed his fist into bunk.

It was a sad turn of events for Fox Company. Morris was well respected and liked as a fair, but firm top kick. The men trusted his judgment and looked up to him as both a leader and protector. And as a commissioned officer even Mulvey was admired, despite his rank. But the disappointment was short lived. Soon all thoughts on the matter were submerged in heavy training and extensive field exercises. The war ground on.

      ❧   ❧   ❧

The *Stars & Stripes* frequently ran stories about the various USO shows, and all the movie stars and performers who were entertaining the troops. The big names were pretty much limited to appearances in London, with only minor revues getting out to towns and villages like Swindon and Aldbourne. F Company did enjoy some of these lesser known acts though, and True was especially delighted by one. It featured a cute young woman who sang a tune he'd never heard before, now wildly popular in the States: "Mairzy Doats." It was pretty simple, and Bill memorized the melody and lyrics right away. Soon he was bugging everyone in the barracks with almost non-stop renditions. It got to be sort of a fun game. Whenever things were dull and he wanted to get a rise out of his buddies, he'd just pick up his ol' Kalamazoo and start in: "Mares eat oats and does eat oats, and little lambs eat ivy…" The general moaning and groaning that followed was entirely predictable.

Some time in August, headquarters set a policy of liberally granting midnight passes into Swindon. They also provided convenient truck rides back and forth from camp. One memorable night True caught a ride into town and headed for a USO dance at the local hall. There he met a local woman named Pat Ball and was immediately smitten. She was a pretty girl and she wore a striking blue dress. As soon as he spotted her across the floor, Bill walked right up and asked her to dance. She accepted, and as they introduced each other, she said "That's really my name, and not a game." When he told her about his unit, and their recent exploits across the channel, she responded with exactly the right words: "Oh, how heroic!" That was it. He knew then and there she was a prize.

In the remaining few weeks that the men were in England, True went into Swindon to see Pat as often as possible. War-time double daylight savings meant it didn't turn dark till after midnight. As a result, the Aldbourne men had to be on their trucks for the return trip to barracks while it was still light. Good night kisses might linger, but the broad daylight did tend to cramp a romantic style.

While in England, Bill learned to love the traditional English fish and chips. It was served in a folded newspaper cone—a nifty example of English economy in scarce times. He especially liked the sprinkle of vinegar, which was new to him. The chips place in Swindon was located near the spot where the Aldbourne trucks dropped and picked up troops. Like many businesses, war-time shortages meant they were frequently out of fish. But on the nights when supplies were plentiful, the ride back to camp was a real pleasure as the men munched their midnight snack.

        ❧   ❧   ❧

As the month of August wore on the 506th experienced the first of what would become several aborted missions. Packing up and preparing their gear and weapons for a jump beyond advancing Allied lines in France, they got as far as trucking to the marshalling area only to have the operation scrapped. Patton's tanks and American ground troops were moving very fast across Europe. More than once, they overran the planned drop zone before an airborne attack could be implemented. For Bill and his buddies this naturally brought a mixture of excitement, disappointment, and relief.

In the midst of this activity, on August 28th the regiment held a memorial service for the men killed in Normandy (see Appendix A). It took place at Littlecote—an English estate that had served as regimental headquarters for the 506th from the time of their first arrival in the Wiltshire countryside. It was a fitting and impressive site for such a ceremony with its imposing manor house and expansive grounds. Though it was not distant from Aldbourne, most of the F Company men had not seen it before.

General Taylor and Colonel Sink both gave thoughtful and respectful talks about the heroic departed. The regimental chaplain offered a prayer. Thankfully these preliminaries were relatively brief since the roll of the dead was very long, and citing each trooper took considerable time. Bill True didn't know most of the KIAs personally of course, but each time the name of an F Company member was called his emotions were deeply stirred. This was especially so for those who had been with him from the beginning days at Toccoa, and whom he knew as friends. Most gut-wrenching were the names of Privates First Class Richard K. Buchter and Don Davis, Lieutenant Freeling T. Colt, and Private John

Supco. The solemn affair ended with a haunting rendition of Taps by a lone bugler.

August 31ˢᵗ found the 506ᵗʰ again heading for the marshalling area at the Membury Airdrome. At these times the food was always excellent: steak, mashed potatoes and gravy, pie and ice cream, the works. These personal comforts helped ease the tension as the men received final briefings and prepared for the upcoming combat mission. Unlike the several before it, this one looked like it might really come to fruition. But then, just hours before the scheduled takeoff, the mission was again called off. The objective had been in Belgium and this time it was the advancing British troops who overran the targeted terrain. There was always some sense of relief when a combat action was cancelled, but everyone knew the high command wanted to get their crack airborne divisions back into the fray. Some time soon they would definitely jump into action and not return to the comfort of their Aldbourne Quonset huts.

ॐ   ॐ   ॐ

RAINCOATS AND JUMP BOOTS
Bill's True Tale

"Why in the hell would they schedule a short-arm inspection on a cold, rainy morning like today?" I'm asking myself. It's early in September, 1944, and we just got back a couple of days ago from another trip to the Marshalling Area for an airborne mission that got called off. The whole Allied offensive appears to be moving faster than anyone can keep track of.

Sergeant Ochipinti just stuck his head in the door and yelled "Fall out in five minutes for short-arm inspection!

Raincoats and jump boots!" He didn't need to add the uniform requirement, since short-arms have called for "raincoats and jump boots" since that first inspection for venereal disease back in Toccoa, Georgia, in 1942.

As I strip down to bare-ass except for my boots, and get my raincoat out of the footlocker, all of the other guys are moaning and complaining, too. "Who's had a chance to get a dose lately anyway?" Joe Flick mutters. "Maybe the battalion doc is just getting bored and these damn short arms give him something to do."

As we fall into company formation wearing our clammy skin-clinging raincoats the chilly rain picks up. Marching the several hundred yards to the medic's hut we're getting really chilled, and the organs about to be "inspected" are shriveling to peanut size.

Lining up to take our turns exposing our privates to Major Kent, I'm reminded again of one of my biggest and longest "standing" gripes about the Army—the standing in line. Beginning with my first days, it's been one line after another. Line up for shots, line up for chow, line up at the PX, line up for a movie, line up for pay, and on and on and on. I've vowed that if I ever get out of the Army I'll never wait in line for anything ever again.

Much of the lining up to wait is done in order of rank and alphabet. Back at Toccoa I remember feeling sorry for Private Roy Zerbe, dead last to collect his pay in those early days. I wasn't much better off with a last name beginning with T, but he and I did improve our positions considerably when we made PFC.

It's raining even harder as I get closer to the door to enter, and I'm really shivering. My apprehension is also starting to rise. The dose of clap that I got in London in July is completely cured as far as I know, and I've already passed one of these inspections since then, but what if it should suddenly flare up?

I'm finally standing in front of the doc and he says "Well, soldier, milk it down and let's see what you've got there." I squeeze my penis and push my fingers forward. Whew! Thank God, nothing comes out! "Okay, you're alright, move on," he says, as I thank my stars and head back for the barracks.

Johnny Jackson and I have a pass till midnight tonight, and we're heading for a town we've not visited before. It's not far outside Swindon, and somebody told Johnny there's a pub in town named the Fox and Hound that is frequented by lots of uniformed women.

When we arrive at the pub we're most disappointed to see a sign that says it's off limits to American soldiers. "Wonder what the hell is the reason for that?" Johnny asks. "I don't know," I answer, "but I don't see any MPs around, so what the heck."

Sure enough there are uniformed females all over the place, and only a few British soldiers. After a few beers Johnny and I are singing up a storm right along with them. We've learned several of the raucous pub songs the English enjoy and join in on one of the favorites.

Oh, 'e touched me on the knee, oi was shimed oi was,
'E touched me on the knee, oi was shimed oi was,
'E touched me on the knee, oi says "You're rather free,"
Oh, Cor Blimey oi was shimed oi was.
Oh, 'e touched me on the thigh, oi was shimed oi was,
'E touched me on the thigh, oi was shimed oi was,
'E touched me on the thigh, oi says "You're rather 'igh,"
Oh, Cor Blimey oi was shimed oi was.
Oh, 'e touched me on the spot, oi was shimed oi was,

'E touched me on the spot, oi was shimed oi was,
'E touched me on the spot, oi says "you're rather 'ot,"
Oh, Cor Blimey oi was shimed oi was.

Before we're able to get another song going, a crew of MPs enters and spots Johnny and me. They come over to where we are and one says "We'll have to see your dog tags, troopers." They're actually pretty courteous, not at all belligerent, so we show them our dog tags. Noticing Johnny's purple heart, they're almost apologetic as they tell us we'll have to be reported. "We have to take you to the bus station, too," the non-com in charge says, "those are our orders for any Americans found in here."

As the group of us are walking to the bus station I ask the MP sergeant why that place is off limits to Americans. "I don't know for sure," he replies, " but someone heard that a quartermaster lieutenant got mugged there last week, and it's been off limits ever since."

❧   ❧   ❧

Acting C.O. Lt. Tuck has just called Johnny and me into his office. The MP was true to his word and reported our off limits violation. "I want the two of you to take your entrenching tools and dig me a five by five by five foot hole. When you're finished come and tell me and I'll check it out."

Johnny and I are heading back to the barracks to get our entrenching tools and I say: "Man, that's one big hole. It'll take us the rest of the day."

"Yeah,' Johnny replies, "but the lieutenant had to do something in the way of company punishment. It's really a lot better than a weekend on KP or Latrine Orderly duty. He's taking it pretty easy on us."

We've been digging for a few hours now, not very vigorously I'll admit, and the hole is slowly growing. "This would sure go a lot faster with a real spade or shovel," I'm grumbling as I toss another small amount of dirt with the entrenching tool. For combat purposes though, these new tools are an improvement over the old set-up where every other man would carry a small pick and his partner a small shovel. Now, at least, each man has his own tool that folds to serve as a pick, and then can be opened up and locked to work as a small shovel.

"Sure would," Johnny says, "but if it was that easy Lt. Tuck might have given us some other and probably lot worse punishment. What if he'd said 'No passes for a month, you guys?'"

"We're not likely to be here in England for another month, anyway," I reply. "I'm betting in the next week or so one of these airborne missions is going to be for real and we'll be long gone."

It's getting close to dusk and I suggest "Maybe this hole is big enough that the lieutenant will buy off on it. I'll go get him and we'll try our luck."

Lieutenant Tuck is looking our hole over with a jaundiced eye. "That doesn't look like a five by five by five to me," he says. It's actually about three and a half feet wide, nearly the same depth, and almost five feet long.

There's a painful pause as Johnny and I look at each other, and then down at the hole. After a bit I look at the lieutenant and say "Well, maybe it's not quite, sir, but you'll notice it's definitely a lot longer than it is wide."

Lieutenant Tuck is almost smiling as he gruffly says "Alright then, cover it up, but stay out of those damned off-limit places from now on."

It's dark as we finish filling the hole. I'm thinking about

the difference between Lt. Tuck and that S.O.B. Sobel the E Company guys were stuck with for a long time. "You know, Johnny," I say, "some officers really may be gentlemen, after all."

$\approx$ $\approx$ $\approx$

On September 13th word came down that another mission was scheduled. Packing got under way to head for the marshalling area the next morning amidst speculation that this one would be for real. That night someone in the 2nd platoon got a crap game going and Bill True decided to join in. It had been a while since the men had been paid so there wasn't a lot of money around. But those with a few pounds decided they wouldn't be needing it for some time anyway. Why not risk it on a game of chance.

Right from the start Bill's luck with the dice amazed him. Time after time he made his points. It seemed the only break was when he threw natural 7s and 11s, as his stack of pounds grew and grew. When he finally crapped out, the dice passed to the next trooper. Now True laid low, waiting till they came around to him again. It wasn't long before bad luck for the others had brought the galloping dominoes back.

"I'm coming out with five pounds," he announced, his third time with the dice in his hand. Willard "Red" Sharp took two pounds and three other guys from the 2nd Platoon took a pound each. True rolled a seven right off the bat and there was general moaning.

"Where the hell did those dice come from?" someone from the 3rd Platoon groaned. "If they belong to True I want to see 'em."

"These are Red's dice, I think," Bill responded, "but if anyone else has a pair let's have 'em." Another set of dice was produced. "OK, the ten pounds rides if any of you are dumb enough to bet against me!" he said.

It took the five remaining shooters to come up with enough money to cover the bet. Bill rolled an eleven, and that was it. The game ended with everyone broke but the one winner, and the men dispersed to their Quonsets.

Bill was undressed and about to crawl into his bunk when Red came in. "I scraped together another three pounds," he said. "You won all that money with my dice, True, so you ought to give me another crack at it."

Bill was agreeable and Red took first turn with the dice, rolling for a pound. He threw boxcars for a loser, bet another pound and rolled a ten. Bill said, "I'll give you two to one for your last pound on that ten." Red agreed, and immediately crapped out with a seven. He picked up his dice and trudged back to his barracks.

The pounds Bill had won converted to nearly $500 American money—a very sizable sum indeed. Next morning he sent almost all of it home. The battalion Red Cross lady, Polly, arranged to wire it to his dad. She also agreed to hold onto his guitar until the next mission ended. As it turned out in the end, the money got home all right but the fate of his Kalamazoo guitar would prove to be less happy.

When the trucks pulled out of Aldbourne on September 14th heading for the Membury marshalling area it was really goodbye to the little English village that had been their home for nearly a year. "Operation Market Garden" would be a go.

CHAPTER VIII

A Narrow Road Too Long
Holland: Operation Market Garden

"Audacious, audacious, always audacious!"
General George S. Patton, Jr.

Operation Market Garden was, indeed, an audacious plan. Its lofty goal was that of ending the war in Europe by Christmas. This would be accomplished by first a lightning-fast invasion of Holland, securing a highway north for tanks and artillery. Next would come the massive pouring of troops and materiel across the Neder Rijn (Lower Rhine), and into the heart of Germany's industrial strength: the Ruhr valley.

Surprise was the key element. To achieve it, an entire army of airborne soldiers was assembled: the first and only such force ever in the history of warfare. In all, 35,000 paratroops from the American 82nd and 101st Divisions, and the British 1st augmented by a Polish unit, were to be dropped along a narrow corridor running the length of Holland. They would take and hold the road connecting Eindhoven in the south with Arnhem in the north. But most important were the bridges along the way. Those were the links that *must* be held long enough for the British XXX Tank Corps to break through the line in Belgium and rush north to secure the invasion path. If even one bridge were lost, the entire plan could be endangered.

Audaciously planned, it required above all else audacity in its implementation. Paradoxically to some, it was the brainchild of Field Marshall Sir Bernard Montgomery, who was widely believed to be the very least audacious of all the

Allied generals. This gave many an uneasy feeling, right down to the lowliest troops of the line. If only Patton could lead the charge, they thought, the plan might indeed work. But Patton was busy tearing through Europe, nearly outrunning his own supply lines in a miraculous string of victories. And Ike, for reasons of his own, had made up his mind to trust "the Hero of El Alamein," Monty.

Holland

For Bill True and his buddies in F Company, the operation would be as different from Normandy as night from day—quite literally. While the June 6 D-Day was a terrifying leap into fierce resistance and the unknown darkness of pre-dawn, this drop would be made in broad daylight with little or no enemy troops waiting. The jump in France had been preceded by hours poring over sand table mockups. For Holland there was an effective, but surprisingly curt briefing. The task was simple for the 506th: upon landing just west of Zon, the troops would assemble and move immediately to take the town and its bridge across the Wilhelmina Canal. This bridge, and that at Eindhoven, were the southern anchor of the highway north. Farther up the road the 82nd would take Nijmegen, and the British had the honor of the northern cap at Arnhem.

Company F was well-prepared after two months of recuperation in England. Replacement troops had filled out the ranks since Normandy. Training had continued, of course, but it was designed more to maintain an edge, than to whet one from scratch. Several missions had been planned and gone so far as transport into marshaling areas, but they were all false starts. Patton's tanks were moving so fast even paratroops couldn't keep up.

Then finally on September 16 the troops assembled at Membury airfield, not far from Aldbourne, ready to go. This time it looked like the real thing. The men were issued Dutch invasion money, as strange and colorful as the French. Final briefings were conducted for a jump the following day, and it was clear that this was a new and different kind of operation. Gone was the desperation of "take no prisoners." In its place was enthusiasm and a hopeful "one last push to end the war, and then we can all go home."

If only it were so.

September 17, 1944, dawned effulgent, presaging a beautiful Indian summer day. Civil War buffs among the troopers might have observed that this was the 82nd anniversary of the Battle of Antietam. It was the bloodiest single day of the war in which the most Americans in history had lost their lives. Doubtless it was best that the coincidence of dates and implications were not noted and dwelt upon.

Bill was anxious as he dressed for his second combat jump. But he was now a veteran and there was confidence, too, in his mind. Most of the guys seemed to have the self-assurance that comes from having "seen the elephant," the term used to denote combat experience. All, that is, but Jerry Ransom†, who had jumped with them in Normandy. He was somehow "off." Avoiding others, his behavior was furtive and circumspect, almost like a caged animal. No friendly greetings to his buddies as they passed; eye contact avoided. True hoped it was only pre-jump jitters and would pass. The job was stressful enough without the added baggage of debilitating fear.

Assembly and loading at the plane was very different than in Normandy. First, there were new parachutes, of English design, with an innovative quick-release harness—no fumbling to get unstrapped once on the ground. There was far less equipment to haul this time around. Lighter now, troopers easily climbed aboard the waiting planes unassisted; a welcome discovery indeed. Consequently there would be far fewer jump injuries in Holland than in France. And this time, they carried rifles pre-assembled and ready to fire. No more clumsy struggle to get a weapon into action, leaving the man vulnerable to attack. Any Germans encountered on the jump would get an immediate and nasty greeting.

Gearing-up on the tarmac next to the waiting C-47, suddenly Bill was startled by the sound of a rifle shot close by. Shocked by the unexpected firing, he and all the others looked for the source. It was a trooper in their stick.

Jerry Ransom.

His rifle had discharged into the ground, presumably by accident. But accidents aren't supposed to happen; not by trained soldiers and in close proximity to so much deadly hardware. A hush fell and hung in eerie silence for a moment. No answer came to the unspoken questions of all. Finally, with no other course of action before them, their preparations continued. Now there was an added nervous edge, not present before.

Strapping of chutes; loading of supply packs through the cargo doors; there was plenty of work to be done. Then, not a minute later, *another* rifle shot rang out! They looked around. It was Ransom again! What the hell!!?? This time the platoon sergeant investigated—he had little choice at that point. A private talk with Jerry was held out of earshot. There were hushed words and furtive hand gestures, seen by others but lending no intelligence. At last the non-com seemed convinced. Perhaps the urgency of take-off played a roll. He waved his hand and shouted for all to board and prep for launch.

It was a striking sight. The huge armada of planes was lined up, engines warmed, ready to go. Ferrying the men to Holland was the 82nd Squadron, 436th Troop Carrier Group. Fox Company lifted off the Membury airstrip at 1025, soaring over the green rolling English countryside to form up with others overhead in a seemingly endless string. People on the ground could be seen waving good luck: they knew instinctively this was an important operation, if only from the sheer numbers of men and machines. By now there was a warm connectedness between the locals and "their boys," who had come as strangers but now lived among them. The tide of war had turned, and these men had helped it be.

The ride across the channel was relatively uneventful. Through the small windows and the open cargo doors, men could see hundreds of other C-47s in the air nearby. And reassuringly, there were also fighter escorts. Mustangs and Thunderbolts zoomed and dived around them, in protective cover. It was a welcome sight indeed. Any Luftwaffe pilots who chose to engage would meet heavy resistance. But none appeared and the airborne army pushed on to the target.

Near the drop zone the calm ride ended. Anti-aircraft fire began, light at first and then increasing. The "krump" of bursting flak grew louder, more intense, until the command finally came: "Stand up and hook up!"

They were scant minutes from the drop now. Planes held formation this time, unlike Normandy, and the pilots had time to do the job right: cut engines back, raise the tail, give the guys in back a nice smooth exit. But there was no getting around the rough air caused by AA bursts. Standing, the men clung to their static lines for balance as the final equipment check was called and the plane lurched and bounced across the sky.

Suddenly there was a loud burst inside the cabin. Bill thought, "That Goddam Ransom! If he's screwing around with his piece again…" Jerry was behind him, not visible in the jump order of the stick. But it was not Ransom's rifle this time. A 20mm explosive round had struck the belly of the plane in mid-fuselage. True felt a sharp "tick" on his hand and, looking down, saw blood. No pain, just blood. Behind him, Ken Steinke fell to the deck, shrapnel cutting deeply into his back, blood flowing. There was little time for contemplation. The green light flashed; the jump master shouted "Go!" as he leaped out the door, followed by the entire stick in rapid order. Scant seconds later they landed in a plowed field north-west of Zon: Drop Zone "C." The time was 1315 on a bright and beautiful Sunday afternoon.

As airborne operations go, it was an almost perfect drop: orderly formations, light winds, soft earth to cushion the fall, and little or no armed resistance on the ground. But it was not "perfect" for everyone. After landing and releasing his chute, Bill looked up. In quick succession two C-47s were hit by AA and, streaming fire and smoke, augured into the ground a mile or so away. He saw few, if any parachutes exit before the planes hit and exploded in huge fireballs. A following pilot jumped his stick and all chutes opened but one. The hapless trooper streamered in, his shroud lines hopelessly tangled in a tight braid, and there was an audible "thud" as his body hit the drop field nearby. The sight and sound made Bill's stomach turn over.

True's injured hand now began to bother him. Still not very painful, it was bleeding profusely. Landing nearby, the platoon medic, Joe Droogan, saw the blood and came to help. He bandaged the hand expertly and then did something even more important: he penciled a note in his log. That entry later turned into Bill's ticket home.

⁊   ⁊   ⁊

Assembly on the jump field was smooth and efficient, considering the size of the drop. Nearly seven thousand men and parachutes had come together exactly where they were supposed to be! F Company was in order within minutes, men sharing their own versions of the landing. Bill met a trooper who had a tale to tell.

"Yeah, Ransom chickened out! Refused to jump and he's on his way back to Aldbourne, right now. Sure wouldn't want to be in his shoes when he gets there!"

Another soldier chimed in, "You know, I kinda thought there was something goin' on with him. Remember when he got wounded in France? Shot in the foot! I just wonder if maybe that didn't exactly happen by enemy fire." The speculation was never confirmed, but nagging doubts remained.

September 20, 1979, Royal Palace, Holland. A cocktail party was given for visiting 101st Airborne veterans and wives by Queen Juliana and Prince Bernhart. Jane True is shaking hands with the Prince, husband Bill is behind her (partially obscured) shaking hands with the Queen. Queen Juliana expressed some surprise at the name "True."

"He was acting squirrelly before the jump," Bill added, shaking his head. "Remember Normandy? He was real shook up at Ste. Mère-Eglise—saw Bill Hale all shot-up hanging in that tree, and Dick Buchter riddled in the town square. I think that stuff hit him hard, but what a lousy way to get out of action. I feel pretty sorry for him." This was met with mixed responses. Every man knew the risks he faced, yet all had volunteered. When a comrade-in-arms left the fold in less than honorable fashion it was a sad turn of events. At the

order, the men moved out. Zon awaited, and with it the
bridge across the Wilhelmina canal.

෧ꝏ   ෧ꝏ   ෧ꝏ

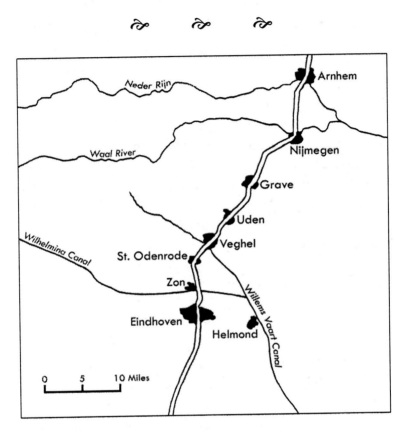

"Hell's Highway"

It was the job of the 506th PIR to capture Zon and secure
its vital bridge. Second Battalion led the way with D
Company in front, followed by F and E. Though no German
resistance had been encountered on the drop field, nearing
town it was a different story. Soon sniper fire began harassing
the men. On the outskirts of Zon, Company D found itself
face-to-face with two 88mm field guns defending the village.

Strength of the enemy presence was unknown, but it didn't matter. The artillery had to be taken out, and so the attack was on! Firing bazookas and Tommy guns, the Americans destroyed both guns and within 15 minutes had a clear path to the center of town.

Time was of the essence now. They had to secure that bridge before the enemy could destroy it. True joined the others in a quick-time march. Several hundred yards ahead were houses and shops—the outskirts of town. They were nearly there. Then suddenly off in the distance, in the direction of the canal, a loud explosion was heard. Wood, stone, and miscellaneous debris flew skyward over rooftops in spectacular destruction, and the men knew at once their first mission had failed. The bridge at Zon, one of the early points of crossing for the British tanks, had been blown!

True and the others were dismayed, but not disheartened. After all, there were objectives beyond that also mattered, and chief among them was the city of Eindhoven to the south. With little alternative, they began moving through Zon. But now their progress was slowed by, of all things, a celebration. The residents had filled the streets, rejoicing in their liberation. Four years, four months, and four days of cruel repression under the Nazi heel had finally ended, and it was as if Christmas, New Year's, and the 4th of July were rolled into one! Delirious with their newly-gained freedom, villagers pressed food, drink, and flowers on the soldiers as they passed along the main road. Troopers were hugged, and kissed, and asked to pose for photographs, even while sniper bullets zinged through the narrow streets from retreating German soldiers. This was in such stark contrast to France! The people of Holland were actually glad to see the Allied soldiers in their town!

It took little time for the residents to cull out

collaborators in their midst, as well. Scarcely an hour after the invasion, Bill passed a corner where two young women stood, faces bleak with fear and shame, while vengeful neighbors shaved their heads to mark them as "fraternizing with the enemy." Their future cloudy at best, it seemed a sad counterpoint to the raucous celebration reigning everywhere around them.

September 18, 1984, Eindhoven, Holland. Following the 40th anniversary jump made outside Zon, Holland, on the same field they jumped in September 1944, Bill True in full World War II uniform handing the Liberation Torch to Prince Bernhart after Bill had led the Liberation Parade in Eindhoven.

Finally arriving at the canal, the men could see that German demolition charges had destroyed most of the Zon bridge, but its center pillar was intact. Now it was the turn of the combat engineers to rig a fix for troops to cross. Salvaging wooden timbers found in the town, a rickety foot bridge was constructed that would accommodate the soldiers single-file. Slowly, cautiously, the troopers made their way one by one to the far bank. Finally, well past sundown, the last of the 506th gained the other side and with it, a clear path to their next target. In their wake a Bailey Bridge for tanks would be constructed, but the invasion path north would now be held up for many precious hours. And, learning from civilian intelligence that a German force in strength awaited them, Colonel Sink ordered that his men bivouac for the night at Bokt, one mile south of the Wilhelmina Canal. The liberation of Eindhoven would have to wait until D+1.

ॐ   ॐ   ॐ

It rained that night, which made the little sleep allowed wet and cold. But September 18 dawned bright and clear as F-Company moved out along with the rest of the regiment toward their objective. Loss of the bridge at Zon would mean a 36-hour delay in the entire operation, and this created real pressure to push ahead with the plan. Colonel Sink gave the word: "If you see any Germans just let them filter on through you. We have got to get to Eindhoven this morning and we can't waste any time killing Germans along the way."

The 3rd Battalion led the 506th into Eindhoven encountering first sniper fire, then artillery and mortars which brought them to a halt. The 2nd Battalion was ordered to swing around to their left, with F Company in a frontal assignment to flank the German forces holding up the advance. Of F Company, the 2nd Platoon became the lead element, with 3rd Platoon in support and the 1st in company reserve. The 2nd Platoon leader, Lt. Russell Hall, was assisted by a local Dutchman in pinpointing the location of one of the German 88's. The lieutenant soon had his squads attacking with rifle, machine gun and mortar fire.

A Dutch woman leaned out of an upstairs window and frantically pointed in the distance, indicating the location of Germans defending the 88. Soon the paratroopers had attacked and hit several of the enemy with rifle fire, but the big gun got off a number of rounds nonetheless. In fierce fighting, the Americans finally scored direct hits on the artillery piece, using mortars and rifle grenades. Shortly thereafter, the 88 and its crew were out of action.

Next a second German gun opened fire from a nearby street, and the troopers knew there was more work to do. Fire from this 88 was intense for a short time, but the gun crew quickly saw the futility of their position and intentionally blew the breach of their own weapon. Attempting to escape through an open field to the rear, all the German soldiers were shot or captured.

While this was going on, Bill True and the rest of the 1st Platoon heard the sound of the fighting while waiting to be called from their reserve position. The call never came. Finally word spread that all the German defenders in the area were dead, wounded or captured.

"By God, I'm through knocking those 2nd Platoon guys from now on," Joe Flick said to True.

"Well, maybe for a while," True responded, "but they'll tick us off again sooner or later. Gotta admit though, they sure did good today."

Fire fights with the Germans had hardly subsided before the people of Eindhoven filled the streets in wild celebration. Drinks, food, hugs and kisses were as rampant as the day before in Zon. By mid afternoon, True and his buddies had finally waded through the raucous throngs and reached their bivouac: a grassy area in what looked like an urban park. They had dug their foxholes and settled in to await further orders when surprisingly, a young Dutch girl—perhaps 12 or 13 years old—approached them and struck up a conversation. Her family lived nearby. Everyone in town was overjoyed at their liberation and wanted more than anything to give comfort to the invading troops, but what could she offer them? Suddenly she got an idea and quickly made off in the direction of nearby homes. In a short while she returned bearing two soft, fluffy pillows for Bill and his partner to furnish their foxhole.

It was a thoughtful and welcome gesture. It was also the first among many such kindnesses the paratroopers would receive. Coming days would bring invitations to dinner at civilian homes—a most inviting break from rations in the foxhole. In short order the bond was forged: Dutch and American friendship might well last forever.

That night, the Luftwaffe began aerial bombing of the town. In the morning, after a fitful night's rest, Bill True and Joe Flick drew a very interesting assignment.

‮ℰ‬   ‮ℰ‬   ‮ℰ‬

ON VOLUNTEERS AND DISPOSABLES
Bill's True Tale

"I'll lead out for starts, Ty Ty," Joe Flick says, "and we can switch off as we go."

"Okay," I answer, "but it won't make much difference. We're going to be way out in front and if we run into any Krauts it won't matter which of us is in the lead. We'll both be goners."

Joe and I have been given the dubious and distinctly undesirable honor of being scouts and leading our whole battalion, and likely the whole regiment as well, on a hurried and massive march toward a town named Helmond. It's apparently several miles from Eindhoven where we've been for a few days, and the word is that the Germans may be building up and preparing an attack from there. "Hit 'em before they're ready" seems to be the idea.

Flick has been busted down again, so our squad leader today is Blackie Wilson. He tells us to take off and we head down the dusty dirt road toward who knows what. Blackie picked Joe and me for scouts on this occasion for his own reasons, whatever they are. It could be that outside of Johnny Jackson, we're the only veterans left in the squad. The other five guys are all replacements and maybe too green for the responsibility. What the hell do you need to know, though, just to walk out in front of everybody and draw first fire?

Joe is hitting his distinctive, long-loping stride, hugging the right side of the road, with me about twenty feet behind him on the left. The rest of the outfit is seventy-five to a hundred yards behind us. Joe's carrying his sub-Thompson as usual, holding it by the grip in his right hand, while I've got my trusty M-1 rifle, also at the ready. There are shallow weed-strewn ditches on both sides of the road which we're prepared to hit in a big hurry if any firing starts. But just in case we see something to shoot at, our weapons are handy.

We've been moving maybe twenty-five or thirty minutes when Blackie gives a whistle and hand signals for us to stop. "Could be we're traveling too fast for the outfit to keep up with us, Joe," I observe.

"Yeah, maybe so," he says, "and I'd just as soon sit a while anyway."

"Remember that first patrol in Normandy that you volunteered us for?" I ask as I flop down beside Joe.

"Sure," Joe quickly responds, "but by God, there hasn't been any repeat of *that* dumb move."

"No, I guess not. But here we are out in front of the whole 506th anyway, and I'll bet some serious volunteering went into this, all the way from division on down."

"Yep," Joe says, "General Taylor calls the regimental commanders together to discuss this foray out to Helmond, and I can just hear our Colonel Bob Sink saying 'Let the 506 do it, General, we're ready and rarin' to go.'"

"Uh, huh," I chime in. "And then Sink has his commanders in for a chat and Strayer can't wait to volunteer the 2nd Battalion for the privilege of leading the regiment. On the parade ground he sticks his pants legs in his boots like some hayseed farmer, but out here in combat he's one eager-beaver soldier."

"Sure, but that's a damn site safer when you're volunteering from a battalion command post several hundred yards back," Joe says. We all used to laugh at Strayer's sloppy looks on dress parade back in training. "Do you suppose anybody is ever going to tip him off how to blouse his pants over his boots with condoms for garters?"

Now Blackie whistles and gives hand signals for us to move on, so we're up and going again.

We extend the discussion as we walk along, me in front now, and I continue. "Next, the company commanders meet with Strayer. Is anyone more likely than our own lovable 1st Lt. Frank J. McFadden, F Company's acting commanding officer, to be hot to trot? Not bloody likely, as the Limeys might say. He'd give his right arm to make captain. So he convinces Strayer that OUR company should be out in front."

"Right," Joe carries the story down another echelon, "then Little Mac gets his platoon leaders together and lays out the situation. Never mind Lt. Tuck's history of caution, he jumps in with a vengeance, volunteering the 1st Platoon to point the way into Helmond."

"Have you ever read 'Appointment in Samarra?' I ask Joe. "It's a novel by John O'Hara, mostly about fate. Kinda reminds me of the fix we're in right now. Maybe since the beginning of time there's been a destiny about you and me leading this expedition. Maybe Sink, Strayer, McFadden, and Tuck all HAD to volunteer today, and maybe Blackie Wilson didn't have any other choice but us for scouts."

"Never read the book," Joe says. "How do things come out?"

"Not so swift, as I recall. Come to think of it, I'm sorry I even remembered reading it."

Blackie whistles again, and this time he signals us to come back. We turn and walk back to the company and learn that the mission has been called off. Late intelligence has shown that there's a concentration of well-prepared Germans at Helmond, including panzer units. It's definitely beyond our capacity without tank support. A rapid return and deployment for defense of Eindhoven now becomes our objective, and no one is happier with the change of events than Joe and I.

I remember now that there was a short tale by Somerset Maugham in the introduction to O'Hara's book. It involved an individual's attempt to avoid Death by fleeing on a swift horse from Baghdad to Samarra. The character learns that he can't escape his destiny. His flight has only *insured* that Death and he keep their "Appointment in Samarra."

"A lot of volunteering took place today," I'm thinking, "but the two guys out front sure had no part in it. They were just the handy disposables."

Fortunately, Joe Flick and Bill True have an appointment in Eindhoven—not Helmond.

෨   ෨   ෨

In the next several days the 506th saw sporadic action in and around both Zon and Eindhoven. Some of this was in collaboration with British tank units, which was a new experience for the Americans. But then, on September 22, came word that a serious breach of the highway had been made by the Germans. It was at the small town of Veghel, and threatened to hinder, or even block, the entire operation. Something had to be done and fast. On the afternoon of D+5, the men of F Company were loaded into trucks to begin the 15-mile rush north.

They arrived by truck amid total chaos, traveling up the main north-south Veghel thoroughfare. German artillery shells fell everywhere around, in a constant barrage. Soon Bill's driver pulled off the main drag onto a parallel side road to the right, and braked to a stop next to a park-like area. As the men began exiting and unloading the trucks, the deafening sound of exploding shells and falling debris filled the air.

In the commotion Bill glanced to his left and saw an odd sight. One of the young lieutenants in the company was behaving very strangely. Short, good-looking, blond, was he 2nd platoon? Cartwright† by name? In any event, it was clear that something was not right. The lieutenant had a wild look in his eyes. He was frantically digging a foxhole by the side of the road, desperate to escape the shelling. But no orders had been given yet! It was *not* time to dig in!

There was no time for Bill to ponder. Soon the non-coms began passing the word: move north, sweep the town house-to-house for Germans and clear them out if found.

True and Flick were ordered to cross the main street to their left, and make their way up the west side of town on a small byway, checking homes and businesses for the enemy. Negotiating the boulevard, they looked up and saw an enemy tank a hundred yards away to the north, at the edge of the village. It was firing artillery and machine guns straight down the street directly at them. Bullets whizzed and cracked over their heads as they crouched and dodged across the cobblestones. In the middle of the street was an American anti-tank gun, probably a 57mm, firing right back at the Germans. "Geez, that sure seems puny compared with what the Krauts are throwing at us," Bill thought. The U.S. gun crew stoically stood their ground and never flinched as they continued firing. Their bravery was "beyond the call" in any soldier's book. But Bill and Joe had orders to move on.

Searching house to house was tedious and scary work. Rifles at the ready, safety off, live grenades handy just in case, they moved slowly through the village. Each home and storefront was another opportunity for a surprise German attack, though none had yet materialized. Eventually they found themselves near the northward end of town with but a few houses left to check. In a residential back yard, Bill saw an outside stairway leading down into an earthen cellar. He decided it had to be investigated.

Creeping cautiously down the dozen-or-so steps, he pulled a hand grenade from its snap. "Here's a likely German hideout," he thought. "Better roll this in just to be sure." But then just at the last minute something inside told him to wait. Returning the deadly pineapple to its place, he kicked in the door and raised his rifle to shoot, then stopped himself.

There *were* people in the cellar, but not Germans. The room measured 25 feet across, with earthen walls and a low ceiling. Dutch civilians sitting on crude wooden benches filled the entire space: mostly old men, women, and a few kids. They were shocked and frightened by the startling entrance of an armed intruder and cowered from him for a moment. But then the tension eased when they saw the American Flag on his right shoulder. Whew! Thank God Bill hadn't gone with his first impulse and pulled the pin on that grenade!

He gazed intently at the group. Not likely that a German would be hiding in their midst, but it's always best to check. Satisfied, he was about to leave when he noticed a different figure than the rest, way in the back. Sitting on a bench all by himself, with his head hung down, was Lt. Cartwright—no question of that. True didn't know what to think or do, so he did nothing. Having made no eye contact, or spoken a word, he turned and walked up the steps to ground level and open sky. "Poor guy really lost it," was all he could say to himself.

True and Flick never did find any Germans hiding in the town. Later it was learned that Cartwright had transferred to Graves Registration—a necessary function in war, but not the place of honor for a seasoned combat veteran paratrooper.

While True, Flick and others of the 1st Platoon had been engaged in the clearing and holding activities in the center of town, others of F Company were involved in intensive firefights on the outskirts. Action continued sporadically through the night and into the next day, September 23rd. Tanks, half-tracks and infantry were rapaciously attacking 2nd Platoon positions when "little" Orel Lev displayed a ten-foot sized courage in killing a number of the enemy attackers. His actions were later described in the citation awarding him the Distinguished Service Cross as follows:

"Orel H. Lev, 39252131, Private First Class, Infantry, United States Army, distinguished himself by extraordinary heroism in action. On 23 September 1944, his company was in action against the enemy in the vicinity of Veghel, Holland. His platoon was protecting the left flank of the defense when the enemy attacked that flank with three half-tracks, one mark

IV tank and infantry troops. The platoon was forced to withdraw, after suffering heavy casualties, but Private First Class LEV elected to remain and cover withdrawal of the platoon. Although exposed to heavy enemy fire, he fired his rocket launcher at the leading half track and killed four of the enemy. At this time, the fire from the tank became a very serious threat to the withdrawing platoon, since its fire was being directed by the commander from an open turret. Realizing this Private First Class LEV killed the tank commander and halted the advance of the tank. He then returned and gave invaluable information to friendly artillery whose effective fire disrupted the enemy attack. In a later action, while moving his machine gun to a better position in order to deliver effective fire on the enemy, he was mortally wounded. His actions were in accordance with the highest standards of the military service. Entered military service from South Gate, California."

Sporadic fights continued in the area, but the town of Veghel itself was secure by 1830 hours on D+6. Mopping-up would last for another four days, when the road could be declared truly back in allied hands. But by then it had become severely impaired by the planting of numerous fresh mine fields. It had earned the nickname "Hell's Highway."

For F Company, there began a period of much moving around, occasionally punctuated by real action. One day they heard the sounds of battle in the distance. Next came the roar of P-47s overhead. The planes streaked toward the fray with machine guns blazing and rockets firing—a great "whooshing" noise that seemed just barely over their heads. This was immediately followed by loud explosions out of sight in the distance. Everyone on the ground knew the devastation that was being wreaked upon the enemy. "Thank God we're not on the receiving end of *that*," Bill thought.

It was in this period that Bill witnessed a puzzling and disturbing event involving Gordon Mather, a sergeant in 1st Platoon who had been with the 506th since Toccoa. His skills and integrity were beyond question.

On this particular day the troops were in loose formation marching down a country road, just moving from one place to another, as had been commonplace of late. There was no action at the time. Mather was perhaps 50 yards ahead, and True could see him suddenly stop near a wounded soldier, apparently German, laying in a ditch off to the side. It looked like there might have been some conversation between the two, but it was too far for Bill to hear actual words. Suddenly, Gordon raised his M-1 rifle and quickly put two bullets into the soldier's chest at point blank range. Then he calmly sauntered off down the road as if nothing important had happened.

Approaching closer, it was plain to see that the soldier was indeed a German. Did Gordon just cold-bloodedly dispatch an enemy who deserved no sympathy? Or instead, badly wounded, had the man asked to be put out of his misery? Bill hoped so, but never did find out and never asked for the particulars. By any measure, it was an unsettling episode that cost him some lost sleep.

After D+10 (September 27), the Division seemed to "settle in" and take a break. Though fighting continued, it was far from constant. There was time for mail, and rest; a "more human" kind of life. In the town of Veghel, part of a dairy facility was converted into a gigantic shower room for the paratroops to use. It was the one and only time throughout the Holland campaign that Bill and others got to wash at once all over. Barber shops were opened. There was even time to launder clothes. The feeling set in that perhaps this operation was over. But such was not the case. And for others involved, Operation Market Garden would prove to be a genuine nightmare.

In Arnhem to the North, things had not gone well for the British 1st Airborne. A variety of supply problems, together with delays of the XXX Tank Corps to move up the corridor and relieve them, had put the Tommies in a real bind. They faced a hardened enemy, well entrenched, and of much superior numbers. Starting on D+5 the Brits had been constantly pushed around and battered. By D+8, September 25, they were surrounded in a small perimeter just west of the city, and in truly desperate straights. Stranded without food or ammunition, it was time to make a strategic evacuation. That night, under cover of darkness, the river crossing was made by all who could. Altogether, 10,095 British troops had been dropped into Holland north of the Rhine. When the final action reports were in, a total of 2,490 had returned.

Meanwhile, back in the American sector, early expectations had been that this operation would be the standard use of airborne troops: a few days of heavy fighting, then relief back to England for a rest before the next big battle. It was now well past that time. Thus it came as a further nasty surprise to learn they would be moving north to replace the British in an area between the Waal and Rijn Rivers. The experience there would prove to be among the most harrowing, arduous, and lengthy for any division in the war.

They were going to "the Island."

CHAPTER IX

The Screaming Meemies
Life on "The Island"

"The efforts which we make to escape from our destiny only
serve to lead us into it."
                    Ralph Waldo Emerson

Most of Holland is low, flat farmland, much of it below
sea level. Extending nearly ten miles west from Arnhem to
Opheusden is an area of this type. It is bordered on the north
by the Neder Rijn, and the south by the Waal River, which
join and form an eastern "point." The land between is nearly
surrounded by water and thus came to be known as the
Island. Earthen dikes lined the banks of the rivers to keep
water out. The famous Dutch windmills dotted the
countryside, their purpose to pump water from the low-lying
central plain.

North of the Rijn near Arnhem is a series of hills and
high ground atypical of the Netherlands. In October, 1944,
this was occupied by the Germans who had dug in well, with
massive amounts of artillery—mostly the feared 88s. From
their vantage point they had complete command of the lowland between the rivers. This would prove the greatest
challenge to the 101st Division for the remainder of the
campaign. For the men of the 506th PIR, that challenge began
on October 2 with a truck ride up Hell's Highway to the
bridge at Nijmegen.

Though the British had failed to hold Arnhem, they did manage to take and keep the Island for themselves. Travel was difficult along this northern end of the road, due to German observation posts relaying instructions to artillery in the area. Simply getting across the Waal River was itself a trial by gunfire, but that was exactly the task before Bill True and his buddies in F Company. Someone had to relieve the much-battered Tommies. The Screaming Eagles had been given the job.

After a relatively quiet night in Nijmegen, it was time for the 506th to make the crossing north of town and enter the Island for the final Holland campaign. In canvas-covered trucks, 12 men to a vehicle sitting on rough benches, they approached the Nijmegen bridge from the south. The men could see what waited ahead. Enemy guns had zeroed in on the bridge and were shelling it in an almost continuous barrage. As the convoy of troops reached the river, each vehicle stopped to wait for a lull in the action.

Bill's lorry took its turn in traffic, slowly creeping forward to reach the bridgehead, then paused at the entrance to the bridge itself. The men in back could hear the driver gun the motor, and felt the vibration in their butts and feet, anticipating the sudden rush forward. Wait for it… wait for it… then when several seconds had passed in silence, the driver popped the clutch and the truck lurched forward, causing all the troops in back to fall against each other. They were in a race for their lives. Suddenly a shell exploded on the bridge support girders not 30 yards behind them. No one was hurt, but shrapnel rained all around as the soldiers were jostled and tossed from side to side with the careening vehicle. "Jeez, this is as bad as the jump in France," Bill thought. With the engine screaming, driving as fast as they could, the northern exit was still 30 yards away! Another blast of artillery, this time in front, but they were really on a roll now. At last! The bridgehead passed behind them as the truck veered left, heading up a winding road to the interior of the Island. They had made it! But further adventures lay ahead, and in short order.

ॐ   ॐ   ॐ

Now the troopers in Fox Company found themselves on a country road, rolling through low farmland and apple orchards, heading north and west. They had an appointment with the British soldiers whom they would relieve on the line. Near the town of Opheusden, 8-10 miles from Nijmegen, they de-trucked next to a tall, sloping dike and began marching to meet the weary Tommies. It was a mile or so to their rendezvous and by the time they arrived, night had fallen.

"No big deal, Yanks. Just stay put in daylight. The Jerrys have this whole area zeroed in from across the river. Bloody hell with their 88s, it is!"

The dike was tall, steeply sloped, with a paved road on the top, perhaps 20 feet wide. There was no vegetation. It was typical of many in the area. Beyond it and out of sight to the north, the Neder Rijn rolled silently through the Dutch farmland. On the lowland American side was a windmill, which was tall enough to be seen from the German positions, and naturally, for any observer in the mill to see them as well. An orchard began roughly 50 feet back from the earthen slope, and it looked like it might be a good place to dig in. This would soon prove not to be the case.

One of the first orders of business was to send out patrols and make contact with American units to the left and right. Bill drew the assignment to check the area to the right.

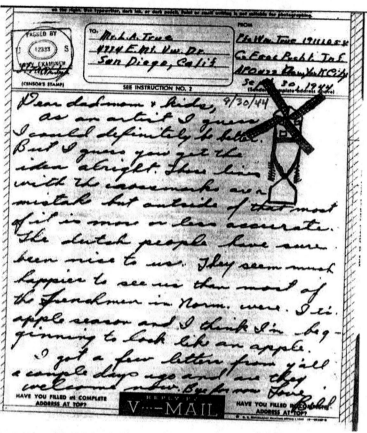

September 30, 1944. V-mail from somewhere in Holland: "Dear dad mom and kids, As an artist I guess I could definitely do better. But I guess you get the idea alright. Those lines with the crossmarks are a mistake but outside of that most of it is more or less accurate. The dutch people have sure been nice to us. They seem much happier to see us than most Frenchmen in Norm. were. It's apple season and I think I'm getting to look like an apple. I got a few letters from y'all a couple days ago and they are welcome now. Bye for now. Love, Bill." Bill later commented on this V-mail's subject: "The difference between the Dutch and the French was remarkable. Of course, in addition to welcoming us with open arms, the Dutch all spoke English and that doubtless made some difference, too. Not many of the French farming people in Normandy spoke English, and very few of us could go much beyond the French language handbooks we had been given."

His orders were to walk east along the dike, looking to be sure there were no German troops in the area, and to locate the boundary with friendly forces on the F Company right flank. It was vital that no enemy forces infiltrate their lines. A new replacement was assigned to accompany the seasoned veteran: a fresh-faced kid with no experience in action.

They did as ordered. Bill took point, walking 10 yards ahead, and put the new kid behind him with the caution to be on the alert for anything unusual. It was quiet in the area. No sound of gunfire or artillery. A thousand yards away they met the friendly forces to their right. This would be an excessive distance between units in normal circumstances. An officer told them that the area separating his outfit from F Company would soon be shortened. With that assurance, Bill and the kid turned and began to make their way back. All seemed calm in the vicinity.

Suddenly True heard a muffled kind of "poof" sound behind him. At the same time he felt something snag his back, a kind of "tick" in the left shoulder blade. He looked back. The kid was on the ground, bleeding profusely. A German mortar round had landed just behind him, and his body had absorbed the brunt of the explosion. Shielded in front, Bill had received only a tiny piece of shrapnel.

There was no time to lose. Quickly he moved the wounded man a short way into a small depression—perhaps 10 inches deep at most, but it might provide some protection in case of further mortar drops. "Damn! Hope this isn't the start of a whole barrage!!!"

He injected the kid with morphine and applied a quick field dressing. The man was seriously wounded, perhaps mortally. Bill made him as comfortable as possible, then left quickly for the company C.P. There he grabbed Joe Droogan, the medic, and together they returned immediately to administer further medical attention. Bill never did learn the ultimate fate of the kid he hardly knew, and who had taken the hit while he himself remained unscathed. This was the second time in Holland that another man had shielded him from serious injury. The first had occurred as they were hooked up and ready to jump back on Sept. 17 when Ken Steinke had absorbed the German fire. How long would this sort of luck hold up? And what did it mean? He would puzzle much on this in the future.

Having established friendly contact, and determined their flanks were secure, F Company was ordered to dig in at the orchard. This was a big mistake. German spotters on the other side of the river could see the Americans moving about and setting up for defense. Any fool could tell that the windmill would be an obvious site for observers and snipers. This analysis was not lost on the enemy.

Using his entrenching tool, Bill started digging a two-man fox hole to share with Johnny Jackson. Suddenly he was startled by a shell exploding 20 yards away behind him. Then another, closer, this time showering him with dirt. Soon artillery shells began falling thick and fast. Some hit the windmill, which was the main target. But when shells missed it, they landed immediately adjacent and in the orchard behind, where F Company was digging in. For Bill True, it was one of the most alarming experiences of the Island campaign. He and Jackson were both repeatedly covered with dirt and debris as the shells plowed the earth around them. The sheer panic brought on by the deafening noise and the battering concussion of an artillery bombardment is probably the ultimate terror in war. The same thought crossed the minds of all the troopers at once: "Let's get the hell out of here, they've got us zeroed in!"

Fortunately, the lieutenant finally picked up on the tactical problem. "Move up to the dike face!" were the new orders. They were quickly followed. The men dug directly into the earthen dike—its "reverse" slope. Now the shelling, though intense, fell harmlessly to their rear. At least a modicum of security had been achieved. But it left the troops shaken and tense: what would life on the Island be like, if this is the start? They would soon find it to be much of the same.

Once the men were out of sight by the German spotters, the artillery barrage slackened and eventually ceased. Ahead was a night of only fitful sleep that gave an unwelcome preview of the future. The most consistent and uncomfortable deprivation for everyone soon became that of sleep. Sleep, blessed sleep, often became a mortally dangerous luxury when alertness for German patrols was worth a man's life.

ॐ   ॐ   ॐ

By the time the 506th took up residence on the Island it had become clear that Operation Market Garden had essentially failed to accomplish its goal. On the plus side, the Allies had liberated large portions of Holland, and the highway corridor between Eindhoven and Arnhem was in American hands. But the dream of British tanks pouring into Germany across the Neder Rijn was gone. Instead, the Americans began a withering campaign to simply hold on to what they'd gained. And their German enemy was not nearly as demoralized or undersupplied as had been thought.

So the Island campaign became one of dreary regimen, punctuated by periods of stark horror. It was common for units to spend five days on the line alternating with five days "in reserve" where men could get at least a modest respite. These were ¼ to ½ mile behind the MLR (Main Line of

Resistance) where troops waited, always ready to respond when and wherever an attack might come.

The weather was bad no matter where they were. It rained more than half the time. And the area had by now been completely abandoned by all civilians, leaving homes and farms empty and cold. Night infantry attacks from across the river were a regular occurrence. The murderous artillery fire from Arnhem made daytime movement very difficult, and even nighttime forays became risky endeavors.

It was on the Island that the troopers first came to know and fear the "screaming meemies." These were special mortar rounds the enemy had developed that made an unbelievably loud and piercing high-pitched whine as they were coming in. As anti-personnel weapons, the added noise factor rendered them "terrorist" in nature. And terror was indeed the effect. Each man knew when the attack was coming, and from whence, but was powerless to avoid the falling bombs. Between the whine of flight, and the explosions on impact, the resulting din was utterly deafening.

Another frightening and common experience was that of combat flares at night. An uncommon occurrence in Normandy, they became all-too commonplace in Holland. Launched by mortar or rocket, they hung in the air and drifted slowly to earth via parachute. They were incredibly bright and instantly turned the pitch-black battlefield into blinding daylight, clearly revealing every detail of ground troop activity. And the only defense was a mind-numbing and counter-intuitive command imperative: FREEZE!

From the earliest days of training, the American soldiers had been taught that the earth was their dearest friend in combat. "When you hear the sound of machine guns, dive for the ground!!" Mother Earth would protect them from the hail of bullets above their heads. But combat flares posed a paradoxically opposite need: to stand still so as to become "invisible" to the enemy. From a distance, details such as individual soldiers are hard to make out on a battlefield. But *movement* draws the eye immediately to it. Combined with the harsh shadows cast by the flarelight, a *moving* soldier was easy to spot—and kill. Hence the command to instantly cease all movement, even if you were caught standing straight upright in the glare of the artificial day. A man was far less likely to be spotted by appearing absolutely motionless, rather than diving for the protection of the earth.

As strange as it seemed, the tactic seemed to work. Several times Bill and his comrades found themselves on reconnaissance patrol, standing upright in the bright light, stock-still in full battle gear and staring across the battlefield toward guns they knew were searching for them. But the crack of gunfire never broke the eerie silence.

❧   ❧   ❧

Friends in other squads and platoons had similar experiences. One night John Taylor, an F Company buddy of True's, had an action-filled adventure.

Staff Sergeant John Taylor and his 2nd Platoon leader Lt. Thomas took a sizable combat patrol out one night with two objectives: Destroy several German positions located along a railroad embankment near a bridge, and bring back prisoners. John, among others, swapped his usual rifle for a Thompson sub-machine gun since this action would be strictly close quarters.

The patrol moved through E Company positions, getting detailed directions on the enemy locations from men of that unit. Sharing the leadership of the patrol, and staying in close contact, Taylor and Thomas led the way. Water-filled ditches, one almost up to their necks in depth, had to be passed in approaching the railroad embankment.

All the men had quietly crossed the ditches and were close to the German positions when a flare suddenly brightened the night. German and American soldiers alike were surprised and shocked at each other's close proximity, and all were now starkly outlined by the artificial daylight. In rapid succession small arms fire and concussion grenades were exchanged. Racing to one of the nearest enemy dugouts, Taylor and Thomas arrived almost simultaneously as the lieutenant threw a grenade into the hole. Following its explosion Taylor fired his sub-Thompson at the Germans and leaped among them.

Taylor found one of the enemy soldiers still alive and shoved him out of the dugout to be taken back as a prisoner. The exchange of fire continued as the patrol moved from dugout to dugout. Another flare went off as Taylor found himself next to a hole where he killed three more Germans and took another prisoner.

The Germans gave nearly as good as they got in the exchange. The paratroop patrol suffered two men killed and four wounded. Since the Americans now had two prisoners and had inflicted serious damage on the enemy positions, the soldiers headed back. They carried their dead and assisted the wounded to waiting jeeps which then drove them the remainder of the way into the American lines.

Reporting to 2nd Battalion Headquarters, Sergeant Taylor and Lt. Thomas critiqued the mission and enjoyed the comfort of warm blankets and hot coffee. They were both awarded Silver Stars for bravery.

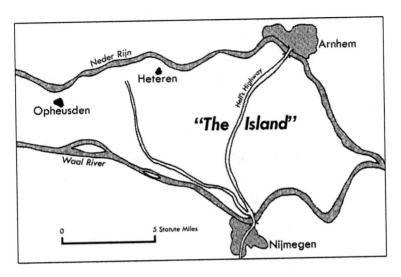

The Island Campaign Theater

The warning of the Tommies as they left the Island proved accurate. German guns held the high ground across the river and up toward Arnhem, with spotters able to pinpoint fire at any target in the American sector. Any activity in daylight continued to be extremely hazardous. But night was little better. Men spent most of their time in the foxholes with nothing to do but wait for the inevitable moments of stark terror that signaled the start of an attack. Sleep became both manifestly dangerous and urgently necessary. It was worth your life to stay alert, yet sleep was utterly seductive to men stressed out by weeks of combat. More than once, German patrols caught troopers dozing off, and took them prisoner back across the line.

Soon it became standard procedure to stand watch in turns. With two men in a foxhole, one was to be fully alert at all times, and watching for enemy activity. If it was necessary for one man to leave, to get ammo or run another errand, the remaining soldier was left alone to stand guard. And it was vital that he do so conscientiously.

One night Bill shared a foxhole with a trooper who had joined the outfit after Normandy. He remembered this kid as one who seemed extremely tough: he beat up another soldier pretty badly when they argued over who would get the lower bunk in their hut back in Aldbourne. But out on the front line, it seemed to be a different story.

"I gotta go check in with the C.P. and see if there are any new orders," Bill said.

"I'll go with you," the kid said.

"No, you stay here. And *keep alert*! Can't have *any* of us getting caught off guard. Remember Kelley, Eldridge, and MacKay in 3rd Platoon? They're probably eating slop in a German POW camp right now. Let's not join them."

"Well, you might need help carrying stuff back. Don't you want some company?"

"No. You know the orders: one man in each foxhole, alert at *all* times!"

After a few more minutes of argument, the realization dawned on Bill: this guy's simply afraid to be out here in the dark alone! Sheesh. Imagine that, and him acting so tough back in England. Soon it was all he could do to break away without the new kid hanging onto his leg like a child afraid of the boogey-man. When a repeat incident occurred later, True felt compelled to report it to the platoon lieutenant, which he did. The replacement soon disappeared from the front lines and was heard from no more by the guys in F Company.

One day Bill was saddened and disappointed to learn that Armand Beauchamp of the 3rd Platoon had been killed. He was a friend from their first days at Toccoa. Although they never served in the same platoon, they had been on pass together. True had seen Armand just the day before his death and noted that he still sported the remains of a shiner given him by Whitey Swafford. Beauchamp was generally quiet and reserved, but apparently had gotten into a heated argument with Whitey while they were still in the marshalling area. Swafford was always more prone to settle a dispute with his fists than his brains, and this incident was no exception. He decked Armand when "intellect" failed to resolve their disagreement. Bill hoped that Whitey would suffer at least some remorse for this, after Armand's demise.

æ æ æ

An artillery barrage could occur on the Island at any time, and frequently did. But infantry attacks took place exclusively at night. One was memorable for its ferocity.

In the quiet of one late evening, suddenly trip flares went up at the perimeter of the American positions. American combat engineers had placed them as early warning devices. German infantry set them off as they attempted to infiltrate for a surprise attack. At the first artificial light of flares, the battle was joined. In minutes enemy artillery began pounding the area, and waves of German riflemen could be seen moving forward in the distance.

True and his friends were in the thick of it, as 88mm rounds began landing in their midst. It was the heaviest barrage to date. Quickly they set up their mortar and began pouring rounds across the dike as rapidly as possible. Soon the battlefield turned to chaos as shells exploded one after another in quick succession. The smell of cordite was thick, and smoke obscured all but the nearby landscape. The men could see nothing of their enemy now and only knew where to fire mortar rounds because of the previously measured distances, and pre-sighted fields of fire. Meanwhile, others in F Company manning machine guns atop the dike were being decimated by murderous enemy action.

Soon the 321st Regiment joined the fray, firing round after round of artillery at the attacking Germans. As with most combat, confusion reigned supreme and whether one man lived or died became a matter of the merest chance of fate. But luck or fate was on the American side. Near dawn, after hours of fighting, at last the action slackened and finally the guns fell silent. The American lines had held, but with numerous casualties.

Later it was learned that the British had added their own artillery to the defense. But there were dark rumors about the accuracy of the gunners and the possibility that some rounds had fallen short. A day after the attack, several men from F Company were assigned to go forward and collect the bodies of company men killed by what was thought to be friendly fire. They knew the dead as buddies. Normally, soldiers would not be asked to collect their own casualties, at least not close friends, for obvious morale reasons. But this time the system failed. Bill saw one of the men later when his personal ordeal was over. The man had a dazed, faraway look in his eyes. His speech, when he talked about picking up the pieces of his comrades, was barely rational. The poor guy was obviously over the edge, unable to handle the traumatic experience. Within days he was shipped out, destination unknown, and Bill never saw him again.

One of the mangled dead was Orel Lev.

Security was tightened greatly following the capture of three men from F Company by Germans who had caught them napping in their foxholes. This included setting outposts on the German side of the dike and manning them around the clock. One pitch black night, Bill True and Johnny Jackson were assigned the task of relieving Bud Edwards and a new replacement who were in their place out front of the American perimeter.

It was about midnight as Bill and Johnny made their way up the well-worn path over the dike and beyond to the foxhole that was the assigned outpost. As they arrived, Bud made a stealthy hand motion and whispered, "Shhh... don't make a sound!"

"What's up?" Bill asked, his voice low.

"I think there may be a Kraut soldier over there. I didn't want to fire, in case it's a trap and they want us to give our position away. But he's just been layin' there, not movin'."

True looked in the direction indicated. Sure enough there was a shape, maybe 50 feet away, that could be a man laying prone. "Well we can't just sit here and stew about this all night. I'll check it out," he said.

Crouching low with rifle at the ready, safety off and finger on the trigger, he crept toward the suspected German. As always on outpost, his bayonet was fixed, though he'd never had occasion to use it. At least not yet. As he got closer, his eyes became more adjusted to the dark as well. Sure enough, it looked like a body. And then, by damn, the distinctive coal-scuttle helmet became apparent as well: an enemy soldier, sure as hell. But there still was no sound, or movement.

Slow and silent, Bill moved to within a few feet of the Kraut and put the tip of his bayonet at the man's shoulder. No movement. With a firm shove, he drove the blade deep into the man's body. There was surprisingly little resistance. A soft "puff" sound emitted The depth of the thrust, and the reality of what he was doing, suddenly produced a sickening knot in his stomach. The man was obviously dead. Thank God.

This would prove to be the first, and last, man Bill ever had cause or opportunity to bayonet. Returning to the outpost, True and Jackson took up their duties as Bud and the replacement returned to their line.

F Company spent its share of alternate duty "in reserve," to the rear of the main line as much as ½ mile. Though this did not in any way put them out of danger—artillery could strike virtually anywhere in the Island—it did provide some measure of relief from the tensions of the front. There was time to relax and read—Reader's Digest being a popular item along with the occasional Stars and Stripes. The latter always gave a morale boost, though the veracity of the stories had become questionable, ever since the "Rangers Take Carentan" flub up. And occasionally the men got to simply sit back for a change and watch as others fought the war. A common sight was of B-17 bombers flying overhead, aiming for Berlin and other German cities. At times the formations seemed endless as hundreds, maybe thousands, of planes streamed toward their targets in Germany. It literally took hours for them to pass. How could the war last much longer with such firepower aimed at the enemy?

Then one day Lt. Tuck picked Bill's squad for an interesting assignment.

LIMEYS AND YANKS
Bill's True Tale

Lieutenant Tuck just walked up to my squad and said "I need you guys to go out on a reconnaissance patrol with some Limey tankers." We've been in Holland about a month and are now up here on what's called The Island, working pretty closely with the British. Don't know if we're attached to them or they're attached to us, but we've been eating their rations for a while and it's a nice change. I like their ready-made tea especially. Just ladle a couple spoonfuls into a canteen cup, add hot water, and with the milk and sugar already in it you've got a real English treat.

"This tank crew is manning one of our Shermans, and you'll get a chance to climb on for a ride out and around the area," the Lieutenant adds. "How about that? A riding reconnaissance patrol. You guys got it made."

"Oh yeah!" I'm thinking. "Tuck is always mindful of the comfort and ease of the men in his platoon. In a rat's ass."

There are five of us in the squad now, Blackie Wilson, Joe Flick, Johnny Jackson and I - the remaining old timers from basic training days at Toccoa - plus a recent replacement. "Can all five of us ride on this thing?" Blackie asks the tanker in charge.

"Surely, my man," the tanker responds. "Just climb aboard and we'll give you Yanks a jolly-good excursion."

I find a spot right next to the tank turret, rest my rifle, and ask where this patrol is supposed to go and what we're supposed to do.

"We'll just be exploring a bit of territory out here to see if Jerry is anywhere about," the tank commander tells me. "Won't be spoiling for a fight. Just want to get some intelligence for the big boys, and you chaps are along to handle any stray infantry surprises we might encounter."

As the other guys clamber aboard and find reasonably secure perches I'm relieved that Tuck was giving it to us straight and this is just a reconnaissance and not a combat patrol.

Off we go on our first ever non-walking patrol and it's quite nice at that. "Sometimes I may be a little hard on Tuck," I'm thinking, "but the odds still favor a solid skepticism."

We've been riding quite a while and I've been enjoying listening to the radio interchange between the tank commander and his headquarters when an artillery shell lands about one hundred yards in front of us. The tank suddenly veers off sharply to the right and our speed increases substantially. Within a few seconds another shell lands behind us but probably only about fifty yards back. Another change of direction is quickly made and we external riders are holding on like a clutch of baby possums clinging to mama's back when there's an explosion to our left front which rattles some shrapnel off the tank hull. No one is hit, but this is getting real dicey in a hurry.

In a coolly controlled voice the tank commander is talking into his radio. "I say old chap, Jerry is doing a bit of heavy shelling and seems to be zeroing in rather close. Perhaps we should consider removing from this area...unless, of course, you have other suggestions."

I can't hear the response he gets over the noise of the tank and the increasing artillery explosions, but I'm hoping his headquarters is giving him the suggestion every one of his paratrooper passengers is mouthing: "Get the hell out of there, and fast!"

Our tank commander's superior probably doesn't have ESP, but his orders obviously reflect our heart-felt wishes as the tank begins a rapid zigzagging course back toward

American lines.

We're back with the platoon, none the worse for wear and tear, and hungry enough to eat anything we can chew—up to and including even the crummy crackers out of a K-Ration carton. For some reason we didn't get any British rations today. We won't go hungry though, 'cause Johnny is going to cook up a stew out of some canned meat and fresh vegetables we got yesterday from an abandoned farmhouse cellar. Only trouble is we don't have a sizable pan or kettle to brew it up in. That was certainly stupid... the house would surely have had plenty of cooking utensils.

"Not to worry," Johnny tells us, "there's a pan by the side of the road back to company headquarters that I noticed this morning and it would work fine." He's off to retrieve the pan, and Joe Flick and I get a fire going in the small circle of large stones which we set up last night to serve as our field-kitchen stove.

Johnny's back, and I guess the pan will serve the purpose, but it's a big hospital-type bed pan. "Oh, no," Blackie Wilson moans, "we're not going to eat a stew cooked in that thing, are we?" The rest of us are sharing Blackie's reluctance to dine on a meal cooked in something with this pan's history, when Joe says he's still got a half bar of the GI soap he swiped from the company cook a while back. We all know that soap would dissolve the balls off a brass monkey, so after a meticulous scrub-down with boiling hot soapy water and a stiff army brush we're reconciled to using our rather innovative cooking implement.

Johnny's been tending our stew for at least an hour now. Meat, potatoes, carrots, onions, and some strange unidentified Dutch vegetable have gone into it, and we're all more than ready to have at it. "Okay, soup's on," Johnny finally proclaims. We've been waiting with eagerly expectant mess kits in hand and quickly move to claim our artfully prepared chow.

When we drew straws I got the short one, so I'm spooning the last of our stew into my mess kit as a couple of our erstwhile British tank buddies walk up. I've tipped the bed pan up to get the last of the juice, when both of the Limies burst into gasps of hysterical laughter. "Blimey, Yank," one of them chokes between guffaws, "if you chaps are that 'ard up we'd be 'appy to do a bit of reverse lend lease to tide you over."

I recall the oft repeated line from the "Fibber McGee and Molly" show where Molly says to Fibber "It ain't funny, McGee." But I have to admit this would surely look more than a bit weird to anyone who hadn't been present for the entire scenario, especially the sanitizing the pan got with our G.I. soap. And I'm also remembering how impressed I was with the British cool of these guys when the Kraut artillery was closely falling. In the interest of Allied solidarity I decide to let them have the last laugh.

On the Island there were houses and farms in the reserve areas, but all had been abandoned when fighting became incessant. These were ripe for looting and no one cared if the troopers helped themselves to a few meager comforts in the midst of their general deprivations. Canned food was plentiful, along with occasional cellars of wine or brandy, which were quickly emptied. And apples, always apples. It seemed as if everyone in Holland grew apple trees, either commercially or just in the backyard, and the varieties were endless. Bill found one tree whose fruit tasted for all the world like bananas! (Of course, that was based on his now distant remembrance of what a real banana actually tasted like.)

When it was possible, the Army managed to provide entertainment for the troops. Once, Bill attended a USO show put on by the Brits, and it was a wonderful break from the dull routine of life in reserve. On another evening, a movie projector was set up in a barn and they showed the film "Double Indemnity," with Barbara Stanwyck, Fred McMurray, and Edward G. Robinson. Bill and Johnny Jackson saw it before retiring back to their foxhole on the main line: a shallow affair with a pup tent erected over it for cover from the weather. They were just about to sack out for the night when they heard the sound of a German artillery shell landing at some distance, perhaps 200 yards.

"Goddam Krauts," True muttered. "I think they're just trying to irritate us—those random shots any time, anywhere. We got no troops out that way. What the hell are they shootin' at?"

A minute or two passed. Then another shell landed, this one closer, about 100 yards away. "Damn Krauts."

After another minute, yet a third round landed 50 yards to their front.

"Hey, this is getting serious. Those guys are creeping up on us," Jackson said. By now both men were fully alert and more than a little nervous about the slinking menace that seemed to be searching for them personally.

Suddenly there was a huge explosion not 15 feet away. It was a direct hit on the neighboring foxhole. The occupants had also gone to the movies, and not yet returned, to their extreme good fortune. But Bill and Johnny were deafened by the blast and their pup tent was showered with dirt and debris. Did the next round have their name on it? Crouched in fetal position, they waited in mortal dread. And waited.

And waited. Finally it was clear that the random barrage was over. Fate had had its fun, scaring the daylights out of them. Then tiring of the game, it had given up and gone to bed.

ॐ   ॐ   ॐ

While in reserve one day, Bill felt a maddening itch in his groin area. It had been getting gradually worse for some time, and he attributed it to the lack of bathing opportunities on the line. But now the itching was intolerable, so he finally gave in and went to see the battalion doctor.

An aid station had been set up in a mobile trailer back of the front lines and this is where True was examined. The doctor took one look and instantly pronounced the diagnosis: "You've got crabs."

"Crabs! I haven't sat on a proper toilet seat since before we jumped and I sure as hell haven't had any contact with women! How did I get *this*?" Bill demanded to know.

"Probably in the marshalling area before the jump. But I can tell you, that's one happy and *large* colony you've got going there. The good news is, I have just the stuff to take care of it," the medic said. He promptly retrieved a tube of medicinal cream from a supply cabinet and smeared it on the affected area. "That'll fix those little bastards."

Bill was grateful for the salve, hoping for an early relief of his symptoms. But within seconds, the opposite seemed to be the case. The cream had apparently driven the bugs crazy in their death throes and they were scrambling and biting like the dickens! Suddenly it became too much to bear. Bill pulled up his pants and, scratching like mad, literally ran from the aid station, frantic to escape the itching pain that was enough to make him nuts. He ran and ran, with no other thought but to escape, while the crabs continued their own frantic dying.

Finally, exhausted from running and now far from the aid station, Bill felt the critters breathe their last, and he himself breathed a welcome sigh of relief. It was the only case of crabs he had ever encountered and, please God, it would hopefully be his last!

∾   ∾   ∾

Food was a little better in reserve than on the front line, though K rations were still a common fare. Often the provisions were British, and these provided something Bill began to think of as a special treat: tea. In the English rations was a packet of powder that was combination tea and milk. It was very tasty, and certainly better than any powdered drink the U.S. Army had provided. On occasion there was even a field kitchen set up—usually in an abandoned house—with real hot meals. What a wonderful surprise! But the best was yet to come.

One day Bill and Doug Roth, from F Company's headquarters unit, looked up an old friend who had long since transferred to the 82nd Airborne: Bill Tucker. Tucker knew how to work the system well, and had set himself up with a very cozy billet in an abandoned home, and gained access to provisions most of the troops could not obtain. Tucker's regiment was only a couple of miles from F Company at the time, and he invited True and Roth over to "his house" for dinner that night. It was an experience so wonderful as to be surreal, in the midst of combat.

Arriving, Bill and Doug found a beautiful house, still filled with furnishings and civilian appointments throughout. A formal dining table had been set, with linen napkins, porcelain dinnerware, and silver cutlery. They were treated to steak and potatoes, French wines, and all the trimmings of an actual, civilized meal in an elegant home! It was a total shock to two foot soldiers fresh from the foxhole. They hadn't experienced such luxury since their last leave home in the States and were duly impressed, as Tucker well intended for his former buddies from the 506th.

❧   ❧   ❧

Not all the time on the Island was spent in foxholes. At one point, Bill and his squad was assigned to occupy and guard an abandoned farm house that had a cellar underneath. They had to be particularly wary of German infiltration. Two nights before, a group in a similar situation had been surprised by enemy attack. The Krauts had traced their telephone communication wire to the building and, sneaking up under cover of darkness, had jumped the squad and demanded to take them prisoner. Fortunately, an American trooper at the back of the cellar had the presence of mind to grab his sub-Thompson in time. With a leap from hiding, he killed the entire German patrol. But from then on, vigilance was doubled for all troops, even when in reserve.

Troops in reserve were often asked to help out with "extra" duties, as well. One day Blackie Wilson, the acting squad leader, presented such an opportunity to True and Jackson.

"There's some Brits stranded on the other side of the river—didn't get out when Arnhem was evacuated. Some of us are going across in boats tonight after dark and see if we can pick up survivors. You want to come along?" Blackie said.

True thought it over. "You really need us, or is this strictly volunteer?" he asked.

"We've probably got plenty of guys to fill the boats. It's volunteer."

Jackson and True exchanged glances, thought for a bit, and finally Bill said, "In that case, we'll leave it to the volunteers." He felt an immediate twinge of guilt, however. Ever since Normandy, when Joe Flick had dumb-ass volunteered the two of them for patrol duty, Bill had followed a strict policy. Getting killed doing your duty was one thing. Volunteering and *asking* for trouble was another. But then again, those Tommies had been given a pretty raw deal and could sure use the help. Well, if they didn't have enough guys to go, that would be different . . .

In his heart, Bill hoped nothing would go wrong with the mission he had opted to avoid. If any of his buddies were hurt or killed in his place it would go hard on his conscience. But his luck held. Next day Blackie reported a completely boring non-event the previous evening: no Brits found to evacuate, and no contact with German troops. Whew! Thank God.

☙   ☙   ☙

November 11, 1944, was Bill's 21st birthday. It so happened that on this day he and his unit were in reserve, bivouacked near a big barn. Talk had turned briefly to the recent election. Ballots had been distributed four days earlier to everyone who was of voting age, but Bill had just missed it. Years later he remarked that it was just as well. Being a staunch Republican at the time he'd have probably voted for Dewey, as much good as that would do. Roosevelt was a total shoo-in.

That evening the guys joined in a round of Racehorse Pinochle, the current favorite pastime. It was a variation of the card game that, like Bridge, depended heavily on skill in "bidding" and involved an exchange of cards by the successful bidders. No money was involved—this was just for fun and diversion from the grind of the front line. But Bill and Johnny Jackson whipped up a scheme to cheat, just for their own entertainment. It was crude, but effective. For example, if Johnny bid in spades, Bill would return with "I'll *kick* that bid," meaning he had the "K" or King of the same suit. In short order, the two cheaters were beating the tar out of everyone else, to the total amazement of all. Nobody ever caught on, and they became the "World Champions of Racehorse Pinochle"—at least as far as F Company was concerned.

As the days passed and Thanksgiving approached, the men of F Company were dog tired and nearing the limits of their endurance. Nearly constant rain had left them cold, wet, and miserable for over two months. Frequent patrols, interspersed with bitter fighting were taking their toll on morale, with no end in sight. Finally, near the end of November, word came down that their Dutch ordeal was coming to a close. A few units began to move out, back down Hell's Highway and into France at a place no one had ever heard of before: Mourmelon-le-Grande.

Just before heading for France, F Company received a wonderful going-away present: turkey dinner with ALL the trimmings. It was a welcome tribute for the pain and sacrifice the men had all endured. On November 27th the last of the 101st Airborne Division left Holland for a well-deserved rest. They had been in combat continuously for a remarkable 72 days.

CHAPTER X

White Christmas in a Foxhole
Bastogne and the Battle of the Bulge

"The first qualification of a soldier is fortitude under fatigue and privation."

Napoleon Bonaparte

Late November, 1944. Finally off the battle line, the men of F Company found themselves in comfortable and pleasant French quarters. Mourmelon-le-Grande was a former military garrison, left over from the first World War. The Battle of the Marne had been fought here and the surrounding land was still scarred by the remains of trenches and shell craters, though time had softened their contours.

Housing consisted of low stucco buildings, in poor repair but infinitely better than the conditions they had all endured in Holland. At least there was a roof over their heads, to protect them from what was hoped to be a long winter lay-over.

Nearby was the town of Rheims, famous for its cathedral and for champagne production. Even better, from the standpoint of 48-hour passes, the city of Paris itself was within easy striking distance for GIs eager to blow off pent up steam. Soon the troops had settled in for a routine of rest, replenishment, and re-supply.

Training continued, as always in rear areas, but now was limited only to short periods of close-order drill. Football teams were organized. A boxing tournament was arranged, much to the pleasure of Whitey Swafford who was always up for any pugilistic opportunity. Mail began to arrive regularly, and there was time for the men to write home. Morale took a decided turn for the better with the arrival of the Red Cross, and Bill True got the opportunity to renew an old acquaintance with one of the women in the battalion's Red Cross Club: Polly.

"Polly," he called out across the recreation building hall, a huge grin on his face, "it's me!"

Her reaction was not what he expected. Her jaw dropped and she appeared to be speechless. Coming face to face, he continued, "You do still have my guitar? The one I gave you for safe keeping when we left for Holland?"

It was a Kalamazoo model, made by Gibson, and a rather nice instrument. He had owned it since he was sixteen. The very morning the 506th moved out to the marshalling area for Operation Market Garden, Bill had given her the guitar to keep for him until they met again. She promised to take good care of it. At the same time he also gave her the $500 he had won in that incredible streak of luck shooting craps with the guys the night before. This she was supposed to wire to his family in the states.

Polly was obviously nonplussed. Finally she stammered, "I'm so sorry. Someone told me you'd been killed and I gave the guitar away."

When asked to whom she had given it, Polly could only make vague references to "a soldier who played the guitar," unable to remember either name or unit designation to help hunt the instrument down.

Feeling very downcast, Bill asked her, "Did you at least send the cash to my folks?"

"Oh, yes. I did that right away," she was quick to reply.

It turned out that this was so. But the loss of his favorite instrument was a blow, and the incident left lingering doubts about Polly's loyalty and veracity. Perhaps some handsome non-combat soldier or officer had garnered Polly's favors while Bill was fighting in Holland. It was a never-to-be-resolved question. Eventually he managed to put it out of mind.

❧   ❧   ❧

Most of the units had left Holland seriously depleted of both men and materiel. Now at Mourmelon they began rebuilding.

Troop replacements began to arrive. These were mostly green soldiers, unseasoned by combat. A training program was set up immediately to integrate them with the "old timers," and help everyone work together as a team.

F Company, along with most of the others, was short on all manner of supplies from basic uniform items to weapons and ammunition. At least two of the men didn't even have jump boots, only galoshes. Of some concern was the lack of specialized winter clothing. Sure, the Allies seemed to have the upper hand in Europe, and no major battles were then underway. No one expected to be sent into combat at any time soon, but who could tell? If it really hit the fan and the division was called up in a hurry, they'd be caught unprepared for a serious winter campaign. Efforts to remedy this were given highest priority.

❧   ❧   ❧

Naturally, the foremost interest for all the soldiers, enlisted and officer alike, was obtaining passes into town. The first troops favored with a weekend leave of absence were sent to the old cathedral city of Rheims. This proved to be a mistake. Supreme Headquarters, Allied Expeditionary Force

(SHAEF) was stationed there and the more-or-less permanent military residents were topheavy with generals, colonels, and other ranking officers. The paratroops had just come off the combat line from more than two months of stress and were ready to sow a lot of wild oats. It proved to be a less-than-compatible mix. A Bill Mauldin cartoon of that era captured the essence of this. It shows a less-than-respectful combat trooper leaning against a lamppost, incongruously cowing superior officers for the unauthorized wearing of the emblematic paratrooper footwear. One general says to the other, sotto voce, "It's best not to speak to paratroopers about saluting—they always ask where you got your jump boots."

Soon Rheims was forsaken for Paris, which was more desirable to most of the men anyway. Not all the troopers got there, but many did. Among them were Bill True and his buddy, Johnny Jackson.

GAY PAREE
Bill's True Tale

"Hey, Jackson, True." 1st Sergeant Charlie Malley, is hollering at Johnny and me as we head for the barracks after morning calisthenics. "We just got word that there's room for two more men from F Company on one of the trucks heading for Paris this morning, so get your asses in gear and be ready to go in an hour."

"Hot damn, Johnny, we're in the next group to hit Gay Paree," I gleefully exclaim as we pick up our walking pace to a brisk trot.

"An hour, hell, Ty Ty, I can be ready in five minutes,"

Johnny replies and we're now in a dead run to shave, clean up and get into dress uniforms.

We've been here in Mourmelon-le-Grande, France, nearly two weeks now after our long ordeal in Holland. Operation Market Garden didn't work and the Germans hadn't capitulated before Christmas as everyone had hoped. It's December 14, 1944, and the road to Berlin now looks to be a long one.

The replacements have been pouring in and they seem to be getting younger and younger. With all of our losses in Normandy and Holland, and my having turned twenty-one in November, I'm now older than many of the men in the company. Not quite old enough to be called "Pop" by even the youngest of the recruits, but grizzled enough to command their obvious regard and respect.

"Here's your forty-eight hour passes," Sgt. Malley says, "and enough pro kits and rubbers to keep you out of trouble." Johnny and I have gotten to company headquarters well before the truck departure time of 0900, but we're traveling light with just toilet articles, an extra shirt, and some skivvies and socks.

"How far is it to Paris?" I ask the sergeant. "We sure hope it's not a long truck trip eating into those forty-eight hours."

"It's only a couple of hours," he replies. "But be damn sure you don't miss the truck coming back, because those passes are for forty-eight hours and not for forty-nine. Understood?"

"Understood," Johnny and I chorus. "We'll be on that return truck like hungry hounds jumping a meat wagon," I hasten to add.

Sergeant Malley nearly smiles as he says "Okay then, get the hell out of here."

The sergeant was right and it isn't more than an hour and

a half before we hit the outskirts of Paris. Of course the truck driver knows how anxious all of his passengers are and he's used a lead foot for the whole trip. If he'd been a taxi driver I know that bunch of grateful troopers would have laid a big tip on him.

We've been dropped off here at the American Red Cross building, where we'll be staying, after a really fascinating drive through the streets of Paris. "Wow! Look at the Eiffel Tower," one of the guys from another company shouted as it first came into view. "This is stuff from our history books," I thought as we passed the Arc de Triomphe.

After getting our assigned bunks in one of the sleeping areas and depositing our few articles in the small lockers supplied, Johnny and I are ready to do the town.

"The first bar we hit I'm gonna order a double cognac and a beer chaser just for starters," Johnny says as we walk the stairs down to the lobby.

"Great—me, too. But wait a couple minutes, Johnny. I want to stop and talk to that chick we saw at the Information Desk as we came in," I answer.

Her name is Mlle. Helene Dubreuil. She's friendly, very French, speaks English like Maurice Chevalier, has lived in Paris all her life, and now volunteers for the Red Cross. I'm guessing she's maybe 22 or 23, but her knock-out looks are no guess. Large dark brown eyes, nearly blond hair down to her shoulders, and lips any soldier worth shooting at would die to kiss.

It's been more than a couple of minutes, and Johnny is pacing impatiently across the lobby. But I can't quit now. I'm already madly in love, and the possibility that I might wangle a date out of her has me totally committed.

I excuse myself and walk over to tell Johnny I've got to try to get to know this beauty. He understands, but indicates he just can't wait. "I'll head down to the left on this street and go in the first bar I come to," he says. "If you get loose any time soon come on down and meet me there. Otherwise, good luck with the babe."

I finally get up the nerve to ask Helene if we might go to dinner or something when she gets off. "I'm sorry," she says, genuinely apologetic I think, "but we're not allowed to date any of the servicemen."

"Well, of course I'm not just a serviceman," I point out. "I'm a paratrooper and I know you're aware that we're something different."

Helene smiles knowingly, and speaking with apparent sincerity she tells me that I am not only different but also sweet and charming, "But the rules against dating are strictly enforced and I must abide by them," she concludes.

A few more minutes of cajoling and polite banter have not advanced my cause much, but I'm encouraged by the fact that my persistence doesn't seem to have turned her off, either. She's perhaps even friendlier than when I started. A hot-flash idea crosses my mind. There was a large flower stand just a couple blocks from the Red Cross building that I'd noticed as we drove here.

"How much longer are you on duty, Helene?" I inquire. "If I step out for a few minutes, will you still be here?"

"I have nearly an hour to go," she says as I move out to implement my plan.

It's a really big flower market, and I keep selecting the brightest colored blooms I can find till I really can't carry any more. I'm glad it's only a couple of blocks back because the flowers are heavy and cumbersome and I can hardly see around them to walk.

I'm back at Helene's desk and the flowers are spread all around and she is laughing and almost crying and I'm pretty sure I've done real well. She agrees to have dinner with me, but it must be discrete. She gives me the name of a restaurant and the directions where we are to meet at 7 p.m. Man, oh man. A date with a Parisian doll. Bill True has "arrived".

The restaurant, the dinner, and the conversation are first rate, but Helene is obviously controlling costs for me as she selects from the menu most modestly, and won't let me order a second bottle of champagne. We're having fun discussing a variety of subjects, but at one point she notes my PFC stripe and asks why I am not an officer or ranking non-com.

Not wanting to get into the complexities of explaining why I had avoided taking on responsibility for anyone other than myself, I pulled out my little French handbook and showed her the English word "stern." Pointing out that I did not like to be "stern," she said that she could see that about me and that she understood.

As our dinner is concluding I offer Helene my parachute wings, but she tells me I must wait and give them to someone I will know better. It becomes clear that the dinner will be the extent of our relationship, and while she wears no rings, the thought that there is a fiancé, or a man close to that, gradually sinks in.

After dinner we walk several blocks and stop and Helene tells me this is where we must say good night. She participates warmly in a good night kiss, and touches my cheek as she turns to walk away into the night. Heartbreak ends my first Parisian passion.

"Well, there's always Pig Alley (Rue Pigale)," I tell myself as I hurry to the first underground station for the directions and a ride to that reputedly iniquitous area. The first troopers to Paris came back and told us Pig Alley was where anything goes: the sky's the limit with booze, rousing music and sex that would satisfy Don Juan himself. Bill True is going to confirm those tales tonight, first hand.

Johnny's double cognac with a beer chaser is a good start for me too, and it's soon followed by more of the same and other potent liquids as well. Soldiers and sailors browse amidst floozies and booze to the accompaniment of loud Can-Can music. That's Pig Alley and man I am in, and of, it.

Somewhere along the line a lady of the evening gets her hooks into me (is that why they're called hookers?), and for what seems a most reasonable price takes me to a room for an intimate tryst. Our session in the bed is unremarkable. I don't even take my pants off, just lower them, but as we finish I have a sudden urge for a bowel movement. I'm really three-sheets-to- the-wind, and spotting what looks like a toilet in a corner of the room I stumble over and relieve myself. It's a weird looking toilet for sure, and there's no paper around, just some towels. The hooker starts hollering something at me, and about that time an old crone comes into the room and the hooker points at me and the toilet and they both start shouting. I don't know any French profanity, but they must be cussing me out a blue streak. It looks like the old one is about to start hitting me with her cane as I yank up my pants and get the hell out of there as fast as I can. Crazy French!

It's our second day in Paris and Johnny and I decide we'd better live a little slower. He'd had some high adventures the night before, too, and since we're nearly broke anyway we take a tour of the city. Napoleon's Tomb, Notre Dame, Champs d'Elysee, and other sites of historic Paris. We even play some ping pong at the Red Cross in the evening. After a few night caps at a nearby bar to spend our last remaining francs, we retire well before midnight for our early trip back to Mourmelon in the morning.

The ride back to Mourmelon is of course utterly boring in comparison with the excited anticipation we experienced heading for Paris. Paris. Paree. Gay Paree. Something reminds me of my Uncle Ellis Trotter, mother's older brother who had been in WW I and overseas in France. And I'm remembering the lyrics to a song he frequently sang when I was a kid. I sing the lyrics as I recall them, and a couple of the guys join in on some of the words.

How ya' gonna keep 'em down on the farm, after they've seen Paree?

How ya' gonna keep 'em off Broadway, from jazzin' around, paintin' the town?

Oh yes and how ya' gonna keep 'em away from harm, that's the mystery.

They'll never wanna see a rake or a plow, and can't you hear 'em Ooh, la, la that cow?

Oh, how ya' gonna keep 'em down on the farm, after they've seen Paree?

৵ ৵ ৵

One day, not long after his Paris adventure, Bill ran into his buddy George Lovell while waiting in the chow line. George seemed to be somewhat down in the mouth about something. It didn't seem in character for the guy he'd known since his first days in the paratroops.

"Hey, George, what's up?"

"Oh, I don't know. Guess I'm kind of feeling my age. We've been in combat quite awhile now. It just seems to me that if we keep fighting long enough, my number's gonna come up."

"Well, I guess maybe that's so," Bill began. "But look at it this way. We also have a lot of experience. We know enough to avoid stupid mistakes, not like these young replacements coming in. I sure don't take chances like I did in Normandy, and neither do you."

"Yeah, I suppose," George replied. "But, don't ya think the numbers gotta get ya eventually, I mean if this keeps on going? How many of us originals are still around? You ever sit down and count 'em up?"

Bill had no reply for this, but he knew that a real accounting of survivors from their first days at Toccoa would be a sobering tally. Lately he, too, had felt a certain fatalistic dread at times. His supportive words to Lovell were meant as much to bolster his own spirits as that of his comrade.

They ate lunch mostly in silence after that. It was a glum counterpoint to the seeming lighthearted atmosphere in camp, what with all the games and relaxation.

Then on Sunday, December 17, an important news bulletin was heard on the radio. German units had launched a major attack on elements of the First Army in the Ardennes.

◈　　◈　　◈

The Ardennes Forest is the prominent geographic feature of south-eastern Belgium. Moderate to highly dense stands of fir trees dominate the flora, and the land is marked by high plateaus, and many deep-cut gorges and valleys. The road and rail nets are sparse and unless a military force commands them, movement of armored vehicles through the Ardennes is virtually impossible. The town of Bastogne lies at the center of railroad and highway hubs, positioned to either facilitate or block any mass movement of tanks and other vehicles through the region. It is these geographic factors which shaped the campaign which would become the greatest trial and triumph of the Screaming Eagle Division.

0 25 50 75 100 Statute Miles

ENGLISH

CHANNEL

HOLLAND

Arnhem

GERMANY

Düsseldorf

Antwerp

BELGIUM

Aachen

U.S. VIII
ARMY

Monschau

LUXEMBOURG

Bastogne

Echternach

F R A N C E

Reims

Mourmelon-le-Grand

Paris

Main Line of
Resistance

Situation, mid-December 1944
The frontline, with German-held territory in gray

In mid-December 1944 the Allies held a line that ran roughly north and south paralleling the eastern Belgium border just inside Germany. Though no major battles were underway, the Allies were engaged in a steady and continual push, forcing the enemy backward toward the Rhine. Of late, the weather had been spotty with worse expected, which would normally discourage any large-scale attack by either combatant.

The U.S. First Army's VIII Corps was headquartered in Bastogne, commanding a front 88 miles wide along the Siegfried Line. It was composed of two battle-weary units (the 4th and 28th Infantry Divisions), one cavalry group, and two green, untested divisions. This was the thinnest and weakest concentration of U.S. forces in the region. Army intelligence believed that the enemy in their path comprised only four German infantry divisions, with perhaps one or more Panzer units in their rear. This thinking was tragically incorrect.

Unknown to the Allies, the Germans had quietly concealed 25 full Divisions at a jumping-off point aimed directly into the Ardennes: 250,000 soldiers, 1900 artillery tubes, and 970 tanks and self-propelled guns, for a last-ditch effort to break through the American line and make a dash for Antwerp. It was Hitler's plan to capture this major seaport, closing the main pipeline pouring Allied materiel into Europe. With a stranglehold on Allied supplies, victory might be possible, or at the very least a stale-mate and truce in situ. Either way, defeat for Germany could be avoided.

At approximately 0530 on Saturday, December 16, the Germans began a massive artillery barrage along the entire VIII Corps front from Monschau in the north, to Echternach in the south. This was quickly followed by infantry and tank attacks. Stretched thin to the breaking point, the American line finally gave way, and German armored units poured into the gap. Within twenty-four hours a "bulge" in the Allied front was threatening the vital transportation hub at Bastogne. Caught by surprise, SHAEF reacted with the only reserves at its command: the 82nd and 101st Airborne Divisions, recuperating in France.

> ↝   ↝   ↝

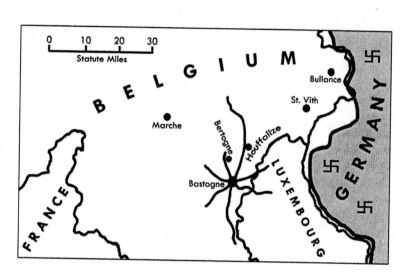

Situation, 15 December 1944
The frontline, with the gray area held by the German forces

While events were unfolding in the Ardennes, activities continued for the Screaming Eagles in Mourmelon. The division officers and men expected to enjoy a lengthy and restful stay, re-building for the next battle which probably wouldn't be until spring. Accordingly, Div. Commander General Maxwell Taylor had returned to the U.S. for high-level meetings. Second-in-command, Brigadier General Gerald J. Higgins was likewise gone and consulting in England. That left the next senior officer, Brig. Gen. Anthony C. McAuliffe, in charge.

At 2030 hrs. on Sunday, December 17, division headquarters got the urgent call to arms: move north to the Belgian Ardennes with all possible speed to stem the flood of German armor through our broken lines. Tony McAuliffe was an artillery man, not experienced at coordinating disparate units at a division command level. Notwithstanding, he immediately jumped to action. At 2100 hrs. he called his staff together. "All I know of the situation is that there has been a breakthrough and we have got to get up there," he told them. Many of his men were away on leave in Paris, and the rest were ill-equipped for battle. No matter. Those on leave were to be left behind and the rest would make do with whatever materiel they had. Quickly, word spread through the camp: prepare to move out.

అ   అ   అ

On the afternoon of December 18, the men of Fox Company were as ready as they could be. Bill knew something big was up, and that the task before them was urgent. Large trucks, pulling ten-ton open-topped trailers were being loaded rapidly and somewhat haphazardly with all the men and supplies they could carry. They looked like cattle cars. With no benches to sit on, the men would have to ride the entire way standing up, bunched together like sheaves of wheat. With little room to move and nothing to hang onto, every lurch and bounce of the spring-less wheels tossed them around like mannequins. If they hadn't been so tightly packed, they would have fallen.

Almost everyone was missing some item of importance: arctic overshoes, heavy winter coats, entrenching tools, ammunition, mortars, sometimes even rifles. As darkness fell on the moving column, the drivers blazed their headlights to allow more speed—an unheard-of practice in combat zones. It was a cool, clear night. The trucks could be seen for miles, and would make for easy strafing by the Luftwaffe. But time was now as much an enemy as the Germans. The trucks pushed on.

They passed through many small towns. Civilians in the

streets watched with curious interest, but seemed as puzzled at this activity as anyone. After what seemed like many hours, the trucks lurched to a stop and the troops disembarked. While everyone relieved themselves by the side of the road, somebody passed the word that they were now in Luxembourg, near the Belgian border. In darkness they began their march toward a town no one had ever heard of. It had a funny spelling: Bastogne. Bill made a mental note of it, and thought it remarkable: he was walking from one country into another, toward an unknown but certainly risky future.

As the men of the 101st walked single file on either side of the road, survivors of VIII Corps, retreating from what was obviously a severe beating at the hands of the Germans, came straggling down the center in the opposite direction. They looked a mess. Completely demoralized, some of them called out words of warning to the paratroops—"Don't go. They'll tear you up like they did us." It was a sorry sight. But Fox Company and the other elite soldiers were not discouraged. They had been trained to win where lesser units might fail. There was anxiety over the coming fight, to be sure. But not panic. Just grim determination for the task ahead.

At last, somewhere outside Bastogne, Fox Company found an open field to rest. Sounds of firefights were heard in the distance, but there was no action in the immediate area. Without digging in, the men lay down on the cold ground for a fitful night's sleep. Some time later a soft rain fell, gradually turning to thin snowfall. By morning they were all lightly dusted when they arose.

The next two days were hectic and disjointed as the 506th, and the entire division, set up a defensive perimeter around Bastogne. The German encirclement was not quite complete, though by now enemy units had flowed around the town on at least three sides. At 1050 hrs. on the morning of December 19, Colonel Sink himself led his regiment as they marched through Bastogne and out the Noville road toward their ultimate goal: establishing a main line of resistance north, near the town of Foy.

Before moving out, those troopers who had them were ordered to remove their heavy army overcoats and put them in a pile on the ground. This was naturally met with some skepticism and grumbling. "What the hell. I'm gonna need that," was the typical reaction. But heavy action was anticipated in the next 24 hours, and they were told to expect rapid movements till things settled down. Heavy overcoats would slow reactions and make the men less agile and responsive. In any case, the weather hadn't yet turned bitter cold. After receiving assurances that the coats would be returned, everyone fell in for the march north.

Bill and his comrades in Fox Company were held in regimental reserve at Luzery that night. Then the next afternoon, December 20th, they found themselves cautiously probing a wooded area just south-east of Foy, in search of a good place to dig foxholes and settle down for the siege to come. The sound of action was now sometimes close, and heard in many directions.

Chapter X – White Christmas in a Foxhole

THE GOOD EARTH
Bill's True Tale

First Platoon has been sent out into a wooded area to see about a suitable defensive set up for our sector. The three squads are almost abreast but with Gordon Mather's First Squad somewhat in the lead. My squad is left of Gordon's with Otto May on the far end and me close to Gordon. The forest here consists almost exclusively of sizable pine trees, only loosely wooded and not nearly as dense as others we've seen.

It's late afternoon and the light is lowering in an overcast sky. If this were back in Nebraska and just a bit colder I'd say it was about to snow.

When we walked through Bastogne yesterday it was our first contact with Belgian people and they speak only French. Nobody knows English here whereas virtually all of the Dutch people did. The main thing I remember about this country is that it's quite small and Napoleon "came a cropper" in a famous place called Waterloo. That can't be too far from here. Yesterday we saw countless bedraggled American infantrymen, drag-assing back through the town. They were a sorry-looking lot who might have been modern counterparts of Napoleon's soldiers of more than a century ago.

We've gone only some fifty to seventy-five yards and I'm thinking this might be a pretty good spot for defense right here. The woods in the distance look to be getting a bit thicker, and we're not likely to find really clear fields of fire anywhere near ahead. It's Mather's call though and his scout George Lovell is still stepping out with no indication Gordon is about to slow him down.

Suddenly a German machine gun opens fire from

somewhere close up ahead. The Kraut gunner is really leaning on the trigger, and the distinctly rapid fire of the enemy's automatic weapons has never been clearer as the buzz of the bullets is like an exploded hornet's nest. No conscious thought is required as I head for the ground—the good earth—and make a slight adjustment in my earthward dive to take advantage of the slightest of depressions. The minor dip of ground that I find has given me perhaps three inches of protection—three inches of precious mother earth. Would that be enough?

The sound of the bullets zipping around my head tells me they are very, very, close. But the feel of the air being split asunder and brushing my cheek is an even starker reality that declares feeling to be the truest of all senses. And my feelings for the earth beneath and around me are both physical and emotional as my fingers clutch and I cling to her as to the mother of my childhood. Oh please, earth mother, please hold me close!

A momentary halt in the hail of fire suggests either a jam, or that a new belt of ammo is being fed into the Kraut gun. A quick look ahead reveals nothing of the enemy's whereabouts, however. I glance to my right to see what Gordon Mather is about as he raises to a half crouch and shouts something to his squad. In a split second of time the gun has opened up again and I see Gordon's head snap back and his body collapse to the ground. A burst has struck him in mid-helmet, and the man many of us have considered the best soldier in our company is dead.

Gordon Mather. He who had stood out so starkly from the rest of we raw recruits right from basic training days back at Toccoa. What possible sense can this make!

August 14, 1999, American Cemetery at Luxembourg. Bill True and Tom Alley at the grave of Gordon Mather, F Company buddy killed at Bastogne, December 20, 1944.

Seconds later the firing stops altogether. The whole thing has probably lasted no more than a minute or two, but the sudden silence is momentarily stunning. Even deafening. We are now able to start moving about to explore our situation, but we still don't see where the Kraut machine gun was set up. The Germans have obviously abandoned the area, and we assume that it was just an outpost and not a main line of defense that we had encountered. Moving ahead we find that Mather's scout, George Lovell, has also been killed, probably with the initial burst of fire since he was in the lead position.

My thoughts go back to the mess hall at Mourmelon-le-Grande some two weeks ago as Lovell and I were in chow line together. George was musing about all the men F Company has now lost in the battle campaigns of first Normandy and then Holland. "You know, TyTy, the longer this war goes on and the more battles we're in, the slimmer our chances get of ever seeing home," he had commented. "The odds just get worse and worse."

Usually a pretty upbeat guy, I'd never heard George sound so pessimistic. Hoping to cheer him a bit, and perhaps to reassure myself as well, I had responded that getting to be veterans had some advantages too. "Combat has taught us some survival techniques, George. More recruits were wounded or killed in Holland than us Normandy vets."

"Yeah," George had said, "but I have a bad feeling about any more combat, and I'm sure not looking forward to it."

I've never been much of a believer in ESP or other occult mumbo-jumbo, but this foretelling of his future by George gives me the creeps. For him to be the first man in the company killed in direct contact with the enemy here at Bastogne has to be more than a startling coincidence.

The First Platoon ends up taking defensive positions and digging in just about where I originally thought we should. If we had done so then might we have avoided the encounter with the Kraut outpost? Maybe so, and maybe Gordon and George would still be with us. But I've given up trying to calculate the "ifs" of war and combat and tactics. I'm still alive anyway, and maybe that's enough to worry about for now.

కా   కా   కా

On December 20th, Fox Company dug in for their part in the Allied defense. They were just south of Foy, in open fields and sparse forest on a line stretching from the town south and east to a rail line. Bill could see the tracks and a small railway building from his foxhole. The tracks set the demarcation between areas of responsibility for the 506th PIR, and the 501st to their right. Later that day he joined others on a reconnaissance patrol to check the area. They saw 3-4 German soldiers, maybe 500 yards away to the north, and fired at them, but certainly missed at that distance. Were the Germans also on patrol, probing the edges of the enemy forces? Probably.

The next two days saw sporadic fighting near Foy, and all around the Bastogne perimeter. Meanwhile, the larger body of enemy forces continued their push westward, expanding the bulge in American lines across a wide front. Bastogne was a critical prize, but its defenders stubbornly refused to yield. Finally, unable to tolerate any further delay in their master timetable, the Germans decided to bypass and encircle the town. Once it was besieged, they reasoned, it should be a simple task to force a surrender. By the morning of December 22, 1944, enemy tanks and troops had flowed completely around the 101st Division, making them the "hole in the doughnut," surrounded and cut off.

Common sense, and most military thinking as well, would count this situation as highly problematic if not desperate for the Americans. The Germans were no doubt counting on damage to morale, among other factors, to hand them the town. But paratroopers are conditioned from their first days to regard encirclement as just another part of the job. After all, classic use of airborne forces is to drop them behind enemy lines to disrupt troop movements, and prepare the way for the main assault which must arrive by more conventional transportation. For a paratrooper, to be surrounded is perhaps serious but in many regards just "another day at the office."

When word spread of their entrapment, the morale of troops out on the line remained high. Their backs against the wall, resolve stiffened rather than collapsing. It was jokingly remarked by at least one soldier that, "Now they've got us surrounded, the poor bastards." And so, the famous demand for surrender, and even more famous one-word reply, was entirely in character for the commanders on both sides of the conflict.

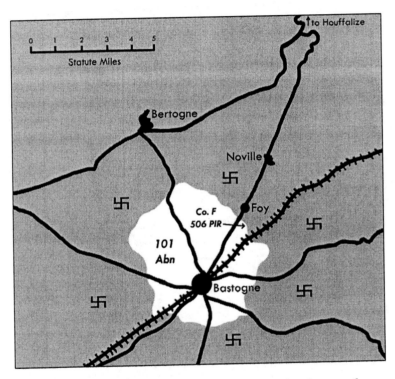

Bastogne besieged. The gray area represents the German forces surrounding Bastogne and the 101st Airborne Division

At 1130 hours on December 22 all became quiet on the front. Four German soldiers—two officers and two enlisted—came through the American lines carrying a large white flag. They announced that they wished to discuss terms of surrender, whereupon the officers alone were escorted through various command posts to division headquarters and Tony McAuliffe's staff.

22.Dezember 1944

An den amerikanischen Kommandeur der eingeschlossenen Stadt Bastogne.

Das Kriegsglück ist veränderlich, diesmal sind die amerikanischen Truppen in und um Bastogne durch starke deutsche Panzerkräfte eingeschlossen. Wietere deutsche Panzerkräfte haben die
Ourthe bei Ortheuville überschritten, Marche genommen und über
Hompré-Sibret-Tillet vorgehend St. Hubert erreicht. Libramont
ist in deutscher Hand.

Es gibt nur eine Möglichkeit die eingeschlossenen amerikanischen Truppen vor völliger Vernichtung zu bewahren: die
ehronvolle Uebergabe der eingeschlossenen Stadt. Hierfür wird
eine Bedenkfrist von zwei Stunden gegeben, die mit der Uebergabe
dieser Note beginnt.

Wenn dieser Vorschlag abgelehnt werden sollte, stehen ein
deutsches Artillerie-Korps und sechs schwere Flak-Abteilungen
bereit, die amerikanischen Truppen in und um Bastogne zu ver-
nichten. Der Befehl für die Eröffnung des Feuers wird sofort
nach Verstreichen der zweistündigen Frist gegeben werden.

Die durch dieses Bombardement entstehenden hohen Verluste
der Zivilbevölkerung sind mit der bekannten Humanität der Ameri-
kaner nicht zu vereinbaren.

Der deutsche Befehlshaber.

Bastogne Surrender Demand (in German), December 22, 1944

Rumors of the surrender negotiations spread to the troops in the foxholes. Such was the attitude of many that they assumed the Germans had come to surrender to THEM! Soldiers came out of their bunkers to relax, wash up and shave, or cook a hot meal at the lunch hour.

December 22nd 1944

To the U.S.A. Commander of the encircled town of Bastogne.

The fortune of war is changing. This time the U.S.A.
forces in and near Bastogne have been encircled by strong
German armored units. More German armored units have crossed
the river Ourthe near Ortheuville, have taken Marche and
reached St. Hubert by passing through Hompré-Sibret-Tillet.
Libramont is in German hands.

There is only one possibility to save the encircled
U.S.A. troops from total annihilation: that is the honorable
surrender of the encircled town. In order to think it over
a term of two hours will be granted beginning with the
presentation of this note.

If this proposal should be rejected one German
Artillery Corps and six heavy A. A. Battalions are ready
to annihilate the U.S.A. troops in and near Bastogne. The
order for firing will be given immediately after this two
hours' term.

All the serious civilian losses caused by this
artillery fire would not correspond with the wellknown
American humanity.

The German Commander.

Bastogne Surrender Demand (in English), December 22, 1944

At his headquarters in Bastogne, McAuliffe had spent
nearly 48 continuous hours dealing with a host of problems:
moving a division-sized body quickly into place, then attacks
by the enemy from all directions, supply shortages
(particularly ammunition), desperate attempts to maintain

communications with higher command. But despite it all, he felt sure he had the upper hand. The Germans had been unable to break through at even a single point in his defenses. His men were beating the enemy at every turn. Morale was high. And despite the temporary setback of bad weather which prevented aerial re-supply, it seemed a good bet that they could hold out until help arrived. So when told that the enemy had demanded his surrender, Brigadier General Anthony C. McAuliffe laughed out loud and said, "Aw, nuts."

The written surrender demand gave the Americans two hours to consider the terms being offered. Then the German emissaries were to be returned to their lines by 1400 hours. The enemy would wait an additional hour for an answer. After that would begin what was promised to be the "total annihilation" of the town.

McAuliffe quickly conferred with his staff. It was unanimously agreed that a U.S. surrender was out of the question. But there remained a need to make some sort of response to the German emissaries. What would be an appropriate answer to their impudent demand? Finally a member of the staff, Colonel Kinnard, said, "That first remark of yours would be hard to beat." This was met with applause all around, and so it was decided. The most famous and defiant stand by any American commander in all of World War II would be captured in the one-word communication: "Nuts!"

The rest of the day remained quiet. That evening, heavy nighttime bombing of the town began. It wasn't long before troops out on the MLR (Main Line of Resistance) stopped envying those in Bastogne with roofs over their heads.

Meanwhile up at Foy, Bill True shared a foxhole with his buddy Otto May. And a fine one it was, if you had to be stuck in one place for awhile. It was five wide by seven long, and two feet deep. They layered logs and dirt on top, which were quickly covered by snow as the weather turned freezing cold. It wasn't long before everyone was doing all they could just to stay warm. Sleeping bags, overcoats, and blankets helped. And no one thought twice about sleeping snuggled up with their buddy for warmth, spoon style—least of all Bill and Otto. No aspersions on any manhood were cast in *that* survival situation. But a problem still remained with cold feet. Arctic boots had not been ordered in time for most of the troops to have them on the front lines. And footwear was not the only thing in short supply.

Cut off from the outside world, the entire division was forced to make do with what it had. And what it had was precious little ammunition. Artillery rounds were strictly rationed, and doled out literally one at a time. Individual soldiers were down to one clip of M-1 rifle bullets. The weather had turned bitter cold—the coldest in 50 years according to some reports—and clouds and fog had made aerial re-supply impossible. Word spread that General George Patton was rushing north with his tank division to end the siege. Would he get there in time? The evening of the 22nd marked the nadir of Allied prospects, but still morale held strong. And then a miracle break in the cloud cover signaled a chance for salvation.

The fleet of C-47s had been standing by, ready at a moment's notice to fly to the rescue, but they had been frustrated by fog and snow. Finally, at 1130 hours on December 23, the first re-supply planes made it through. A large, clear field just west of Bastogne was designated the drop zone. By that afternoon 241 aircraft had delivered 144 tons of materiel, to the wonderment and joy of troops on the ground. Bill and Otto could see the operation from their foxhole at Foy and it was indeed a cause for celebration. With enough ammunition on hand, everyone knew it was only a matter of holding out till the cavalry arrived. And no one doubted that Patton would get through.

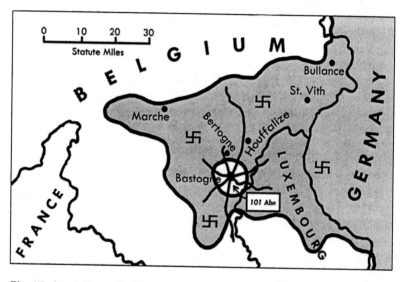

The "Bulge," December 25, 1944. The gray area represents the extent of the German advance with the 101st Airborne Division surrounded in Bastogne

The same day Len Hicks and Edgar Bishop found themselves on a scavenging mission to augment supplies for the troops on the line. In a small storage building on the north end of town they struck pay dirt. Len pried the lock with his "Arkansas screwdriver" and there before them was a huge pile of burlap gunny sacks. It was apparently a baking supply house of some kind and the sacks had been used to carry the loaves of bread. But Len knew at once their value to the men on the line. "Ed, find us a truck to drive these things up to the guys!" he shouted. Quickly he and Edgar commandeered a vehicle, loaded up, and headed north out the Noville road to Foy.

Bill and Otto had settled into their bunker and were doing as well as anyone else keeping the cold at bay. But those damned jump boots just couldn't keep their feet warm. Some of the men were starting to get frostbite, which could be extremely hazardous. Then up drove Hicks and Bishop.

"Here. Take these gunny sacks and wrap your boots with them. Use that twine to tie them off. They'll keep your feet warm and dry," Len told his compatriots.

Bill was a little skeptical, but willing to try anything. His feet were freezing. The misery never seemed to let up and made it almost impossible to sleep, even when that was practical. He and Otto did as Len suggested. The twine arrangement seemed a little slipshod, but then again if you weren't marching or moving around a lot, just hunkered down in the foxhole, it might hold OK. And in short order, by damn if it didn't work! True and May were shocked at how much difference that burlap could make in personal comfort. After days of cold torment, warm feet were simply the next best thing to being home and safe. They luxuriated in it, wallowed in the pleasure of warm, dry toes.

る る る

On Christmas day, Bill and Otto found themselves temporarily relieved from the front line. Their job: ration detail, carrying chow, water, and supplies up to the other guys on the MLR. On one pickup they were handed a mimeographed page. It was a message from McAuliffe to the troops. Someone on the general's staff had found a printing press in town, and run off the leaflets as a little holiday cheer.

HEADQUARTERS 101ST AIRBORNE DIVISION
Office of the Division Commander

24 December 1944

What's Merry about all this, you ask? We're fighting - it's cold
we aren't home. All true but what has the proud Eagle Division accomplished
with its worthy comrades the 10th Armored Division, the 705th Tank Destroy-
er Battalion and all the rest? Just this: We have stopped cold everything
that has been thrown at us from the North, East, South and West. We have
identifications from four German Panzer Divisions, two German Infantry
Divisions and one German Parachute Division. These units, spearheading the
last desperate German lunge, were headed straight west for key points when
the Eagle Division was hurriedly ordered to stem the advance. How effectively this was done will be written in history; not alone in our Division's
glorious history but in World history. The Germans actually did surround us,
their radios blared our doom. Their Commander demanded our surrender in
the following impudent arrogance:

December 22nd 1944

"To the U. S. A. Commander of the encircled town of Bastogne.

      The fortune of war is changing. This time the U. S. A. forces in
and near Bastogne have been encircled by strong German armored units. More
German armored units have crossed the river Ourthe near Ortheuville, have
taken Marche and reached St. Hubert by passing through Hompres-Sibret-Tillet.
Libramont is in German hands.
      There is only one possibility to save the encircled U. S. A. Troops
from total annihilation: that is the honorable surrender of the encircled
town. In order to think it over a term of two hours will be granted beginning with the presentation of this note.
      If this proposal should be rejected one German Artillery Corps
and six heavy A. A. Battalions are ready to annihilate the U. S. A. Troops
in and near Bastogne. The order for firing will be given immediately after
this two hour's term.
      All the serious civilian losses caused by this Artillery Fire
would not correspond with the well known American humanity.

The German Commander"

      The German Commander received the following reply:

22 December 1944

"To the German Commander:

      N U T S !

The American Commander"

      Allied Troops are counterattacking in force. We continue to hold
Bastogne. By holding Bastogne we assure the success of the Allied Armies.
We know that our Division Commander, General Taylor, will say: "Well Done! "
      We are giving our country and our loved ones at home a worthy
Christmas present and being privileged to take part in this gallant feat of
arms are truly making for ourselves a Merry Christmas.

/s/ A. C. McAULIFFE
/t/   McAULIFFE
      Commanding.

**Christmas Message to the Troops. Mimeograph flyer from Tony
McAuliffe delivered to the 101st Division, December 24, 1944**

It had the desired effect on True.

"Hey, look at this," he said to Otto. "The damn Germans wanted us to SURRENDER! And get what Mac said back? *NUTS!* That guy has balls. The newspapers are gonna eat this stuff up, that's for sure." Even at the youthful age of 21, True could easily see the historic importance of events unfolding around him.

That night the men were served hot bean soup in the foxholes. Compared to K-rations, it seemed like a feast. No one was much concerned that they were still completely surrounded by the German army.

      ∽   ∽   ∽

The day after Christmas began much as the days preceding it. On that morning, German units attacked the western Bastogne perimeter, leaving other points around the defensive line relatively quiet. Though they exerted strong pressure on the Screaming Eagles, the American positions held firm. Meanwhile, the tanks of Patton's 4th Armored Division had been steadily fighting their way north, meeting heavy resistance since they had begun the relief operation on the 22nd.

Bastogne was the key to victory in the very last chance the Germans would have to reverse the fortunes of war in the west. They put up fierce resistance, costing the armored U.S. column dearly in men and machines, nearly equal to the sacrifices of the encircled defenders. Over 1,000 American soldiers were lost in action. And by the afternoon of December 26, Patton's entire division force of medium tanks had been reduced to the equal of only a single battalion. But finally, at 1650 hours, three tanks from Company C, 37th Tank Battalion, drove to within sight of the 326th Airborne

Engineers of the 101st.

It was the beginning of the end for the German army in the Ardennes. A few days' fighting would be needed to secure supply lines leading into Bastogne from the south. But the encirclement had been broken, and the tide of the offensive had turned. Among the first American forces to enter the defensive perimeter was General Maxwell D. Taylor, commander of the 101st Airborne Division. He arrived in time to take charge of what would prove to be the heaviest fighting of the entire campaign.

∾   ∾   ∾

To Bill True and his buddies the aerial re-supply of December 23, and the subsequent breakthrough by U.S. armored forces on the 26th, were certainly joyous occasions. But any celebration was well tempered by the arduous task still before them: reverse the tide of battle and offensively advance out of the Bastogne pocket toward the heart of Germany. In the weeks to come the men did considerable moving about, as forces were repositioned. Often the command would come, "OK, dig in. You'll be here awhile." This would then be countermanded within hours, as the plan changed. Adding to the frustration was the difficulty of setting defensive positions. The weather was bitter cold and the ground frozen hard. G.I. issued entrenching tools were barely up to the task. Much colorful and creative language was heard throughout the Ardennes as the soldiers faced their duty with grim determination.

As always, outpost and patrol duties were a regular feature of life on the MLR. On one daytime patrol, Bill ran across a rather large group of dead German soldiers—perhaps as many as 25 or 30. They had been terribly chewed up by what looked to be 81-mm mortars. As usual, the bodies were searched for pistols. Finding none, it became obvious that this was not the first American patrol to pass that way.

Another patrol, this time at night, proved to be much more risky though not from enemy fire. The task was this: move out in front of the American lines and make a large half circle clockwise, coming back through our defenses at a carefully designated spot occupied by the 501st, on the right. Bill was in the lead. Unfortunately, his map reading skills hadn't improved much from those days in early training when his squad was as likely to get lost as find the right destination. It had become almost a joke among the first platoon, so frequently did it happen. But unlike those risk-free days, this time there were a few moments of real confusion and terror. Bill had taken them to the wrong point for re-entry.

At about this time, rumors had been circulating about enemy troops disguising themselves in American uniforms and infiltrating behind allied lines. When True and the others approached within earshot, and without the correct password, the first impulse on the part of the 501 guys was to shoot. Fortunately, caution prevailed. Eventually a convincing tale led to safe passage through the lines. But there was much consternation, and plenty of swearing about incompetence, and the typical Army SNAFU. "We shoulda' killed all you assholes!" was heard from one soldier as the F Company men departed. Bill was rightly shook up and plenty mortified as well.

It wasn't the last night adventure that would cause real concern.

Chapter X – White Christmas in a Foxhole

SCHLAPP DAT PIECE
Bill's True Tale

It's colder than a well digger's ass! Don't know which of
the guys I heard use that expression first, or whether it's
native to a particular part of the U.S., but it sure fits the
weather here in Belgium ever since it stopped snowing last
night. Those bitterly cold January days delivering the Omaha
World Herald through snowy high school winters come
readily to mind. Back then an occasional warm respite broke
the freezing monotony though, while here in a fox hole it just
goes on and on and on.

Those burlap gunny sacks Hicks found back in Bastogne
should earn him a medal. I continue to be amazed at the
warmth they bring to my feet by simply wrapping one around
each boot and tying it with heavy cord. If we were on the
move and doing much marching they probably wouldn't stay
on too well, but just standing or lying here in a cold hole this
burlap keeps your feet as warm as the 4th of July. What a truly
delicious and wonderful thing warm feet are.

Otto May and I are again sharing a hole since our platoon
dug into this defensive spot a couple of days ago. Not a
standard fox hole, it's only about two feet deep, but wide
enough and long enough for us to lie down in and try to sleep
when we're not keeping tabs on the squad. The frozen
ground makes digging mighty tough, and when you don't
know from minute to minute when you might have to move
out, a compromise on something less than a deep fox hole
seems to make sense. Anyway it allows us to lie below the
ground to avoid artillery or mortar fire, and to assume a good
firing position in the face of an attack.

"It'll be dark in an hour or so," I mention to Otto as we
both cut open a supper K-Ration with our jump knives.

"How about having Smitty and Sam take the first watch while you and I get an early nap before we relieve them?"

"Sounds okay," Otto says, as he tears his ration box in strips to make a bit of a fire, and opens his can of meat. We both like to sprinkle some of the bouillon powder over the supper can of meat and heat it when we can.

The wax covering on the K-Ration boxes lights readily and I add mine to the small pile and light it. We have to get our cooking done before nightfall, because the fire will give us away to the enemy. I save most of my bouillon powder to put into a canteen cup of water and put it next to the fire along with the canned meat. Some of the guys gripe like hell about the K-Rations, but I've gotten so I like them. If you switch the combinations around and use a little imagination it's at least something to do. And having something to do can get damn important when the hours of boredom drag on endlessly. Of late it's been cold, cold, boredom, and that's even harder to take.

Otto and I have tried to get a little shut-eye as Smitty and Sam took the first night-shift guard duty, but with little success. The bitter cold makes for fitful sleep even when you're bone tired. As we relieve the guys it's apparent that the night has gotten even colder, and the wind is whistling and moaning through the trees like someone out there dying.

Time slowly and reluctantly passes and snow is being blown off some of the heavily laden tree boughs. Every once in a while there's a thump that could be the stomp of an approaching jackboot.

"Those Krauts would have to be nuts to attack on a night like this," I observe to Otto.

"Seems unlikely," Otto replies, "but they sometimes do crazy things. It wouldn't be too surprising if they at least had some patrols out. That snow falling out of the trees makes some pretty weird sounds and I'm uneasy as hell. This figures to be one long night."

As twilight gives way to night, we hear odd sounds in the distance—voices. "Fock Yahnkees! Amerikaners kaput! Fock Prasident Roosenfelt!" Loud voices with thick German accents are shouting at us out of the darkness. What they're saying is hardly distinguishable—the guys who are yelling clearly haven't taken many English conversation classes—but the intent to insult us and arouse a response is obvious.

"How the hell do they know where we are?" I whisper to Otto, as I recover from my utter surprise and shock. "It's too dark to see a damn thing out there."

"I'll bet one of our stupid replacements lit a cigarette or something," Otto replies. "It may be a combat patrol trying to get us to give away our positions."

Otto and I decide to split up, crawl out to the other guys in the squad, and tell them to keep quiet and fix bayonets.

Fix bayonets. Fix bayonets. I'm back in Toccoa, Georgia, and Lt. Kenneth J. Havorka is putting First Platoon through bayonet drill. The Lieutenant has had military training at a school that featured a stern and awesome German Instructor named Schmidt. Master Sergeant Wilhelm Schmidt had had experience as an infantryman in World War I.

"We will now do the Long Thrust," Havorka orders. Left hand on the front stock of the rifle, right hand on the rear stock just behind the trigger guard, crouching position with left foot forward and right foot behind, we wait for his command. "Lunge," he shouts, and we plunge forward throwing our right foot forward some two yards or more while simultaneously thrusting the bayoneted rifle as far as we can reach. We have skewered an enemy soldier through and through.

"Left hand away from the rifle as you hold," he

commands. We're holding ten pounds of rifle and bayonet fully extended with our right hand only, the rear stock pressing up under our right forearm. "Hold," Havorka barks..."hold...hold." Minutes pass as our right arms seem near to breaking before the ardently longed for command finally comes: "SCHLAPP DAT PIECE!"

We smack the forestock of the rifle a resounding whack with the full strength of our left arm and hand. The force of our Long Thrust has driven our weapon through the enemy's chest and out his back causing the bayonet to become lodged in the bones. Thus, the necessity for us to "slap that piece" in order to dislodge the bayonet and pull it away.

"Withdraw...bayonet," the Lieutenant shouts. Bayonet withdrawn, you make a half turn left and bring the butt of your rifle smartly up with the full strength of your right arm, uppercutting and smashing the next enemy's chin to claim your second victim.

"You're doughboys, men! Infantry! Queen of Battle! Il ne pas passé! Great bayonet drill. Sergeant Schmidt would be proud of us all."

Lt. Havorka dismisses the platoon.

ॐ   ॐ   ॐ

The German taunts have gradually diminished as none of our squad has made a sound. Muffled footsteps follow a tension filled silence of a minute or more, and as the sound slowly recedes we presume the enemy has withdrawn.

"Can you imagine those bastards hollering 'F... Roosevelt?'" Otto finally whispers. "We should have yelled back 'Hitler's mother wears army boots,'" he adds.

"I really couldn't understand all they were calling out to us, Otto. If they really were saying 'F... Roosevelt' though, it sounds like some Republicans might have gotten to them."

My attempt at a bit of humor seems lame indeed, but I need something to cover my true feelings of consummate relief. While fixing my bayonet I had silently prayed... and my prayer had been answered. It had not been necessary for me to SCHLAPP DAT PIECE.

෨ ෨ ෨

One morning dawned cold and overcast, with a light ground fog obscuring no-man's-land and the enemy territory beyond. Bill and Otto May had been up for awhile and were building a small fire to heat coffee when as they watched, suddenly two figures emerged from the mist. Obviously Germans, they were in full uniform wearing garrison caps instead of helmets. Their hands were on top of their heads, with fingers interlaced, holding small white flags. And to Bill's great interest, both were wearing pistols at their sides.

"Nicht schiessen! Nicht schiessen!" they shouted as soon as within earshot. Don't shoot! Don't shoot!

Normally in war an act of surrender is one filled with tension. The party giving up has no way of knowing what the enemy will do, nor if they will honor the usual code of safe conduct for POWs. For this reason one might expect a surrendering soldier to throw away all weapons in order not to appear aggressive or dangerous, which might elicit an armed response. But here these two carried weapons on their hips in plain view. Bill had to wonder. Then a thought occurred to him. These soldiers were obviously turning themselves in. A deception and quick-draw of pistols at the last minute seemed unlikely; American rifles were trained on them with safeties off, ready to fire at an instant. Ah, but the pistols! Everyone in the war zone knew how desirable it was to capture an enemy handgun, both for protection and as a highly prized trophy. These guys were coming in bearing gifts! Yeah! And True would be only too happy to relieve them of their burden.

"Kommen zie mit mir," Bill ordered in one of the few German phases he knew. Quickly he and Otto took the pistol belts. Inside the holsters they found two very nice P-38s, in excellent condition, each with a full clip in the gun and a spare in the holster. A very nice haul indeed, even if they weren't the fabled Luger. This was the first pistol of any kind that Bill had personally possessed at any time in the war. Within fifteen minutes the prisoners had been marched 50 or 60 yards behind the MLR to company headquarters where they were turned over to the Company Commander. From there they would be taken further behind U.S. lines to battalion headquarters for interrogation, and whatever fate awaited them in some POW camp. They were certain to find kinder treatment there than if the Russians had captured them.

☙   ☙   ☙

As is common in war, in between the stark panic of artillery barrages and infantry attacks there were periods of absolute boredom. Then thoughts turned to personal comforts and the almost complete absence of the same. Food was always a prime focus, especially when the troops were stuck with K-rations, which seemed most of the time. At Bastogne, field kitchens were rarely seen anywhere near the front lines, so the men had to make do with what they had. Bill and Otto May managed some fairly creative ways to doctor up their meager provisions. And this not only helped pass the time, but improved the quality of their fare.

For example, they found that putting the lunch ration of cheese on the usually dry biscuit, and roasting this over a fire, something approaching a grilled-cheese sandwich could be made. The tin of breakfast meat was pretty bland by itself. But if the evening packet of beef bullion was sprinkled over it, the flavor was immensely enhanced and actually quite palatable. They often used the trick learned in Normandy of shaving the dark, hard, semi-sweet chocolate bar with a trench knife, then dissolving the pieces in hot water to produce a reasonable ersatz cocoa drink. And on rare occasion there were the more desirable "C" rations available. These had larger cans of one-dish meals such as beef stew with vegetables which were fairly tasty, provided there was means to heat them.

Two meals from this period, however, stood out forever in Bill's memory as being very special. On the first occasion, his squad ran into a group of Catholic nuns who ran a school or convent in the area. The sisters were exceedingly gracious and invited the dirty, unshaven troopers into their home for lunch. It was an ancient stone structure, quite in keeping with the classic image of cloisters and cathedrals that dot the European continent. The elaborate habits worn by the nuns added a touch of genteel civility to the occasion. Though their pantry was certainly as spare as any other non-combatants in the war zone, they offered all they had. Soon the soldiers were seated at table in the common dining hall. All the sisters scurried about to serve what seemed a veritable feast, wonderfully prepared and—praises be sung!—HOT. Tired and hungry, the men ate ravenously and soon had devoured every speck of food in the place. It was probably an entire week's supply of tightly rationed goods. The nuns never said a word about their sacrifice, and lunch was delicious!

But the biggest surprise was yet to come. Incongruously, it was out on the MLR. On later reflection, it seemed to many of the men to be almost a dream or hallucination. Some, including Tom Alley, later claimed that it never even happened, so bizarre was the very thought of it.

Steak.

It happened one night, without warning or preamble. Somewhere, somehow, scroungers had found a sizable cache of beef. Morale was generally high among the troops, but it could be unimaginably improved with a special treat for dinner. So the cooks all got together and set a plan. They'd cook the meat over open fires, and then have drivers ready at the instant they were needed to deliver the still-hot food to the men in the foxholes. Slabs of cooked steak were piled high inside 55-gallon drums to keep them warm as they were hauled to the front lines. There the men took turns leaving their shelters to visit the "welcome wagon." Grabbing hunks of meat with their dirty bare hands, they ate them like breadless sandwiches till all were devoured. Bill True remembers it as the finest steak he ever tasted before or since, though the quality was probably enhanced more from the circumstances than by any culinary skill of the Army cooks.

                                   ॐ   ॐ   ॐ

Some time after the breakthrough of Patton's tanks, Bill came down with an infection in his groin. It was a bad one. He had developed a terrible rash that itched unbearably, and the open sores oozed pus in a continuous, messy goo. In serious pain, he went first to the field hospital where a corpsman and then the battalion doctor looked it over. "You'll need to get to the hospital in town for this," the medico said. So the next stop was Bastogne itself, via bumpy jeep ride. There, another doctor took one look and wrote out a prescription for salve that he said would do the trick in short order. Then he left it to the female nurse on duty to administer the medicine.

The nurse had been present for Bill's examination and knew the extent and location of his ailment. The salve would have to be rubbed liberally and thoroughly all around the affected area, and she was obviously uncomfortable at the prospect. "Do you want me to put it on, or would you rather do it yourself?" she asked. Bill was as much relieved by her question as she was by his answer. "I think I can do it myself," he replied. And at that she left him to his own ministrations.

The doctor had also prescribed one night in the hospital. Bill was scheduled to return to duty on the front line the next day, taking along a supply of the salve. That evening another soldier from F Company's third platoon was brought in, and assigned to the next bed.

"What happened to land you in here?" Bill asked. Actually, he could guess at the cause just by looking at the guy. His left leg was missing, with a stump just above the knee heavily bandaged.

"We were out at Foy a while back, holding off the Krauts from that little railway station. You know it?"

"Yeah, I was out there, too. We could see the rail line from our foxholes. I know the place."

"Well, we're in the station house, shooting out the windows, and the Germans are real close, see? All of a sudden this potato masher came through the window, and I didn't have time to hide before the grenade went off. BOOM! Tore my foot and leg up pretty bad, I guess. Anyway, they had to take it all off."

"God. That's rough, fella. Now what happens?"

At this question the man's face lit up with a huge grin.

"I'm going home in a week or two. War's over for me, that's for sure, and I can't say I'm sorry one bit!"

Bill could not detect any dissemblance. The man seemed genuinely glad to be getting out of Bastogne alive and in mostly one piece. True envied him the trip back to the States. Everyone on the line was equally tired and scared and yearning for the security of home. But this wasn't a good way to get there.

                                                          ∾   ∾   ∾

Next day, as Bill was preparing to leave the hospital, he overheard two soldiers in a heated discussion.

"That G.I. Bill is just bullshit!" one was saying. "The Army needs us to keep fighting no matter how long it takes to beat the Krauts and Japs, and they'll say anything to make us think we're getting a good deal in return. They don't care if we get blown to bits, just that we keep fighting!"

"It can't be all lies, can it?" said a second. "I mean, all these guys counting on going to school when they get home? Hey Doc, you know anything about this G.I. Bill stuff?" he asked a young, friendly internist that happened to be passing by.

"Oh, it's for real all right," the doctor said. "Congress already passed the law and made a whole ton of money available. All you guys will be able to go to college, tech school, or any place you want, all on the government's tab. It's going to change a lot of things, that's for sure!"

Right then and there, Bill knew he had to look into this new prospect. He'd heard of the upcoming benefits package for veterans but hadn't given that much thought to his plans after (and IF) he survived the war. But suddenly a spark was lit. He'd go to college, be the first in his family to graduate.

And he'd really make something of himself!

That die was cast.

❧   ❧   ❧

It took the American forces some time to re-group, re-supply, and get organized after their encirclement ordeal. But with the breakthrough, and once all the pieces were in place, the Screaming Eagles moved out to wreak some serious vengeance on the enemy. The division was on the move, pushing the Germans out of the Bastogne perimeter and back toward their homeland. F Company soon found itself covering a lot of ground, rather than maintaining their fixed defensive positions as before. The action heated up, and the Air Corps was there to back them.

On a gray, overcast afternoon, Bill and his F Company cohorts were marching north in a coordinated, regimental-level attack. In the distance were their comrades on the left flank, where an enemy artillery barrage was in progress perhaps a quarter mile away. Suddenly a formation of P-47s streaked overhead toward the fight. As they neared the front line, a stunning salvo of rockets fired from beneath their wings at Kraut positions. The effect on the ground was devastating; the attack vicious and concentrated.

"Hey, aren't they a little close to our guys with those rockets?" someone asked.

"Nah, they know what they're doin'. But I wouldn't want to be anywhere near the target, that's for sure," was the reply.

Some time after this it was learned that, in fact, a number of American soldiers had been killed by "friendly fire." Sgt. Willie Morris, F Company's original top kick, had been among them. The P-47's had mistakenly strafed their own lines.

Days later, Bill's company was attacking directly in the face of artillery fire from big German guns out of sight in the distance. Shells landed in what looked like random patterns all around the area. Amid the din and smoke and falling debris, True noticed a wounded man leaning against a tree trunk, being attended by an Army corpsman. The corpsman was holding a lit cigarette up to the man's nose so that he could take a puff of smoke. This was necessary because his jaw had been completely blown away by shrapnel.

August 13, 1999, Bastogne, Belgium. Deryck and Bill True in front of the monument.

As late afternoon faded toward evening, F Company found itself moving up a hill in a wooded area. Johnny Jackson was ahead of True when the artillery shells began to fall with ever more frequency. Soon the woods were inundated with explosions: trees ripped apart like toothpicks, earth and debris flying everywhere, smoke and the smell of cordite thick in the air. It was hard for a sane man to think straight and keep marching in the face of such constant fire, but they trudged onward. Then suddenly there was a devastating burst close by. Bill hit the dirt and managed to avoid injury, but Jackson wasn't so lucky. Shrapnel from the shell ripped through his back and buried itself in his spine as he went down like a sack of potatoes.

The attack continued. More explosions, more deafening roar of artillery shells. True passed by his friend Johnny, who was bleeding badly but fully conscious. Dude Stone was attending him, injecting a morphine syrette. This was hardly the first time Bill had seen comrades felled by enemy fire. Ordinarily, there wasn't time to dwell on it. Empathy or mourning would wait, as the combat at hand took all of a man's attention. But this was different. Johnny was his absolute closest friend, and had been since their early days at Toccoa. In something of an emotional daze, the chaos all around seemed to momentarily dim in Bill's consciousness. Even the sounds of battle became strangely muffled. It lasted briefly, then reality came back to focus. *There was no time to stop.* He *had* to keep the squad moving toward the enemy. Dude would take care of Johnny, who would be out of the war after this injury. With thoroughly mixed feelings, True pushed on.

The shelling continued with unabated fury. Then, when it seemed impossible that the barrage could increase any further, suddenly it *did*. Explosions everywhere, one after the other in deafening cacophony. Bill knew he had to find temporary shelter and desperately looked for any kind of depression in the ground. It was dark now, and difficult to see in the gloom. Bright flashes from shell bursts made it worse; shrank the pupils to pinpoints, making it harder to see when the strobe-effect of gunfire briefly ceased. And suddenly there it was, not ten feet away! An old, abandoned foxhole was now his only refuge. In sheer panic he dove for it, landing at an odd angle on his left foot. Pain seared through his knee, almost blinding him with its intensity. But he had made it and was safe inside the arms of mother earth, yet again!

∂o   ∂o   ∂o

When the pain in his knee subsided enough to think straight, Bill looked out from his borrowed foxhole. His unit had moved forward and he was now in the rear of the action. Agonizingly, he managed to crawl out of the hole and, leaning on his rifle as a crutch, started working his way back to where an aid station would likely have been set up. It took what seemed like hours to finally arrive at the tent with the familiar red cross on it. There, medics examined his injury and pronounced it severe. He would have to be transported further back to a real hospital for treatment. For him, too, this particular battle was over for now.

Though not as serious as thought at first, the knee injury was bad enough to require days of rest and recuperation. All in all, Bill didn't much resent this a bit. And the resulting Purple Heart would later prove to be one of the keystones in his getting out of Europe with the first troops to go home. But by the time he left the hospital, his unit had traveled far beyond the last position he had known them to occupy. He was unsure how to get back with his buddies. Then the ubiquitous "repple-depple" came into play.

Officially they were called "Replacement Depots," and consisted of a small complex of tents or barracks with various support facilities and personnel. Their purpose was to move unattached or displaced military personnel to wherever they might be needed in the area. Someone who got lost from his original unit, like Bill, would report to a repple-depple for re-assignment. From there he would ordinarily be transferred to whatever outfit had a need. But paratroopers were a different breed.

Once he had made it known that he was with the 101st Airborne, True was treated differently than other soldiers being cycled through the center. For one thing, he was immediately issued a standard Army .45 caliber automatic pistol. This was because, as the supply sergeant explained, all paratroopers get side-arms. It was certainly news to Bill, having never been issued one before. But he wasn't about to object. Next they set about to find his old outfit: Company F, 506th PIR, so that he could rejoin them. Unlike ordinary soldiers, the paratroopers were considered elite troops whose task required them to stick together as units. So Bill found himself stuck for a few days while Fox Company was located. He decided to spend some of the time at the local firing range, getting acquainted with his new handgun.

The main weapon of a rifleman is, naturally enough, a rifle. Bill was very comfortable with his old M-1 and depended on it totally. Pistols were strictly for personal *defensive* use, not to attack anyone. As such, officers were routinely given handguns, but line soldiers mostly went without. True knew the basics of how to handle and shoot the .45, but this was the first time he'd had a chance to actually do some serious practice with it. His first thought was that they must have screwed up the sights at the factory. He couldn't hit the broad side of a barn with it! What the hell??!!

Soon he came to realize that this was normal. *Nobody* could hit the broad side of a barn with a standard issue .45. It was made to such loose tolerances that the sights were more decoration than useful appendages. This was intentional on the part of designers. The inherent sloppiness did make for inaccuracy; which meant that a soldier had to be *very* close to the target to hit anything. On the other hand, that same looseness made for extreme reliability. A U.S. pistol could be dropped in the mud. Sand and dirt could encrust it and get inside, and it would still go BANG every time you pulled the trigger. In war this is a good thing.

Deryck and Bill True on top of the Bastogne monument at the marker which shows where Bill's F Company, 506th PIR, fought during the battle near the village of Foy.

By contrast, the German Luger was an extremely elegant, refined, and accurate weapon. But it had so many complex moving parts, and they were so finely machined and hand-fitted, that the least contamination rendered them inoperable. Everyone in the European Theatre wanted Lugers for war trophies. But the fact was that they were pretty worthless to the average foot soldier who spent his time in the muck of a foxhole.

Bill allowed as how he'd stick to his trusty old M-1 in any event. But he didn't give up the pistol. It was still an extremely valuable commodity, if only for the purpose of barter. And he was soon to learn that it was highly pilferable, as well.

In his several days at the repple-depple True met up with another soldier: a regular Army type, who seemed quite friendly. His name was Joe. One day Joe approached him to ask a favor.

"I'm going into town tonight and I'd sure like to carry some personal protection. Any chance I could borrow your .45? I'll bring it back in the morning." he said.

Bill thought this over with somewhat mixed feelings. But after all, Joe had seemed an OK guy. And he'd be here tomorrow, so what the heck? "Sure, just don't lose it." he said.

"Great!"

Next day, Bill went to Joe's tent to retrieve his pistol. Joe was gone, and was nowhere to be found throughout the complex. So much for trusting a new buddy. But when this was explained, the supply sergeant cheerfully issued a brand new pistol and everything was right again.

Eventually True did make it back to his old unit, which had done some pretty intense fighting in his absence. There was still more to do in the Bulge campaign, but things were really winding down now. Sporadic action gradually petered out. Finally word came to move out after being relieved on the line. They were going to their old, familiar home in France: Mourmelon-le-Grande. But Bastogne would prove to be a seminal chapter in the story of the 101st Airborne; a place and a battle with which their name would be forever linked. Its importance would be summarized in the official 12th Army Group After Action Report for December, 1944, as follows:

"Preoccupation with the key position of Bastogne dominated enemy strategy to such an extent that it cost him the advantage of the initiative. The German High Command evidently considered further extension to the west or north as both logistically and strategically unsound without possession of Bastogne, as that town overlooks the main roads and concentration areas of the spearheads. By the end of the month, the all-out effort in the north had become temporarily defensive; in the west there was a limited withdrawal, and the array of German forces around Bastogne clearly exposed the enemy's anxiety over that position. Until the Bastogne situation is resolved one way or the other no change in strategy can be expected."

The Screaming Eagles were the pivotal element in foiling the last, desperate attempt by fascist forces to salvage their grip on Western Europe.

CHAPTER XI

Wie Eins Lili Marlene
From Alsace to Berchtesgaden

"I feel like a fugitive from the law of averages."
Anonymous soldier at war's end

There were no regrets when word came down that the 101st would be pulling out of the Bastogne area. The Germans had been stopped cold (both literally and figuratively) in the "Bulge" area of Belgium, but were reported to be mounting attacks south and east in the Alsace region. Fighting Krauts was never a picnic, but movement in a southerly direction might at least provide a few degrees of warmth.

Loading once again onto the open-topped trucks that had taken them to Bastogne just a month earlier, the mood of the men was nearly festive. "Anything sounds like a vacation after the miserable freezing we've had in the Belgian woods," True observed to his squad as he pulled himself up into the truck bed.

One of the new recruits who had arrived at Mourmelon in early December spoke up. "If I live to get back to Tampa I'm never gonna be anyplace where it snows again, so help me, God. How the hell anyone with one brain cell would voluntarily live in a place that gets this cold is a mystery to me," he added, as several of his southern compatriots chimed in with soulful agreements.

The weather was still below freezing with light-to-moderate snowfall as the trucks crawled slowly along icy, slick roads. It took days to traverse miles that normally could be covered in mere hours under normal weather and road conditions. Several villages and towns provided nighttime stopovers along the way until arrival at Drulingen, France. There, the 2nd Battalion would spend some days before moving into line at Haguenau near the German border.

By this time the German line jutted out to encompass a small town only a couple of miles from where F Company was billeted. Battalion headquarters was interested in any intelligence that might be obtained. Thus, not long after arriving, Fox Company was ordered to send out a night patrol to capture one or more Kraut prisoners for interrogation.

Lieutenant Ben Stapelfeld, new to the company after Holland, was selected to lead a large patrol, which the higher-ups ordered to be platoon-sized. It was expected that the Germans would have outposts set well in front of their main line. But if the patrol could either bypass the outposts, or get close enough to overwhelm them before a general firefight broke out, there would be an excellent chance to bring back prisoners.

Bill True was now in Stapelfeld's 1st Platoon, so the ten men of his squad were among the 30 constituting the patrol. Bill Green, a sergeant in the company headquarters unit, volunteered to go along as well. Green had extensive experience in leading patrols and the lieutenant happily accepted his offer to join in.

Some time after dark the men blackened their faces with burnt cork. Then, after stern warnings to carry nothing that might rattle or otherwise give off sound, the patrol set out. Green, along with one of the squad scouts and Lt. Stapelfeld, led the patrol as they advanced at a brisk pace toward the German lines. Soon considerable ground had been covered. Hopes began building that any nearby outposts had been bypassed. Then suddenly there was an explosion up ahead. Either a land mine or a booby trap had gone off at the lead point of the patrol. Immediately after that a Kraut machine gun opened fire with its characteristic "brrraaaappp" staccato sound. It was soon joined by another. Any chance of surprise was now lost as every man dove for the safety of Mother Earth. Next a parachute flare lit the area like a night baseball game at Yankee Stadium. No one dared move as ever more machine guns joined the din. Bullets cracked the air inches above their heads as the flying lead broke the sound barrier. They were really "in the shit."

True's squad was at the rear of the action, but he could feel the crackling gun fire almost as much as the men at the front. Mercifully, as the flare finally died out, word quickly passed back: "Abort the patrol, return to our own lines." That was all they needed to hear. Between bursts of fire the troopers raced back, hitting the ground repeatedly as the lead from the ultra-fast Kraut guns rattled overhead. The Germans seemed to be firing high, perhaps because the ground fell away with distance. For awhile it seemed that everyone might return safely.

But such was not the case. Bill Green, leading the advance near the front of the column, had been hit in the first surprising burst of fire. So had the squad scout. Stapelfeld and others near the point had dragged them back, but unlike the scout, Green did not survive his wounds. True learned of this only after arriving back at the company area. Upon hearing the story he was reminded of the first days at Bastogne, when Mather had been mortally wounded. "Another exceptional soldier dead," he thought. "And this one only because he volunteered."

As he pondered the senselessness of battle, and the utter randomness of who would live or die, his internal monologue continued. "I decided back in Normandy never to volunteer. At least *that* makes sense. I'll keep on doing my duty, sure, and be the best squad leader I can. Gotta do that for the guys. But volunteering? Not on your life. Odds are getting better every day that I won't make it home. If that happens it's *not* gonna be because I went out of the way looking for trouble. My mother didn't raise any fools."

Bill was not alone in this view.

The 2nd Battalion went into reserve for the next several days. The sun came out, snow started melting, and everyone got to take a shower in portable units that came around. Life was starting to seem a bit livable. A few movies from home were even shown, and issues of the Stars and Stripes became available.

One of the features in the Stars and Stripes that was followed avidly was the advance of the Russian lines against the Germans. True and his buddies found themselves rooting whole heartedly for the Russians with each issue of the Army newspaper. Every advance made on the Eastern Front was greeted with an eager "Go you Russkies!"

In a V-mail letter home on February 1, 1945, True wrote:

"We're still keeping quite busy but I'm really anxious about our Russian friends. Hope they can keep going."

Bill Mauldin's cartoons in the *Stars and Stripes* were another feature eagerly anticipated. One capitalized on Mauldin's theme of satirizing commissioned officers. It showed two of them gazing out over a panoramic scene as one of them observed: "Beautiful view. Is there one for the enlisted men?"

News of the war in the Pacific was much more sobering.

Japanese soldiers were recognized as far more fanatic than the Germans. By most accounts, they'd all gladly fight to the death defending their emperor. It seemed to some a likely prospect that the 101st Airborne Division would be making a trip to the Far East when the war in Europe ended. And a D-Day-like invasion jump in Japan was not a cheering thought.

The Final Campaign Theater

401

☙   ☙   ☙

In early February the 506th relieved infantrymen of the 79th Division and moved into Haguenau, France. It was a big city and the Moder River ran directly through it, varying in width from as narrow as 40 or 50 feet to as much as 100 yards. Wooden frame houses, usually two or three stories, and a hodgepodge of commercial buildings were strewn along both banks of the river. Germans occupied those on the north and Americans on the south, with only the water separating them.

F Company took a stretch of buildings that had been extensively damaged by mortar and artillery fire. Nevertheless the ruins would provide welcome protection from both weather and enemy alike, and the men were happy for the novel luxury of occupying civilian homes while on the front line of combat.

The relief itself was carried out at night since experience had shown that movement during daylight hours frequently brought on heavy cannonades from the Germans. Silence was important as well, since the Krauts were so close across the river as to distinguish individual human voices. Everyone was especially cautioned to avoid shouting or clanging of equipment.

Bill True's squad drew a large two story house that also had a half-basement. Several windows faced the river on all three levels. About 75 yards directly across the river was a long brick building stretching almost a city block. It looked to be some type of warehouse and it was *definitely* occupied by Germans. Before leaving, the guys from the 79th told True there had been machine gun fire from that building at night on several occasions.

The real danger though was from the heavy artillery

which could come at any time of day or night. Some very big stuff, reputed to be huge railway guns well back of the German lines, had rocked the whole area more than once. "Of course there's nothing you can do about those," said the sergeant from the outgoing unit as he was relieved. "If one of those babies hits your house there'll just be pieces to pick up. Keep the daylight movement outside to a minimum, and the window blankets tight at night. With luck you might just make it." And on that cheerful note, the infantry moved out as the paratroops moved in.

The house had suffered substantial damage from shell-fire and mortars, but the 79th had made it quite livable. One of the three bedrooms on the second floor still had curtains and a large mahogany armoire with no bullet holes in it at all—remarkable under the circumstances. The kitchen, dining area, and a master bedroom on the ground floor were in good condition as well. The basement had also been part of the regular living quarters for the original occupants, and the addition of a few army cots made useful bunking for several guys in the squad.

True and two others took the large bed in the ground floor bedroom for sleeping, and the second floor bedroom would serve the rest. The remaining rooms had been severely damaged, with walls blown out, and thus were open and exposed to the elements.

The water system was still up and running in the house. This was a real break, and not the case with many of the other houses the company occupied. Two gas-operated lamps and a portable stove in working order completed the facilities and made for a more than adequate front-line home. To be this comfortably situated, with the enemy only yards away, was more than any of the men could have dreamed of during their weeks at Bastogne.

Two-man outlooks were maintained around the clock, with the windows in the basement determined to be the best post. Standing on the basement floor, a man could look out at eye level and observe the entire area, with a clear field of fire extending to the brick building across the river. For this reason, the squad machine gun was set up there. By moving one of the heavy wooden tables down from the kitchen and bracing the gun tripod with sand bags found in a corner bin, an effective portable firing unit was created. The machine gun could be pulled back from the window for concealment, and readily slid back up into firing position as needed.

Their first night was a quiet one with only sporadic incoming artillery, none of which landed very close. The expected machine gun fire from across the river never opened up and most of the squad got a good night's sleep. Taking a regular two-hour guard tour with Marv Crawford on the fourteen-to-sixteen hour post, True had been pleasantly surprised. "What do you think, Marv?" he asked. "Maybe those Krauts in the warehouse got word that it's the 506th up here now, and they figure they better lay low."

"Man, wouldn't that be nice," Marv said. "But don't forget about those big railway guns. They don't figure to worry much about which Americans are in these houses."

"Yeah, you're right. If you're pulling the lanyard on a canon twenty miles back you don't give two cents for paratroops sittin' on this river. But ain't this peace and quiet a wondrous good thing?"

Crawford nodded. "Let's enjoy it while we can."

❧   ❧   ❧

Bill's squad had hauled in several days' supplies with them when they moved into their new house. There were a couple of ten-in-one rations (rations for ten men for one day), as well as some boxes of both C and K-Rations. Of the three different types, the ten-in-one were by far the most desirable, since there was much more variety in them. They even had some canned items, such as bacon.

Soon the men settled into an occupation routine. Mostly-boring days were shortened a bit by mixing and experimenting with the different foods provided in the rations. Everyone in the squad took a turn cooking meals, each trying to outdo the other with something both appetizing and filling. No one acquired Primo Chef status, but all participated with gusto and no one screwed up enough to be relieved of duty.

Weeks later, True wrote in a letter home on March 24th.

"We were all living in houses with the Krauts about 75 yards away in homes and buildings across the river. Our squad had a pretty nice house with 2 good bedrooms. There was plenty of coal in the shed to cook with, and potatoes, onions, canned fruit etc. in the cellar. These plus our regular rations … made some pretty nice meals."

One day word came down from Army intelligence that civilians in the town might be fifth-columnists, alerting the enemy about American movements. The Alsace region had repeatedly switched back and forth between France and Germany over the decades. There were known to be people with "unreliable allegiances" in the area. Everyone was put on alert for spies, which made it even more important to limit daytime activities to a minimum.

The necessity for minimizing daylight movement was soon brought home with sobering clarity. The first full day in town, Len Hicks had liberated a Citroen auto for use by all the squads to transport materiel. One bright sunny morning Ed Bishop and "Dutch" Ostrander were using it to ferry supplies to all the houses. Suddenly an artillery shell landed in the street 30 yards ahead, showering them with dirt and bits of cobblestone. Soon they were in the middle of a full scale barrage, and it was obvious they were the main target. German gunners had them zeroed in. Before there was time to duck down a side alley, a round burst close at hand, upending the vehicle. Food rations, ammo cans, and various first aid supplies were scattered everywhere, and both Bishop and Ostrander were seriously wounded by shrapnel. The car was utterly demolished: a twisted, smoking pile of metal, glass and rubber that once was a civilized mode of transportation. Luckily, the whole event was witnessed by others in F Company who quickly dragged the troopers to safety. The wounded survived, but barely. And never again were supplies delivered except by hand under cover of darkness.

One ration run about a week later had a major payoff. In addition to the regular food rations, there was real PX food, several cans of beer, the latest issues of Stars and Stripes, and mail from home. The last mail call had been some weeks before, so reading longed-for letters from home got immediate priority. Having a couple of cold beers (the weather was still cold enough to keep the beer chilled), while reading about the Russian advances in the Stars and Stripes ran a close second. And the PX rations were the frosting on the cake.

Like the mail, the most recent distribution of PX rations had been weeks before. Smoking lousy Fleetwood and Chelsea cigarettes from K rations was getting really old. Luckies, Camels, and Chesterfields were a fabulous treat for the men, most of whom now had taken up the habit. Added to that were candy bars, gum, soap, toothpaste, and razor blades, all of which were eagerly snatched up. Everyone felt like the Christmas they'd missed at Bastogne had finally arrived.

As always, mail from home was the main attraction. Bill had half a dozen envelopes to open and savor, each one a breath of fresh air from home. His sisters told of their new dresses for the high school prom. Dad was planting new flowers in the garden. All the mundane details of life in the "real" world made for welcome and interesting reading. However, as had happened before, the incongruity of it all struck home. Was his father tilling the earth in his rose garden at the same instant that an artillery tree burst nearly killed Bill and others in his squad? Were the girls shopping for dresses the very moment he and his buddies were fixing bayonets, preparing for an enemy charge? How could the world be divided so neatly into two such disparate parts: the regular, safe doings of civilized people back home, and the life-or-death moments of the combat soldiers who defended their freedom? His own life could be snuffed out at any moment, yet others carried on theirs as usual, in their untroubled corner of the world. Bill didn't resent this at all. But the comparison seemed somehow surreal and, on reflection, hard to assimilate.

As the days rolled on there was artillery and mortar fire, punctuated by rounds from the Big Bertha rail guns, at random times both day and night. However, the machine gun in the brick building across the river had been silent ever since True's arrival. Then one night in the second week he found himself on guard-post in the basement.

For a time all seemed boring and quiet. Then suddenly several short bursts of automatic weapons fire crashed and rattled off the house, fortunately without effect on the inhabitants. Bill thought, "That's probably those guys across the way, just reminding us they're still around." There was no apparent reason for the attack. No lamps had been lit for several hours, so light leaking past a blanket over the windows couldn't have invited it. Regardless of the cause, True and one of the new recruits immediately began moving their machine gun table into position. But by the time they got it into the window, the Kraut gun had ceased firing. It was a very dark night. Without a visible muzzle flash it would be impossible to tell where the enemy was located, and the German gun remained silent the rest of the night. There was no opportunity to return fire. The troopers were left frustrated, and vowing to somehow "get back" at the enemy if they could.

Next day True and the recruit spied through field glasses at the warehouse across the river, trying to pinpoint the machine gun nest that had vexed them the night before. It was hard to be precise. But they both agreed that the angle of the tracers pointed to a single window as the most likely spot. Bill positioned his machine gun to zero precisely on that spot, but with the muzzle set a bit back in the basement and not visible from outside. If the Germans opened up again, even if they didn't use tracers, there'd be a good chance of nailing them.

True took the first guard-post that night. Nothing from the Germans. He decided to spend the full night in the basement so he'd be close by if they opened up later. All was quiet. Then next morning Bill advised his squad to leave the machine gun in place and zeroed in. "If the Krauts decide to spray our side again, and are dumb enough to use the same window, we'll make 'em sorry."

F Company had just learned that the former commander of E Company, Dick Winters, had been moved up to battalion headquarters and promoted to major. It was widely known that the men of Easy Co. greatly respected and admired Dick, compared to their original C. O., Captain Sobel. So it was a pleasant surprise when Major Winters himself paid a visit to Bill's squad in their makeshift billet.

Winters explained that he was taking a look at all of the battalion's positions, and asked True to show him his set up. After a tour of the upper floors Bill took him down to the basement and explained their plan with the machine gun. "Unfortunately, the Krauts were quiet over there last night, but we're hoping they'll give us another crack at 'em," he told the major.

"Looks good, soldier. Keep it up," Winters said, as he wished the squad luck and moved on to further inspections.

As it turned out, the German guns would never again fire from the brick building across the water. It became just one more frustrating disappointment for the men during their stay in Haguenau. But True remembered ruefully a snippet from Robert Burns: "The best laid schemes o' mice an' men Gang aft a-gley." Life in the army surely proved that point with maddening regularity.

One morning not long after this, Bill was sitting in the kitchen drinking coffee. The wonderful smell of frying bacon filled the room as everyone eagerly anticipated a hearty breakfast. Suddenly there was a tremendous explosion in the adjacent bedroom. It was the room True shared with two others. As a blinding cloud of smoke and dust burst through the bedroom door and into the kitchen, a tiny piece of shrapnel or debris struck the tip of True's nose. It drew one, then two drops of blood. He felt his nose and looked at the blood with surprise. Then before the dust had even settled he stepped into what was left of the bedroom. The view was sobering.

The outer wall was entirely gone. The bed was in shreds, and the few other meager pieces of furniture were completely demolished. "I was in that bed not five minutes ago," True thought to himself. "OK, so Fritz has missed me again. But can this kind of luck last till the whole damn war is over?" he mused. Recurrent doubts about his ultimate survival again nagged him.

"Guess we're all pretty lucky when you think about it," Crawford commented as the rest of the squad gathered to observe the destruction. "That was probably only an 88. If it had been one of those railroad guns, F Company would be scratching this whole squad off right now."

There wasn't any sense in belaboring the point. Everyone pitched in on the clean up, and construction was started to completely close off the now useless room. It was especially important to block out light streaming from the kitchen through the gaping maw. A large piece of the wall had fallen but remained intact. Working together, several troopers heaved and grunted it back into place. It would serve much of the purpose, but more was needed. Some scrap lumber found in the basement, and upholstery material from a useless sofa, ultimately provided a fully blacked out separation of the bedroom from the kitchen. True had to relocate his sleeping quarters. But at least he was alive to need them.

As the days expanded into weeks, the men grew increasingly accustomed to the easiest combat experience F Company had yet known. "Jeez! There hasn't even been a single patrol, day or night," Bill thought gratefully one dark evening as he and Crawford headed to their command post to pick up rations. On arrival at headquarters though, Operations Sergeant Tom Alley put a damper on that line of thinking. "Yeah, well try tellin' that to Taylor," he said. Second Platoon Sergeant John Taylor had had a harrowing patrol just the night before, and Tom filled them in on the details.

Taylor had been chosen along with several others, including Borden, Noody, Segal, and Wright, for a reconnaissance mission. They were to make a night-time foray across the river to find out what they could about the German positions and intentions. From a 3rd floor window in their platoon command post they had selected the spot where they'd cross the river, and the route they would follow. The path skirted through a graveyard and crossed behind some houses that might yield a prisoner or two. This would be an obvious bonus for the intelligence guys. It was important not to get into a firefight, however, since alerting the Krauts would make re-crossing the river next to impossible.

Combat engineers supplied them with two rubber boats for the patrol and gave them an opportunity to try them out on a safe pond well back of the lines. But the practice with the boats was a fiasco. The men weren't able to control their craft even on the calm pond. What the hell would they do on a swift moving river?

Back at F Company Headquarters, Sergeant Studs Malley provided the answer. "I'm a strong swimmer," he said. "We'll tie a rope around one of the trees on this side. I'll swim across with it and hold while you guys pull yourselves over in the boats."

The crossing had worked just as Malley outlined it. His swimming prowess in the swift flowing and nearly freezing water impressed the hell out of everyone. Luckily, Malley's long johns were olive drab since starkly white underwear might have attracted German attention.

The boat landed ashore on the German side near a road leading past the graveyard. Taylor sent two men out to the left with a BAR where they could take up positions to cover a nearby house suspected as a hideout for enemy soldiers. By prior arrangement there were also two machine guns back on the American side, trained on the same house. But this was just a precaution. A firefight was still to be avoided if at all possible.

Easing over a wall into the graveyard the patrol crawled slowly through the tombstones toward their objective. The gravel on the graveyard paths made silent movement impossible though, and their scrabbling over the stones seemed loud as hail on a tin roof to the nervous troopers. Adding to the tension, someone suddenly whispered loudly to Taylor, "Check your watch! Your watch!" Looking down, John was shocked to see that his large dial wristwatch, with its brightly fluorescent face, was beaming almost like a flashlight. Sheepishly, he quickly stuffed the offending time piece into his pocket.

Now easing up to a wall adjacent to the house they sought, the men stopped and listened for the sound of movement. Nothing. Move a bit, stop and listen repeatedly, all the while remaining as quiet as possible and straining to hear any sound of enemy threat. Their stealth was soon rewarded. As they neared the house casual scuffling could be heard. The Germans had positions both inside the building and out, and no alarm had yet been sounded. The Americans might just be able to grab an inattentive Kraut and kidnap him quietly back

412

to headquarters. What a coup that would be!

Tense minutes passed, every man hugging the ground hardly daring to breathe. Taylor cautiously eyed the situation, looking for his chance. But soon it became clear that luck was not on his side. The Germans were relaxed, talking and joking among themselves, but all in groups of three or more! There was no opportunity to take a single soldier captive without the risk of alerting the others. And avoiding an all-out firefight was more important than the intelligence value of a single prisoner.

Disappointment had to be tempered by reasonable expectation. Any intelligence gained of enemy positions is better than none, and they had already gained some. John had to content himself with that. His mind set, Taylor gave the word to move out. He had to get the patrol back across the river as quickly as possible, and report their findings to command.

Slowly, deliberately crawling back through the graveyard they arrived again at the river bank. Taylor counted heads. Where the hell were the BAR guys? *Damn!* In the stress of their tense retreat, no one had thought to alert the troopers manning the Browning. There was nothing to do but go back. So another painful and scary trip was made through the tombstones, to retrieve the forgotten comrades.

Thank God, the Germans still seemed unaware of their presence. But how much more screwing around could they get away with on the enemy side of the river? Surely the sentries must have heard their clumsy scrambling through the gravel, back and forth *twice* now! In his imagination John could see the enemy flares going up, and machine guns blowing his entire patrol straight into the hereafter. His heart sank with fear.

No time to waste now; they had to get moving and fast!

413

Standing on the river bank Taylor, Borden, and two others held the rope while the first boat made it safely across. Every man held his breath and prayed the Germans would give them just a few more minutes grace. Then they realized, on the second trip there would be no one holding the rope! As John and the others watched with dismay, their boat drifted uncontrollably with the current. Where the hell would they end up?

But again their luck held. Though further downstream than planned, the new landing spot worked out OK, and made for a challenging but manageable climb up the embankment. The boat emptied quickly as the troopers made a mad scramble ashore and up the bank to safety.

John Taylor had seen a number of action-packed patrols over the months since D-Day in Normandy, but this was one of the scariest. Not because of any real action; he was almost used to lead flying at him. It was the spookiness of the scene. All those creepy tombstones, and the men slinking up on what he knew was a superior enemy force secure on their own turf. Then there was the wild, almost uncontrollable, boat ride both ways, knowing they were fully exposed to machine gun fire if even one German discovered their presence. Just thinking about it raised the hair on the back of his neck. It was a vivid, nerve-wracking memory to last a lifetime.

True and Crawford heard the details of this account with sympathetic alarm.

Bill had been on some chilling patrols himself. Night-time excursions were always the scariest. He could see how being on the other side of that river would add a most frightening element. And since the battle lines were right on the river itself, *any* patrol would have to make two crossings in close proximity to the enemy. "Man, oh man. I'll sure keep my fingers crossed that our squad isn't called on for one of those," he muttered to himself.

                                     ॐ   ॐ   ॐ

For some time the platoon sergeants, along with acting 1st Sergeant Malley, had been very unhappy with the current F Company C.O., Lt. Nye. Now at Haguenau this tension finally came to a head. Nye was a stickler for grooming and uniform standards, sometimes in the most inappropriate situations. Worse, and unforgivable, his leadership in combat was weak and indecisive. Word about this eventually got to Col. Sink, the regimental commander. He called the other officers and upper non-coms to a meeting at headquarters for a pow-wow on the problem.

By now True had promoted, but only to buck sergeant. As such, he was not invited to the party. But his platoon sergeant, Bob Vogel filled him in on the doings when it was all over. Apparently, everyone in the room had been of the same mind: Nye had to go. Colonel Sink was convinced, and cut orders for his transfer out immediately. As a general rule, the Colonel was careful to support his officers so long as they did their jobs. But a man who couldn't lead in combat was a danger to himself and everyone around him. This one would be offered a "less demanding" assignment. The offer was both imperative and irrevocable.

Shortly after this incident a number of replacements, both officers and enlisted men, started coming into F Company. It was unusual for this to happen while they were actually on the combat line. New troops normally arrived when the entire regiment was in reserve, fully pulled back out of action for replenishment of arms, equipment, supplies, and uniforms. That allowed the new men to get acquainted and blend into their units before undergoing actual combat.

True received no enlisted replacements for his own squad. But a gung-ho lieutenant fresh out of West Point and jump school came in as assistant leader for his platoon. Bill had scarcely met the man, but it was clear from his demeanor at their first encounter that he was avid for combat. At a meeting in the squad quarters, their new leader briefly explained his background, and declared his admiration for the paratroops. It was clear that he could hardly wait to kill Germans himself. When he left, the men wasted no time exchanging views about this latest change of platoon officers.

The less experienced soldiers were inclined to accept the lieutenant at face value, drawn to his enthusiasm and elite military training, with little reservation about his leadership. But Crawford and True were of a very different opinion. They were now the oldest men in the squad, both in calendar age and combat experience. They wasted no time expressing their reservations.

"Listen you guys, the lieutenant knows the training manuals backwards and forwards, and he sounds plenty gutsy as well," True told the men. "But surviving this war is getting to be damn important to me. I'd rather have an officer who'll just do his duty. This guy looks to me like he's out to win medals and hasn't much time to do it. I don't want to be cannon fodder for his personal glory!"

"That's sure as hell the way I look at it," Crawford echoed. "Give me an officer who sees the survival of his men as a mighty important part of his duties. I didn't hear much of that from this yokel."

Finally, all present agreed to just wait and see how the new lieutenant would pan out.

One morning the communication wire to the company command post went out suddenly and unexpectedly. True decided to make a rare daylight trip outdoors to see what might be done about it. Running all out from covered doorway to doorway, he paused at each and waited cautiously for possible sniper fire. Dashing to each protected spot along the way, he finally made it back to the C.P. without incident. There, Tom Alley told him that the repair crew would be working that night to restore communications. A couple of other houses out on the line were having the same trouble. It was thought to be just a hardware glitch—no sabotage or Nazi shenanigans.

Then Tom told him about the latest regimental orders that had come down. Battalion was sending a patrol across the river to bring back prisoners. Luckily E Company had been selected for the assignment. They were mounting a sizable force to do the job. Everyone knew that F Company had just received its new commander, Captain Philip Dean, and he was just getting settled into the new assignment. Tom thought that might have helped the Fox guys avoid being chosen for the patrol.

F Company positions were situated immediately adjacent to those of E Company. All the Fox men were briefed about the patrol. In protection, they would return any German machine gun fire in their area. True didn't know exactly what time the patrol would set out across the river, but it was important to be ready regardless. As soon as it was dark he posted men at the windows on all three levels of the house.

Night fell. Several hours passed quietly with the usual random 88 or mortar shell incoming from the enemy side. There seemed to be no American artillery or mortars at work. This was surely part of the plan: to lay low until it was time to launch the patrol. But then, without warning, American artillery opened up from far back behind their lines.

The intensity of cannon fire quickly built to a level far beyond anything yet seen at Haguenau: it was a massive barrage. From True's vantage point at his 2nd floor window, he couldn't see precisely where the shells were landing. But soon hundreds of projectiles whistled overhead like rockets on Independence Day, and bright orange flashes showed their targets starkly lit by fire and destruction. Thunderous booms in the distance made it clear that some really big stuff was being thrown at the enemy. Amid the din, American machine guns began to sound with their recognizably slow chug-chug-chug rate of fire. They were soon joined by the more rapid brrrrrrp of the Kraut small arms. And the distinctive whuump of 81mm mortars made it clear that second battalion's headquarters company had also joined the fray. All in all it was a fireworks show of massive proportions.

"Man, that's one hell of a show going on over there," True observed to Crawford.

"God, I hope the patrol's okay," Crawford answered. "That big stuff doesn't know the difference between Krauts and us. Wish to hell we could see something to shoot at from here and help out at least a little. Wouldn't it be nice if our German friends across the way would start firing from that window we've got zeroed in? We'd sure answer 'em back!!"

"I think that whole building has been abandoned for the last couple weeks," Bill said.

"You're right," Crawford said. "It'd be good to join the action, but only if we do it from here. I don't envy the Easy guys on that side of the river one little bit."

It wasn't long before German artillery responded with equal intensity. Soon explosions were raining all over the American side of the river. Nothing hit True's house, but a big mortar round whooshed in near enough to shake the whole building. Flares occasionally lighted a large area on both sides of the river, and machine gun tracers skittered off into space, but True and his men were never able to see any of the close actions of the patrol.

By general agreement, True's men thought the fireworks display was more colorful (and certainly more exciting) than any 4th of July show back in the U.S. But it finally petered out, to everyone's immense relief. Returning to the standard two-man guard post drill, those not on duty called it a night and turned in. There would be time enough tomorrow to inquire how E Company had fared.

As it turned out the patrol had been successful, returning with a number of live prisoners. But two Americans had been killed in the action. One of them was the new lieutenant in True's platoon, who had insisted on going along. Someone said he had tripped a land mine. Bill was saddened but not greatly surprised. "A damn shame his family will now be getting their telegram," he thought to himself, "and the lieutenant's earned his Purple Heart. Hell of a price to pay."

ॐ   ॐ   ॐ

In late February the 101st was relieved and moved from Haguenau to the smaller town of Saverne. They would be there for a few days prior to the big move back to Mourmelon. In the lull, training was ordered by regimental headquarters. It was nothing very strenuous. Just some close order drill and manual of arms practice to help integrate the replacements they'd received at Haguenau into their units.

The time at Saverne passed quickly, and soon the division was on its way back to Mourmelon-le-Grande, their old home in France. Everyone looked forward to this with anticipation. Not only were they leaving the combat front, there were comfortable barracks waiting for them, and maybe even leaves in Paris!

This trip was an interesting first for the men. They traveled by rail on old box cars called *Forty and Eights*. They got this name because on the side of each was printed the words Quarante Homme, ou Huit Chevaux, which translates in English as "Forty Men or Eight Horses." These trains had been ridden by some of their fathers in World War I. Liberally supplied with straw for sleeping comfort, it was fun for the troopers to sit in the open doors and wave to the mademoiselles as they moved through the French countryside. Good food was supplied along the way as well. Together with generous supplies of hard cider, wine, and even a bit of schnapps to cheer their spirits, life had never seemed much better.

Arriving at Mourmelon after a few days' travel, they were disappointed to find their previous barracks now occupied by the 17th Airborne Division. The 101st was relegated to 12-man tents. To describe the latrine and washroom facilities as "less than adequate" was to put the best possible face on it. But at least they were off the line, out of combat, and there were no dreaded night patrols to fear. The food was good, and sleeping on an army cot in a tent was several notches above what they'd been through in the past. All in all there was little grousing. But what looked to be a soft life was short lived.

Soon orders came down from Regiment for rigorous training. This was necessary to blend in the numerous replacements that had been added since Bastogne. The companies were up to full strength, at least in numbers. But the new men could only be properly "teamed" with hard, sweaty work along side the veterans who were their mentors. Daily routine became filled with vigorous calisthenics, close order drill, manual of arms, bayonet practice, and the myriad of strenuous infantry activities all the old timers had long ago mastered. Then long marches and overnight field problems were added. After that, some of the men began grumbling that maybe combat wasn't so bad after all. But they knew, too, that all this was necessary to build a cohesive fighting unit fit for combat.

ॐ   ॐ   ॐ

Late February 1945. Riding forty-and-eights from Haguenau to Mourmelon le Grande, France. Tom Alley and Bill True shirtless sitting in door of boxcar.

The men had often read in the Stars and Stripes of big-name USO shows playing in the European Theatre, but the 101st had somehow managed to miss almost all of them. Now at Mourmelon, however, there was finally some redress of this grievance. In a V-Mail letter home dated March 3rd Bill True reported on the weather and some shows. "Our weather is still pretty cool. The sun did come out one day last week and it was pretty warm. I did my laundry yesterday tho and it hasn't been out since. Fine thing—my clothes are still drying. Several shows have been here at camp since we got back. Bobby Breen gave one last week, also Mickey Rooney. They were both pretty good. Tonight Marlene Dietrich will be here. Hope I see it too."

There were other diversions as well. Perhaps to compensate for the harsh training regimen, passes into Mourmelon-le-Grande and occasionally Rheims were granted with increased frequency. Boozy brawls between the paratroopers and tankers, and even with troopers of different units, were a natural result as the men got loaded and blew off steam. To counter this, Headquarters came up with a plan to use regular troops as temporary MPs. There had never been very much respect among the common soldiers for professional army "cops." But if the peace were kept by some of their own... well, maybe the riots would at least be tempered by a sense of camaraderie for the enforcers. Soon two-man teams consisting of a lieutenant and a sergeant were drawn from the line companies to patrol both towns.

Bill True and a new lieutenant from the 3rd Platoon were F Company's contribution for two weekend nights in Rheims. Donning their MP arm bands and each sporting a .45 sidearm, they were both a bit apprehensive about the assignment. Their uniforms made it clear that they were not regular MPs, and the two of them decided early on that that was a clear asset for which they were mighty grateful.

Their first patrol in Rheims was quiet, except for a single incident at a popular watering hole. Hearing loud shouts and screams coming from a neighborhood bar, Bill and the lieutenant entered and pushed their way through a crowd who were egging on a pair of very drunk, brawling soldiers. Both were buck privates, one sporting the Screaming Eagle of the 101st and the other wearing the Eagle Claw of the 17th. The Claw man was a real bruiser with long arms that looked like the proverbial simian "knuckle dragger." The 101st trooper had a flattened nose that looked like it had been busted up pretty good on previous occasions. If he ever had a pretty face for the ladies, it was long gone now.

"What's the beef, guys?" the lieutenant asked in a loud but amiable voice, as he and Bill pulled the two combatants apart. True measured the surrounding crowd with apprehension, and fervently hoped he wouldn't find himself in the middle of a knock-down, drag-out melee.

"Aw, theesh friggin jumpers think ridin' a glidersh a picnic. Lemme tell ya those are flyin' coffrins we're in, Lootent, and I didn' even volunteer for this crap," the 17th man slurred through booze-contorted lips. "They jush shtuck me with it!"

Bill noticed that there were a number of paratroopers and glider men from both divisions in the boisterous group. Most of them were drunk. This was exactly the right mix for a full scale riot, and he wanted no part of it. He half spoke, half whispered to the lieutenant, "Let's split these guys up."

The lieutenant took the gliderman's arm in a friendly fashion. "Hey man, I know you glider riders gotta have plenty of guts," he said as he started edging him toward the door. "The time I took a ride in one it scared the shit out of me. Whadda ya say we go outside and talk about it!"

Late February 1945. Riding forty-and-eights from Haguenau to Mourmelon le Grande, France. Conrad Ours, Bob Vogel, and Bill True standing outside one of the boxcars.

Meanwhile True kept the paratrooper occupied by offering to buy him a drink. Squeezing through the crowd, and half holding up his charge under the arms, he managed to muscle the two of them up to the bar for a cognac and beer chaser. It turned out the trooper was also from California. "Here's to Shan Franshisco, the besht f...in' town there ever was!" the trooper slurred. After downing the shot, he slumped his head to the bar and passed out, unconscious to the world. His beer chaser remained untouched nearby.

Bill saw this as a sign that "my work here is done," and made it out the front door where he met the lieutenant. The gorilla from the 17th lay face down on the sidewalk, snoring contentedly. The two temporary MPs congratulated themselves on their handling of the situation, and continued on their patrol.

Next night the two had an easier time of it. Patrolling past a large establishment—more a nightclub than a "bar"— they heard a live band playing a popular American tune. "You know Sarge," the lieutenant said, "it might be very important for us to stop in here and be sure no American troops get into any trouble."

Bill quickly picked up on the implied message. "Probably the most important thing we could do on our whole patrol tonight," he responded, as they entered and found a table near a small stage. A four piece band made up of trumpet, saxophone, piano and drums was playing a very creditable version of "Brazil." Better yet, a sultry brunette dressed in a brief skirt and the sheerest of blouses was seated on the stand. She appeared to be the vocalist for the group.

The band finished that number with a flourish, then picked up another as the singer came to the microphone. This brought her closer to the light, and also the table where sat the temporary MPs, who knew quite well the game of "hooky" they were playing.

"Holy Christ, Lieutenant, would you get a look at those

knockers," True exclaimed. It was clear that the woman was wearing nothing under her transparent blouse. The bright pink nipples on a pair of bold, firm breasts were like wild cherries on a marshmallow topping.

"That's the best set I've ever seen," the lieutenant answered. "By God, if those beauties didn't make a man hungry he'd have to be dead."

As she began to sing it was apparent that she had a polished voice as well as magnificent tits. The song was "I'll Walk Alone," and her pleasing tonal quality more than offset her minimal command of English. She had obviously learned the lyrics phonetically, and had no real idea what the words meant. Occasionally she'd come close to understandable English, as when she sang, "to tell you ze truce I be lonely." But who cared if she fractured the language? She was a feast for the eyes and the voice was soothing and sexy.

The two reluctant peacekeepers stayed for several more songs and band instrumentals, but finally their consciences got to them. Without enthusiasm, they left to resume their duties. "We sure kept the peace in that place, didn't we?" Bill observed later as they walked up the main drag. The lieutenant had to agree, and noted that Rheims was undoubtedly a quieter and more lawful city because of their sterling work. Bullshit was piling up.

ॐ   ॐ   ॐ

One day there was an announcement that the 101st would be honored by a visit from General Eisenhower himself. He'd be accompanied by a host of bigwigs, including some from Washington. The whole division would march in review for the VIPs, and it was said that the Screaming Eagles would receive a Presidential Distinguished Unit Citation.

Late February 1945. Riding forty-and-eights from Haguenau to Mourmelon le Grande, France. Conrad Ours, Tom Alley, and Bill True, shirtless and standing outside one of the boxcars.

Soon all the troopers were polishing and cleaning weapons and uniforms for the parade. Everyone wanted to look their very best. Wings and ribbons and other dress decorations were refurbished and proudly pinned on, even by men who had disdained their display before.

General Eisenhower gave a brief talk in which his praise of the 101st was unstinted. One brief sentence caught the essence of his speech. "You were given a marvelous opportunity (in Bastogne), and you met every test."

In a letter home on March 18th Bill True wrote about the visit by Ike. "General Eisenhower was out to review the division last week. We're really getting famous. He gave us the Presidential Citation (cluster this time, we had one from Normandy already) and told us we were the first division ever to receive the citation as a whole. Maybe I'd better explain that. The citation we got in Normandy didn't include the whole division, while the whole 101 got it for our show in Bastogne."

                          ☙   ☙   ☙

Rumors began to circulate about a jump across the Rhine River, or even on to Berlin. This made sense with the division now back up to full strength and the latest replacements acclimated to their units. It was not to be, however, and General Eisenhower decided to give the 17th Airborne Division its first crack at a combat jump into Germany.

On the morning of March 24th, the men of F Company watched the formations of C-47s circle into their Vs and head east. Bill True was filled with mixed emotions. He had never before watched people head out for a combat jump that he wasn't to be part of. He was not sorry to be left behind. There was certainly no envy that he wasn't participating in this action, and yet there was a peculiar sorrow he couldn't describe. Was it guilt? Rationally, that made no sense. He didn't give orders, only followed them. But there was something—an emotional tug—that said he should somehow be there with those guys. At last he satisfied himself with fervently wishing them luck, and just resumed his duties.

As the month of March came to a close the men of the 101st themselves boarded trucks and headed for the Ruhr Valley. For the first time they would be in the homeland of the enemy. They would be billeted in German houses as they advanced, and this news was greeted with happy anticipation. At Haguenau the troops had enjoyed the pleasant advantage of occupying civilian dwellings instead of foxholes. They looked forward to repeating that experience.

The first night following entry into Germany True's platoon was directed to occupy several houses in a middle-class section of a small city that had seen no war-time devastation. It was a lovely town, typical of the region, with ginger-bread homes that looked as much like fancy baked goods as real abodes. Bill's squad ended up in a house occupied by a middle-aged couple. Being the sergeant and now in command of such decisions, he allowed the residents to remain in one of the several bedrooms, rather than turning them out in the street. (A few less sympathetic soldiers had done exactly that.) The man of the house was disabled. His wife was quick to explain that his condition was the result of a childhood disease, not due to wounds received as a German soldier.

Both residents spoke fluent English, and they wasted no time declaring that they had never been members of the Nazi party. There was no evidence to the contrary, such as photos or other mementos in the house, to suggest that this was not so. Nevertheless, Bill and his men took the protestations with a bit of skepticism. The homeowners expressed great pleasure over the conquest of their area of Germany by the Americans, rather than the Russians. They enthusiastically welcomed the end of the war and would do all they could to assist in restoring peace and order for all concerned. But over all their protestations wafted a slight aroma of mendacity.

That night the woman prepared a sumptuous dinner for the squad, and she did not appear to withhold any of her provisions of food or wine from the soldiers. The Americans left the next morning with all pockets stuffed with goodies. At parting the woman and her husband both managed weak smiles and a reasonably pleasant "auf Wiedersehen."

"They know very well how lucky they are," Bill thought to himself as he and his men walked to the waiting trucks. "If we were Russian troops they'd be fortunate to still be alive, and their home would doubtless be a shambles, probably burned to the ground."

℔   ℔   ℔

The 506th traveled further north and took up defensive positions on the west bank of the Rhine River opposite Dusseldorf. True's squad again found themselves billeted quite comfortably in an undamaged house. A few blocks down the street sat a large home right on the bank of the river, which served as an outpost for Bill's platoon. Manning it proved to be soft duty as each squad only had the outpost assignment every fourth day. The remaining days consisted mainly of "goof-off" time, although the company did have an occasional formal inspection. This was probably more to give the troops a bit to do than out of necessity.

March 1945 studio photo of Bill True in full uniform, Mourmelon le Grande, France.

There were occasional American patrols across the river, but True's platoon never had to participate. On one, a regimental headquarters patrol failed to alert the 2nd Battalion front outposts regarding an upcoming operation. The regimental men were to cross the river, obtain intelligence and possibly a few prisoners, then return. But coming back to the American side of the Rhine they had to pass through friendly outposts who knew nothing about the movement. As a result, the group suffered heavy casualties. Bill recalled his own similar mistake and near-miss at Bastogne. It sent a chill down his spine.

Everything was going so quietly that one night True, Crawford and one of the newest replacements decided to take a walk just to break the monotony. They took their weapons but didn't really expect to need them. They strolled through several blocks of houses that constituted the village, and found themselves out in the country passing a large farm house that had a light on in the window. Singing could be heard coming from inside. Thinking that it was probably some 506th men who'd come across a cache of wine or booze, Bill and the others knocked on the door to join the party.

The door was opened by a large man holding a jug. Still boisterously singing, he gestured with the jug for them to enter. Inside were some five or six rather disheveled men, definitely not Americans, sitting or standing around a large table. Several bottles and a huge chunk of cheese were piled in the center. None of them could speak English, but by sign language they made it clear that the paratroopers were welcome to join in the festivities.

One of the men played a guitar as the rest sang a rousing song that seemed to repeat the words "Tito" and "Yugoslavia." The Americans wasted no time in joining the drinkers, and Bill soon offered to play the guitar for the hosts. His rendition of "Ragtime Cowboy Joe" caught their fancy right away. Gesturing for him to repeat it, they even joined in with some fractured efforts to sing along.

Many drinks and many songs later, as the Americans walked back to their house in the village they pondered who in the heck they'd been with, and how these strangers had come to be in this place. The general speculation was that they were Yugoslavian, forced laborers for the Nazis, and had recently escaped or been liberated. "Whoever they are, and wherever they came from, they put on a hell of a party," True said, summarizing the feelings of the three Americans.

ॐ   ॐ   ॐ

Now that they were in Germany, the importance of maintaining a high alert status was constantly hammered home to the troops. That notwithstanding, outpost duty soon became very dull. No German patrol or other intrusion ever marred their quiet "watch on the Rhine," and there was certainly no complaining about this lack of activity. The paratroopers were quite happy with the boredom of their calm days and nights.

One morning in April, when True and his squad returned from outpost duty he learned of the death of President Roosevelt. Most of Bill's relatives were Republicans, but he could hardly remember a time when someone other than the Democrat FDR was president. He did recall a time during the 1932 election when his grandfather Charlie Trotter, a lone and ardent Democrat in the clan, had argued vehemently with his dad about Roosevelt and Hoover.

"That damned Hoover doesn't give a rat's ass about us common people," his grandpa had raved. "Les True, you're a cockeyed fool if you vote for him," was his final advice.

Like Bill, some of the younger replacements couldn't recall any president other than FDR either. They reacted with considerable emotion to the loss of their great war-time leader. For his part, True thought it was too bad that Roosevelt hadn't lived to see the victory over Germany that was about to be achieved. But other than that, he didn't feel much either way about the passing. In fact, Bill's first reaction was to recall Dude Stone's great imitation of FDR back during basic training at Toccoa: "I hate wahr! Eleanor hates wahr! Our little Scottie dog Fala hates wahr!"

Most of the replacements had never heard Stone's realistic, but irreverent satire. Bill knew this was not the time to drag it out of mothballs.

Not much later, word spread of a general collapse of German forces in the Ruhr area. It was rumored that hundreds of thousands of soldiers had surrendered. Soon afterward the 506th was loaded onto boxcars—German this time—and headed for Bavaria. The 101st had been attached to the 7th Army by General Bradley. Munich, and eventually Berchtesgaden, were their ultimate objectives. Many believed that Hitler would make a last stand in his Alp Mountain redoubt. Speed was now of the essence to move American forces into the area.

By this time the German rail system had suffered wide devastation. As a result, the train carrying the paratroopers was considerably delayed, making numerous detours. This was just fine by Bill. None of the men were in a hurry to re-enter combat. Die-hard SS Troops might be expected to put up a furious fight in heavily fortified mountain positions. So riding in the relatively comfortable boxcars, with bales of straw for resting and sleeping, the Americans relaxed as they sat in the open doors, swinging their feet outside. There was plentiful food and drink along the way, and they spent the time singing bawdy songs and otherwise just enjoying the vacation-like interlude.

March 1945 studio photo of Bill True in full uniform, Mourmelon le Grande, France.

The train trip seemed to meander over half of Europe, passing through parts of Holland, Belgium, Luxembourg, and France before arriving at Ludwighshafen, Germany. There, the men transferred to a totally new means of transport for the 506th: the DUKW. This was an amphibian land/water all wheel drive vehicle which had come into use with the Normandy Invasion. Its great utility was matched by excellent performance on either land or water, and its smooth riding comfort made the paratroopers wish they'd had such vehicles for transport throughout the war.

Traveling on side roads as well as the Autobahn, they headed for Munich. On the way they passed thousands of surrendered Kraut soldiers marching to the rear. It seemed there were virtually no American troops assigned to guard the prisoners. From this fact alone, it was apparent that the fight was totally gone from the Germans. The paratroopers began to hope that the rumored "Gotterdammerung" by elite SS Troops would never come to pass.

બ   બ   બ

Late in April the 2nd Battalion, 506th PIR stopped near Landsberg for a night. Nearby they discovered a former Nazi slave labor camp. Some of True's 1st Platoon, including Lt. Ben Staplefeld and a few others, were sent into the camp to check on conditions and report to battalion. Bill's squad was not in on this assignment, but his buddies E.B. Wallace and Jesse Orosco told everyone about it on their return.

"It was the most awful thing you could imagine," E.B. said. "Half-dead people, just skin and bones, lying among others already dead. And a stench that made me puke right on the spot. We wanted to get some food for those that were still alive, but the regimental surgeon stopped us. Said we'd best leave that to the experts. Too much food, too fast, could kill people that far gone. Apparently they were making something in a factory there. But I don't see how in the hell anything worth making could have come out of that place in any recent times."

Jesse echoed E.B.'s remarks, and added another story. The two of them plus Whitey Swafford had come across a German official of some kind in one of the offices, as they swept the building for enemies. "The guy spoke English and made some smart-ass remark about how we Americans didn't understand total war," Jesse said. "That was a mistake, with Whitey in the room. The two of us took turns showing him we at least know something about close action hand-to-hand combat."

E.B. described the scene as he watched Jesse and Whitey's pummeling of the German. "He looked like he'd probably survive when they finished with him, but he'll sure need a mouth-full of dental work. And that nose will take a major overhaul to ever be close to normal again."

General Taylor also visited the camp and became utterly incensed at what he saw. How could the German people do this to fellow human beings? The following day he ordered that every adult in the city of Landsberg be taken to the camp, handed burial equipment and clean up tools. Then American soldiers stood guard over them with loaded weapons while they worked. No one was allowed to leave until the dead were all interred and the camp restored to order.

The next stop for the regiment was Munich, and the squads were told once more to pick a civilian house in which to spend the night. Bill and his squad again chose a good one.

LILI MARLENE
Bill's True Tale

We've been in Munich a couple of days now, and to steal a line from a George Gershwin song, "the livin' is easy." Nice house the squad's in, with the whole company spread throughout an upscale neighborhood. Not much real action of late, but we don't know what we might run into as we drive farther south in Bavaria. Possibly the last holdout of Adolph and some of his SS Storm Troops. "Eat, drink and be merry" is the story today, and tomorrow could be another tale.

I've decided it's a good idea after all to let the German family stay in their home with us. Ike's "no fraternization" policy might make sense to some, but it's sure not natural around women and kids. I'll bet the rule is being bent, if not fractured, all over the place.

The matron of the house is about forty years old, friendly, and a very good cook. The daughter appears to be less than twenty, with long dark hair, beautiful features, and a Betty Grable figure. She is likely aware of her extreme good luck that it's American troops occupying her town rather than Russians. The remaining member of the family is a boy of nine or ten who is well mannered, obviously impressed with soldiers and their weapons, and speaks English almost as well as his mother and sister. It's difficult to think of the three of them as anything other than a typical American family with only the father missing.

Between the family's cellar-store of food supplies, and our K and C rations, the mother and daughter have been putting some first-rate meals together. We're enjoying a bit of real home cooking, and this morning we even had fresh eggs—"medium over" for me. Wow! I can't even remember the last time I had eggs like that.

There's a lovely large upright piano in the living room, and both the mother and daughter play quite well. They've entertained us a couple of times, and we've joined in some singing with them when they played a few American standards. Alan Summers in our squad knows some piano too, and this afternoon he's playing and all of us are sitting or standing around listening and singing along on occasion. I came across the lyrics to the German song Lili Marlene recently. Maybe it was in our Army newspaper The Stars and Stripes. Included was a verse in German. Alan knows the song and we join him.

Underneath the lamplight, by the barracks gate,
Darling I remember, the way you used to wait,
There where you told me tenderly,
That you loved me, you'd always be,
My Lili of the lamplight,
My own Lili Marlene.

Vor der kaserne, vor dem grossen tur,
Stand eine laterne, und steht sie nock davor,
So wollen wir uns da wieder sehn,
Bei der laterne wollen wir stehn,
Wie eins Lili Marlene,
Wie eins Lili Marlene.

As we finish the song the daughter, tears streaming, rises from the sofa, covers her face, and hurriedly leaves the room. We all turn to the mother, unspoken questions in our eyes, and she too stands and says "I'll be right back." She returns shortly holding a large framed studio photo. It is her daughter and a handsome German soldier in uniform, looking at each other with obvious adoration. "He was her fiancé," she explains. "They often sang that song. He was killed in Normandy."

Is it possible that we, by some strange chance of fate, faced the fiancé's unit among Normandy's hedgerows? Might one of us have ended his life? Surely no group of soldiers ever felt the humanity of their enemy more than my squad on this occasion.

ϕ   ϕ   ϕ

On the first day of May the 506th left Munich and continued its drive southeast toward Berchtesgaden. At one of the stops along the Autobahn someone discovered what looked like a whole squadron of German planes hidden in the woods adjacent to the road. It was possible that the autobahn had been used as a runway, for the planes could then be hidden in the woods. Whether true or not, the men had a rollicking good time exploding hand grenades throughout the makeshift aerodrome. The planes would never fly again.

By now, Joe Flick and Bill True had been in different platoons for some time, but they got together to reminisce on the road to Berchtesgaden. Joe had just run into Bert Barnamm,† who had been supply sergeant for F Company since way back in basic training days at Toccoa. It brought back memories of Bert's "special" position in the company.

"Remember that time in London after Normandy when Bert and I ended up with a couple of women in a pub? He really laid it on those broads about how many Germans he'd killed single-handedly! Well, you should hear him now, bemoaning the fact that all these Germans are surrendering and denying him the chance to kill a few hundred more. As if he ever killed anybody. Sheesh! What a load of bullshit!!!"

"Oh, yeah," Bill responded. "And do you remember how he never got beyond that first bend in the road when we ran Mt. Currahee? Plenty of guys flunked out in basic because they couldn't handle *that*, but not ol' Bert!"

"That's the one thing I always held against Captain Mulvey," Joe said. "Giving Barnamm that special pass home to California just so he could bring his Cadillac convertible to Toccoa. Hell, it was just so the officers could ride around in it and make like big shots to the women! Bert wouldn't have made two weeks of basic except for that. And how about that big photo of Maureen O'Sullivan he kept by his bunk? Took it with him every time we moved, too. Inscribed 'To Bert, from one Mick to another'. I'll bet he signed it *himself*, the lyin' son of a bitch. What a pain in the ass!"

General Nikolaus von Vormann (Left) conferring with General Erwin Rommel, obtained from German files by Bob Thomas. Bill True "confiscated" von Vormann's uniform at the end of the war.

"When Barnamm gets home he'll have a slew of hair-raising stories about slaughtering Krauts, I'm sure. It might actually be fun to hear how fanciful his tales will get," Bill added.

అ   అ   అ

There was intense competition between French, British and American troops to be first into Berchtesgaden. At least two powerful reasons were behind this. Symbolically, Berchtesgaden represented Hitler and all of his Nazi power. Thus the first conquering forces into the city would reap the glory of essentially "defeating" Germany. But overriding even this was the promise of looting. It was well known that for years the Nazis had plundered Europe of gold, jewelry, fine art, and other treasures. Rumor had it that much of this was hidden in and around the Eagle's Nest. Whichever Allied army got to it first could do what they wanted, with no one to stop them.

The French, in particular, seemed intent on purposely delaying advance of the 101st into the city. Their interference must have been utterly frustrating for both General Taylor and Colonel Sink. Together, those two exercised what must be considered the ultimate "Allied solidarity," as they struggled to maintain order. At one point it appeared there might be an actual exchange of gunfire between their men and De Gaulle's. The Americans have never received proper credit for showing such admirable restraint.

Debate continues to this day over exactly what elements of which units were the very first into Berchtesgaden. It's a moot argument at best, since there were no gallant displays of heroism in taking the city. Bill True recalled that he didn't hear a single rifle shot, artillery round, machine gun burst, or mortar blast, as his 2nd Battalion entered the town. But if the psychological glory of conquering Berchtesgaden was absent, looting more than made up for it. The "liberation" of valuables was thorough and sweeping. And it was by no means confined to the enlisted ranks. From lowly private to general officer, all ranks participated in the plunder.

General von Vormann's house at 3 Gmundberg Strasse, Berchtesgaden, photo taken by Bob Thomas, September 1998.

As F Company hiked up a hill lined with luxurious homes, True recalled how beautifully picturesque all of Bavaria had seemed. Even modest abodes looked like fairy tale cottages that Hansel and Gretel might run out of at any time, with the wicked witch in hot pursuit.

෨   ෨   ෨

Chapter XI – Wie Eins Lili Marlene

THE LIFE OF RILEY
Bill's True Tale

We're strolling into Berchtesgaden, Germany, like it might be some little town in Tennessee from maneuver days back in '43. It's early May, 1945, and I never heard a shot fired as the 506th moved into this fabled Alps Headquarters of Adolph Hitler. What a breeze! Word was that the 101st had been sent down here to do final battle with the cream of Adolph's SS Troops, as the Fuehrer went to his Valhalla in a flame of glory. Man, oh man, it's great that the wild rumor was a mile off the mark.

Everybody in the company is smiling and laughing and joking and just loving this beautiful turn of events. And the gorgeous surroundings add to our feelings of joy as we drink in the loveliness of the snow capped mountains and the dark green forests.

We've been enjoying the beauty of Bavaria for some days now as we traveled south. Droves of surrendered German soldiers marching north were cheerful to see as well. For the past several nights we've slept comfortably as we took over civilian houses that looked like cuckoo-clocks magically enlarged to accommodate people.

I'm recalling the home we'd stayed in a couple of nights ago. We allowed the middle-aged man and woman of the house to remain, and as they spoke English reasonably well had conversed with them some. They told us how very happy they were that we Americans had gotten there before the Russians, and the woman assured us: "My husband and I never supported Hitler."

We took that assertion about their allegiances with a huge hunk of salt, of course, but since they'd been both civil and hospitable I didn't think it necessary to confront them about

444

their politics. They had a modestly stocked cabinet of wine near the kitchen which we depleted in short order, and some of the guys were searching the house and cellar for more.

The woman of the house said she hoped that as their sergeant I could restrain my men from taking all of their wine since with the wartime conditions they would not be able to replace it. I informed her that my men felt they were entitled to any and all food or drink whenever and wherever they found it in Germany, and that I shared their feelings in that regard. The thought of what the Russians would be taking from her, had we not arrived first, may have crossed her mind. She showed me only a cheerful countenance thereafter.

One of the guys discovered a sizable stock of wine and booze secreted in a far corner of the cellar. Next morning we left with pretty fair hangovers, and pockets stuffed with bottles.

We've been walking up a fairly steep street here in Berchtesgaden when the column is halted. We're sitting on the curbs having a smoke when Bob Vogel, now platoon sergeant, comes over and tells us: "The captain wants to meet with all the squad leaders in a house around the corner."

All of the company's non-coms are now together, and the C.O. tells us that each squad is to pick a house to stay in and then let him know where we are. The house we're meeting in will be company headquarters, and we're all to stay in touch with him there. Until further orders: "Just relax and enjoy," he says.

We go back to the column and I get my squad together and give them the good news. "Any house we want," I tell 'em, "so let's head out and find a good one."

We've gone less than a block when I spot a nifty looking villa. It's three stories tall and has typical Bavarian gingerbread decorations. There are wide surrounding verandas and the site provides panoramic views of the encircling snow-topped Alps. "This is it," I tell the guys and walk up a few steps to the front door and knock. The door opens almost immediately, and two women, one middle aged and the other possibly a daughter, nod quickly at me and walk down the steps past my squad and out into the street. They are carrying small suitcases and continue walking without looking back.

We're all rather non-plussed, but at least we won't have to make room for them or throw them out. "They've been expecting us," I think to myself as we enter a spacious entrance hall. "And they're taking no chances on what soldiers might do whether American or Russian."

"Okay, guys," I announce. "Let's explore what we have here, but remember who gets first crack at the best bedroom."

The men are more interested in what food and booze are available and take off for the back of the house as I go up the stairs to check bedrooms. There are several of them and I pick the biggest with its own private bathroom. Wow, talk about luxury. I lean my rifle in a corner and leap into the middle of a huge canopied bed. "Have I died and gone to heaven?," I think, as I stretch into the softest mattress I've ever known.

One of our latest replacements comes tearing up the stairs hollering: "Hey, Sarge, they got the biggest wine cellar I ever did see, and the produce and canned stuff is unbelievable."

"Okay," I tell him. "Now you get back to the C.O.'s house and tell him where our squad is. The food and booze will still be here."

I wander over to the bedroom closet just to check out my full accommodations in this lap of luxury. Jeez! A German general's uniform no less, with a whole chest full of medals.

"Probably not surprising that a general would have a home like this down here in Bavaria," I say to myself, "what with Berchtesgaden being the famed German city of beauty it is."

Exhibit at the National Infantry Museum, Fort Benning, Georgia, displaying the uniforms of General von Vormann and Sgt. William True.

I'm trying on the jacket and find it's a bit big around the waist but short in the sleeves. The overall fit suggests that the general was probably about five eight or nine and stout in the middle, but this is going to be my best war souvenir ever. I wrap the jacket and the overseas cap in a sheet from another closet, and secure it in a duffle bag for mailing home at the earliest opportunity.

The guys are whooping it up downstairs so I know the wine and booze are already flowing. I descend the stairs and head for what I presume to be the kitchen to get in on the celebration myself. Numerous bottles have been popped and a couple of jars of some kind of meat have been opened as well. "Here's where they keep the bread," one of the men announces as he comes out of a spacious kitchen pantry waving a long loaf in each hand. Another trooper comes through the door from the cellar with his arms full of more sealed jars of various canned goods and several bunches of fresh produce.

"Okay guys," I pronounce, "let's get a little organized on how we're going to live for the next couple days. Archie and Kelly, you two can be our bartenders for starters, and you can get all the wine and booze collected on that big side board in the dining room. Pete, you've always been good at making those ten-in-one rations taste like something, so you can be our head chef for the next twenty-four hours. Smitty can help you, and the rest of us will clear out of the kitchen while you and he get a dinner ready. Holler when it's time to start setting that long dining room table, and those of us still sober enough not to bust up the dinner ware will pitch in, too."

It's nearly ten o'clock in the morning on our second day in Berchtesgaden when I'm finally fully awake and remember the fabulous feast and party we had last night. At least I recall parts of it, and that slight ache above my eyeballs confirms that I surely consumed my share of the liquid refreshments.

As the full awareness of my luxurious surroundings again registers with me, I remember my private bath and the spacious tub. Filling it with hot water nearly to the top, I slip in and find myself wondering if this can truly be happening to me. With nearly three years in the army, including two years of hard training, and the last year wondering frequently if I'd live through the war, the feeling is almost as if I've been transported to another level of existence.

"This war in Europe is over," I'm thinking, "and I've made it. While it's conceivable that they'd send us veterans over to Asia to fight the Japs, too, it seems unlikely. I'll actually be going home and attending college before long." The fighting and dying over the past year had gradually brought growing and despairing doubts about the likelihood of that lovely outcome.

Thoughts of Bill Green cross my mind. He was the last man to be killed in our company. It happened during a night patrol. I was there as well, but Green had volunteered whereas the rest of us had been ordered. The utter randomness of who lives and who dies in a war, and the ultimate question of why I'll be going home while others like Bill Green won't, will probably haunt me for a long time.

Raucous laughter is lofting from downstairs, and I am brought back to the reality of the here and now. My squad is happy and joyous with the wonderful circumstance of our condition at this moment, and I rise from the tub to join them in living this, "The Life of Riley."

Summer 1945, Kaprun, Austria. Part of Bill True's squad during the occupation of Austria after the end of the war in Europe. Left to right: Talbot, True, Monley, Revier, Summers, Ratliff, Hisamoto, Hewitt. Bill and Alan Summers were the only old-timers dating from Toccoa.

On May 8, 1945, Bill True wrote a letter home, conveying his pleasure at the ending of hostilities in Europe. The joy was somewhat muted, however, by the continuation of the war in the Pacific which remained to be won.

"It's all over but the shouting in this theatre. I'm not quite so elated as I thought I would be, but of course I'm happy.

"I don't know whether I'm permitted to tell you where we

are or not, so I won't mention it. But I think it's probably one of the most beautiful spots in Germany. Quite well known for a small place too.

"The weather is strictly A-1. Sun shining all the time but not hot. If I were a fisherman this would really be paradise. There are a couple streams and several small lakes close, with beaucoup trout.

"Of course everyone is talking about home, and no one knows anything. We still have that other war to win. I'll try to write again soon."

Unfortunately, True's sojourn in the large and lovely alpine villa lasted only a few short days. As the war in Europe ended, all of F Company, as well as others in the 2nd Battalion, were moved to quarters that appeared to have been used as military barracks before. A German man and woman were in charge of cleaning and maintenance of the facility. The man's frequent and vehement expression was "Alles kaputt!"

The couple were extremely accommodating and pleasant with the American soldiers. This was entirely expected, of course, since their fate depended completely on the whims of the conquering soldiers. Even the "Alles kaputt!" was always meant to show disgust with Hitler. There was never any kind of criticism of the Americans.

The woman had an attractive face. She was slightly plump and always pleasant. And except for her advanced age (late forties), she would have been tempting for many of the men even during their increasingly rare sober stages. But with the war in Europe ended, little discipline was exercised in limiting the consumption of wine and other intoxicants. Except for the few tee-totalers among them, most of the men were half-swacked a good deal of the time.

One night 1st Sergeant Malley of F Co. was in his cups a

bit more than usual. In that condition, he apparently decided it was time for a romantic interlude with the housekeeping matron. True only witnessed part of this episode in person, but as he saw Malley chasing the woman up the stairs and around a corner, Bill was afraid his top-kick was headed for real trouble. Luckily, the woman's husband and one of the lieutenants from battalion happened along just as Malley and the woman were wrestling on a hallway floor. The attempted rape was somehow kept quiet and no permanent harm was done. But it served as an object lesson and warning to everyone of the dangers and punishment that a proven rape charge carried.

By and large these were pleasant days, spent swimming and boating at the nearby Konigssee Lake which was located in as lovely a setting as could be imagined. With snow-capped mountains all around, surrounded by deep green forests, the view in every direction was breathtaking. Luxurious resort buildings merely added to the splendor of the place.

Transportation was never lacking. Every squad had acquired some means of locomotion ranging from three-wheel motorcycles to thirty-man busses. The myriad of German vehicles the paratroopers had acquired was astounding. But when accident rates climbed, all unofficial vehicles were ordered to be turned in. Days at Berchtesgaden were nearing an end. Occupation duty in Austria was about to begin for the troops of the 101st Airborne.

CHAPTER XII

Kilroy Was Here!
85 Points Gets a Ticket Home

"What war has always been is a puberty ceremony…
you went away a boy and came back a man…"
Kurt Vonnegut, Jr., "City Limits," March 11, 1983

The few days the 506th spent in Berchtesgaden seemed short indeed. The war in Europe was over and everyone reveled in that knowledge, but it was sad to pick up and leave so quickly from such a lovely place. Forsaking the leisurely life they had briefly enjoyed, Bill and his comrades loaded onto trucks and headed south into Austria.

The ride was short: about 25 miles to the resort town of Zell Am See. It was pleasant to see that the countryside remained lush and verdant with snow capped Alps on all sides. The town itself was located on a large and beautiful lake fed by alpine streams. It consisted mostly of lavish hotels and other resort accommodations, along with a few affluent private residences. Zell Am See would serve as regimental headquarters, while F Company and other units of the 2nd Battalion would move on to lesser towns.

Five miles farther south was the town of Kaprun, which would be home to F Company for the next several months. As in Berchtesgaden, the men were bunked in private homes. But this time each squad was assigned to a house selected by the officers, rather than getting to pick their own.

"Occupation duty" was the term for their new responsibilities. Thousands of German soldiers were rounded

453

up, disarmed, and sent to P.O.W. stockades. None had any thought of further armed resistance. Over and over, Bill heard the expression "Alles Kaputt!" (everything is demolished) sadly and often repeated as his unit moved into Germany, but now it seemed to be almost a continual mantra... nearly as pervasive as the American soldier's commentary that everything was SNAFU (situation normal, all f...ed up) to describe conditions in the Army.

Organized guard duty assignments gave the men something to do as the Americans settled into routines of occupation. True had never been fond of guard duty as a private, standing sentry at a post with two hours on and four off, around the clock. But "Sergeant of the Guard" was an even worse task. It meant shaking the men awake throughout the night and escorting them to their posts, to guard against only phantom enemies. All the troops were naturally grumpy to be roused from a sound sleep for such drudgery.

For the first few weeks everyone served numerous guard stints, until all of the German soldiers were removed from the area and the civilian population returned to its normal routines. Each non-com took his turn as C.Q. (charge of quarters), answering phone and radio calls at company headquarters, and maintaining contact with battalion and the regiment. Time began to hang heavy for the whole company.

The Austrians were eager to perform routine tasks for their conquerors such as washing clothes, cleaning their living quarters, and serving KP duties in exchange for food, cigarettes or money. F Company even had two Italian P.O.W.s who were whiz-bang cooks. The meals were sumptuous beyond imagining for troopers accustomed to C- and K-rations. Home-made wine and hard cider were easily available as well, so life was pretty close to the proverbial "bowl of cherries."

In a V-mail letter home dated May 18, 1945, Bill described the situation.

"We're not doing much nowadays. Mostly athletics, etc. I've been swimming a few times and have a start on a tan. There is a very swift stream about waist deep near here and is it cold. The stream is fed mainly by the snow melting in the mountains so you can see what I mean. I saw a show the other night in a regular theatre. Seemed a long time since I'd done that."

The "regular theatre" was in Zell Am See, and in another letter, True wrote home about a different experience.

"Saw a swell show the other night. 'Objective Burma.' Errol Flynn was a paratrooper in it, and the jump was so real I think I sweated it out more than Errol."

As it turned out, the return trip to Kaprun after that movie became something of an adventure in itself. Transportation was a small German Army bus, crammed full of F Company men. The driver had elected to skip the movie in favor of several steins of beer which he swilled at the Hotel Austria, in downtown Zell. By the time he fired up the bus and pointed for home, he was "feeling no pain." The truck was still fitted for wartime blackout conditions, with headlamps that gave only weak illumination to the pitch-dark road ahead. Fortunately, the driver took this into consideration and did not use excessive speed. Unfortunately, he was too shit-faced to drive safely, even at slow speed. While rounding a sharp turn the bus careened off the road, tore through a barbed-wire fence, and ended up on its side in an adjacent field.

Inside the bus, it was something like being in a martini shaker wielded by a strong bartender. The resulting jumble had troopers so mixed together they looked like a can of earthworms on its way to a fishing hole, but they somehow managed to untangle themselves and crawl out the windows. The bus was fairly light. With the help of many hands it was easily turned upright and pushed back onto the road. By some miracle, the engine started immediately. With no one seriously injured, the journey into Kaprun continued without further incident. The original driver, however, was forcibly strapped into a passenger seat.

ॐ   ॐ   ॐ

Upper echelons knew that high living and free time would likely lead to increased trouble in the enlisted ranks, so a schedule of organized training and recreation was arranged. There had already been a few fist fights in F Company between erstwhile friends. Constructive activities were definitely needed to keep the men occupied and out of mischief.

Morning hours became filled with calisthenics before breakfast, followed later by close order drill, manual of arms practice, and classroom instructions in infantry tactics. Afternoons consisted of athletics including soft ball, volleyball, boxing, wrestling and even some horseback riding.

In a V-mail letter home dated June 10, 1945, True noted the change.

"Well we've started some training now but still have sports all afternoon so the vacation isn't entirely over. We have a little pool right here in town now, and the water is nice and warm, at least compared to the streams. There's still snow on top of the mountains so I guess it must stay there the year round."

Bill became part of a skilled volleyball team the company put together. First Sergeant Studs Malley was their leader. He learned that D Company had what they thought was a good team, too, so Malley and one of the D Company non-coms arranged a competition. More was at stake than just company pride. Each team put up $300, winner take all, in a 50-point match.

A couple of neutral officers were selected to officiate the match. Regular amateur rules would be followed, except rotation of players through positions wasn't required. Malley and True were the best at "spiking" the ball at the net so they played the front line throughout the game. The most skilled server was a recent replacement who had competed in college, and he took that post.

At the outset the teams were evenly matched, and the score went back and forth with never more than a two-point spread. As the game wore on, however, Malley and True found they were unable to dominate the net as they had with opponents in their own company. Soon F Company trailed 42 to 46. Malley asked for a two minute break, which the captain of D Company readily agreed to, panting breathlessly.

Malley told his team, "Listen you guys, I got $75 bucks ridin' on this thing, and a week's pass to Nice, France, comin' up. Let's by God take it to 'em from here on in! Okay?"

"Okay, Okay," the team wheezed in response.

"But these guys are sure as hell no pushovers," True added between panting breaths.

It might have been Malley's pep talk, or maybe just D Company running out of gas. But whatever the cause, a series of weak serves by their opponents saved the day for Bill and his buddies. Fox Company won the match, 50 to 49. Malley would have some dough to spend in Nice.

Volleyball wasn't the only game in town. Several of the men had gotten cozy with the owner of a nearby stable, and were riding horses on a daily basis. This gave rise to the idea of staging a competition, and a makeshift race track was laid out in a nearby pasture. Interest grew rapidly as riders described the prowess and speed of the horses they would ride. A pair of enterprising troopers developed an informal pari-mutuel betting system to make the race "interesting."

By race day a goodly sum of money had been wagered. When the horses lined up to start, a rowdy bunch of troopers were gathered to cheer on their favorite. With eight entries in the race, and none heavily favored, every bettor figured he had picked the winner and was ready to root him home.

A shot from an M-1 started the race as one of the judges hollered "They're off!" But the animals weren't prepared for the loud bang of the rifle. Two stallions screamed, reared, and gave their paratrooper riders a real "airborne" trip to the turf. As the remaining competitors thundered down the track and into the first turn, four of them continued on a straight course right through the bordering fence and into the open fields beyond.

Only two of the starting horses ever finished the race, so all of the "show" bets were off. While the winners happily pocketed their lucky earnings, there was little general enthusiasm for a repeat of organized racing. The "bookies" who had hoped for continuing profit from the endeavor were disappointed, but everyone else was content to seek other diversions.

One night Bill's platoon was suddenly called out to load onto trucks and travel south. Their destination was hours away: a railroad tunnel some five miles in length that ran downhill through the mountains and connected Austria with Italy below. The Army needed to control the flow of refugees and displaced persons passing north. But this mission had a specific purpose beyond that. There was a train scheduled to transport a load of civilian goods along the same route, and it was said to be worth $20 million, minimum. Valuables of every description were aboard, owned primarily by Hungarians who had managed to escape with their belongings in advance of the invading Russians.

True's squad took their turns guarding the train day and night There seemed to be no suspicious or unusual activity, and the regimen of posting his men soon became routine. He was not aware, however, of the surreptitious entry two of his newest replacements made to one of the railroad cars. As his men were preparing for relief by another unit, Bill happened upon one of the soldiers as he unabashedly showed off the booty he had stolen: several large gold pocket watches heavily encrusted with jewelry, one of which had miniature figures which struck the time musically with tiny hammers. His partner in crime had "liberated" an entire case of miniature spy cameras.

True was in a bit of a quandary regarding what to do about the thefts. It was widely known that others, including non-coms and officers, had looted civilian valuables from the beginning of combat days. Bill's own participation in this had been mainly stealing wine, booze and food wherever they were found. These served to relieve the personal discomforts of life in a foxhole. Other than that, it was only "historic" memorabilia that interested him. The pistol taken from his prisoner at Bastogne, and the German general's uniform he purloined from the home in Berchtesgaden, were possessions he prized beyond anything. Gold and jewels held no attraction for him.

Bill didn't dwell long on the dilemma. Amid the chaos and devastation of war, he and many others came to rationalize a stunning array of behavior that would have been unthinkable back home in Podunk, Iowa, or wherever they were raised. The likelihood was remote that any of the goods on this train would ever get back to their rightful owners, anyway. And there was always the question of why he should get his own men in trouble for doing something others had practiced with impunity. In the end, that tipped the scale. As they were trucked back to Kaprun, Bill shed all personal sense of guilt and contented himself with the philosophy of "live and let live."

$$\approx \qquad \approx \qquad \approx$$

A big 4th of July celebration was arranged by regimental staff in Zell Am See, and all of the 506th came to participate. In a letter home dated July 8, 1945, Bill briefly discussed it.

"It's raining like the dickens again today. There were a couple nice days last week though—and we had a 4th of July celebration the 6th. It was held over at Zell Am See, a town near here that is regimental headquarters. It's a very nice little town, right on the edge of a big lake. There were boat races, swimming races, horse races, etc. The natives in full costume danced and sang for us during lunch. There was also a ten man parachute jump into the lake that the Austrians got quite a thrill from."

In addition to the horse races there were track events with performances by several exceptional athletes in the regiment. These included a pole vaulter who apparently held several collegiate records. The native costumes were colorful indeed, and included men in traditional short leather pants with bright suspenders (lederhosen) and women in flouncy big dresses with flamboyant hats. They sang and danced to the music of an "oompah" band, and the American soldiers found it very entertaining, many of them having never seen the like before.

The ten-man jump was unfortunately marred by a very foolish and insensitive prank, thought up by some lame-brained lieutenant. As the C-47 approached the lake drop zone, a man apparently jumped out and fell 2,000 feet to the water as his parachute streamered and failed to open. Bill's heart leaped into his throat, and many of his trooper buddies were white-faced with shock and fear at the apparent fatality of a compatriot. Then the loudspeaker came on and announced that what was seen had been for fun, and it was only a dummy thrown from the plane. "That is *not* funny!!" True mused aloud. "Somebody ought to kick the shit out of the wise-ass who dreamed *that* one up," he thought to himself.

The "real" jump which followed was a spectacular success, however. Each of the men dropped smoke grenades and different colored flares on their way down. The "oohs" and "aahs" from the Austrians left little doubt of their appreciation for the performance. Bill was a bit apprehensive about the lake landing for the jumpers, since the dangers of drowning in a water landing had always been stressed in training. But motor boats were standing by to quickly retrieve each of the wet but happy men from the sharply cold waters of the snow-fed lake.

From their very first days in Berchtesgaden, men of the 506th had been driving a wide variety of captured German vehicles. Colonel Sink personally appropriated the special Mercedes-Benz, purportedly custom-made for Hermann Göring. But men of all ranks had acquired a collection of vehicles ranging from motorcycles with side cars to huge transport trucks.

True's squad had a medium-sized truck that had benches along both sides of the truck bed, meaning it was probably used to transport German soldiers. Whatever it's original purpose, it served his squad well in getting around the countryside. Occasional trips to Zell Am See to swim in the cool waters were always a great diversion on hot afternoons. Once the squad even took a drive up the nearby mountain to a ski lift.

The ski lift had been restored to operation by the engineers of the 101st after extended disuse by the Austrians. War demands had caused the locals to discontinue its use, and they were very happy when the Americans put it back into working order.

Bill found that riding the lift to the top of the ski run and then back down again was a harrowing experience. The traumatic plane ride on furlough two years before had left him with a chilling fear of heights, which he hoped by now might have subsided. It had not. Looking down from on high without a parachute on his back gave him goose bumps, a roiling stomach, and an upper lip wet with perspiration. This wasn't a condition he wanted the men in his squad to know about, so he forced a grin during the ride. But it was with great relief that he stepped off the lift as it reached the bottom.

One afternoon not long after this unpleasant ride, True's squad decided to take a swim at Zell Am See. Bill chose to sit in the back of the truck on the benches, instead of his usual place in the cab up front. A brand new recruit from Arkansas had just joined the squad. He had been a truck driver before joining the Army and asked if he could take the wheel. "Okay, Arkie," True said, "but this thing can be hard to handle on turns, so watch it."

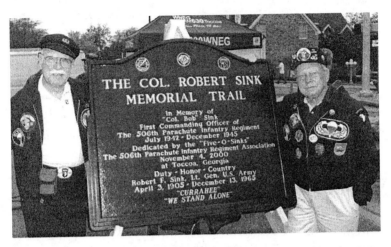

November 4, 2000, Toccoa, Georgia. Bill True (Left) and Tom Alley at large plaque honoring Col. Sink, which will stand near the beginning of the trail up Mt. Currahee which the regiment ran during basic training at Camp Toccoa in the summer and fall of 1942. Taken during mini-reunion of the 506th PIR to honor their World War II C.O., Col. Robert Sink.

Half way to the lake Bill noticed that they seemed to be going pretty fast. He was about to lean over the side of the cab and tell the driver to slow down when they started around a curve. The sharpness of the turn, combined with excessive speed, was too much for the truck. Losing control, the driver flew off the road and into a steep ditch. Luckily, no one was injured, but the truck's front axle was a lost cause. There was no point in trying to get the vehicle out of the ditch since only a new front end would ever put it into running condition again. The group abandoned it, hot and disappointed, and walked a sweaty two miles back to Kaprun.

This mishap was by no means unique. Vehicle accidents were now becoming common throughout the regiment. Freed from the concerns of combat, the natural exuberance and often reckless attitude of paratroopers led to risky driving habits, and the easy availability of hard cider and other alcohol didn't help. Finally it was time to call a halt.

An order came down from Regiment directing that all unofficial vehicles be turned in. Furthermore, anyone caught driving even authorized autos under the influence of alcohol would be severely punished. The directive noted that recent accident figures made for casualties almost as high as the Battle of Bastogne!

Unfortunately, the regimental order came just a day too late to avoid a tragedy that struck close to home. Three men were involved. Lt. Andrew H. Tuck, III had been Bill True's platoon leader at various times during the preceding three years. Conrad Ours joined Bill's platoon when he transferred into the company at Fort Bragg, just before it was shipped overseas. A third man from D Company, whom Bill did not know, rounded out the trio.

On a rainy night, Ours had been driving the three of them back from Zell Am See in a jeep when it slid off the road. The vehicle ended up wrapped around a tree. Lt. Tuck and the D Company man were both killed. Ours was only slightly injured.

Lieutenant Tuck had been with F Company since its founding in Toccoa, Georgia, and had taken part in all the campaigns across Europe. Bill didn't think much of Tuck as a combat leader, but the lieutenant had always been amiable and fair-minded. To die in an automobile accident after surviving all those combat actions seemed like such a senseless waste. A formal funeral service was held as everyone in F Company and a number of friends from other units gathered in memoriam.

As it turned out, the new Arkansas recruit liked singing as much as Bill did, and knew the lyrics to lots of country and folk songs. Arkie taught him new verses to the "Crawdad" song he'd never heard before. It was a good number to sing while marching, and one of the new lines went like this: "Yonder come a nigger with a pack on his back, Honey; Yonder come a nigger with a pack on his back Ba-a-a-by; Nigger fall down and break that pack, watch them crawdads back and back; Honey, Sugar-Baby, Mine." Bill had reluctantly grown accustomed to the common use of the word "nigger" by the boys from the South, but he was never comfortable with it. Try as he might, he never could get the guys to substitute the preferable word "fella" in the song.

One of the other platoons occupied a house that had a piano in the living room. Arkie used it to teach Bill to play simple chords. Bill's dad had also played chords and sung, using the same system. A letter dated July 15, 1945, contained this:

"By the way, Dad, you're not the only one that can chord a piano and sing 'She's Only a Bird in a Gilded Cage.' One of the Arkies in the squad taught me a few chords. Two keys yet, C and G."

ತಿ   ತಿ   ತಿ

The war in Europe was over, but there was still a conflict with Japan to resolve. With their experience and seasoned combat skills, the men of the 101st Airborne Division seemed likely candidates to invade the Japanese home islands. Along with all the other veterans, Bill was naturally anxious to get back to civilian life. The very thought of shipping out for what might be an extended Asian campaign was chillingly repugnant. For the men who had already endured long periods of nearly continuous combat, it was hard not to feel that in due time their "number would come up."

By some miracle, the Army chose fairness as a policy and established a way to discharge soldiers early, based on service rendered. Thus a point system was developed. Men with the longest record and most combat experience would be given the most credit, and released even before the Japanese conflict ended. Points were awarded for months served, with overseas duty counting double. Battle ribbons and individual medal awards also added to the score. Anyone with a total of 85 or more was all set for the first boat home.

By July of 1945 everyone was calculating points, hoping to get to that magic number and head for home with the first dischargees. Bill's Purple Heart for the knee injury at Bastogne was worth 5 points. He had also earned the Meritorious Service Bronze Star (worth another five) which General Taylor awarded to each man who participated in all four of the 101st battle campaigns. Together with his service and campaign points, this brought True to 83. Agonizingly close, but no cigar.

John Taylor, Platoon Sergeant of the 2nd Platoon was also close, but had never been wounded. He was one of the very few old timers in the entire company who had not received at least one Purple Heart. Checking the company records, he found that there were only five soldiers in the same category. It was an odd paradox, indeed, to find himself wishing that he'd taken a bullet at least once in his long ordeal across Europe. ("Could you make it just a little wound, please?")

YA YA, WILHELM, YA YA
Bill's True Tale

Our 2nd Battalion has moved from Berchtesgaden down across the border into Austria. F Company is situated in a little town named Kaprun, and each squad has been assigned to a civilian home. Ours is a two story with a cellar and several bedrooms, so there's plenty of room for all ten of us plus the Austrian family to whom the home belongs. The family consists of a middle-aged couple with one daughter, and they've stayed on, occupying the cellar and one of the bedrooms.

The father in the family walks with a limp and explains right away that he was never in the Army because of his infirmity. The mother is a somewhat plump but quite pretty hausfrau, cheerful and squeaky clean in her starched cap and apron. The daughter appears to be about twelve or thirteen, as pretty as her mother, and understandably shy with the houseful of American soldiers.

Allen Summers and I are sharing the largest bedroom, which is also closest to the one bathroom, but all of the men have a reasonably comfortable set up with at least an army cot to sleep on. Allen and I are among the few Toccoa veterans left in the platoon now, and our squad consists mainly of young guys who came as replacements after Bastogne. A couple of them are only eighteen years old.

Occupation duty becomes very routine and mostly boring as our days roll by, with regular calisthenics in the morning sometimes followed by a bit of close order drill, and occasional classroom instructions from one of the officers on weapons or tactics. Regular guard duty does take place every night, of course, and I've had Sergeant of the Guard assignment a couple of times. All of us non-coms are also assigned in rotation to Charge of Quarters functions in the Company Headquarters office, manning the phones and keeping in contact with Battalion and Regiment.

Our youngest squad member, an eighteen year old Texan (who we happen to call Tex), told me last night that someone in E Company had come across a small swimming pool just at the edge of town. He said he thought he could find it, so this afternoon, after the class by a lieutenant from 3rd Platoon, we're going to locate it and enjoy a dip.

          ❧   ❧   ❧

Tex would have made a good tracker because he's taken us straight to the pool. It is quite small, but one end is eight feet deep, and guys are doing some fancy dives off a low board.

Tex and I are down to our skivvies in a hurry, and he hits a contorted position off the board with his rear end sticking up and his hands in a Hail Mary clasp that I remember Leo Gorcy performing in one of the "Dead End Kids" movies. Everybody is laughing, while at the same time we recognize that Tex knows his way around a diving board.

Somebody brings out a couple of big jugs of hard cider, and we're having fun drinking and splashing up a storm. The effect of the cider becomes apparent as we get to laughing uproariously at anything anybody does off the board, especially the flat belly flops. Finally Tex says "I'll bet y'all ten American bucks I can do a back flip off the board and get my shorts off before I hit the water."

"Nobody's got ten American bucks," I say, "but if you can do it, I'll do it even better." I've never even done a back flip, I'm suddenly remembering, let alone pull my shorts off in mid-air. Why in the world didn't I keep my mouth shut?

"All right, I'll go first," Tex says as he saunters to the end of the diving board and turns around, grabbing the waist of his shorts with both hands. He takes a tremendous spring high up off the board. I'm just sober enough to follow his motions as he spins, curling into a kind of ball, with his shorts clearing his feet just as he hits the water.

"Okay, True," a guy from E Company hollers. "Let's see you top that one."

I can't back out now, I'm thinking. Can a person break his neck doing something like this? Naah, I'm loose. I watched how Tex did that. I'll just get a hold on my shorts, jump high off the board, and do it the same way.

I jump as high as I can. I flip my head backwards. I pull my legs up. My shorts catch on my knees and I hit the water with a resounding splat that could probably be heard back at Regimental Headquarters in Zell Am Zee.

Sharply stinging pain accompanies my crawl out of the pool, but the laughs and guffaws of the guys steel my determination to give it at least one more try.

Again I jump as high as I can. Again I flip my head backwards. Again I pull my legs up. And yet again I smack the water like a dead goose, peppered and leaded with buckshot. And my shorts are still on.

As I laboriously pull myself from the water, hurting all over, Tex takes pity and says: "Hey, Sarge, that wasn't too bad, but maybe we should practice it some more another time,"

"Yeah," I reply, feeling really grateful for the out, "I think I'm beginning to catch on, but we ought to get back to F Company before chow time, so let's go."

I've learned that Greta, the young girl at our house, is actually fourteen. A bit older than I had thought but still much too young for any shenanigans. She's taken an obvious shine to me, though, as I've made the effort to speak to her in

German using my little handbook.

This morning she made a meringue for me with some eggs I swiped from the mess hall and gave to the family. Between my handbook, gestures, and facial expressions, I had shown her quite clearly how delicious the meringue tasted, and expressed my "danke shoen" to her delight.

"Ya ya, Wilhelm, ya ya," she says with her mischievous smile. That has become her regular response whenever we've made a pretty good communication. Every time she says it, it gets to me, and I wish fervently that she was five or six years older.

Greta's parents appear to have no concern for her safety as she mixes freely with all of the soldiers of the house. It strikes me that that is surely a tribute to the generally good reputation of American soldiers, but I know there have been some exceptions to the rule. This afternoon after chow the whole company will experience the result of an exception.

We're in a company formation at full attention as the captain comes out of our headquarters house accompanied by an attractive young woman. We've been told in advance what it's all about, and the captain and the lady pass along the squads in each platoon as she looks every man in the face. She'd been raped by a soldier a few nights before, and the regiment is making every effort to identify the offender.

I have weird and eerie feelings as she slowly passes along my squad and looks straight at me. What if I should be mistakenly identified, I'm thinking? We're probably all having similar thoughts, and we know the penalty for rape is big time. Do they still use firing squads, or would it just be a life sentence at Leavenworth?

Whew! The lady has finished reviewing the entire company, and to the great relief of everyone, no one has been identified. After her departure, 1st Sergeant Malley says we have the afternoon off and gives the command to fall out. Our uneasy talk is punctuated by nervous laughter as we saunter back to our quarters.

~∂~   ~∂~   ~∂~

When I tell Greta about my guitar playing and singing (didn't even need the handbook to communicate that), she squeals with delight and goes to retrieve an old relic that has apparently been stored away for some time. It looks to be a quality instrument, but the strings are pretty far gone. I manage to get it into some kind of tune, however, and when I sing "Lili Marlene" in both English and in my improvised German Greta beams and claps with enthusiasm.

They've been playing a new American song on the radio of late, "Don't Fence Me In," and I'm anxious to try it out. I've heard it often enough that the words have sunk in, and the chords don't sound too tough. They aren't, and soon I'm doing a half-decent version of this catchy western-style tune. I've even got Greta singing along with me a bit, and her Germanized version of the title line "Don't Fence Me In" has me in stitches.

We've been here in Kaprun a couple of months now, and the "point system" for going home to be discharged has been announced. Points are given for time in service and for battle campaigns and medals earned. If yours add up to 85 or more you're eligible to ship out with the first lucky group. Mine add to an agonizing 83.

Most of the old timers meet the 85-point minimum, and I'm heart-sick that I'm so close and yet not quite there. Nearly all of the guys who've gone through it all from Normandy have at least two Purple Hearts. I have the one from my knee injury at Bastogne, but I'm still a miserable two points short.

The high-pointers are due to ship out and head for home a week from tomorrow, and I'm talking to Joe Flick and Dude Stone about it at mid-day chow. They're both just over the 85, and are excitedly talking about home. I'm quite glum and envious, of course, but I try to put a good face on it and remark that maybe it won't be too long before the next group will be eligible to go.

"Hell, no, TyTy," Joe says, "they'll probably be lowering the points you need real soon." Dude chimes in with a quick agreement, but I know they're just trying to make me feel good.

As we're leaving the mess area, Tom Alley calls over and says "Hey, TyTy, I've got some great news for you." He's been Charge of Quarters today, and manning the company headquarters office. "A report just came down from regiment. You just got another Purple Heart for that wounded hand Joe Droogan treated in Holland."

Wow! That's 88 points! I'll be heading for home next week. Joe and Dude are real happy for me, too, and I'm walking on air.

I'd completely forgotten the minor hand wound I got just before we jumped in Holland. The guy behind me took the brunt of the shrapnel from the flack and was out of the war. My wound was superficial and didn't keep me from jumping, but it was bleeding badly and our platoon medic, Joe Droogan, had bandaged it for me. "Thank God for Joe Droogan and his meticulous record keeping," I'm thinking when I get back to my room.

Greta has been crestfallen since I told her about my good fortune in getting to go home. As a matter of fact, parting from her is the one thing that detracts just a bit from my own elation. My feelings for her certainly couldn't be described as "being in love," but maybe they aren't entirely foreign to that emotion.

We're leaving this morning, and I'm trying to tell Greta how much I'll miss her. She's managing a "stiff upper lip" but some tears are starting to leak. As I shoulder my bags I give her a quick kiss on the cheek, the first time I've ever done that, and try to tell her that I'll write to her from California when I get home.

"Ya, ya, Wilhelm, Ya ya," she says chokingly, as I walk down the steps with a large lump in my throat.

❧   ❧   ❧

The high-pointers said their goodbyes, and loaded on trucks for the ride from Kaprun up to Berchtesgaden. There, they were officially transferred to the 501st Parachute Infantry Regiment to make the trip back to the states with them. Tossing his barracks bag up and climbing to take a seat, Bill remembered a recent pep talk all the guys got. It was from a recruiting sergeant who tried to convince them to reenlist.

"Just sign up for one more hitch and we'll give you two stripes for free: buck sergeant to tech sergeant in one jump. You could be a company top-kick in no time!"

Bill wanted to respond, "If you made me a full bird colonel I still wouldn't take it!" but instead he settled for a simple "Thanks, but no thanks." He looked forward to attending San Diego State College in the fall, if he could just get home before September expired. His sister Betty Jean and step-sister Dona were already enrolled, and he couldn't wait to join them.

When he joined the Army in 1942, True still suffered from a slight lack of self-esteem when it came to academics.

His high school career had certainly been less than stellar, though he did graduate with his class. His first impression of the officers in F Company was that they were smarter than he. Most of them did have at least some college credits to their name. But as time went on, Bill came to know that he was every bit as smart as his superiors, and often smarter. Gradually, the idea formed that if he survived this war, his first priority would be getting a college degree. When the G.I. Bill of Rights was passed, his determination took solid form.

As new members of the 501st. Bill and his buddies spent several pleasant days once more at Berchtesgaden. Nearby Konigssee lake was as luxurious as that at Zell Am See, and cooling swims along with leisurely sailboat rides became the order of the day. At the resort, gorgeous blond women in skimpy bathing suits had everyone drooling for dates, but the men all bombed out. Not one of the girls would even join in small talk. Soon all the troops had given up the effort. "If I wasn't ecstatic to be on my way home, I'd be good and pissed off with those arrogant bitches," Bill thought to himself.

In a letter home dated July 27, 1945, he wrote a bit about these days in Berchtesgaden.

"They just informed us that the Belgian government has awarded our division the Croix de Guerre, with Palm, or something like that. Some of the guys say it's a rope-like affair worn around the right shoulder, but I don't know."

Additional foreign awards earned by the division included two French Croix de Guerres, and the Orange Lanyard from Holland. All of these were shoulder devices of like design.

"Marshall Stalin is going to be here in Berchtesgaden tomorrow and Sunday so if I get any hot oil from him about how the big three's conference is going, I'll let y'all in on it. Some of the boys saw General Marshall and Admiral King at Konigssee today. That's a pretty famous resort about two miles from here...There's a nice big lake surrounded by mountains...

"Billy Rose's Diamond Horseshoe Revue, or at least part of it, played here yesterday. The M.C. was very good and of course the girls were very lovely, but otherwise there wasn't much to it."

                            ॐ   ॐ   ॐ

The lazy days at Berchtesgaden ended as the men again piled into trucks and headed west toward France. After nearly a week of daily truck transport, stopping overnight at various points in the French countryside, they transferred to "40 and 8" railroad cars once more.

Now long, boring days on trucks were simply replaced by much of the same riding the rails. The monotony was relieved a bit by playing cards and reading. Someone picked up a piece of white chalk at a stop along the way and printed the slogan "Kilroy was here!" in extra large letters on the side of Bill's car. Joe Flick, the artist, added the characteristic picture of Kilroy peeking over a fence with his long nose and fingers hanging across. No one in the rail car knew how that

ubiquitous graffito started, though Europe was certainly covered with it. In point of fact, it began as a chalked inspection notice in a Quincy, Massachusetts shipyard. After the war, it was said that this cartoon had literally "launched a thousand ships."

The troops happily disembarked for a few day's rest at the small town of Bar-le-Duc, not far from Nancy, France. It was good to no longer be riding the less than commodious boxcars, but they hoped the stay would not be long.

In a letter home from Bar-le-Duc dated August 8, 1945 Bill wrote the following.

"We've been moving all over here lately and I expect we'll do some more shortly, but I'll keep y'all posted as we go along. The 501 P.I.R., of which I'm a member right now, is going to be broken up here shortly and everyone in it sent to the 17th A.B. Division. I believe the 17th is composed of men eligible for discharge, and on arriving in the U.S. will be deactivated. Don't quote me on this, but as far as I know we're scheduled to be heading homeward in September. Sounds nice, doesn't it? Gosh but sometimes I can't hardly imagine being home.

"I'm writing this from a Red Cross club downtown in the heart of Bar-le-Duc. As you can imagine it's a pretty small town. We got here a couple days ago after riding beaucoup time on a 40 and 8. In case you don't know what that is, it's a French boxcar (even smaller than ours) that's supposed to carry either 40 Hommes (men) or 8 Chevaux (horses). I understand they were quite well known in the last war, too. They weren't quite as uncomfortable as they sound though— cause we only had 20 hommes in each car, plus a couple bales of straw; so it was really quite like riding in a Pullman—only different."

In the same letter Bill referred to the last letter he'd

received which included pictures. One of them showed his dad wearing the German general's uniform, sent home from Berchtesgaden. "That's a swell picture of you too, Dad. You look at least as good in the uniform (better in fact), as these Kraut officers."

On an evening not long after this, True was in town having a drink at an outside café with one of Bar-le-Duc's ladies of the evening. She spoke only a little English. Bill managed to do a bit better in French, with the aid of his Army handbook. Thus they haltingly discussed the news of the day, including the startling story of atomic bombs dropped on Japan. Both agreed that this probably meant that the "guerre" was almost "fini."

A popular song at that time was "Amour, Amour, Amour." As he ordered a second round of cognac for the two of them, Bill started humming the tune. His companion wrinkled her nose in disdain. "That song," she said. "The words are... how you say?... stupide!"

True found this very puzzling. Why would a bonifide member of the "world's oldest profession" find the lyrics "Love, Love, Love," anything but charming? He decided not to pursue the matter. She never raised the subject of any commercial transaction and at the end of the evening, they simply parted without a tryst. That was fine with Bill. He had enjoyed drinks and the company of a lovely woman, on a fine and balmy evening in the heart of France, headed for home. There seemed little indeed to complain about. He would remember her fondly ever after, though not as vividly as another girl: Yvette.

Chapter XII – Kilroy Was Here!

BAR-LE-DUC
Bill's True Tale

It's late August, 1945, and we're in Bar-le-Duc, France, headed for Marseille. The U.S Navy will be taking us from that port to either New York or Boston, and we're expecting the trip to be a big upgrade from the voyage on the English ship, the Samaria, that took us overseas back in September, 1943. The high-pointers from the outfit have been transferred to a temporary unit for transport home, leaving the guys with less than 85 points to remain on occupation duty in Austria. We apparently don't have very high priority in terms of either trucks or train clearances though, because we seem to make stopovers every few days.

Here in Bar-le-Duc we're billeted in old military barracks that must date back to WW I. But it's not the antiquated quarters and spartan facilities I'm frustrated with, it's the delays. I'm real anxious to get back to San Diego in time to enroll at State College for the fall semester. The days are mighty long and boringly dull as we have no training or duties to perform, just falling out for roster check in the morning and killing the rest of the time as best we can.

A few days ago Burr Smith from E Company collected dues from some of us for membership in a 101st Association being formed. It's an organization that will help us to keep in touch with war-time buddies and to continue the deep friendships we've formed over the last three years. That sounds great, but initial membership isn't cheap. The receipt Burr gave me reads: "18 Aug. '45. Received of Wm. True the sum of 1,250 francs for membership fees in 101st A.B. Assoc. Robert B. Smith III, Enlisted Assoc. Rep." That's twenty-five dollars, American, but most of us are pretty loaded right now.

Evening chow was a couple hours ago, and I'm lying on

478

my upper bunk reading the latest Stars and Stripes when Whitey Swafford makes a noisy entrance into the barracks, loudly extolling the talents of a local prostitute. "A gal named Yvette down at the cat house in town is unbelievable," he announces. "Man-o-man, I've never had anything like her, and I've screwed whores all the way from Indianapolis, Indiana, to London, England, to Paris, France, and plenty of places in between. This little broad here in Bar-le-Duc outclasses 'em all by a country mile."

Some of the guys are asking Whitey for particulars and he's glad to oblige with extended anatomical specifics. I'm thinking about how risky a visit to that cat house might be. We've been warned that it's off limits, and that the MPs are making examples of any guys they catch there. Wouldn't that be a sorry situation if one of us got caught and the delay kept him from getting home with the others?

Well, of course it would be just God-awful bad if a guy got caught. Sure would be. Very bad. But, on the other hand... What if Swafford isn't just bullshitting us? What if this Yvette is truly the love marvel of the world? What if a guy were to miss this once-in-a-lifetime opportunity to experience the ultimate in sex? When was the last time I went all the way with a woman, professional or otherwise? London furlough after Normandy more than a year ago? No, there was at least one bimbo when I got blotto on that 48-hour pass to Paris just before Bastogne last December. In any event, as that line from the hit song goes "It's been a long, long time."

I'm in town and I'm casing the large multi-story cat house for any sign of MPs. No jeeps anyplace in sight, but they could be hiding, of course. A couple of GIs come casually sauntering out the front door, a very encouraging sign, and they're followed shortly by two staff-sergeants beaming from ear to ear. That's good enough for me. Besides, if worst comes to worst, I was one of the fastest sprint men in F Company when we had the mini-olympics back in basic at Toccoa. I should be able to outrun any MPs.

The madam, an older woman of around forty or so and not unattractive herself, greets me in a most friendly and inviting way as I enter. There are a few soldiers sitting around the spacious, comfortably-furnished room talking to some of the girls. "Je voudrai Yvette" I say in my hand-book French, and the madam replies "Oh, Yvette, elle est tres occupe." "I'll wait till she's available," I say, and her fluent English is evident as she responds "Very well, I'll call you when she's ready."

There's a small bar in the room, tended by a large beefy man about the age of the madam, perhaps her husband. I'm nursing my third beer and wondering if the MPs are taking the night off or something and how long my luck is going to last when the madam beckons me, thanks me for my thousand franc note, and escorts me up a long stairs to the first of an apparent string of bedrooms.

Yvette is a flat-out beauty. Young, she can't be more than eighteen, with long blonde hair, bright blue eyes, and even white teeth. Generous lips fashion an enticing smile, and through her sheer short kimono a petite but still voluptuous shape is stirringly visible. She drops the kimono and says in a seductively husky voice: "Ah, mon cheri, comment allez-vous?" "Just great," I manage to mutter. Love-struck, gaping, gulping and tongue-tied, I can't think of anything to say in French. Or anything else in English for that matter. Yvette is already loosening my tie. Between us I'm shortly as unclothed as she.

My sexual encounters prior to this time have been relatively simple and doubtless amateurish. Certainly not polished or worldly in any sophisticated sense. But I know instinctively, incontrovertibly, that with Yvette I am experiencing something most extraordinary. Thrilling sensations she renders are exciting me into new and novel performances I never before imagined. But even the astonishing and wonderful things she is doing with her body and with her mouth are equaled in my mind, and in my appreciation, by the utter delight she is taking in every passionate movement. Yvette has great fun in giving great fun! When I reach climax, completion and exhaustion, I collapse with the sure and gratifying knowledge that I've thrilled to something very, very special. Whitey Swafford's seeming hyperbole back at the barracks was anything but that.

Yvette is helping me dress and I've got my underwear, socks, pants, shirt and cap on, with only my necktie, Ike jacket and boots to go, when there is a loud racket below with a police-like whistle blasting and someone shouting "MPs, MPs!" I grab my jacket and boots, and Yvette scoops up my tie as she leads me to the room's one window indicating that's the way to go. As I throw open the window I see her rush to the door and turn a key that's been in the lock, just as there is a loud pounding with shouts of "MPs, MPs, open up, open up!"

As I exit the window I'm on a steeply slanted roof and I slide down holding my jacket under my left arm and my boots in that hand. It's utterly black below me and I slide farther along feeling the roof shingles with my right hand. As I feel my left foot go over the edge of the roof I look to see how far I'll have to drop. It's too dark to see what's below, but I know that since the room was only on the second floor, and that I've already slid down several feet, I can probably make the jump all right. "Talk about your night jumps" I'm thinking as I slip over the edge. It's a pretty far fall at that, but luckily I land on some bushes that cushion the impact, and

I'm off and racing away from the house toward some distant lights.

My feet are lent mercurial wings of speed as I consider the dire consequences of not escaping the MPs. To miss getting home with my buddies would be a monstrous penalty for a short period of bliss, and I know I'm doing the fastest, most important, 100-yard dash of my life.

As I round the second corner in my elusive sprint I take time to look back and gradually realize that no one is in pursuit. Donning my Ike jacket, I drop down on a curb to pull on my boots, and think almost aloud: "I'm going to try with every fiber of my being to make the remainder of this trip home so utterly quiet and uneventful that, by comparison, even Sunday mornings at church will constitute extreme excitement."

     ﻋﻮ   ﻋﻮ   ﻋﻮ

Delays all along the route from Berchtesgaden had been frequent, but the troopers found the long days at Bar-le-Duc most aggravating yet. August was wearing thin by the time they finally loaded again onto 40 and 8's, heading for Marseilles.

The train obviously had a low priority, as there were frequent switches onto side tracks to make way for other passenger and freight carriers. The 300-mile trip seemed endless. Even when they were lucky enough to get a clear track ahead, their progress was slow. What in normal times would be a journey of only hours turned into several days of frustration.

The accommodations at Marseilles were makeshift, with army cots set up in ten-man tents. The food was excellent, however, and seconds on everything included deliciously extravagant desserts. USO entertainment groups offered shows every day. It was there that Bill heard the song "Paper Moon" for the first time. It was the only tune he would remember from the many troupes that performed.

November 4, 2000, Toccoa, Georgia. Several F Co. and E Co. ("Band of Brothers") men at the banquet honoring Col. Sink and the occasion. Left to right: "Babe" Heffron, Deryck True, Don Replogle, Tom Alley, Bill True, Bill Guarnere, Ralph Robbins, Mario Patruno. Heffron and Guarnere are E Co. men.

One night a large symphonic orchestra put on a performance for the men. A sizable stage was erected at the foot of a hillside. Rude benches ascended the gradually rising slope, accommodating several hundred soldiers. The orchestra played several classical compositions, with repeatedly diminishing applause at the conclusion of each number. Few of the soldiers were accustomed to such "long hair" music. Their boredom soon became manifest. Several men at the top of the stands started blowing up condoms, tying them off like toy balloons, and wafting them down over the crowd. Men farther down the hill gave them an added bounce as they floated over. Soon inflated condoms were finding their way down and onto the stage. The orchestra conductor was nonplussed at this peculiar offering, but perhaps thinking it was just an American custom, continued with the concert.

Most of the soldiers soon tired of the condom-floating sport and, utterly bored by the music, they gradually drifted away. The few who could appreciate the performance remained, and the orchestra showed its class by continuing to play for the now greatly diminished audience.

Joe Flick, Dude Stone and Bill True stayed for the full program, as much to apologize for their compatriots' boorish behavior as for appreciation for the concert itself. Walking back to their tent they were in a talkative mood.

"It was pretty funny at that," Joe said," but I felt a little guilty with those rubbers flying up there on the stage."

"Yeah," Dude added, "Those musicians went to a hell of a lot of trouble to come out here and play for us. But I guess I was laughing as much as anybody when the rubbers floated down."

"There was one really good looking gal playing violin I'd like to talk to," Bill said, "but she probably thinks American soldiers are pretty uncouth after *that* concert!"

"By the way," he continued, "A letter from Johnny Jackson caught up with me in mail call this afternoon. He's in California with Sylvia and they just visited my folks in San Diego. Kind of funny how things worked out for the four of us, don't ya think? I mean, being together from our first mortar training in Toccoa, then through this whole shootin' match."

"Yeah, I guess," said Joe. "The main thing is that we all *made* it. Too bad about Johnny getting hit bad at Bastogne.

But at least it got him home to marry Sylvia a lot sooner."

Reaching their tent, they all stripped for bed on what would be their last night in Marseille.

❧   ❧   ❧

Next morning, the men boarded a U.S. Navy ship for the final journey home. It was a far cry from the Samaria they'd sailed on just two years prior. The sleeping quarters were clean, commodious, and comfortable, and the food was so good they actually looked forward to every meal.

At their first lunch as they steamed out of port, True asked Flick, "If you knew the Navy eats this well, would you have joined the Army?"

"Well... I wouldn't want to be anything but a paratrooper," Joe replied, "but I might have thought twice if I'd known there was food like this."

Awakening the first morning at sea, Bill was startled by a loudspeaker announcement: "Now hear this! Now hear this! Sweepers, sweepers, man your brooms. Sweep down fore and aft all decks!"

"Did you hear that, Dude?" he called over to Stone. "Sweepers, man your brooms! What the hell kind of an order is that? You think they say 'Cooks, man your paring knives! Pare down those potatoes fore and aft?'"

"I don't know," Dude answered, "but they sure have their own lingo. 'Head' for latrine, 'bulkhead' for a wall, and 'port and starboard' for left and right. They say the Navy is big on tradition, and I can believe it."

The trip to Boston from Marseille was a lot shorter than that from New York to Liverpool. There was no need for zig-zagging to avoid any U-boats now, and the Navy ship was much faster than the old Samaria.

The pace toward discharge picked up. A few brief days at the Army Post in Boston left just enough time to say fond adieus to never-to-be-forgotten buddies. Promises were made to always keep in touch. Then, miraculously, Bill True was on a train headed for California.

෴   ෴   ෴

HOME… SWEET, SWEET HOME
Bill's True Tale

This train ride heading west from Boston to Fort MacArthur, California, seems even longer than that interminable eastern trip from the Fort to Camp Toccoa, Georgia, back in August, 1942. Three years and one month ago that train-car load of Californians was mighty impatient to get to Georgia to begin training to become paratroopers. But that impatience pales in comparison with the eager anticipation of the troopers now headed for discharge and home.

We're a collection of high-point airborne soldiers from various regiments, and I'm only acquainted with a few of them. A PFC, Charlie Johnson from Tulare, California, has been very friendly from the start of the trip, and we've spent quite a bit of time together. He was a glider infantryman, not a paratrooper, though, so our experiences have had more than a little variance.

"Bill, did you ever think about whether you'd rather ride a glider into combat than jump out of a C-47?" he asks as we light up for a smoke with coffee following a substantial lunch.

"Sure did," I reply. "The extra fifty bucks we got for jumping was an incentive for starters, but once I saw those smashed, busted up and mangled gliders in Normandy, I sure didn't envy you guys one whit. I'll take a parachute jump anytime!"

"That's for sure," says a nearby staff sergeant who's from my regiment but not my company. "I never knew a paratrooper who didn't admire the hell out of you glidermen for the guts it took to ride one of those flying coffins down."

Charlie is obviously pleased with the response he has gotten, and I'm glad we've made him feel good about his role in combat. But I wasn't just trying to make him feel good. I really think that paratroopers had an easier time than the glidermen. In fact, the straight infantrymen who found themselves leading an assault up a beach or attacking a pillbox had it every bit as tough as we did.

At last we've finally made it to Fort MacArthur, and it doesn't seem to have changed much in three years. While I was only here for a few days back in 1942, I remember it well. The officers' houses up on the hill, with the neatly manicured lawns, are a clear and unpleasant memory. The work details I'd been put on to manicure those lawns still rankles a bit.

The lieutenant who's doing my final processing for me is a pleasant guy, and it becomes clear that my combat record is something he respects. He appears to be about twenty-one, same age as I am, or possibly even younger, and his lack of ribbons suggests that he's not seen real action.

"Have you received any of these medals shown on your record?" he asks.

"No, sir. They gave us the ribbons, but no actual medals."

"Well, here's your Bronze Star," he says as he reaches back into one of several boxes and cartons behind him. "And here's the Purple Heart as well," he adds reaching into another carton.

Looking again at my records he says: "You obviously qualify for the Good Conduct Medal, too."

"The Good Conduct Medal?" I'm thinking. I was AWOL four days and got busted from PFC on that first furlough from Fort Benning in December, 1942. And I also lost a few days of credited service for the time I was hospitalized for that dose of clap I got in London in July, 1944, right after Normandy. Well, who am I to question what the Army considers "good conduct?" I'll take any medals they want to give me.

"You've also got a good amount of pay coming," the Lieutenant informs me and starts counting out the money.

It's in cash and comes to over $600. That's as flush as I've ever been, and I carefully stash it in the breast pockets of my uniform that I can button down.

"Have you finished typing his discharge?" the lieutenant asks a corporal across the room.

"Yes, sir," the corporal answers and brings some papers over.

"We both need to sign this now," the lieutenant says, and we put our signatures at the designated places on the back side of the document. "This is your Honorable Discharge, Sergeant True. It's a mighty valuable piece of paper. You should take real good care of it."

"I'll do that for sure, lieutenant," I say, as I salute and head out for the bus station.

The bus to San Diego seems "slower than a yoke o' terrapins," as Dad used to say to me when I showed a lack of enthusiasm in performing one of my chores around home. It's not much more than a hundred miles, but we make stop after stop along the way and it's dark when we finally get to the bus depot at the foot of Broadway.

It was just over two years ago when I had my last furlough home right before we went overseas. As I walk up Broadway toward the center of downtown San Diego, my nostalgia is all-consuming and I'm observing everything through misty, teary eyes. My feet are hardly touching the pavement as I stroll past the noisy bars, tattoo parlors, and other brightly lit establishments of every variety that cater to servicemen. Soldiers and sailors and marines and every description of military dress are evident among the crowd of revelers.

I could grab a street car and probably be home on East Mountain View Drive in a half hour or so, but I'm in no hurry at all. The delicious anticipation of walking in on my folks and surprising them is to be savored, and my walk is a saunter at best. I'm home, I survived the war, and except for knees that sometimes get to clicking, I'm hale and hearty. These are the happiest moments I've ever known. I must stretch them to the limit.

I've slowly walked some twenty-four blocks when I notice another of my Adams Avenue and Mountain View Drive streetcars approaching. I board it and continue to relish my surroundings as we pass through Balboa Park, cross University Avenue and El Cajon Boulevard, and turn up Adams Avenue for the final run for home.

A sailor gets off at my stop, but I decide to ride for a few more blocks. The quiet walk back up a darkened East Mountain View Drive is at least as emotional as my stroll through downtown.

I have not told the family just when I'd get home, and my welcome as the door is opened is as raucous as it is joyous. Mom and Dad and the kids and even Skippy the dog are as excited as I am, and I'm being hugged and kissed by everyone. Except Dad. Grown men don't hug and kiss each other, of course. But an escaping tear accompanies Dad's firm handshake, and I know his joy is deep. Skippy can't hug me either, but he sure makes with the wet kisses.

Within minutes the popcorn is popping, and the root beer is pouring. The soldier is being welcomed home. Home…sweet, sweet home.

Epilogue

by Bill True

I was three weeks late in enrolling at San Diego State College for the fall semester of 1945. An exception was made for the returning veteran who was among the very early enrollees taking advantage of the G.I. Bill. I was determined to reverse the poor showing I had in high school, and to excel in college. My success in that aim was achieved as I graduated in June, 1948, With Honors, and With Distinction in Economics. I completed the full four-year course in less than three years through attendance at all summer school sessions offered.

In the interim I had married Clarissa Jane Tufts in September, 1946, and our first child, Deryck Tufts True, was born in January, 1948. I was studying for final exams at the hospital the night Deryck was born, and received A's in all five courses that semester.

Following graduation we moved to Richmond, CA, so I could attend graduate school at the University of California, Berkeley. During the summer of '48 I worked for Armco Drainage Aluminum Company while waiting for the fall semester to begin. I found myself the most highly educated of the labor crew, loading and unloading every conceivable configuration of pipe from railroad flat cars and trucks heading in and out of the plant. The work was heavy and exhausting. It gave some real incentives and significance to my educational desires.

Graduate school was a degree tougher than my work at San Diego State, but I managed to keep an A- average, even while working to supplement my veteran's allotment. However, our second child appeared to be on the way in the

491

summer of 1949, and the G.I. Bill money was about to run out. I decided to forego my goal of a PhD. and settle for a Master's Degree in Economics. So in January, 1950, I received the M.A. from Cal and went to work in the real world.

June 1948. Bill True's graduation from San Diego State College (with Honors and with Distinction in Economics). He is holding his first child, five-month old Deryck Tufts True. Bill was the first of his family to graduate from college.

My first job was Budget Analyst with the California State Department of Finance in Sacramento. I spent more than ten years with the State of California and the Cities and Counties of Los Angeles in financial and administrative positions. During this time my family expanded to include three sons and a daughter, and we bought our first home using the G.I. Bill. Watching that home being built in the San Fernando Valley, and knowing as we visited its progress weekly that it would soon be ours, gave us heartfelt pleasure difficult to describe.

I played a major role in the merger of the Los Angeles City and County Public Health Departments in the 1960's. This led me to a career shift away from government and into the management of health care delivery in the private sector. That's the field where I found my ultimate success and satisfaction as I managed both for-profit and non-profit hospital facilities. I became active in professional and community organizations which included publishing articles in professional journals, and serving in numerous offices.

Sometime back I read an article listing what the author thought were the 100 most important pieces of Congressional Legislation during the 20th century, and the G.I. Bill was among them. I don't recall if the bills were listed in the author's order of importance, or where the G.I. Bill fell if he did so, but I know it would be at or near the top if my family were ranking them.

I was the first of my family to attend college, let alone obtain a graduate degree, and the G.I. Bill gets full credit for that accomplishment. The professional success which followed was certainly due to my education. All four of my children have also gone on to obtain at least bachelor's degrees, undoubtedly influenced by my example.

Initial home ownership through a G.I. Bill loan, and the

resulting healthy environment, undoubtedly contributed to the wholesome growth of our family. All four children are happily married and have produced a total of six grandchildren who have added greatly to the happiness of Janey and me. We recently celebrated our 56th anniversary, and anxiously await becoming great-grandparents. Alas, however, the new generation appears much slower to get into marriage and production of offspring.

❧   ❧   ❧

When I retired in 1988 at age 65, after seventeen years as chief executive officer at the San Gabriel Valley Medical Center, it was with great expectations for productive years of retirement. That expectation has been more than met as my wide range of interests includes writing, developing family history and photo albums, participation in local political issues, and semi-weekly bridge sessions. It keeps me pretty busy. Add to that a weekly golf game (with rising handicap), and occasional guitar playing for the amusement (or amazement) of myself and friends. The latter activities cannot be attributed to the G.I. Bill. But nearly all of my other endeavors have been enhanced, if not actually induced, by that legislation. I can find no words that would overstate my gratitude to the 78th Congress for passing the original G.I. Bill of Rights.

❧   ❧   ❧

On the way home for discharge in August, 1945, I had joined the newly formed 101st Airborne Division Association. "Burr" Smith of E Co. was collecting dues and signing people up. After several years of busier and busier times, however, I dropped my membership and much time passed before I again became interested in things military.

May 1984, Los Angeles, California. Bill True in full World War II uniform. Photo taken after his return from a parachute jump in Orange, Massachusetts, on 6 May 1984. Bill is holding mementoes of the Orange jump. CBS News covered the event.

❜❜❜❜❜❜

In 1978, a chance meeting with a wartime buddy resulted in my rejoining the 101st Association, and I became active in the Southern California Chapter. Then in 1983 a story in the Los Angeles Times caught my eye. It was about a group of young World War II buffs who were planning a 40th anniversary parachute jump in Europe in 1984. I contacted them, and before I knew it I was not only involved in helping with their planning, but making practice jumps with them in preparation for the overseas trip.

On September 17, 1984, in cooperation with the Dutch Army, our group re-enacted Operation Market Garden, the invasion of Holland 40 years before. More than a dozen World War II veterans were among us. It was again a bright sunny day as I landed on the very same field, just outside the town of Zon, as I did in 1944. A big difference, of course, was the absence of German anti-aircraft fire we had encountered then. But one thing was the same. It was the sincere welcoming of the Dutch people.

The 506th captured Eindhoven on September 18, 1944, the day after our landing. Every year since then the large city has celebrated its liberation in a grand fashion. One feature of the festivities is a huge "Liberation Day" parade which includes presentation of the "Liberation Torch" to Prince Bernhart. On September 18, 1984, I was given the honor of leading the parade by carrying that torch, and presenting it to the Prince.

I've returned to Europe numerous times since the war. On almost every occasion I've paid a visit to the American Cemetery at Normandy which is located just above Omaha Beach. Standing at the graves of fallen comrades brings forth emotions that were stifled and smothered when those men fell in those tumultuous days of combat.

The carnage that occurs in the heat of battle permits little thought but that of killing the enemy and personal survival. Even when the immediate conflagration has ended and there is time to take stock of who survived and who didn't, there is more of a selfish feeling of gratitude for surviving than a sorrow for comrades killed. But when you stand at the graves of those same comrades 35 years later, as I did on my first re-visit to Normandy in 1979, things are different. You know then that you've been blessed with all that life can offer: career, wife, children, grandchildren, and many years to enjoy and appreciate them. But the brothers in arms that lie at your feet will always be just the boys you each were back then. It's a real kick in the belly, and each visit I've since made has evoked similar fervid emotions. The essence of this is captured eloquently in the film "Saving Private Ryan," when the title character stands before the headstone of his protector, Captain Miller. Seeing that film literally churned my stomach nearly as much as my actual pilgrimages to that heart-breaking place of tranquil repose.

APPENDIX A

Normandy KIAs

Bill True was one of sixteen men to share his Quonset hut in Aldbourne, England, as Fox Company prepared for the Normandy Invasion. Of those, seven were wounded and six killed in that first combat. On August 27, 1944, a formal memorial service was conducted for all the men in the regiment who had died in action, including those six. Bill knew each of the men, described below, and felt their loss keenly.

Richard K. Buchter and John Supco were both from the same small town of Pottstown, Pennsylvania. Richard had been a star baseball player in high school, and as Bill could testify from experience, his ability to hit fungo fly balls with pinpoint accuracy anywhere on the field was phenomenal. John was among the smallest of the men in F Company, and his retiring, almost shy, manner belied the size of his courage. He evoked a "big brother" feeling among some of the larger, rougher men of the First Platoon, but he was no "little brother" when it came to performing his duties.

Donald P. Davis (nicknamed "Pedro") was the platoon Jack of All Trades, and master of several. He could sew, wash, press, or shine anything, and did so at quite reasonable prices. His haircuts were sought after throughout the company, and his pre-war experience as an itinerant fry cook came in handy whenever anyone found a raw provision that called for expert handling.

William C. Hale was a Kansas farm boy who was a whiz at the checkerboard. He had never learned the game of chess, however, until Bill True decided to teach him. True won the first game during lesson one, but none thereafter. If Hale had lived, he might very well have become a "game theory" genius.

Walter J. Hult and Raymond Kermode were both replacements who joined the company in England. They were thus not as intimately known in the platoon as others. But in the hard training months before D-Day, the two proved to be trusted team-mates alongside the old-timers. Both were killed on the jump at St. Mère Eglise, as were Buchter and Hale.

The memorial service included the following "506th Parachute Infantry Prayer," written by Lt. James G. Morton:

Almighty God, we kneel to Thee and ask to be the instrument of Thy fury in smiting the evil forces that have visited death, misery and debasement on the people of the earth. We humbly face Thee with true penitence for all of our sins for which we do most earnestly seek Thy forgiveness. Help us to dedicate ourselves completely to Thee. Be with us, God, when we leap from our planes into the dread abyss and descend in parachutes into the midst of enemy fire. Give us iron will and stark courage as we spring from the harnesses of our parachutes to seize arms for battle. The legions of evil are many, Father; grace our arms to meet and defeat them in Thy name and in the name of freedom and dignity of man. Keep us firm in our faith and resolution, and guide us that we may not dishonor our high mission or fail in our sacred duties. Let our enemies who have lived by the sword turn from the violence lest they perish by the sword. Help us to serve Thee gallantly and to be humble in victory. Amen.

August 9, 1999, American Cemetery in Normandy above Omaha Beach. Bill True and Tom Alley have applied sand to Supco's head stone marker so the lettering will show in photos.

Bill had known from basic training on, of course, that paratroopers would be killed in the war. He had seen both friends and enemies killed in Normandy. But the six with whom he had lived so closely for so long, who were now forever gone, brought the reality home as perhaps nothing else could.

Most of the F Company men killed in Normandy were brought back to America for burial after the war. The families of five of them, however, made the decision to leave their loved ones at the place where they died for their country. Viewing the American Cemetery above Omaha Beach one is deeply touched by its serene beauty. The wisdom of the relatives who left their men there cannot be questioned. Those five represent nearly all the ranks of the fallen. They are:

501

PRIVATE JOHN SUPCO
P.F.C. CHESTER J. NAKIELSKI
CORPORAL THOMAS B. WOLFORD
SERGEANT JULIUS A. HOUCK
1ST LIEUTENANT FREELING T. COLT

"I visited these graves several times over the many years since World War II. My feelings of awe and wonderment grow with each revisit as I ponder the mysteries of who lives and who dies in war. Why I was given a life of fulfillment as a husband, father, and grandfather, while these five comrades will always be boys, is an enigma."

—Bill True

APPENDIX B

Old Army 849
A Fond Remembrance by Harold Wayne King

In the years following the war Bill True became active in the 101st Airborne Association, at one point even serving as president of his local chapter. In August of 1983 the Association held its annual national gathering in Dallas, Texas. For Bill that was a particularly important meeting. Among the attendees was Harold Wayne King who, as a 1st lieutenant, piloted the C-47 which carried stick #76 into their first combat on June 6, 1944. Months later King and True corresponded by mail. In a letter dated December 16, 1983, Wayne described at length the ordeal of the Normandy flight, from his perspective in the cockpit. That account is the basis for part of the story contained in Chapter V of this book. In the same letter Wayne gave a lengthy and eloquent account of the airplane he flew throughout the war, which he dubbed "Old Army 849." That portion of the letter is reprinted verbatim below.

Dallas, Texas
December 16, 1983

Dear Bill,

Please forgive the delay in response to your—much appreciated—pictures and information from the August, '83 reunion in Dallas.

For whatever it might be worth to you, at this late date, all of the above does bear witness to the fact that I did retain a deep and abiding concern for what happened to my first load of troopers into combat. I'm sure that all of the official pictures that were taken prior to take-off which wound up in my scrap-book had a bearing on all this, but your part of my war time experience seemed to have struck harder than most of all the rest. I suppose the gravity of beginnings carries a lot of weight in memories, but it's like there was more than just that here.

As a matter of fact I recall being pretty highly impressed, once, through some reading I did concerning the religious beliefs of the Polynesians-of-old relative to this sort of thing. Though some may scoff, they operated under the premise that when two people or objects touch that a permanent bond has been established, thereby creating what might be thought of as an ethereal-universal web that somehow ties into what might be called the big IBM system of life.

With this in mind, let me first say that if I'm an inordinate sentimentalist, I don't recall ever having been called such to my face. But I must confess sentimentality toward one of my memories out of that period, which was a lowly piece of machinery, "Old Army 849"; the airship you rode into the war. Over the years I seem to have come to accept 849 as a lucky number, and openly admit that it stems back to the memory of that airplane. It goes without saying that much impressive happenstance with this machine had to have been necessary for it to stand—head and shoulders—in my memory, above seventy odd other types which I have flown.

Though I may be overplaying the point, it occurs to me that it might be of interest to you, too, to glance over a few of the highlights of this particular ship's career, as it related to that period; especially in the face of the fact that you, without doubt, left minor scars and a couple of drops of sweat on her floor.

At the time, this should hopefully serve as an insight into the mysteries of the difference between "the Troop Carrier Command" of which 849 was a proud member, and "the Air Transport Command" which the American press so ignobly misconstrued. Lest one might be interested, the ATC served as a non-scheduled military airline, from whatever, up to the edge of what was known as the communication's zone. Quite separately, Troop Carrier seldom left the battle zones in the execution of its daily chores. It is in this context that, I'm sure, "Old 849" would be happy to have me defend her heritage!

She, along with 100 of her sister ships which comprised the 439th Troop Carrier Group, were factory-new in January of 1944 when we left Fort Wayne, Indiana. Suffice it to say, weather-wise she required the services of a 13-ton cleat-track to snap her frozen brakes loose before she could taxi out amid man-made mounds of snow, for the take-off into an unknown destiny. Shortly after dark of that same day, en route to Fort Lauderdale, Florida, she drew her first blood. I remember thinking of something on the order of a christening she had undergone, when she collided with a bird of such size as to loosen some of the rivets in her nose section near my left foot. Disintegration was the only word for the bird!

In the morning of the second day, on a southerly heading out of Fort Lauderdale, we learned of her destination. One hour after take-off, sealed orders revealed that the Group, along with 50-odd sundry other airplanes, were to proceed to Prestwick, Scotland, via the southern route. i.e. South America, and Africa, with several overnight stops along the way.

The third day took us into the steaming, jungle-like

atmosphere of Georgetown, British Guiana, where we remained over night. 849 spent the night on the so-called airport where part of the Jim Jones massacre occurred many years later.

About 11 p.m. on the night of the fifth day, she shut her eyes and headed out across 1600 miles of ocean, in order to arrive at the Ascension Islands after daybreak. This leg of the trip was out of Natal, Brazil, and put her to the test of seeing if she could find the seven square miles of rock in the middle of the Atlantic. This, incidentally, is where the British based their operation for the retaking of the Falklands in '82.

Out of there, en route to Monrovia, Liberia, she weathered a South Atlantic squall that was so severe that it claimed two airplanes; one of which was my Squadron Commander, never to be heard of again.

En route up the west coast of Africa, she spotted three crash diving German Submarines, radioed ahead to Dakar, in what was then French West Africa, alerting the British Air Patrol, and got them all sunk.

In an attempt to reach Marrakech, Morocco, she succumbed to a raging dust storm in the Sahara and had to go into Tendouf, Algeria (a desert fort) to get the sand out of her system. Four days passed before the storm subsided.

At Marrakech she fell victim to mass-cowardice, refusing for two weeks to head north to England under the excuse that the head-winds were too strong—that she could not make it on her fuel supply. The truth finally came out; secret information had come through that the Germans were patrolling too far out to sea, off the French Coast. The whole mob was simply afraid that they might be shot down. But she did finally make it up into the Midlands of England, where she immediately went to work practicing for the eventful day with which you are familiar.

It was during this period that 849 had her first real brush with disaster. While practicing mass formation one extremely cloudy day over England, a British bomber nicked her belly with his vertical stabilizer as he passed—90 degrees—underneath her. But she survived this and a couple of other minor scrapes. By "D-Day" she was honed to a razor's edge, and was ready to get on with whatever we were there for.

When your part of her duties had passed she really went to work, doing a little bit of just about anything that could be expected of an airplane of this type, in the execution of a war.

A few of her—individual—claims to fame came in sundry ways, as the war rolled on to its conclusion

After the Saint Lo breakthrough in Normandy, it was decided that the ground forces should be given a brief rest in Paris, and it was quite clear that they would need money—lots of money! 849 joined another ship, in London, hauling half of the 25 million dollars necessary across to Paris.

On a later occasion, she met Winston Churchill's party in Paris, to team up with an RAF Dakota—one of her first cousins—to take them across to England. It was decided that she would haul General Allenbrooke (Great Britain's "George Marshall"), and most of the guard entourage. She managed to survive a Royal chewing out by the Dakota pilot, later in London, for having dared to come within a couple of hundred feet of Sir Winston's ship—in the air—when, all the while, she was totally dependent upon the Dakota for routing on an incredibly cloudy day. However, I suppose it all balanced out in the end, as General Allenbrooke invited her crew into the terminal to have tea with him.

On another occasion, in London, she found herself in the position of being asked, as she was preparing to leave Heathrow Airport for a trip to Paris, to keep a sharp lookout for Major Glen Miller's ship which had just been declared overdue. 849 was the first ship out on the route, after his disappearance. Believe it or not—I am currently in semi-touch with a couple of individuals who are continuing to investigate that case. They are out to prove that Miller did not die in the aforementioned fashion, that this was a cover-up for what they believe to have been a devious murder.

Among the myriad activities she performed, her group seemed to have been looked upon with favor on three or four occasions, when General George Patton's tanks had driven up to fifty miles into enemy territory and run out of fuel. She and her sisters, as per instructions, went in under the trees—single file—and five minutes apart, loaded with Jerry-cans of fuel.

If you were there, perchance, in the vicinity of Nijmegen, Holland, on September 23rd , and saw the glider armada that brought the 82nd Airborne in, she was out front, leading the right column. She won the Distinguished Flying Cross that day, over the coast of Holland. This was the mission which the British Press proclaimed "the fulfillment of President Roosevelt's prophecy, that we would put an umbrella of airplanes over Europe." They also stated that it took three and a half hours for this armada to pass over the English coast.

And 849's final role—above ordinary duty—was to take the British Brigadier and his official party into Oslo, Norway, to commence negotiations with the German Commander there for dismantling his 500,000-man army. She felt somewhat queasy in the early stages of—in a sense—offering herself up to the enemy, but finally settled down to an enjoyable couple of weeks. Her crew's American uniforms were a novel revelation to the Norwegians, who couldn't seem to ask enough questions about what had really been happening down in Europe. It seemed that the Germans might have been lying to them.

In the interim periods of participating in the seven major battles of the European War, she and her ilk never ceased to be amazed at what they were asked to do next. Their basic effort was to help supply the ground forces, all the way from the North Sea to North Africa, hauling anything from bales of tank tracks to Eskimo Huskies out of Iceland, winter clothing, ammunition, and rations. Along toward the end, she almost became embarrassed over the notion that they had just about turned her into a lowly damned truck. She was very often called upon to perform through rain, snow, mud up to her prop-tips, and ceilings so low that she often found it difficult to find the quagmires that were referred to as landing-strips.

One extremely dark night, over central France, while on a peaceful mission, she was forced to do a belly-up landing in a remote part of the country-side. This was during a period of "pull back and destroy" on the part of the Germans, and a time before our side could install any radio or light facilities. But even this didn't seem to deter her indomitable spirit; with her band-aid patch job, and her brand new paddle-blade props, she was stronger than ever, and could outrun any airship in her league.

After the Rhine crossing she was tired; too many 16-hour days, too many heavy loads, too many nights of sleeping out in all types of weather. More than 2000 hours of war effort had taken their toll. She and her sister ships begged for a rest, but under the cloak of military indifference, I was never certain that they got it. All I ever knew was that higher headquarters made the decision that we would trade them in for a like compliment of larger ships—the Curtis C-46.

I can still recall the sharp anguish I felt when the

departing pilot of 849 climbed aboard her creaking floors to take her away, and the flippant remark he flipped over his shoulder, to his co-pilot, "Jesus Christ, do you suppose this damned thing will get us home?" Had it not been for military decorum, I might well have taken him to task for having desecrated a friend.

Watching her disappear from sight, on a northerly heading—in the general direction of Paris—was a sad and final knowledge of her existence for me, and fell into the category of a heartfelt departure.

Many times since, I have wondered if she, like so many of her peers, fell into the position of having grown older than the pilot that was flying her. Has she been just around the corner—somewhere—that I might have passed in the night, or has she crossed my trail somewhere along the way. I have often wondered if she might still be doing duty in some distant Banana Republic, possibly catering to the whims of some minor potentate, or might she have wound up in a commercial melting pot to become a part of something new.

I've never really been able to dislodge the notion that she's still out there somewhere, waiting—waiting to say a final "so long, friend, remember what we all went through together?"

If all of this sounds a little too "buttery" for any of you guys that went out her door that night, then please indulge me in the consideration that a soul that can feel like this toward a mere piece of machinery can't be all bad, and—if for no other reason—keep in touch.

Sincerely yours,

H.W. King, P.T.F.Y.I.C.

☙　　☙　　☙

P.S.

I hope that the foregoing will fit into your memoirs sufficiently to do some degree of justice to our brief encounter during those times.

I cannot help wondering if your progeny will view this period in the light of antiquity, due to the headlong advancement of the horrors of warfare, or is it likely that someone of their time may be instrumental in helping overcome the shortcomings of Mankind, which may be something as fundamental as learning how to overcome greed.

Can it be rationalized that man has been irresponsible in his failure to watch over his Khans, Napoleons, Hitlers, Khomaniacs, and their types closely enough, or is he a mere victim of celestial machinations, over which he has no control? That all of the disastrous side of life is part of a Grand Design, for the purpose of recycling souls, in an ever climbing reach for the Sublime.

It seems to be a sad commentary on the human race to have to face the fact that each generation seemingly "must" have its destructive war, and if he *is* responsible, man may be in more trouble than he's capable of realizing, when you stop to consider the present state of things,

In the vernacular of—seemingly declining—twentieth century phraseology—hey, man, like I don't know what's diggin' either—hey, you tell me! Know whad I mean?

Frankly, forty years of reflection has me wondering what wars are really all about. It seems to me that they are merely a deterrent to what might, otherwise, be a more righteous path, and only wind up lessening man's status on this spaceship called Earth.

Here's to those of us that didn't make it!

APPENDIX C

A Coincidence of Dates

In the course of each year, two dates stand out as significant in Bill True's life.

They are June 6 and November 11.

Bill's birth date of November 11, 1923, is coincident to at least two interesting historical events.

The very day that Bill's mother brought him into the world, Adolph Hitler was arrested in Bavaria for leading the infamous Munich "beer hall putsch." It was a bold but ill-planned power grasp which earned him 9-months in Landsberg prison. Hitler used the time productively, dictating "Mein Kampf" to his sycophant and cell-mate, Rudolph Hess.

This was also five years to the day after the Armistice was signed ending World War I. Many historians attribute the oppressive reparations imposed on Germany by the Treaty of Versailles as contributing to the rise of Hitler and National Socialism. In that light, World War II was merely an extension of the first. True's birth date would thus seem to have fated him to be involved in that most disastrous of all human conflicts. America entered the war very shortly after his eighteenth birthday.

Throughout Bill's youth, Armistice Day parades were held each year on November 11 with marching bands, military units and their equipment, floats, and patriotic paraphernalia of all sorts. Betty Jean, Bill's younger sister by four years, was impressed as everyone was by all this hoopla. Her older brother managed to convince her that the celebrations were in his honor, as they always occurred on his birthday. She had no reason for doubt, though it seemed grossly unfair. Her own birthday was on the 11th, too—but in February. She had to concede, however, that February was a shorter month than November. Her big brother somehow always won the argument over whose birth deserved celebration.

June 6 also carries great significance. That day in 1941, Bill graduated high school in Omaha, Nebraska. His high school career had been academically "less than distinguished," but that would later be reversed in college, when experience and maturity finally motivated him to succeed in life. The war was a significant contributor to that metamorphosis, particularly as it led to the G.I. Bill of Rights.

Of course June 6, 1944, carries with it the fame of history. Three years to the day after graduating, Bill took part in the greatest military invasion the world has ever known (and perhaps with luck, ever will know).

Finally, on June 6, 1970, Bill stood to witness the wedding of his first-born child, Deryck, to Anna Margaret (Peggy) Burnette. It was a lovely garden ceremony, held in the yard of a well-loved neighbor. As he watched and listened to the vows exchanged, this thought ran through Bill's mind: "If 26 years ago I'd known I would be standing here today, the leap into Normandy machine gun and anti-aircraft fire would have held far less terror for me."

APPENDIX D

"The Recruit"
A Ballad by Bill True

In 1991, Bill attended a course in creative writing at Los Angeles Valley College. One of the assignments was to "write a ballad." The following is the poem he submitted.

THE RECRUIT

Just two good men, the sergeant said,
       Now who will volunteer?
The captain's ordered night patrol
       Men going get free beer!

I'll go, the new recruit pipes up
       The rest of us stand tight,
Patrol's the pits, we've all learned well,
       Especially at night.

Just one more soul is all I need,
       Must I order him to go?
There'll only be the three of us,
       A small, exclusive show.

We're going for a walk this eve',
       It's safer in the dark,
No shooting, just a recon job,
       A hike, a stroll, a lark.

No man steps forth, it's clear to see,
        The Sarge must make his choice,
He's chosen Corporal Endicott,
        NOT ME! Each inner voice.

The dawn has come, where are the three?
        Have our patrollers flown?
At last in comes the new recruit,
        Legs dragging, all alone.

The sergeant's gone, the corporal too,
        Those burp guns killed 'em dead,
I never saw the enemy . . .
        His voice trailed off in dread.

The new recruit, no longer new,
        Has learned what can't be told,
Old soldiers never volunteer,
        To live beats being bold.

Acknowledgements

Bill True first became seriously involved in writing about his wartime experiences at the behest of Dr. Stephen E. Ambrose, who solicited thousands of first-person accounts of the era for his best-selling work: "D-Day June 6, 1944: The Climactic Battle of World War II." Much to his pleasure, Bill's stories were included in that volume. Even more importantly, Dr. Ambrose encouraged the writing of this book, which might otherwise never have come to be. It seems fitting that the authors render first gratitude to him.

The remaining acknowledgements are in no particular order of importance, and the authors intend no "ranking" by the sequence in which they are here named. All made significant contributions without which this book would not have been possible.

Chris Anderson, editor of *World War II Magazine*, is another writer who has encouraged us. In his professional capacity he has doubtless seen hundreds of wartime manuscripts, so we are most pleased and grateful that he found our efforts worthwhile.

Bill Brown is a World War II buff too young to have participated in those unpleasantries. But he has devoted extensive time and effort to research the tales of Company F, 506th Parachute Infantry Regiment. In that regard, he has compiled a history of the unit entitled "Fighting Fox Company," based on personal accounts of the men who lived them. Our book owes much to that work.

Harold Wayne King was the young Air Corps Lieutenant who piloted Bill's C-47 into combat on June 6, 1944. He and Bill didn't meet up again until many years later at a reunion of the 101st Association, but they corresponded closely after that. The wonderful detailed account he provided of that action is matched only by his warmth and humanity, as revealed in his memoir of Old Army 849, appended here unabridged.

Many men of the 506th PIR have contributed to our book by simply talking about their wartime experiences at reunions and other get-togethers. It is likely that some of their names will be unknowingly omitted here, but the following come to mind. For any who do not appear in this list, but should, the authors beg sincere forgiveness and offer grateful thanks.

Gaston Adams	Bill Galbraith	Art Peterson
Ray Aebischer	John Gibson	Loy Rasmussen
Tom Alley	Eldon Gingerich	Don Replogle
Manny Barrios	Frank Griffin	Ralph Robbins
Joe Beyrle	Marion Grodowski	George Rosie
George Blain	Bill Guarnere	Doug Roth
Jim Bradley	Keith Havorka	Russ Schwenk
Bob Brewer	Les Heglund	Merlin Shennum
Linus Brown	Babe Heffron	Jim Shuler
Ralph Campoy	Clark Heggeness	Ben Stapelfeld
Burton Christenson	Ben Himmelrick	Bob Stone
Lou Cioni	Jim Hollen	Allan Summers
Bill Clemens	Bob Hopkins	Lou Truax
Nick Cortese	Johnny Jackson	Bill Tucker
Harry Dingman	Bob Janes	George Vanderslice
Joe Dominguez	Dick Mandich	Bob Vogel
Duke Dukelis	Paul Martinez	E. B. Wallace
Dave Edwards	Bill Murphy	Dave Webster
Joe Flick	Jesse Orosco	George Yokum
Robert Flory	Mario Patruno	Roy Zerbe

Bob Thomas is another young enthusiast of World War II history. Though willing, he was never able to serve his country as a paratrooper himself. But Bob's intense desire led him to seek private personal training which culminated in actual parachute jump qualification. His extensive knowledge contributed a variety of technical data on equipment and hardware used during the war, which the authors were otherwise unable to obtain. He is a good friend and loyal patriot.

Several members of the 506th, in both E (Easy), and F (Fox), Companies have formalized their recollections into self-printed book form, and the authors are greatly indebted to them as well. Many, many thanks to each of the following:

The late Leonard F. Hicks, for his "War Memoirs." Len was older than most of the Fox Co. men—enough so that the nickname "Pop" might have been a natural. But his exuberance for the exhausting basic training at Camp Toccoa belied his age, and that moniker was never applied. His memoirs are wonderful accounts in themselves, and the authors are sincerely sorry that he is not here to read this account.

Vincent Occhipinti, also deceased, wrote of his experiences in the account "Lessons of War." Vince was recognized right off as a fine soldier, and made squad leader in Fox Co. early on. Grievous wounds at Bastogne put him out of the war at that point, but the "lessons" he had learned contributed to our work.

Robert J. Rader is another friend who is no longer here to grace us with his wisdom and foresight. Bob was an Easy Co. non-com, and he and Bill True did not become close friends until after the war. They corresponded extensively however, and often joined in close vocal harmony at reunion singalongs A sharply observant and outspoken man, his

"Anatomy of a Paratrooper" helped the authors to focus and develop numerous episodes in their own work.

John H. Taylor is a modest man, but one with a remarkable memory for details of his wartime experiences. His personal memoir, "Fortunate Soldier," depicts his own journey through war-torn Europe. He was far more than simply "fortunate" (never wounded), however, because to his Fox Co. buddies he is one of the established heroes of the company. His writings reflect his marvelous aptitude for recollection, and we are very much indebted to him, especially for his detailed descriptions of Holland and Haguenau patrols.

George Koskimaki, 101st Airborne historian, contributed significantly to this book. His detailed accounts of the division's three major campaigns in Europe, as well as specific suggestions reflected herein, were most helpful.

Cecil Newton is a long-time resident of Aldbourne, England, and has become a good friend and contributor to this work. It was he and the Aldbourne Civic Society that offered source material for the map of the village and information about Bill's stay in that lovely community all those years ago. A veteran of the same conflict that Bill survived, Cecil has earned the love and respect of his countrymen, and certainly of us.

Mark Bando's books covering the 101st Airborne were an important resource. He also provided factual details that added to our book's accuracy.

In addition to the above, numerous family members and friends made contributions to the work at hand and the authors would be remiss, indeed, if those efforts were not listed here:

Jon Dobrer is a good friend and published author in his own right. He lent valuable editorial insights at the earliest stages of the project and helped set it on the right course.

Bob Wright, another friend and respected Hollywood screenwriter, lent encouragement and a very special contribution to our book: its title.

Kelly Jane True, Bill's eldest granddaughter, performed yeoman service transcribing numerous taped interviews and her help is greatly appreciated.

Dean Leslie True, Bill's youngest son, gave a final, "objective" read-through of the entire text and provided one last, unbiased point of view on continuity and flow before submitting it to the publisher. By that time the authors were far too closely involved in their own work to really edit effectively, so this was an invaluable service.

Dedra Lynn True-Scheib, Bill's only daughter, got the very last crack at proofing the book before actual printing. By then hers were the only "fresh eyes" in the family, so this was a vital contribution. Any typos you find in this work can therefore be attributed to her. (Just kidding, Dee Dee.)

Devin Paul True, Bill's second son, provided an unusual and vital graphic element to the dust jacket design. On his farm in West Virginia, Devin photographed a number of his cows which, coincidentally, are a French breed: Limousine. However, Devin's cows speak English exclusively.

Bill's sister, Betty Jean True Gruen, and her son, Christopher True Gruen, both contributed writings to this family project as did Janey's cousin Bryan "Bud" Reese. For that we are grateful and honored.

Janey (Tufts) True, Bill's wife of 59 years, was instrumental in numerous ways. Her recollection of stories from countless reunions was remarkable. She provided a vital "reality check" when the authors threatened to spin a tale out of control, or drive it into the ground. And she kept us both from getting on each other's nerves when the project seemed

Acknowledgments

to stall. Without her, the book would probably have never been finished.

Lastly, and certainly not least, is Deryck's wife of 35 years, Peggy. She was the mail clerk, typist, editor, transcriber, research assistant, supporter, nag, and generally essential behind-the-scenes gal-Friday we could not have done without. And if she doesn't receive photo credit for the beach picture of the authors, taken in 1984, there will be some serious repercussions in at least one household.

To all these, and the many that we surely have forgotten, our sincerest thanks.

Bibliography

Ambrose, Stephen E. *Band of Brothers*. New York: Simon and
Schuster, 1992.

— *Citizen Soldiers*. New York: Simon and Schuster, 1997.

— *D-Day, June 6, 1944*. New York: Simon and Schuster, 1994.

— *The Victors*. New York: Simon and Schuster, 1998.

Bando, Mark A. *The 101st Airborne at Normandy*. Osceola,
Wisconsin: Motorbooks International, 1994.

Brown, Bill. *Fighting Fox Company of the 506th Parachue Infantry
Regiment*. Self-published.

Burgett, Donald R. *Currahee*. New York: Ballantine Books,
1967.

Crookendon, Napier. *Drop Zone Normandy*. Great Britain:
Charles Scribner, 1976.

Department of the Army. *Utah Beach to Cherbourg*. Nashville,
Tennessee: The Battery Press, Inc., 1984.

De Trez, Michel. *American Warriors*. Belgium: D-Day
Publishing, 1994.

— *At The Point of No Return*. Belgium: D-Day Publishing,
1994.

Drez, Ronald J., editor. *Voices of D-Day*. Baton Rouge:
Louisiana State University Press, 1994.

Heintz, Joss. *In The Perimeter of Bastogne*. Belgium: Omnia
Ostend.

Hicks, Leonard F. *War Memoirs*. Self-published.

Keegan, John. *Six Armies in Normandy*. New York: Penguin
Books, 1982.

— *The Face of Battle*. New York: The Viking Press, 1976.

Koskimaki, George E. *D-Day With The Screaming Eagles*. New
York: Vantage Press, 1970.

— *Hell's Highway*. Kingsport, Tennessee: Arcata
Graphics/Kingsport, 1989.

— *The Battered Bastards of Bastogne.* Kingsport, Tennessee: Arcata Graphics/Kingsport, 1994.

Mackenzie, Fred. *The Men of Bastogne.* New York: An Ace Book, 1968.

Marshall, S.L.A. *Bastogne, The Story of The First Eight Days.* Washington, D.C.: U.S. Government Printing Office, 1988.

Mauldin, Bill. *Up Front.* New York: Henry Holt and Company, 1945.

Moore, Harold G., and Galloway, Joseph L. *We Were Soldiers Once...And Young.* New York: Random House, 1992.

O'Brien, Tim. *The Things They Carried.* New York: Penguin Group, 1990.

Ochipinti, Vincent. *The Lessons of War.* Self-published.

Rader, Robert J. *Anatomy of a Paratrooper.* Self-published.

Rapport and Northwood. *Rendezvous With Destiny.* Madelia, Minnesota: House of Print, 1948.

Renaud, Alexandre. *Sainte Mere Eglise.* Paris: Julliard, 1984.

Ryan, Cornelius, *A Bridge Too Far.* New York: Simon and Schuster, 1974.

— *The Longest Day.* New York: Simon and Schuster, 1959.

Taylor, John H. *Fortunate Soldier.* Self-published.

Tucker, William H. *Parachute Soldier.* Athol, Massachusetts: Haley's, 1994.

Van Horn, W.R., editor. *Currahee: Scrapbook of the 506th Parachute Infantry Regiment, July 20, 1942—July 4, 1945.* 101st Airborne Div. Assoc., Fort Campbell, KY.

Vassaux, Willy, and LePage, Pierre. *Nuts: Bastogne, the Battle of the Bulge.* Brussels, Paris: Lombard Editions, 1984.

Webster, David Kenyon. *Parachute Infantry.* Baton Rouge and London: Louisiana State University Press, 1994.